USING
MICROSOFT® WORKS 4.0
FOR WINDOWS® 95

USING MICROSOFT® WORKS 4.0 FOR WINDOWS® 95

Richard T. Christoph / Glenn T. Smith

James Madison University

Prentice Hall, Upper Saddle River, New Jersey 07458

Acquisition Editor: Carolyn Henderson
Marketing Manager: Nancy Evans
Interior Design: Suzanne Behnke
Cover Design: Lorraine Castellano
Design Director: Patricia Woscyzk
Senior Manufacturing Supervisor: Paul Smolenski
Editorial Assistant: Audrey Regan
Production Coordinator: Renee Pelletier

Cover Art: Don Baker, Illustrator

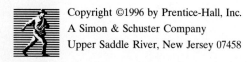

Copyright ©1996 by Prentice-Hall, Inc.
A Simon & Schuster Company
Upper Saddle River, New Jersey 07458

ISBN 0-13-456344-1

Prentice-Hall International (UK) Limited, *London*
Prentice-Hall of Australia Pty. Limited, *Sydney*
Prentice-Hall Canada Inc., *Toronto*
Prentice-Hall Hispanoamericana, S.A., *Mexico*
Prentice-Hall of India Private Limited, *New Delhi*
Prentice-Hall of Japan, Inc., *Tokyo*
Simon & Schuster Asia Pte. Ltd., *Singapore*
Editora Prentice-Hall do Brazil, Ltda., *Rio de Janeiro*

Printed in the United States of America
10 9 8 7 6 5 4 3 2 1

CONTENTS

3

An Introduction to Word Processing   31

4

Working with Documents   67

5

Advanced Word Processing Features   109

6

An Introduction to Computer Spreadsheets   147

7

Using Spreadsheet Functions   185

8

Advanced Spreadsheet Operations   217

9

Creating and Using Charts   245

10

Introduction To Database   275

11

Form Design and Database Filters   305

12

Creating Database Reports   341

13

Integrating Works Applications   367

Appendix A: Telecommunications   405

Appendix B: Works Add-ins   419

PREFACE

Development of the Text

When we designed the outline of this text, we followed two fundamental concepts. First, we felt that coverage should start from the beginning, introducing basic concepts and terminology, and move to advanced topics as the user's knowledge builds. This allows users of all experience levels to use this text. The second but equally important premise is that a new user needs more than simple, technical information about using a computer program. They also need information on how to apply the computer skills to real-world problems. These two concepts resulted in a book that describes how the computer and the Works 4.0 for Windows 95 software can be used as a powerful tool. Further, the text provides detailed, hands-on tutorials that allow the new user to try out their new-found skills.

Microsoft Works 4.0 for Windows 95

Microsoft Works 4.0 is specifically designed to run under to the very popular Microsoft Windows 95 operating system. The Microsoft Works 4.0 program provides the user with an easy-to-learn but powerful set of application modules that can perform the common tasks required by an individual or small business. These functions include word processing, electronic spreadsheet use, charting techniques, database development, and telecommunications. The key element in the Works program is its ability to *integrate* data between modules. This provides a new user with a program that is both easy to learn, yet powerful in its capabilities.

Enhancements in Works 4.0

Perhaps the most significant enhancement is complete Windows 95 support provided by the Works 4.0 release. This provides the user with all Windows 95 features including the easy to use visual interface, enhanced file naming abilities, and excellent disk management tools.

Additional improvements include a "push-button" Toolbar for fast, mouse-oriented access to common functions. Additionally, an appointment calendar, enhanced compatibility with other programs, and support for more printers are included.

Some of the new features in the word processing module include reorganized menus to give the program a more intuitive feel, Easy Text and Easy Formats, improved thesaurus, and improved bullets and paragraph numbering. Further, the insertion of pictures, or clipart, into a word processing document is enhanced as is support for color printers, word counting, and line and column indicators.

Changes to the spreadsheet module include an easier-to-use graphic window, a *best fit* column width, an Easy Calc summation feature, the continued ability to define colors for negative numbers, and the formatting of numbers in fraction form such as 1/2 or 1/4. Charting procedures have also been enhanced.

Improvements to the database module include an easier approach to database creation, form design and simplified report design procedures. In addition, database files can be much larger.

Structure of the Text

Using Microsoft Works 4.0 can be used to fill the void between computer concepts and applications. The first chapter introduces general microcomputer concepts that are essential for the user's understanding of the terminology of microcomputers. The second chapter introduces essential Windows 95 operations that most users will need to accomplish common, computer-based tasks. We strongly suggest that these chapters be covered by all students, even if they are proficient with microcomputer use.

The remaining chapters are focused on the Microsoft Works 4.0 program. Each chapter begins with a narrative introduction to the terminology and concepts covered in the chapter. This section of the chapter explains how Microsoft Works 4.0 performs certain tasks and through extensive screen displays, shows exactly how each feature is used. This is followed by a self-test in a short answer format.

The second section of the chapter presents a self-paced, step-by-step tutorial that guides the user through the development of a document, a spreadsheet, or a database. The concepts and principles covered in the first section of the chapter are implemented in the second section. This allows the user to learn computer concepts and then apply them in a hands-on environment. The tutorial exercises can be used in a classroom, lab, or individual user environment.

Features of the Text

Each chapter is written with a minimal amount of computer jargon that often interferes with the understanding of the concept presented. Each chapter also presents aids to assist the user in applying concepts with hints on when certain approaches should be used.

Self-paced, hands-on tutorials are included that guide the user through an application of the material presented in the chapter. These applications are oriented to the *real world* as much as possible. This allows the user to gain an understanding of not only of the computer concepts used to accomplish a task, but also how to do it. A collection of tutorial data files is provided on the data disk to provide the user the chance to use a Works application with large data files without spending endless hours of typing.

Each subject offers special hands-on practice exercises in which the user can use the computer to solve problems independently. These computer-based exercises allow the user to apply techniques learned in the chapters to new problems without the guided assistance of the textbook.

Perhaps the biggest difference between this text and many others is the use of the detailed tutorial concept. This allows the user to both understand what he or she should do, and then shows them exactly how to do it. These tutorials include actual screen displays so the user can check his or her progress throughout the tutorial to be sure the assigned task is completed correctly.

To the Instructor

Windows 95 is a very powerful operating system. One of the primary sources of this power is the built-in flexibility that allows the user to perform functions in different ways. For example, the Taskbar and Start menu are easy to customize in different ways. This means that one student may change the Start menu so that it appears in a different form than is displayed in the text. For this reason, we have attempted to describe a set of procedures that will work regardless of customized choices. This also means that there may be shortcuts that are set up on your computers that are optional. In this case, feel free to alert the students to this and allow them to use it.

The text also features an accompanying instructor's guide. The guide includes a chapter outline, additional approaches to performing tasks covered in the chapter, things to consider before covering the chapter, answers to each chapter self-test, objective questions for the chapter, and transparency masters for many of the screen displays in the text. Additional exercises for the word processing, spreadsheet, and database modules are also provided. The instructor's guide is available in printed form and on diskette in the Works format. Solutions to all assignments are included on the instructor's disk.

Acknowledgments

It is impossible to acknowledge every individual that contributed to the development of this text; however, we would like to express our special thanks as follows. First we would like to express our thanks and appreciation for the many suggestions we have received from those individuals that incorporated our earlier book, *Using Microsoft Works 4.0*, in their classes. Their suggestions have made this text dramatically better.

Special thanks go to our editor, Carolyn Henderson, and Audrey Regan, her able assistant. Without their support this project would have never been completed.

We would also like to thank Joan Moogan for editing the manuscript and for key testing the tutorials. You all did a great job!

We would be remiss if we did not thank our wives, Orinda and Terri, for their unselfish patience and understanding. Finally, we would like to thank our children: George, Erica, Wesley, and Jacob. We love all of you.

USING
MICROSOFT® WORKS 4.0
FOR WINDOWS® 95

PERSONAL COMPUTER CONCEPTS

When you've completed this chapter, you will be able to:

- Describe the central processing unit.
- Understand random access memory (RAM).
- Identify the parts of a computer system.
- Identify different kinds of computer software programs.
- Describe how data is stored on a disk.
- Know how to buy the correct disks for your computer.
- Describe the concept of disk files.
- Understand how to name a file.
- Know how a file is saved on a disk.
- Understand how files are grouped in directories.

LEARNING THE PERSONAL COMPUTER

This book will introduce you to the fun and power of the personal computer and some of the software programs that make the personal computer a productive tool. You will learn to produce professional-looking documents using a word processor, as well as to create electronic spreadsheets to help prepare budgets and manage numerical information. You will discover how easy it is to express information on spreadsheets and in different types of graphs. You will also learn how to maintain information about inventories and personnel-related items such as names and addresses using a database. Finally, you will find out how to combine documents created by the Works word processor with spreadsheets, charts, and drawings that you have created. You will even be able to prepare newsletters and to print form letters by combining documents with names and addresses in a database. These functions are easy to use with the Works software and the graphics-based Windows 95 operating environment.

Although these topics may seem foreign at first, each will be presented in a step-by-step fashion and will become second nature as you develop skills using the computer. Perhaps the real key to success is to experiment and have fun.

Before you can begin to learn how to use any new tool, you need to learn some concepts and terminology, and the personal computer is certainly no exception to this rule. Let's start with the computer equipment, or "hardware."

COMPUTER HARDWARE CONCEPTS

Computer hardware refers to the actual equipment, machines, and physical devices of a computer system as illustrated in Figure 1.1.

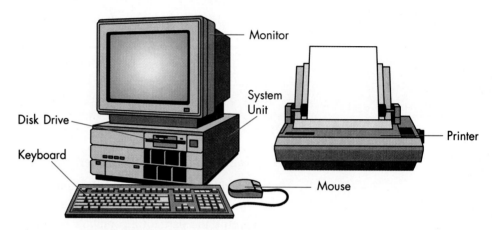

FIGURE 1.1   A typical personal computer system.

System Unit and Central Processing Unit

The **system unit** is the cabinet that contains many of the computer's working components as shown in Figure 1.1. One of the most important of these components is the **central processing unit** (normally referred to as the **CPU**). The CPU, a small electronic circuit chip, is the heart of the computer system and is the device that allows the machine to perform its complex mathematical and logic functions. Although it is not important to know how the CPU works in order to be able to use the personal computer, it is important to know that it is a major part of the machine.

The CPU chip is identified by a number that indicates its computing capabilities. For example, a basic computer might have a chip called an 8086 whereas a more powerful system would have an 80386, 80486, or the Pentium chip. Higher-numbered CPU chips will perform tasks faster and allow the computer to do more things.

CPU chips are also rated in terms of processor speed, which is measured in **megahertz** (MHz). When comparing two Pentium chips, the higher processing speed will normally indicate the more powerful computer. Typical processor speeds range from 25 MHz to 100 MHz. It is important to remember when evaluating a computer that the chip type (80386, 80486, or Pentium) will determine the overall computer performance to a greater degree than the processing speed.

Random Access Memory

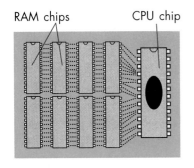

RAM chips   CPU chip

FIGURE 1.2 RAM chips are connected to the CPU.

As you work on a computer, the programs used to run the computer and the information you enter are in a temporary area of computer memory. The amount of temporary computer memory available depends upon how much **random access memory**, or **RAM**, the computer contains.

RAM is stored on electronic chips connected to the CPU as seen in Figure 1.2. The amount of RAM in a computer depends upon the size and number of RAM chips. As RAM increases, more information and programs can be used at one time.

RAM is measured in bytes; you can think of each byte as one character. RAM chips come in kilobytes (kilo means thousand; abbreviated K) or megabytes (mega means million; abbreviated MB). Less-powerful computers come with 640K RAM; newer, more powerful computers come with 4, 8, 16, or more MB. Many newer programs, including Windows 95 and Works 4.0 operate more efficiently with increasing amounts of RAM. Windows 95 requires a minimum of 4 MB and computers with 8 MB or more of memory are preferred. Fortunately, it is easy to add additional memory to most personal computers.

The most important thing to remember about RAM is that it is *volatile*; that is, whatever is in RAM exists only while the computer is on. As soon as you turn off the computer or close the program with which you are working, the information is lost. In addition, if the computer is accidentally shut off — such as with a power failure, lightning storm, or the plug coming out — everything is lost. There is, however, a way to save your program and information by storing it on disks, which is discussed in the following section.

Disk Drives and Storage

Since RAM is volatile and everything in it is lost when you turn off the computer, you need a way to store the information you enter and documents you create. A fairly permanent way to store information is on computer disks. (We say "fairly permanent" since unforeseen things can happen, even to a disk. Later we discuss how to create copies of all your data to avoid losing it.)

The component of the computer used to store information is called the **disk drive**. Most computers come with a **hard disk drive** (sometimes called a fixed disk drive) located inside the computer and one or two **floppy disk drives** in which you can put **floppy disks**. **Hard disks** come in different sizes, measured in megabytes. Sample sizes of hard disks include 220 MB, 540 MB, and 730 MB. Floppy disk drives can hold 3.5″ or 5.25″ floppy disks (see Disk Concepts, page 6).

Each disk drive is identified by a letter. By convention, the first floppy drive is called drive A and the second drive B. The hard disk drive is called drive C. Note that even if the computer has only one floppy disk drive, the hard disk drive is still called drive C.

The advantages of hard disks over floppy disks are that they are faster and hold much more information. The disadvantage is that they can crash and destroy all your data. For this reason, it is important to make copies of your files on floppy disks, a procedure called backing up your data.

CD-ROM Disks

CD-ROM

CD-ROM disks are a new method of storing vast amounts of computer data. CD-ROM stands for Compact Disk-Read Only Memory. These small, plastic disks look the same as the typical music CD and can store up to one billion bytes of data. CD-ROM computer drives can even be used to play a standard music CD.

Although CD-ROMs provide outstanding amounts of data storage, you cannot record new information to them with your computer as you can with other disks. This fact accounts for the "Read Only Memory" part of the CD-ROM name. Thus, CD-ROMs are usually used for storing new programs, computer graphics and similar material from the software manufacturer.

Keyboard

Keyboard

The **keyboard** is the standard device used to enter information into the computer's memory. It looks and operates much like a standard typewriter keyboard and includes the 26 letters of the alphabet, the 10 digits used for numbers, and some special characters such as the @ # $ % & * ( ) ?. In addition to these standard keys, the keyboard also has special sets of keys.

On the right-hand side of the keyboard is the **numeric keypad**. These keys also allow movement around the computer screen when used as arrow keys: Home, End, Pg Up, and Pg Dn. At the top or left-hand side of the keyboard are keys labeled F1, F2, F3, . . . F12. They are referred to as **function keys**. These keys perform special functions such as getting help on the computer or saving your data, and are not used to enter information into the computer.

Other special keys you will use include the following:

Shift: The shift key works like the familiar shift key on a typewriter.

Alt: The Alternate (Alt) key is used in combination with other keys to send special commands to computer programs. For example, in Microsoft Works you use the Alt key in conjunction with a second key to work with special computer commands called menus.

In this book, when the Alt key is used with another key, it will be printed as Alt/X where X represents a second key. To use the alternate key, press the Alt key and, while holding it down, press the second key. For example, to use Alt/P:

Hold down the Alt key and press the P key.

Ctrl: The Control (Ctrl) key works similarly to the Alt key. It causes a second key to execute some special function. Like the Alt key, it is always used in conjunction with some other key. When you are asked to enter a control key, it will be printed as Ctrl/X where X represents the second key.

Esc: The Escape (Esc) key is used to escape or leave some function you have selected. The Escape key is always used by itself.

Enter: The Enter key may be labeled with an arrow symbol (⇔) or simply be called Enter. Usually, you press the Enter key to signal the computer that the last instruction you are using is completed and should be "entered" into the system.

Tab: The Tab key is used in two different ways. First, the Tab key can be used to move across the screen to the next tab stop, in the same manner as a tab key on a typewriter. The Tab key is also used to move between options within a computer program. The Works program will make extensive use of the Tab key in this manner.

All the keys on the keyboard are auto-repeat keys. This means that if you hold the key down, the character or function that the key performs will be repeated as long as the key is held down. This idea is especially important when you use Alt or Ctrl keys. Since these keys usually perform a function, if you hold them down for several seconds, you will perform the function several times. To avoid problems, hold down the Alt key then quickly tap the second key once.

The Mouse

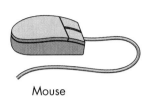

Mouse

A **mouse** is a special device used to move a position indicator called the cursor around on the display screen and to select options from screen menus. The bottom of the mouse contains a small ball that rolls when you move the mouse. As the ball rolls, it causes a signal to be sent to the computer, moving the cursor in the same direction in which you are moving the mouse. The mouse usually has two buttons. By pressing one of these buttons, you can instruct the computer to perform some action where the cursor is resting. Windows software, such as Microsoft Works, makes extensive use of the mouse.

Video Monitor

Monitor

The **video monitor** looks much like a TV screen. It is sometimes called a cathode ray tube (CRT), or video display terminal (VDT), or simply a monitor, and serves as the standard output device for the computer system. In practice, there are two different types of monitors: a monochrome monitor and a full-color monitor. If the monitor is monochrome, it can display one color and black. These monochrome monitors are usually available in amber and black or in green and black. Most of these monochrome systems can also display different shades of either the amber or green, much like a black-and-white television. Color monitors are available in different resolution levels, or clarity. A higher-resolution monitor will provide the sharpest picture, but will be more expensive than a lower-resolution system. Both monochrome and color monitors come in different sizes such as a 14", 15", or 17" screens.

Dot Matrix Printer

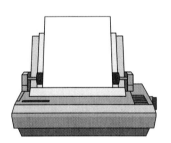

Dot Matrix Printer

A printer is used to produce a "hard" or printed copy of the information stored in the computer system. A **dot matrix printer** prints letters, numbers, and other characters by arranging a series of dots on the page to represent each character. It is an impact printer and works by striking the paper with wires (that makes the dots) to form the character. Dot matrix printers are rather loud when printing, and since each character must be printed individually, are not very fast.

Laser Printer

Laser Printer

A **laser printer** provides superb quality print and is capable of printing any graphic character. They are more expensive than dot matrix printers, but their quiet, high-quality print provides the best output possible, especially when you are printing charts or other types of graphics. Laser printers can print an entire page at a time and are usually faster than dot matrix printers. These are the printers that you would like to use when you want the best print quality possible.

COMPUTER SOFTWARE CONCEPTS

The term **software** refers to the programs that enable the computer to perform its tasks. There are basically two types of software programs that the computer uses of which you need to be aware: the operating system programs and the application programs.

Operating System

An **operating system** controls the resources and components of the computer. It consists of many specialized programs, each of which performs a specific task. One task controlled by the operating system is the allocation of the computer's RAM to application programs. The operating system is also responsible for the synchronization of hardware components such as the monitor, printer, and disk drive(s). Most personal computers use a disk-based operating system called the **disk operating system** or **DOS**. Commands executed within the operating system are called DOS commands.

Windows 95 is a picture-oriented operating system that is more advanced than DOS and makes the computer easier to learn. Chapter 2, <u>Learning and Using Microsoft Windows® 95</u>, discusses some of the functions of Windows 95.

Application Programs

Application programs are written to perform useful functions. Examples of application programs are word processing programs, accounting programs, and programs that handle business inventory. Many application programs perform a specific function. Others, called **integrated programs**, provide word processing capabilities, electronic worksheet and graphing capabilities, database management capabilities, computer communications, and drawing capabilities. The Microsoft Works 4.0 for Windows 95 program that you will be using is an excellent example of an integrated program.

DISK CONCEPTS

Computers have the ability to process and manage vast amounts of information quickly and easily, but to do so they must have the ability to store the information so it can be retrieved when needed. Today, the hard disks within the computer and the floppy disks used in the computer's disk drives are the most popular devices used to store information.

As mentioned earlier, hard disks come in different sizes such as 40 MB, 220 MB, 540 MB, and 730 MB. The larger the hard disk, the more data you can store on the drive.

Identifying Floppy Disks

Floppy disks come in two sizes — 5.25″ and 3.5″ as illustrated in Figure 1.3. The 5.25″ disk consists of a round, floppy, magnetic disk housed in a flexible, square case. The 3.5″ disk consists of a magnetic disk within a hard plastic case. The case has a sliding metal cover that protects the magnetic disk.

Each size of floppy disk comes in low (also called double) and high densities. The density of the disk determines how much information it can store; the higher the number, the more information. The 5.25″ low-density (double density) disks store 360 K of data; the high-density disks store 1.2 MB of data. The 3.5″

low-density (double density) disks store 720 K of data; the high density disks store 1.44 MB of data.

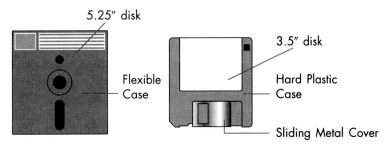

FIGURE 1.3   The two types of floppy or removable disks.

In addition to size and density, disks differ in whether they store information on one or both sides. Early computers used disks that stored information on a single side and in a single-density format, called SS/SD. Today's computers use disks that store information on both sides in a double-sided, double density (DS/DD) format or in a double-sided, high-density (DS/HD) format. Figure 1.4 summarizes the available floppy disks for a PC.

Diskette Specifications

Label	Meaning	Size	Capacity
DS/DD	Double Sided/Double Density	5.25″	360,000 (360 K)
DS/HD	Double Sided/High Density	5.25″	1,200,000 (1.2 MB)
DS/DD	Double Sided/Double Density	3.5″	720,000 (720 K)
DS/DD	Double Sided/High Density	3.5″	1,440,000 (1.44 MB)

FIGURE 1.4   Choose disks based on both size and density.

To better understand the amount of information you can store on a disk, consider that a 360 K, 5.25″ (DS/DD) can hold about 100 single-spaced typed pages. A 1.2 MB, 5.25″ (DS/HD) disk can hold about 400 single-spaced typed pages. And a 1.44 MB, 3.5″ disk (DS/DD) can hold over 500 single-spaced typed pages.

Formatting Disks

When something is written to a disk, the information is recorded magnetically in concentric circles called **tracks**, as illustrated in Figure 1.5. These tracks are then further subdivided into **sectors**, also shown in Figure 1.5. The computer's operating system and disk drives know where information is stored by maintaining the track and sector numbers.

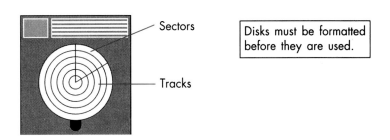

Disks must be formatted before they are used.

FIGURE 1.5   Disks are formatted by creating tracks and sectors.

Tracks and sectors are not on new disks and must be created by the computer before you can store information on the disks. The process of creating tracks and sectors is called **formatting**. (Note that some disks come preformatted.) You can format a new disk or a disk that has previously been formatted and has information on it. An important point to remember is that *when you format a disk, it wipes out all information on the disk*. The computer command used to format a disk is covered in Chapter 2, <u>Learning and Using Microsoft® Windows® 95</u>.

PURCHASING DISKS

Purchasing disks can be confusing and it is very important to buy the correct disks for use in your computer. There are several considerations, but the two most critical deal with the disk size and density.

When buying disks, first identify the size you will need and then consider the density that is used by the computer. Check the computer's owner manual for the recommended disk specifications. Once you have identified the size and density, look for the label on the disk box (DS/DD, DS/HD) that matches the required density. NOTE: If the computer can read high-density disks, it can also read low-density disks, so either disk density can be used in a high-density disk drive. However, a computer with a low-density disk drive cannot read a high-density disk.

Care of Disks

The disks available today are reliable; however, they are not indestructible. You must use reasonable care to ensure that the disk does not become damaged. If it does, the data stored on the disk could be lost.

To appreciate the care you must take to protect your disks, you should understand that the disk is coated with an iron oxide material. The information stored on the disk is recorded as magnetized spots next to each other. When data are transferred from the disk to the memory of the machine, the reading device must be able to interpret groups of spots as a character. If it encounters a spot that cannot be interpreted, the reading device gives an error message and stops reading. Depending upon where the error is, you may lose all the information on the disk or you may lose only a small portion of the information.

In general, use the same care for a disk as you would for your best cassette tapes or compact disks. They are constructed in similar fashion and store their data in somewhat the same way. The biggest difference is that if you destroy a CD, you can buy a new one. If you destroy a disk that contains important information you entered, you may need to recreate the information manually. Figure 1.6 provides information on how to care for computer disks.

Caring for Diskettes

---

1. Avoid storing the diskette in extreme hot or cold temperatures. If the disk has been exposed to extreme temperatures, allow it to return to room temperature before using it.
2. Keep diskettes away from magnetic fields since magnets will erase the data. Some computer monitors and most electric motors emit a magnetic field that can damage a diskette.
3. Do not fold or bend the diskette.
4. Keep food, drinks, and smoke away from the diskette.

FIGURE 1.6 Observe these precautions while using disks.

When you store information on a disk, you store it as a *file*. A file on a disk serves much the same purpose as a traditional paper file folder. A paper file folder is labeled by the name of the report it holds. A disk file is similarly labeled by the information it has about a specific subject. For example, if you created a resumé using a word processor, on the disk the resumé could be in the Resumé file on the disk.

Naming Files

Disks, especially hard disks, can contain many (sometimes several hundred) files. Therefore, to be able to find a file and access its information, each file must have a different name from any other file on the same disk. The file name consists of two parts: the actual file name and an extension. For example, a file could have a name such as **EMPLOY** and an extension such as **WPS**; the entire file name would then be EMPLOY.WPS. The name is generally used to identify the file and the extension to identify the type of information in the file. For example, EMPLOY might indicate the file has information about employees, and the WPS would indicate it is a Works word processing file. These file-naming conventions are discussed in Chapter 2.

Loading and Saving Files

To use a file on a disk, you must load the file into memory. This process creates a second copy of the file in random access memory. The copy that is on the disk remains there and is not changed until you save your work.

When you make changes to the copy of the file on the screen, only the copy of the file in RAM, not the copy of the file on the disk, is altered. *No* changes are made to the copy of the file on the disk until you instruct the computer to *save* it to the disk. Then, the new copy of the file in the computer's memory replaces the copy that is on the disk. This process is shown in Figure 1.7. You will learn how to save files in Chapter 3, An Introduction to Word Processing.

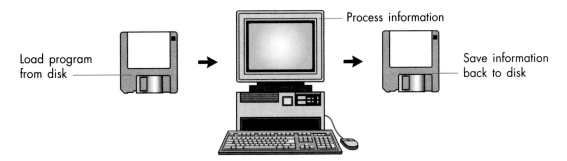

FIGURE 1.7   A program is first loaded into the computer's memory from a disk before it can be used. Finished work is then saved back to a disk.

FOLDERS

After you have been working with a computer for a while, you will probably have many files. The computer provides a way for you to organize your files so you can retrieve them quickly and easily. You can create **folders** using Windows 95 that let you organize files that are related under some common topic or area. Each folder can contain documents, programs, graphics or other related material. Think of these computer folders as an electronic manila cardboard folder in which you can save your electronic files.

For example, suppose you want to organize your computer work according to the subjects you are interested in, namely, history, English, and other information under a folder called Mywork. You would set up folders for each subject area so that you could quickly find the information you were looking for. Figure 1.8 shows an example of a disk with folders that can contain other folders of files. Folders are also helpful to store different kinds of application programs on the same disk. You could have one folder for Microsoft Works, another for a graphics program, and another for the Windows 95 operating system.

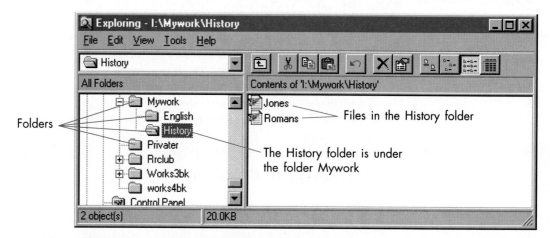

FIGURE 1.8   Windows folders contain disk files in which data is stored.

CHAPTER 1 SELF-TEST

1. Describe the hardware components of a typical personal computer system.
2. What is the function of RAM?
3. What does the term volatile mean?
4. When would you use the Alt or Ctrl keys? How would you use them?
5. When would you use the Esc key?
6. If you have a machine with one floppy disk drive and one internal hard disk drive, what are the names of the drives?
7. What are some differences between a dot matrix printer and laser printer?
8. How is the mouse used?
9. What is the function of an operating system?
10. What happens when you format a disk?
11. What is a DS/DD disk? A DS/HD disk?
12. List four things you should not do to a disk.
13. What are the two parts of a file name? What does each part tell you?
14. When you load a file from a disk into memory and make changes, what happens to the file on the disk?
15. Why are folders used?

2

LEARNING AND USING MICROSOFT® WINDOWS® 95

LEARNING OBJECTIVES

When you've completed this chapter, you will be able to:

- Understand what the Windows 95 software does.
- Be able to start Windows 95.
- Move between different windows with the mouse.
- Understand how icons are used.
- Open the Windows Explorer.
- Format a disk from the Explorer.
- Use the Explorer to copy or delete files on disks.
- Describe how files and folders are used in Windows 95.
- Start Works 4.0 and other Windows programs.

THE COMPUTER OPERATING SYSTEM

As we discussed in Chapter 1, the personal computer is one of the most powerful tools available. It can help you with a variety of tasks, including word processing, financial analysis, and the storing information in databases. The computer, called hardware, uses programs, or software, to accomplish these tasks. These programs are the instructions that tell the computer what to do and how to respond to your commands.

One of the most important software components of the computer is the operating system. As you may recall from Chapter 1, the operating system is a collection of programs that controls the functions of the computer, including presenting information on the screen, printing the information, and storing the information on disks.

In the past, personal computers compatible with IBM systems have used the MS-DOS (Microsoft Disk Operating System) or PC-DOS (IBM disk operating system). The systems are basically the same, and in this book we will refer to these operating systems simply as DOS.

When DOS was used, the computer screen was empty except for what is called the DOS **prompt**; for example, C:\>. To communicate with the computer, you would type DOS commands at the DOS prompt. Most users found it difficult to remember these detailed commands. They wanted an operating system that would use the graphics capabilities of computers enabling them to become more "user-friendly." Early efforts by the Microsoft Corporation to develop a graphical interface resulted in the Windows software. Original versions of Windows required the use of DOS to control the computer and was limited by a number of DOS shortcomings.

Windows 95 represents an entirely new operating system and replaces DOS. Windows 95 also offers simple-to-use menus of commands and program icons, or pictures, to run the computer. Figure 2.1 shows some typical Windows 95 icons. Windows 95 is a complete operating system that runs best on a powerful CPU, such as a 386, 486, or Pentium. It also needs a computer with a hard disk, or one that is attached to a network of other computers that are connected together.

Msworks

jmu

Officecp

FIGURE 2.1   Some typical Windows 95 icons.

STARTING WINDOWS 95

Windows 95 will automatically start to run when the computer is turned on. You will not have to enter any special commands, so simply turn your computer on now as follows:

1. Turn on the monitor, printer (if there is one), and the computer.

THE WINDOWS 95 ENVIRONMENT

When you power up the computer and start Windows 95, the first thing that will appear on your screen is the desktop window. This window acts as an electronic work surface on which you can place items you are currently using. This is similar to the function of the surface of a standard office desk. Further, your office desk has drawers where work can be kept. This function is also provided in Windows 95 through the taskbar and Start buttons which allow you to move programs or information to the desktop.

The desktop window can be set up in as many different ways as there are computers and users. This means that your computer screen may look different from everyone else's and from the figures in this book. Do not be concerned. One of the features of Windows 95 is its flexibility in allowing people to work in a comfortable way. Regardless of how your desktop looks on the screen, it will most likely have the taskbar and Start button as shown in Figure 2.2.

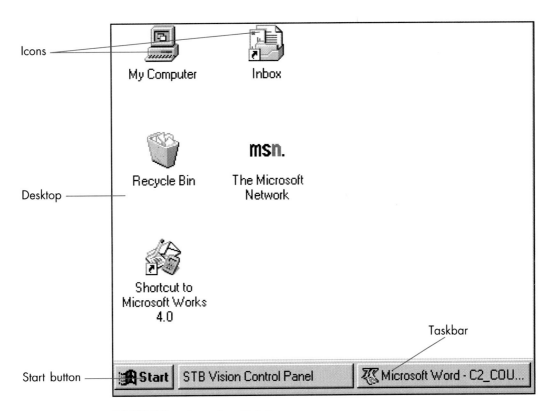

FIGURE 2.2   The Windows 95 desktop

Windows 95 Components

No matter how your Windows 95 system is set up, screens will consist of several components:

Desktop: This is the background area of the screen. Think of this work space as the top of a standard desk where you will work on projects and tasks.

Windows: These allow you to see inside the computer so you can recall data or programs whenever you wish. Opening a Window is analogous to opening a drawer in your desk. Windows can contain check boxes, selection boxes, and buttons as shown in Figure 2.3.

Icons: These pictures represent various programs, data, or information that you can select with a click of a mouse or press of a key. Icons make it easy to run the computer without having to learn complex computer commands.

Buttons: Windows 95 uses pictures of buttons that you can "press" with the mouse or keys. When you press a button, you will cause Windows to perform some specific operation, such as making a word appear in **boldface** type.

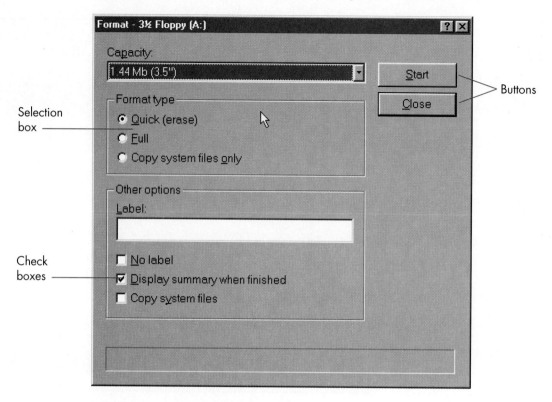

Selection box ——

Check boxes ——

Buttons

FIGURE 2.3   A Windows 95 disk format window.

MOUSE TECHNIQUES

Windows 95 software such as Microsoft Works 4.0 is designed to be used with a mouse. The use of a mouse makes it easy to point at and select icons in a window. You can use Windows 95 with the keyboard, but you will be missing out on much of the power and ease-of-use Windows programs offer.

Using the Mouse

The **mouse** is a device that allows you to move a **pointer** on the screen. By moving the mouse on a flat surface such as your desk, you cause the pointer to move in a corresponding fashion on the screen. This provides a fast and accurate method of selecting icons or other material, such as text. You can also use a mouse to draw in a drawing program and in many other ways, such as moving text or figures from one location to another.

Usually, a mouse has two or three buttons on the front as shown in Figure 2.4. You press, or **click**, these buttons to cause an action to take place. Treat the mouse with respect and make sure that dirt and other objects are not in the area over which you move the mouse or the mouse movement will become erratic.

Press (click) the left button to begin an action.

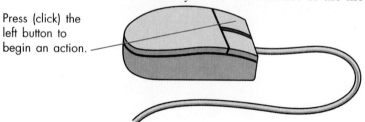

FIGURE 2.4   A typical mouse for use in Windows 95.

To use the mouse in Windows 95, move the mouse pointer over the icon you want to execute and click the left mouse button. The easiest way to learn how this works is to try it. First, try accessing a menu from the Start button. Follow these steps:

1. Be sure that Windows 95 is active and your screen appears like Figure 2.2.
2. Move the mouse pointer until it is resting on top of the item Start in the taskbar as seen in Figure 2.5. You will see a small box appear containing the text "Click here to begin."

Shortcut to
Microsoft Works
4.0

1. Move the mouse pointer over the Start button.

2. The "Click here to begin" box appears

FIGURE 2.5   Move the mouse pointer to Start to begin a Windows 95 session.

Move the mouse pointer until Help is highlighted.

FIGURE 2.6   Click the Start button and move the mouse pointer to the Help option.

3. Click (press) the left mouse button once and release it. This will "press" the Start button and activate the Start menu.
4. With the Start menu displayed, move the mouse pointer up until it rests on the Help option as shown in Figure 2.6. Notice that you do not need to press the mouse button to do this.
5. Click the mouse button with the Help option highlighted to initiate the Windows 95 help function. The Help Topics window will appear as seen in Figure 2.7. To select the Help Index, click the Index Tab as shown in Figure 2.7; you will then be able to enter the topic you would like to seek help on.
6. Type the word "mouse" and notice that as you type, Windows automatically finds the closest match to your topic. Feel free to investigate different topics in the Help index by clicking the mouse pointer on a specific entry.
7. To exit the Help function, click the mouse pointer on the Cancel button located in the bottom right corner of the Help screen.

The mouse works in a similar fashion throughout all of the Windows 95 screens as well as in the software programs that run under Windows, such as Works 4.0 for Windows 95.

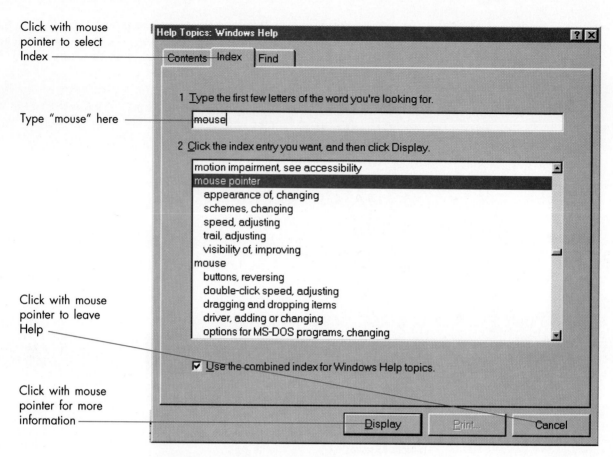

Click with mouse pointer to select Index

Type "mouse" here

Click with mouse pointer to leave Help

Click with mouse pointer for more information

FIGURE 2.7   The Windows 95 Help Index.

WINDOWS EXPLORER

The Windows Explorer provides a convenient control point for computer operations and makes running Windows 95 even easier. The Explorer will be found under the Programs listing of the Start menu. Again, the easiest way to learn about the Explorer is to use it.

1. To use the Explorer, click the Start button as you did for the Help function, but move the highlight up until it appears on the word Programs. Do not press the mouse button at this point.

2. Your computer will display a window with many different programs that are available for your use; find the Windows Explorer program as seen in Figure 2.8.

3. Move the mouse highlight over the Windows Explorer option and click the left mouse button. The Explorer will appear as seen in Figure 2.9 Note: If your Explorer screen does not display the Toolbar or Status Bar shown in Figure 2.9, click the mouse pointer on the View menu item as seen in Figure 2.9. Then, click either the toolbar or Status Bar options under the View menu so that a check mark appears next to the option. This will cause the selected bar to be displayed.

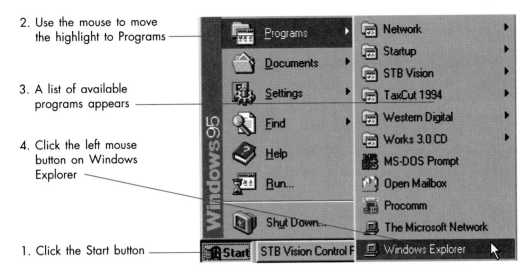

2. Use the mouse to move the highlight to Programs

3. A list of available programs appears

4. Click the left mouse button on Windows Explorer

1. Click the Start button

FIGURE 2.8 Select the Windows Explorer to find out more about your computer.

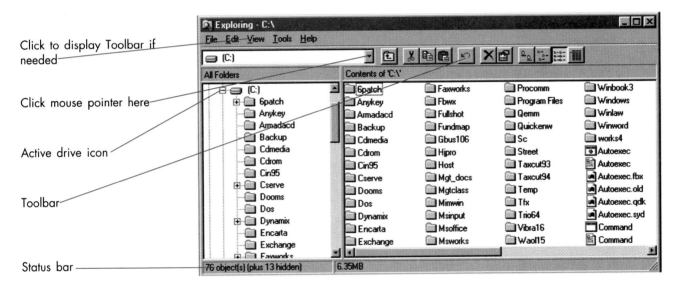

Click to display Toolbar if needed

Click mouse pointer here

Active drive icon

Toolbar

Status bar

FIGURE 2.9 The Windows Explorer Screen.

USING THE WINDOWS EXPLORER

Windows Explorer gives you a pictorial representation of the information in your computer. By clicking the mouse on the small arrow next to the active drive, as shown in Figure 2.9, you can see all the components of your computer. Get acquainted with your computer now.

1. Be sure the Windows Explorer screen is still displayed on your computer. If it is not, repeat steps one through three above.

2. Click the mouse pointer on the down arrow symbol next to the active drive icon as shown in Figure 2.9. Note: if the Toolbar does not appear on your screen, click the word View to pull down the View menu and then click the word Toolbar.

3. You will see the computer components for your system as shown in Figure 2.10. Do not be concerned if your computer has somewhat different components showing on your Explorer screen when compared to the screen shown in Figure 2.10, as all computers will be set up differently.

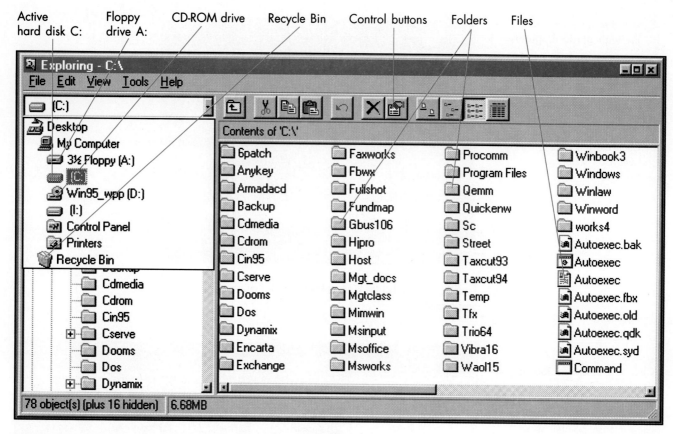

FIGURE 2.10   The Windows Explorer can display your computer configuration.

The Explorer provides you with quite a bit of information on one screen. Let's take a look at some key components.

Active hard disk C: This highlighted icon represents the hard disk you are currently using. The contents of this active disk are displayed on the right side of the Explorer screen. Notice that the information on the disk is stored in *folders*. Conceptually, disk folders are much like ordinary paper file folders you might use to store related documents or information concerning one topic. Folders contain files that are the actual computer documents used to perform a task. Here is some additional information on the importance of computer files.

File: A file is any named collection of characters that is stored on an area of a disk. These characters may make up a program, document, spreadsheet, picture or chart, or almost anything that can be stored on a computer. Virtually all information stored on a computer is stored in a file. The Explorer displays icons in front of the file names that show you what kind of file it is.

File name: Each file on a disk must have a unique name that will identify it. The file name consists of two parts: the file name and an optional extension. When a file extension is used, the file name must be separated from the extension by a period (.). Programs developed for Windows 95, such as Works 4.0, allow the use of filenames of up to 40 characters, not including these special characters $ % @ - { } ! #. However, earlier versions of Windows were limited to filenames of up to eight characters including letters, numbers, and any of the following special characters $ % @ - { } ! #. This means that older programs, while useable with Windows 95, still require filenames of eight or less characters.

File type icon: The file type icon makes it easy to identify the kind of information in a file. For example, an icon depicting a sheet of paper and pencil indicates that the file is a word processing file. Similarly, an icon showing a small chart or graph indicates a spreadsheet file. The Works program will automatically assign a file type icon to your file depending on the contents. Figure 2.11 displays several common file type icons.

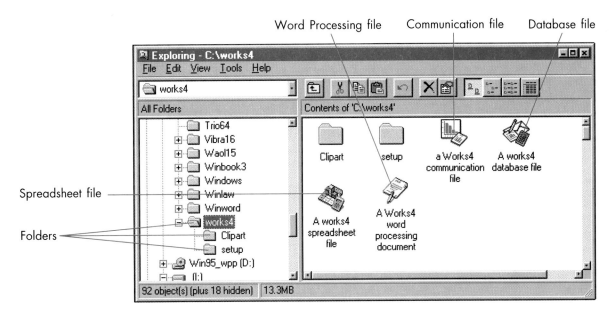

FIGURE 2.11   File type icons used with Works 4.0.

Earlier versions of Windows used file extensions in place of file type icons. These extensions consisted of a period followed by a three character string added to the end of the filename. For example, word processing files were identified with an extension "WPS." Do not be surprised if you see file extensions on some older files; Windows 95 will automatically display the appropriate icon even for older files using extensions. You will not need to add file extensions to files created in Works 4.0.

The Explorer provides many powerful functions that will make it much easier to use your computer. These functions include procedures for copying files from one disk to another, erasing old files, and checking the contents of a disk. The Explorer uses icons, buttons, and menus to perform these tasks. For example, if you want to view the contents of a disk in disk drive A:, you would place a disk into drive A:, then click the mouse pointer on the icon representing floppy drive A: shown in Figure 2.10. If you forgot to put a disk into drive A:, Explorer would display the error message shown in Figure 2.12. Note: If your computer has more than one floppy disk drive (drives A: and B:, for example) and you wish to use drive B:, simply substitute the B: for A:.

FIGURE 2.12   This error message informs you there is no disk in drive A:.

Formatting a Disk

Disks need to be formatted (as described in Chapter 1) before you can use them to store data. To format a disk using the Explorer, follow these steps. Note: If you are using drive B:, substitute B: for A: in the following instructions.

Notice that the dialog box also contains options for making your formatted disk a system disk as well as for using the Quick Format option. When you select the Copy System files option, Windows will copy information to your disk that will enable the disk to be used as a boot or start-up disk, which prepares the disk to be used to start the computer. Usually you will not need to use this option. The Quick Format option is used to reformat disks that have been formatted before. This option saves time.

IMPORTANT: When you format a disk that contains data, all the data will be lost! Be sure you want to format the disk before proceeding.

1. Insert a new, blank disk into drive A: of your computer.
2. Pull down the drives window by clicking on the down arrow pointer next to the active drive icon as shown in Figure 2.13.
3. Use the mouse pointer to click on the My Computer icon which will display all the components of your computer on the right side of the Explorer window.
4. Click the icon for the Floppy A: drive on the right side of the Explorer window as seen in Figure 2.14. This step informs Windows 95 that you want to use the A: drive. If the Floppy A: icon is not highlighted, you will not be able to format the diskette.
5. Click on the word File located in the upper left corner of the Explorer window, then click the word Format as shown in Figure 2.14.
6. The Format 3½ Floppy (A:) window shown in Figure 2.15 will be displayed.
7. Select the correct disk capacity in the Capacity box (for DS/DD 3.5 (disks, this will be the 1.44 MB or 720K option).
8. Click the Full format option. You will not have to change any other options.
9. Click the Start button to format the disk.
10. The format process will begin and the Format dialog box will show you a bar graph displaying the progress of the format.

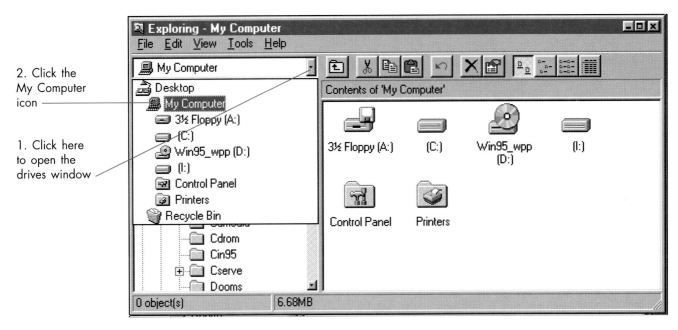

2. Click the
My Computer
icon

1. Click here
to open the
drives window

FIGURE 2.13   Opening the Explorer drives window and selecting the My Computer icon.

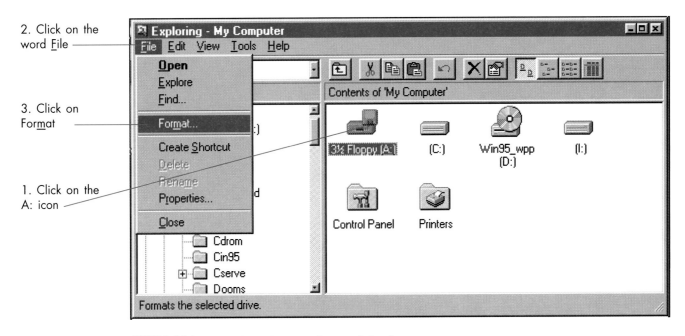

2. Click on the
word File

3. Click on
Format

1. Click on the
A: icon

FIGURE 2.14   Select the 3½ Floppy (A:) drive icon before formatting.

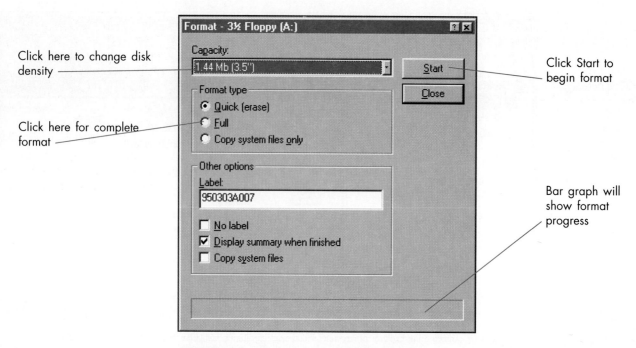

Click here to change disk density

Click here for complete format

Click Start to begin format

Bar graph will show format progress

FIGURE 2.15   The Format — 3½ Floppy (A:) window.

When the format is complete, an information box illustrated in Figure 2.16 will be displayed showing how much room is available on the disk. Click on the Close button to complete the format process. Finally, click the Close button on the Format box to close the Format option.

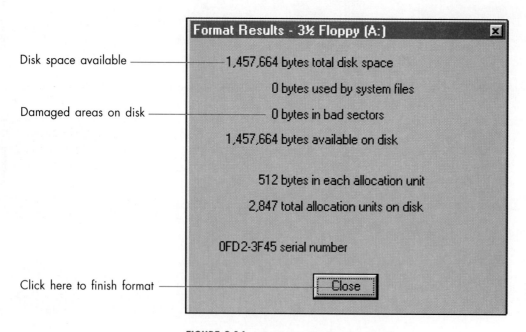

Disk space available

Damaged areas on disk

Click here to finish format

FIGURE 2.16   The Format Results information box.

Note: Occasionally, you might be notified that the disk contains damaged areas (sectors). The disk can still be used (Windows will write around the damage), but it is probably good insurance simply to use a different disk.

Once you begin to work with the computer, you will probably find that you are saving quite a few disk files and it is hard to recall what is on each one. One way to relieve this problem is to use folders, which allow you to subdivide a disk (either floppy or hard) into many different areas. This technique lets you group related files together. Then, even if you forget what the name of a file is, you can have a good idea of where to look for it. For example, you might elect to set up folders for different subject areas. Such a file organization might look like the one in Figure 2.17. Note that this directory structure has a **root folder** as its highest level. The root is the directory or portion of the disk you will be in when the system first boots up.

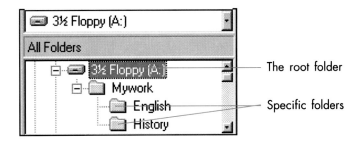

FIGURE 2.17 The file structure of a disk in drive A:.

This type of directory structure is especially helpful when you are using the large storage capacities of a hard disk. It can, however, also be helpful when using floppy disks so that data can be easily identified.

Creating New Folders

You can create new folders through the Explorer. First, highlight the disk or folder under which you wish to place the new one. Next, pull down the File menu and position the highlight over the New option. When the submenu appears, click the mouse on the Folder option as shown in Figure 2.18. Windows will create the new directory, but prompt you for a name as shown in Figure 2.19. The name for a folder can be up to 255 characters, including spaces, but cannot contain any of these special characters: \ ? : * ? " < > | .

Note: The directory will be created *under* the currently active or highlighted directory, so be sure to make the root directory active if you want it created there.

1. Pull down the File menu

2. Move the highlight to New

3. Click on Folder

FIGURE 2.18 Creating a new folder.

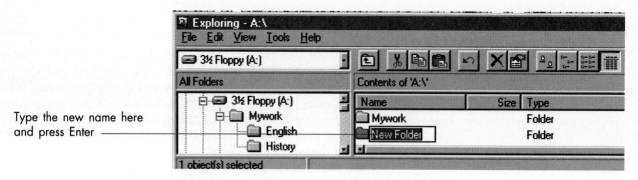

Type the new name here and press Enter

FIGURE 2.19   Naming the newly created folder.

Control Button Descriptions

The Windows Explorer allows you to manage files and folders quickly and easily through the use of control buttons. These buttons, illustrated in Figure 2.20, are located at the top, right-side of the Explorer window and are used as follows.

Up one level: Move to the next higher folder or disk.

Cut: Remove the file or folder from current disk and hold it to copy to a different destination.

Copy: Copy the file or folder, but do not remove it from the current location.

Paste: Pastes the cut or copied file or folder to the highlighted destination.

Undo Copy: Removes the copied file or folder from the new location, but will not erase the original file or folder. This is not available when using a floppy disk.

Delete: Will move the highlighted file or folder to the Recycle bin where it can be erased permanently.

Properties: Allows you to determine when the file was created, the program it is used with, and so forth.

Explorer display: Changes the way files and folders appear in the Explorer window.

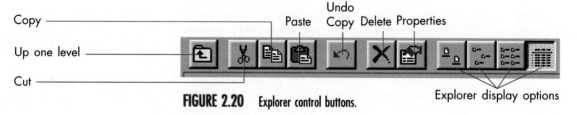

Copy
Up one level
Cut
Paste
Undo Copy
Delete
Properties
Explorer display options

FIGURE 2.20   Explorer control buttons.

Copying Files to Disks

You will often need to copy an existing file of information onto a disk for backup purposes or to take the information with you to work on a different computer. The Explorer allows you to copy individual files, groups of files, or entire folders. The general procedure you will follow is first to highlight the file or folder you want to copy. Next, using the control buttons located at the top of the Explorer screen, (illustrated in Figure 2.20), select the Copy button. Finally, highlight the destination you want the file copied to (a disk or folder), and press the Paste button. Try this yourself by copying a file now.

1. Be sure a new formatted disk is in Drive A: (or B: as appropriate).
2. Click the mouse pointer on the C: drive (your hard disk) icon on the left side of the Explorer screen as displayed in Figure 2.21. You may have to scroll up or down in the Explorer screen to find the C: icon.

The up scroll arrow ——

Click on the C: icon ——

The down scroll arrow ——

Click on these scroll arrows to find the C: icon

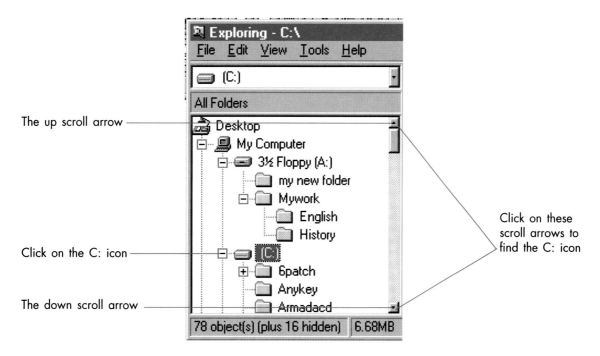

FIGURE 2.21   Selecting the C: drive.

3. When you see the contents of drive C: displayed, you will notice a series of file folder icons on the left side of the Explorer screen and under the C: icon. Click the down scroll arrow shown in Figure 2.21 until the Windows folder is displayed, then click the Windows folder with the mouse pointer by pressing the left mouse button. This will display the files in the Windows folder on the right side of the Explorer screen.
4. On the right side of the Explorer screen you will notice a number of folders. Directly above them, there are four buttons labeled Name, Size, Type, and Modified as shown in Figure 2.22. By clicking these buttons, Explorer will order the folders and files according to the button parameter. For example, click the name button to organize folders alphabetically in ascending (A,B,C, etc.) order. Click the name button again for descending (Z,Y,X, etc.) order. Similarly, you can arrange folders by Size (smallest to largest), Type (folders to files) and date of last modification.

Right now, click the Name button so that folders are selected in ascending order so that the Explorer window appears as shown in Figure 2.22.

5. Click the Help folder on the right side of the Explorer screen twice. You will see a number of Help files on the right side of the Explorer screen.
6. Click on the first Help file on the right-side of the Explorer screen. Click on the Copy button in the Explorer window as shown in Figure 2.23. To be sure you have selected the Copy button, hold the mouse arrow over the button for a few seconds before clicking it. The word Copy will appear to confirm your selection.

Click to change folder diplay

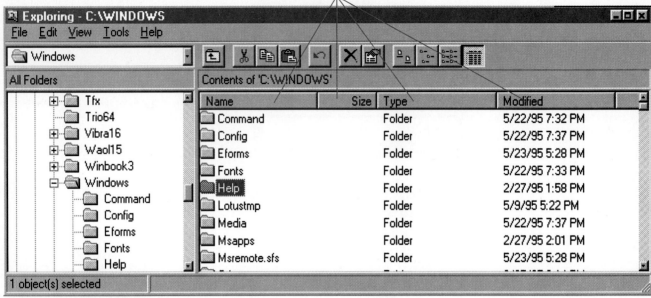

FIGURE 2.22   Using the Explorer.

7. Finally, select the A: icon from the left side of the Explorer window by clicking in the top opening as shown in Figure 2.23. You will see available drives displayed from which you should click on the A: icon. After selecting the A: drive, be sure the A: icon is highlighted (you may need to click the icon one more time).

8. Move the cursor over the Paste button. The word Paste will appear to confirm your selection. Click the Paste button to finish the copy procedure.

9. You will see the Explorer graphic showing the file being copied and then it should appear on the listing for drive A:.

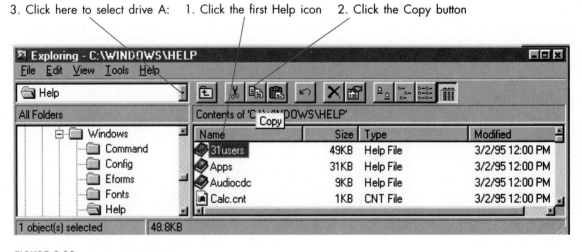

FIGURE 2.23   Copying the Help file.

Copying a Group of Files to a Disk

You will often encounter a need to copy several files from one disk to another. While you could do this one file at a time, the Explorer allows you to copy many files in a single step. Try copying a group of files now.

1. Copying a group of files is similar to copying a single file, except you must highlight several files instead of just one. To highlight several files listed next to each other, click the topmost file. Then, move the mouse pointer to the last file you want to copy. Hold down the Shift key and click the left mouse button. You will see all the files between the first and the last ones you selected are highlighted. Copy these files using the Copy and Paste buttons as you did earlier.

What happens if the files you want to copy are not next to each other? The Explorer also allows this operation. Explorer uses the Ctrl key in a fashion similar to the way the Shift key was used to copy files that were next to each other. Try copying multiple files with the Ctrl key now.

1. Click the C: drive icon to display the contents of the hard disk. Then, click the Windows file folder in the left window of the Explorer and select the Help folder as you did earlier.
2. Position the mouse pointer over the first file in the right side of the window and click the mouse button to highlight it.
3. Move the pointer down to the third file. Press and hold down the Ctrl key while you click the mouse button. Release the Ctrl key and the mouse button. Notice that now both files are highlighted, but not the one in the middle.
4. Move the pointer down to the sixth file. Highlight it using the mouse button and Ctrl key.
5. Copy the files to your disk in drive A: using the Copy and Paste buttons.

Copying Folders to Disks

Just as you can copy files to disks, you can also copy entire folders by highlighting the folder on the left side of the Explorer window, then using the Copy and Paste buttons in the Explorer. Copy a folder now.

1. Select the Windows folder icon in the left window. Then, highlight the SendTo folder located under the Windows folder if it is on your computer. If your system does not have this folder, try to find a folder with only a few files so the copy process goes quickly.
2. Use the Copy and Paste buttons to copy the folder to the A: drive.

Searching for Files

Hard disks can store a vast amount of information; however, it can be hard to recall where all that information is. For example, suppose you wrote a paper two months ago and wanted to look at it again. You might not recall where the file is located or even the name of the file. Fortunately, the Windows Explorer has a search facility that will look for files or folders on the disk. The search is initiated from the Tools menu using the Find option. The Explorer allows you to enter all or just a part of the folder or file's name. Search for any file whose name contains the word windows now.

Be sure the Explorer displays the directories for the C: drive by clicking the C: icon to highlight it.

1. Pull down the Tools menu and select the Find option. Next, select the "Files or Folders" option from the choices that automatically appear. This will cause the Find dialog box to be displayed.
2. Type *windows* in the Named box as shown in Figure 2.24.
3. Click the Find Now button to start the search and display matching entries.
4. Exit the Find dialog box by clicking the 3 located in the upper right corner of the Find dialog box as illustrated in Figure 2.24.

Click here to exit Find

2. Click Find Now

1. Type windows here

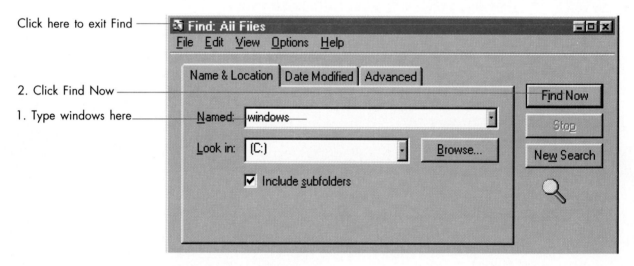

FIGURE 2.24   The Find dialog box.

The Explorer Find facility allows you to search for folders or files based on many other factors besides the file name. Notice you can search for files based on the date of the last modification or where they might be located (a disk or folder). Experiment with this tool to learn other search techniques and use the Windows Help facility for advanced topics.

Deleting Files and Folders

You can delete files and folders in much the same fashion in which you copy them. To delete a file, group of files, or a directory, highlight the file(s) desired, then click the Delete button on the Explorer window. The Delete dialog box will appear as shown in Figure 2.25 and ask you to confirm the file(s) deletion, so respond with Yes if you are sure you want to proceed. You can delete directories in the same fashion. Files deleted from the hard disk are actually copied to the Recycle Bin, so if you make a mistake, you can easily undelete the file by opening the Recycle Bin, by clicking it, highlighting the file you want to restore, and choosing Restore from the File menu.

If you wish to remove the file or folder completely, click the Recycle bin and select Empty Recycle Bin from the File menu. Please note that this will permanently remove the file or folder from your computer, so be sure that is what you want to do! Files deleted from the floppy drives are deleted permanently, so be sure you want to delete them before continuing.

Shut Down (Turn Off) the Computer

When you are ready to turn the computer off, click the Start button and choose the Shut Down option. Click the Yes button to shut down the computer. This will help you to avoid any data loss, so always use the shut down option before physically turning off the machine.

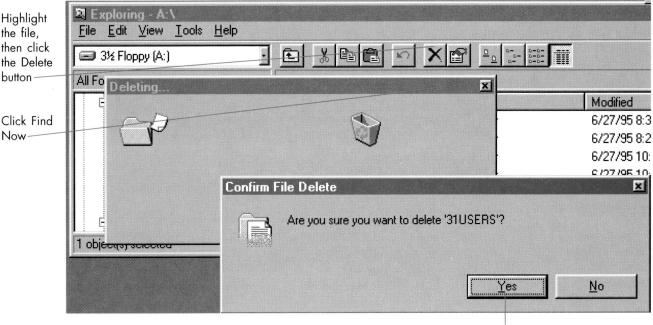

Highlight the file, then click the Delete button

Click Find Now

FIGURE 2.25   Delete files with the Delete button and dialog box.

Click Yes to complete deletion

Quick Tour of Works 4.0 for Windows 95

Microsoft Works is very easy to use, and one of the best ways to be introduced to it is to use the Works tutorial that is part of the program. Let's try it now.

1. Click the Start button, move the highlight to Programs and find the Microsoft Works 4.0 icon and click it to start the Works program. Note: Check with your instructor if you cannot find the icon.
3. You will see the Works Task Launcher box appear on the screen.
4. Click the Cancel button to remove the Task Launcher.
6. Activate the Help menu by clicking the word Help in the upper left area of the screen.
7. Click the Introduction to Works option. When you will see the Introduction screen displayed, click the mouse on the right arrow to begin. This short introduction will acquaint you with some of the many features of Microsoft Works 4.0.
8. When you are finished, the Task Launcher will again appear. Exit the Works program by clicking the Exit Works button located on the bottom left corner of the Task Launcher window.
9. Choose the Shut Down option after clicking the Start button, answer Yes at the prompt, then turn off the computer when the instruction appears on the screen.

Conclusion

You should now be able to start Windows 95 on your computer and understand the basic concepts of files, folders, and icons as used in Windows 95. You should be familiar with the use of the mouse, menus, and dialog boxes. Finally, you should be able to copy and delete files and folders using the Explorer. These important concepts will be used throughout the rest of the text.

CHAPTER 2 SELF-TEST

1. Describe what you can expect to find in a disk file and a disk folder.
2. How would you use the Windows Explorer to list all files on drive A:?
3. Describe how to format a disk in drive B: using the Explorer. Why do you need to format disks at all?
4. Describe how to copy a file from drive C: onto a disk in drive A: using the Explorer control buttons.
5. What is the procedure to copy four files that are not adjacent to each other from drive A: to drive C:?
6. Describe how to delete a file called HISTORY PROJECT from the disk in drive C:. Once deleted, how can you remove it permanently from the disk?
7. How can you create a new folder called SAMPLES on a disk in drive A:.?
8. How would you search for files whose name contains the word "English"?
9. How can you search for help on windows folders?

HANDS-ON PRACTICE

To complete this session, you will need one 3.5″ or 5.25″ inch DS/DD or DS/HD disk, depending on the type of computer you will use.

1. Turn on the computer and make sure Windows 95 is loaded. Format a new floppy disk using the Windows Explorer. If you need assistance, refer to the instructions "Formatting a Disk" earlier in this chapter.
2. Use the Explorer to search for any files in the C:/ directory that contain the word "mouse". How many files did you find?
3. Use the Explorer to copy two adjoining files from the Windows Help folder to your disk. If you do not have a Help folder, ask your instructor for another directory to use.
4. Select the View menu under the Explorer and choose the Large icons option. See how the screen listing changes. When you are done, select the View menu item again and click on List.
5. Be sure your disk is in drive A: (or B:). Click the A: (or B:) drive icon in the Explorer Toolbar to display the contents of your disk.
6. Highlight one of the files you copied to the A: (or B:) drive. Use the Rename option on the File menu of the Explorer to rename the file My New Project.
7. Delete all the files on your floppy disk. Click on the drive A: icon again to make sure there are no files left on this disk.
8. Remove your disk, choose the Shut Down button on the Start menu, and turn off your machine, printer, and monitor.

AN INTRODUCTION TO WORD PROCESSING

LEARNING OBJECTIVES

When you've completed this chapter, you will be able to:

- Create a word processing document.
- Understand word processing terminology and the Microsoft Works word processing screen.
- Use the toolbar.
- Enter, change, and delete text.
- Create bold, italic, and underlined text.
- Align text.
- Copy and move text.
- Undo changes.
- Preview and print documents.
- Save a document.
- Use Works Help routines.

ABOUT MICROSOFT WORKS

Microsoft Works is a software package that consists of four basic productivity tools. These tools are the Word Processing tool, the Spreadsheet tool, the Database tool, and the Communications tool. Each productivity tool provides a set of tools that will help you perform a particular type of task to solve a personal or business problem. In this chapter you will be introduced to the Word Processing tool of the Microsoft Works software package.

Starting the Microsoft Works program may use different approaches on different systems. This is because Windows 95 can be tailored for each user. For most systems you should be able to find the Microsoft Works icon in the Microsoft Works 4.0 folder on the Programs section from the Start button. Once you find this icon, simply click the icon and the Microsoft Works program will start. This process was discussed in Chapter 2.

When Microsoft Works starts, a brief Works screen will be displayed, then the Works **Task Launcher** window shown in Figure 3.1 will be displayed. This window has three distinct folders — Task Wizards, Existing Documents, and Works Tools, as shown in Figure 3.1.

Folder tabs

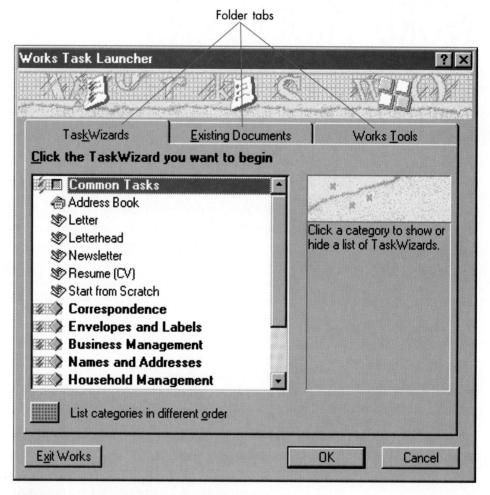

FIGURE 3.1   The Microsoft Works Tasks Launcher.

Creating A Word Processing Document

To create a new word processing document, first click the **Works Tools** tab at the top right of the Works Task Launcher screen. These tabs are shown in Figure 3.1. This will bring the Works Tools folder to the front of the screen. Next, click the Word Processor button on the Works Tools folder. This step will start the word processing tool of Microsoft Works and create a new word processing document.

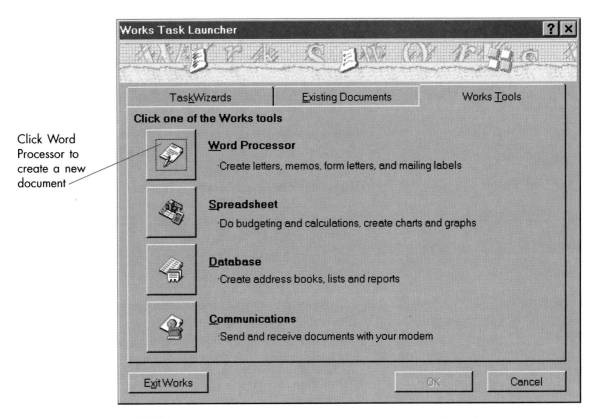

FIGURE 3.2   The Works Tools folder of the Task Launcher is used to access the Word Processor.

WORKS' WORD PROCESSING SCREEN

Before discussing how to perform word processing tasks, some of the items on the word processor's screen need to be explained. Examine the top part of the word processing window shown in Figure 3.3.

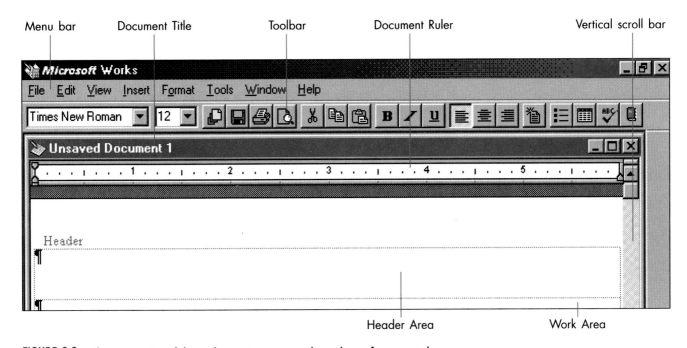

FIGURE 3.3   The upper portion of the word processing screen can be used to perform most tasks.

The upper portion of the word processor's screen includes the menu bar, document title, toolbar, and document ruler.

Menu bar: The menu bar allows access to other pull down menus.

Toolbar: The toolbar shows several icons or tools. Each icon or tool performs a special function. To execute the tool's function, use the mouse to point to the tool and click the mouse button.

Document title: The document title is the current name of the document with which you are working. Note that the current name of the document in Figure 3.3 indicates that the document has not been saved.

Document ruler: The ruler provides information about the length of the line. The ruler is normally specified in inches and marked each 1/8 of an inch. The ruler may also show the left and right margins and the location of tab positions.

Vertical scroll bar: The vertical scroll bar shows the current location in the document relative to the beginning or end of the document. As text is entered, the block in the scroll bar will move down the bar. Click the scroll bar's arrows or use the mouse to drag the block to move through the document.

Header Area: The header area is used to place text at the top of each page of the document. This area will be covered in detail in Chapter 4.

Work area: The majority of the screen is the work area. It is in this area you enter and work with text.

There are also several items at the bottom of the word processor's screen. These items are shown in Figure 3.4.

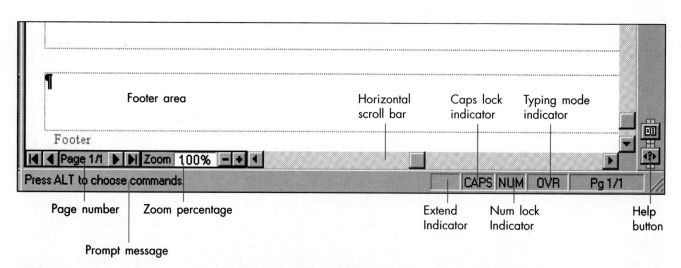

FIGURE 3.4 The lower portion of the word processing screen contains information about the document and keyboard.

Footer area: This area is used to place text at the bottom of each page. This area will be covered in detail in Chapter 4.

Horizontal scroll bar: The horizontal scroll bar is similar to the vertical scroll bar except that it indicates the relative horizontal position on the line, rather than the vertical position in the document. Since a line may be too long to fit on the screen, this will help you know the relative position to the beginning or end of the line.

Page number: The page number is the page the cursor currently appears on out of the total number of pages in the document. The buttons on the left and right sides of the page number allow you to move quickly from page to page through the document.

Zoom percentage: These buttons allow you to magnify or reduce the screen display. The percentage displayed shows the current magnification.

Prompt message: The prompt message tells what needs to be done next or what the selected option on a menu will do.

Extend indicator: This area will display EXT when the F8 function key is pressed. Extending is one technique used to select a block of text.

Num Lock indicator: This area will display NUM if the Num Lock key is on. It will be blank if Num Lock is off.

Caps Lock indicator: This area will display CAPS if the Caps Lock key is on. It will be blank if Caps Lock is off.

Typing mode indicator: This area will display OVR if overstrike mode is on. It will be blank if overstrike mode is off.

Help buttons: Help buttons are used to display the step-by-step help window or the Help Index window.

USING THE PULL DOWN MENUS

The menu bar at the top of the word processing screen lists several options for working with a document. Each option has a **pull down menu**. Figure 3.5 shows one of the pull down menus.

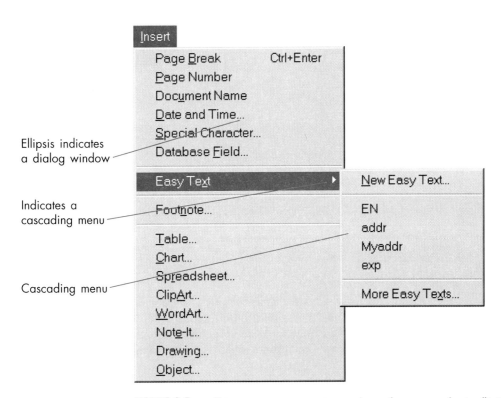

FIGURE 3.5 Pull Down menus contain options used to perform many tasks. An ellipsis indicates the option will need more information in a dialog window.

The first technique used to activate one of the pull down menus is to use the mouse. To pull down a menu, point anywhere in the menu name on the menu bar and click the mouse button. To select an option on the pull down menu, click anywhere in the option's entry on the menu.

The second approach to pulling down a menu uses the keyboard. To use the keyboard, press the **Alt** key followed by the underlined letter in the menu name. With the menu pulled down, press the underlined letter of the option you want to select.

Some menu options have a **cascading menu**. These cascading menus allow you to select sub-options of the menu option. A cascading menu is shown in Figure 3.5.

Using Works Dialog Windows

Sometimes when an option is selected from a Works menu, a new screen, or dialog window, is displayed. Menu options that have an **ellipsis** (...) following them use these dialog windows. **Dialog windows** have additional options that need to be set to complete the Works menu option.

Examine the dialog window shown in Figure 3.6 which has several options. To select an option, click the name of the option. A small black dot will move to the option indicating it has been chosen. Other options in dialog windows require that you enter values in an area. Still others contain an X indicating that you can select several of the options or a check indicating that the option is turned on.

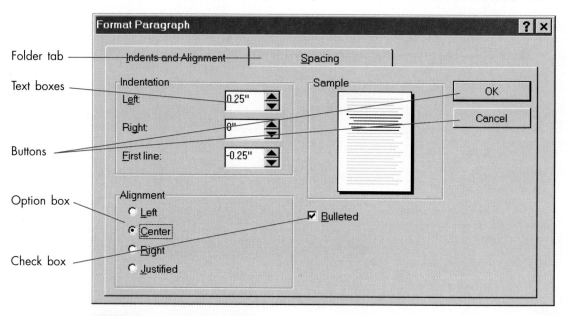

FIGURE 3.6   A Works dialog window.

Dialog windows such as the one in Figure 3.6 also may contain several folders, one behind the other. Each folder contains different options. To set options on a folder, bring the folder to the front by clicking the tab at the top of the folder. Then set the options in that folder's dialog areas.

WORD PROCESSING TERMINOLOGY AND CONCEPTS

As you work through this chapter, you will need to understand some common terms that apply to word processing and Microsoft Works. These terms are defined in the following paragraphs.

Cursor: In Microsoft Works, the cursor is a small, flashing vertical bar(|). It is sometimes called the insertion bar. When text is inserted into a document, the text is placed to the immediate left of the cursor.

Word-wrap: Word-wrap means the word processor will sense the end of a line and wrap to the next line when a line is full. You do not need to press the Enter key at the end of a line.

Formatting: When text is formatted, special characteristics or effects are applied to the text. Underlining or making text appear in italics are examples of formats. Sometimes individual words or characters are formatted. Other times entire paragraphs are formatted.

Alignment: Text alignment indicates where the text appears in relation to the left and right margins of a document. The text can be on the left side, right side, centered, or spread across an entire line (justified).

Selecting: When something is selected, it is marked so that the next function you choose is applied to it. For example, to underline a sentence, you select or mark the sentence before applying the underline format.

Toggle: A toggle is like a switch that is turned on or off. If a toggle is on and you press the switch, the switch is turned off. If the toggle is off and you press the switch, the switch is turned on. Many options available in Microsoft Works function like toggle switches to set the options on and off.

Insert mode: Insert mode is a typing mode. If you enter text anywhere in a document while in insert mode, the new text is added to the document. If you enter text between existing text, the new text is inserted between the existing text and text to the right of the cursor is moved forward.

Overstrike mode: When you enter text in overstrike mode, the new text replaces the old text. As you type over text, the original text is destroyed.

Paragraph: In Microsoft Works, a paragraph is all text that appears between two paragraph marks. A paragraph may be as large as an entire document, or it may be as small as nothing. The word nothing is used here to be precise in the definition of a paragraph; for example, if the Enter key is pressed two times in a row, two paragraphs are created. The first Enter key would terminate one paragraph, and the second Enter key would create a new paragraph. The second paragraph would appear as a blank line, but Microsoft Works would treat it as an entire paragraph.

Working with Text

In a word processing program, text is the characters and words that make up the content of a document. Works allows operations to be performed on the text such as inserting, deleting, changing, moving, copying, and many other operations.

INSERTING TEXT To insert text into a document, you need to be in "insert typing" mode. The Insert key toggles between overstrike and insert mode. To select the insert mode, press the Insert key until the typing mode indicator in the lower right corner of the screen is turned off. Once in insert mode, move the cursor to the point in the document where the new text is to be inserted and begin typing. Figure 3.7 shows what happens when text is inserted.

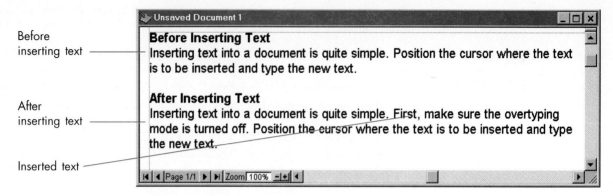

Before inserting text ——

After inserting text ——

Inserted text ——

FIGURE 3.7 When text is inserted, existing text is pushed onto new lines.

DELETING TEXT   There are several ways to delete text in Microsoft Works. The simplest way is to delete one character at a time. Two keyboard keys can be used to delete a single character. The Backspace key deletes the character to the left of the cursor. The Delete key deletes the character to the right of the cursor. Another way to delete text is to select the text as a block and use either the Cut option from the Edit menu or press the Delete key. Use this blocking approach if large segments of text need to be deleted. If only a few characters need to be deleted, use the Backspace or Delete keys.

CHANGING TEXT   There are several ways to change text. The two most common approaches are to overstrike the text and delete the text and then reenter it.

To use the overstrike approach, position the cursor to the left of the text to be changed and press the Insert key until the overstrike indicator appears at the bottom of the screen. Once in overstrike mode, type over the old text, replacing it with the new text.

To replace text using the delete method, delete the old text, then insert the new text. Be sure you are in insert mode when entering the new word or you may overstrike adjacent words. For example, to change the word *mini* to the word *micro*, delete the word mini and enter the word micro.

A large block of text can also be replaced with new text. To do this, select the old text as a block and begin entering the new text. The **Typing replaces selection** setting window in the Options reached from the Tools menu must be turned on for this approach to work. Figure 3.8 shows this approach.

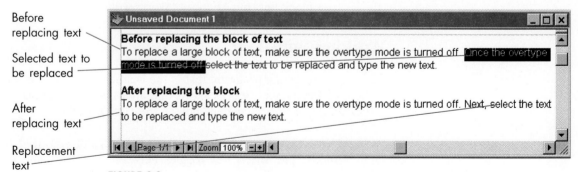

Before replacing text ——

Selected text to be replaced ——

After replacing text ——

Replacement text ——

FIGURE 3.8 To replace a large block of text, select the old text, then begin typing the new text.

Selecting a Block of Text

To perform operations such as copying, moving, deleting, and assigning attributes to a large area of text, the text must be selected as a block. When text has been selected, it will be shown in reversed video or in a different color.

There are several ways to select a block of text. The first approach is to press the **F8 function key**. The letters **EXT** (for extend) will be displayed on the status line. The arrow keys, or other movement keys, can be used to highlight the text to be selected.

A second way to select a block of text is to hold down the Shift key and cursor movement keys to highlight the text to be selected. Any of the cursor movement keys can be used including the left, right, up, and down arrow keys, page up and page down keys, and the Home and End keys.

The mouse can also be used to select a block. To use the mouse, place the mouse's pointer on the first letter of the block to be selected. While pressing the mouse's right button, drag the mouse until the text is highlighted, then release the mouse button. Once the text is highlighted, most of the options discussed in this chapter can be applied to the selected text.

To deselect text that has been blocked, use the arrow keys or the mouse to move the cursor. When the cursor is moved the text will lose the highlighting and will no longer be selected.

FORMATTING TEXT

Microsoft Works can format text in several ways. The three basic text formats are underline, bold, and italics. Any combination of these three attributes can be used. For example, text could be formatted as bold and underlined or as bold, underlined, and italic. Figure 3.9 shows the formatting tools and examples of different formats.

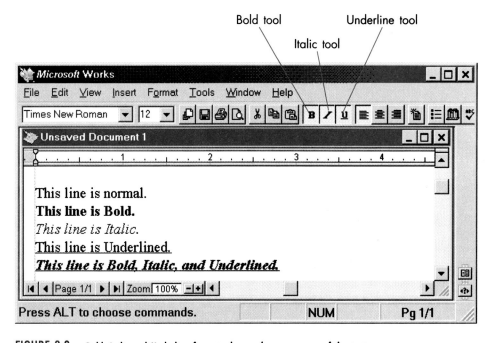

FIGURE 3.9   Bold, Italic and Underline formats change the appearance of the text.

Formats can be applied to the text as it is entered, or they can be applied to existing text. In either case, the toolbar can be used to turn a formatting option on and off. To turn a format on and off, simply point to the correct tool on the toolbar and click the mouse button.

The format tools on the toolbar work like toggle switches. To turn a format on, click the tool for the format. To turn a format off, click the tool a second time.

To apply a format as text is entered, click the tool before entering the text. If this approach is used, remember to click the tool a second time after the formatted text has been entered. This second click will turn the formatting option off.

To apply a format to text that has already been entered, select the text as a block and click the formatting tool. To remove a format from a block of text, select the text that has the format to be removed, and click the appropriate formatting tool to turn the attribute off.

Aligning Text

Three types of text alignment can be set using the toolbar. They are left, right, and center alignment. A fourth type of alignment, called justified, can be set using the *Indents and Alignment* folder of the Paragraph option on the Format menu. All four alignments are shown in Figure 3.10. The left, center, and right align tools are also shown in Figure 3.10.

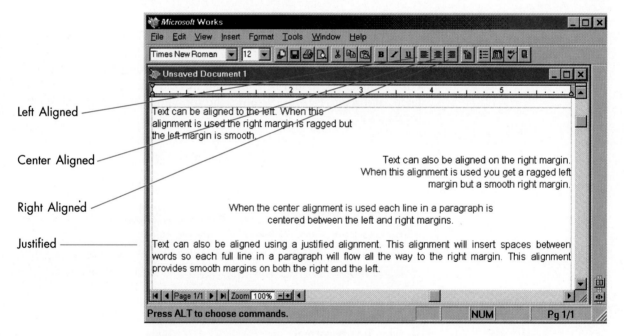

FIGURE 3.10   Alignments change the way text is oriented relative to the left and right margins.

Left alignment will start the first character of a line at the left margin. This provides a smooth left margin, but a ragged right margin. **Right alignment** will align the text against the right margin. This provides a smooth right margin, but a ragged left margin. **Centered alignment** will center the lines between the left and right margins. **Justified alignment** will spread the text all the way across the line, inserting spaces to guarantee smooth margins on both the left and right sides of the document. Most of the text in this book is printed with justified alignment.

Text alignment can be set using the toolbar buttons or the Indents and Alignment folder of the Paragraph option on the Format menu.

Text alignment always works with entire paragraphs. This means if alignment is set for any part of a paragraph, the entire paragraph will use the alignment. Remember that a paragraph is any text between two paragraph markers and can be a single line or even a single character. To align a paragraph, place your cursor anywhere in the paragraph and click the correct tool on the toolbar. To align several paragraphs, select the paragraphs as a block and click the appropriate tool or use the Indents and Alignment option.

THE UNDO OPTION

There is an **Undo** option on the Edit menu. This Undo option will remove the last change made to a document. This is especially helpful if a mistake is made while editing a document. If you make a mistake, pull down the Edit menu and choose Undo Editing. The last change to the document will be removed.

It is important to remember that only the last operation can be undone. For example, if a paragraph is deleted and the Undo is used immediately, the paragraph will be returned. If a paragraph is deleted and a new word is entered, or any other operation is performed, the deleted paragraph cannot be recovered. Also, any operation performed on a disk cannot be undone by Works. For example, if a paragraph is deleted and the document is saved, the save cannot be undone.

If the last operation performed is an Undo operation, the Edit menu will only display a Redo Editing option. This option will reapply the editing that was just undone.

USING THE ALL CHARACTERS OPTION

When entering text or modifying a document, you normally see only the text or characters that will be printed. There are however many characters in the text that do not print. These characters mark spaces, paragraphs, tabs, end of lines and other special entries in the document. To display these special characters, turn on the **All Characters** option from the View menu.

The All Characters option operates as a toggle. The first time it is chosen, the option is turned on and the special characters are displayed. The next time it is chosen, the option is turned off. The check beside the option indicates it is on. The All Characters option is shown in Figure 3.11.

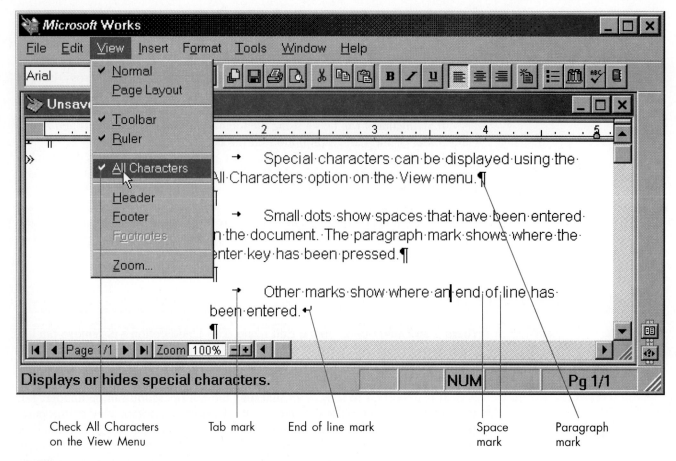

Check All Characters on the View Menu   Tab mark   End of line mark   Space mark   Paragraph mark

FIGURE 3.11   The All Characters option will display special characters on the screen.

COPYING AND MOVING TEXT

At times you may want to copy text and place it in a different location. At other times you may want to move text from one location to another. To accomplish both the copy and the move operations, use the Works clipboard or use an approach referred to as drag and drop.

Using the Clipboard

The Cut, Copy, and Paste tools can be used to delete, move, and copy text and other items in a document. When these operations are used, the text is placed on the Windows **clipboard**. The clipboard is an area of memory where data are temporarily stored. The data remain in the clipboard memory area until it is replaced by other data.

There are three tools on the Toolbar that can be used with the clipboard. These are the Cut, Copy, and Paste tools. These tools are shown in Figure 3.12.

Copy tool

Cut tool   Paste tool

FIGURE 3.12   The Cut, Copy, and Paste tools can be used to delete, copy, and move text in a document.

To place text on the clipboard, select the text as a block and use either the Cut or the Copy tool on the toolbar. The **Cut tool** deletes the selected text from its current location and places it on the clipboard. The **Copy tool** leaves the selected text in the document and places a copy of the text on the clipboard. To place text from the clipboard into the document, use the **Paste tool**.

To **copy text** from one location to another, first select the text and choose the Copy tool. This places the selected text on the clipboard. Next, to place the copied text in a different location, move the cursor to the new location and choose the Paste tool from the toolbar. The text on the clipboard can be pasted as many times as necessary. The text on the clipboard is not changed until another copy or cut operation is performed.

To **move text** from one location to another, first select the text as a block and choose the Cut tool to place the text on the clipboard. Next, move the cursor to the location where you want the text to appear and choose the Paste tool. The Edit menu also has the Cut, Copy, and Paste options available. They work in the same fashion as the tools on the toolbar. Just pull down the Edit menu and choose the option from the menu.

Remember that you have the Undo option. If you accidentally move or copy the text to the wrong location, you can use the Undo option of the Edit menu to undo the copy or move. You will want to move text when it is in the wrong location and needs to be placed in a new location. You will want to copy text when you want to leave the original text where it is and want the same text in a different location.

Using Drag and Drop

You can move text with the clipboard, or you can **drag and drop** text to a new location. To move text, select it as a block first, then place the cursor over the selected area. A small drag pointer will appear. Hold down the mouse button and a vertical bar with the word *move* will appear. While holding down the mouse button, drag the mouse until the bar is at the location where you want the text placed, then release the mouse button. The selected text will be moved to the new location.

To copy a block using the drag and drop method, hold down the Ctrl key while dragging the text. The move pointer will change to a copy pointer to indicate text is being copied.

MOVING THE CURSOR

There are many ways to move the cursor while working in a document. To use the mouse, hold down the mouse button while pointing to the up or down arrow in the scroll bars. This scrolls the screen. Once the correct area is displayed on the screen, move the mouse's cursor (I-beam) to the location and click the mouse. This will move the cursor point to the new location.

The keyboard can also be used to move the cursor. The arrow keys are the simplest way; however, they are also usually the slowest way. Figure 3.13 shows other keys that can be used and how they move the cursor.

Key	Movement
←	Left one character
→	Right one character
↑	Up one line
↓	Down one line
Ctrl / ←	Left one word
Ctrl / →	Right one word
Ctrl / ↑	Up one paragraph
Ctrl / ↓	Down one paragraph
Home	To beginning of line
End	To end of line
Ctrl / Home	To beginning of file
Ctrl / End	To end of file
PgUp	To beginning of page
PgDn	To end of page

FIGURE 3.13 Cursor Movement Keys.

USING PRINT PREVIEW

Before actually printing a document, it should be previewed. The preview option shows what the document will look like when it is printed. To preview a document, choose **Print Preview** from the File menu or click the magnifying glass tool in the center of the toolbar.

Since the printed output is much larger than what the screen can show, the preview reduces the size of the type. Although the document is too small to read, you can get a general feel for the way the finished product will look.

In the Print Preview, the cursor is a small **magnifying glass**. If you want to enlarge an area of the document to see it more clearly, move the magnifying glass over the area and click the mouse button. Click the mouse button once more to enlarge the document even more. To cancel the Print Preview, press the Esc key or click the Cancel button. An example of a print preview is shown in Figure 3.14.

Document to be printed   Preview buttons

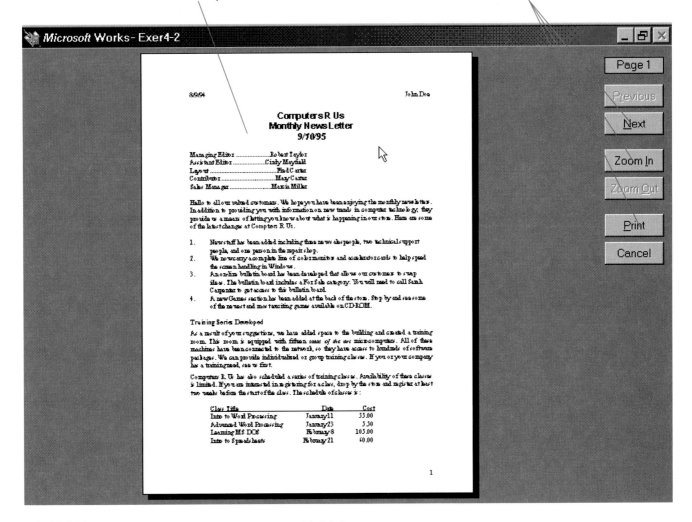

FIGURE 3.14   Use the Print Preview to see how a document will look before printing.

PRINTING A DOCUMENT

To print a document, use the Print option from the File menu. This option will provide a Print window similar to the one shown in Figure 3.15.

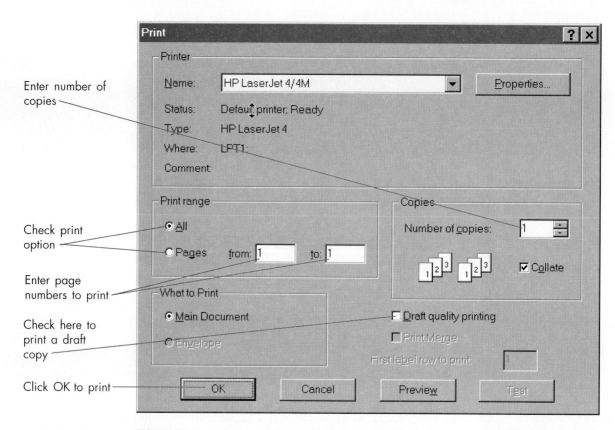

Enter number of copies

Check print option

Enter page numbers to print

Check here to print a draft copy

Click OK to print

FIGURE 3.15 The Print dialog box is used to specify the printer, number of copies, pages to print, and the print quality.

The top portion of the screen indicates the type of printer that is being used to print the document. Other entries indicate how the printer is connected.

To print multiple copies of the document, enter the number of copies needed in the **Number of copies** area.

To print only certain pages of the document, click the Pages option in the **Print Range** area. Next enter the starting and ending page numbers. If the Draft quality printing box is left blank, the document will be printed using letter-quality printing. If the Draft quality printing box is marked, the document will be printed faster, but the print will not be as clear and crisp as in letter-quality mode.

Documents can also be printed using the **Printer tool** on the center of the toolbar. This approach provides a quick way to print the entire document, but does not provide an opportunity to set the printing options on the Print window. Use this tool only if you are sure all the printing options have been set for the document.

SAVING A FILE

When a new document has been created or changes have been made to an existing document, the document will need to be saved. Saving a document will copy the contents of the computer's memory to a file stored on a disk. To save a file, pull down the File menu and select one of the two save options.

The first option is the **Save** option. When this option is selected, the file will automatically be saved under the same name, in the same folder, and on the same disk drive where it originally exists. This Save option can also be selected from the toolbar using the small disk tool. If this is the first time you are saving the file, Microsoft Works will present the **Save As** window discussed next.

The second option is the Save As option. Use the Save As option the first time a file is saved, to change the name of the file, or to change the disk drive and folder in which a file is saved. When this option is selected, the Save As window shown in Figure 3.16 is displayed.

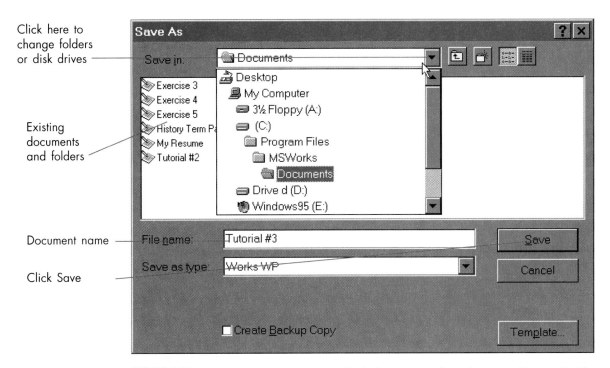

FIGURE 3.16   Use the Save As option to save a file the first time or to change the name and location of a file.

At the top of this window is the name of the current folder. There are several ways to change the folder. The first method is to click anywhere in the entry to the right of the words Save In. This will pull down a list of drives and folders available. To select a drive, click on the drive letter or name. To change folders, click on the folder name to move to the folder. You can also click on the first folder icon, shown to the right of the folder name, to move up one folder level.

The next step to saving a new file is to enter a file name in the File name area. You can enter any valid Windows 95 file name.

The **Save as type** option on the Save As window allows the file to be saved using different file formats. Use this option when you want the file saved so that it can be used with some other program.

GETTING HELP

Microsoft Works provides an extensive **Help** facility. When you are not sure how to accomplish a certain task, try using the Help facility. There are several ways to use Help. We will explain the simplest and most direct approach here.

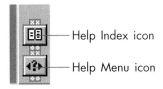

Help Index icon

Help Menu icon

FIGURE 3.17   Use the icons at the right of the screen to get help.

Along the right side of the screen you will find the two small icons shown in Figure 3.17. The first icon will provide a **Help index** screen. If this icon is clicked, the screen shown in Figure 3.18 is displayed.

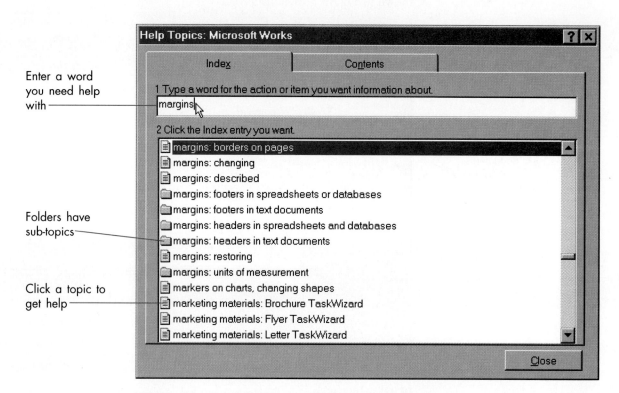

Enter a word you need help with

Folders have sub-topics

Click a topic to get help

FIGURE 3.18   Use the Help Index to look for help on a specific topic or task.

The contents window displays an alphabetically sorted list of Help topics. To see the help on a topic, click on the name of the topic. Another window will appear that describes the topic selected. If the Help topic displays a folder to the left of the topic, more topics will be displayed that deal with the subject selected.

You can also type a word or even a few letters in the entry at the top of the Help index window. As you type the letters, the topics will scroll through the index displaying topics that start with the letters typed. To get detailed help, find the correct topic and click the topic.

If the Help menu icon is clicked, the menu is displayed on the left side of your document as shown in Figure 3.19. To get help on one of the topics listed in the Help menu, click the topic. For example, if you click the "Change how text looks" topic shown in Figure 3.19, the help screen on the left in Figure 3.20 will be displayed. To see how to accomplish a task, for example applying an italic format to text, click on the "To make text italic" option. The window shown on the right in Figure 3.20 is displayed.

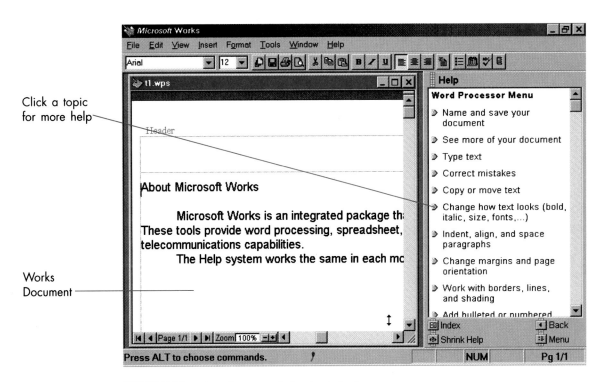

Click a topic for more help

Works Document

FIGURE 3.19 The Help Menu is displayed with the document.

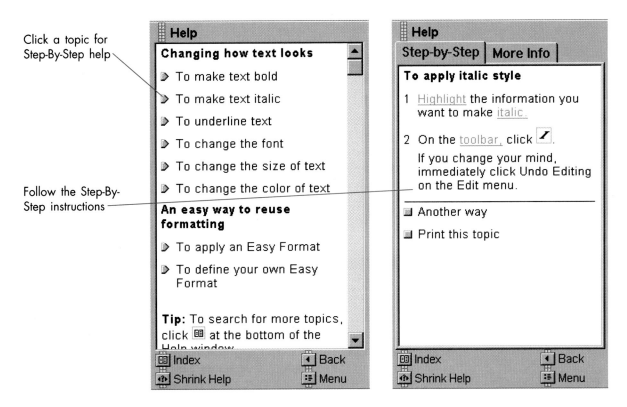

Click a topic for Step-By-Step help

Follow the Step-By-Step instructions

FIGURE 3.20 A second level help allows you to obtain help on a specific task.

If you click on underlined words that are in a help window, a text box that defines the term is displayed. Notice also that some of the help windows have a **More Info** tab. If the tab is clicked, you can get background information, troubleshooting, and related information on the topic.

There are four buttons at the bottom of the help window. The Index button will display the help index explained earlier. The **Shrink Help button** will remove the help window and allow you to see more of your document. The help icons will return to the right side of the screen. The **Back button** will display the previous help screen and the **Menu button** will display the beginning help menu for the word processor.

CHAPTER 3 SELF-TEST

1. How do you execute a function on the toolbar?
2. How do you pull down a menu from the menu bar?
3. What is meant by word-wrap?
4. Describe three different ways to select a block of text.
5. Explain the difference between the Insert and Overstrike typing modes.
6. What does Microsoft Works consider a paragraph?
7. What is the difference between using the Backspace and the Delete keys to delete text?
8. When using drag and drop, what key is used with the mouse button to copy text rather than move text?
9. What is the function of the Undo option? How many changes can be undone?
10. Explain the difference between left alignment, right alignment, centered alignment, and justified alignment.
11. List the steps necessary to copy a block of text from one area to another.
12. Explain the difference between moving and copying text.
13. Explain how you move text using the Drag and Drop method.
14. Explain the purpose of the Print Preview option. Which tool on the toolbar executes this option?

TUTORIAL

In this tutorial, you will create a new word processing document. Throughout the tutorial, we will assume that you are using a mouse to access menu options or the toolbar. To use the mouse, point to the menu option on the menu bar and click the mouse once. This will pull the menu down. To choose a menu option, point to the option on the menu and click the mouse again. To use the toolbar, simply point to a toolbar tool and click the mouse.

Make sure you read the text material to get a full understanding of the procedure you are going to perform.

To start the tutorial, boot the microcomputer using the appropriate steps for your machine. If you are not sure how to start Works on your machine, use the procedure below. See Figure 3.21 for an example. If this procedure does not work, you will need to see your instructor for the correct procedure.

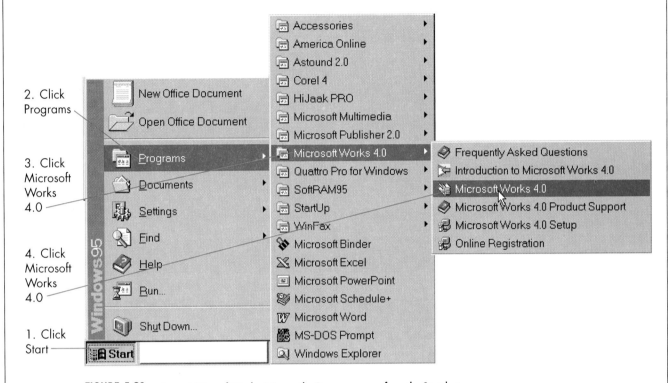

2. Click Programs

3. Click Microsoft Works 4.0

4. Click Microsoft Works 4.0

1. Click Start

FIGURE 5.21 To start Microsoft Works 4.0, use the Programs group from the Start button.

1. Start the microcomputer.
2. Once Windows 95 has started, click the Windows Start button.
3. Click the Programs entry on the Start menu.
4. Click the Microsoft Works 4.0 entry on the Programs menu.
5. Click the Microsoft Works 4.0 entry on the third menu.

Open A New Document

After Works has started, the **Task Launcher** shown in Figure 3.22 is displayed. Now you will need to move to the Works Tools folder and select the Word Processor tool.

1. Click the Works Tools tab at the top right side of the Task Launcher.
2. Click the Word Processor button.

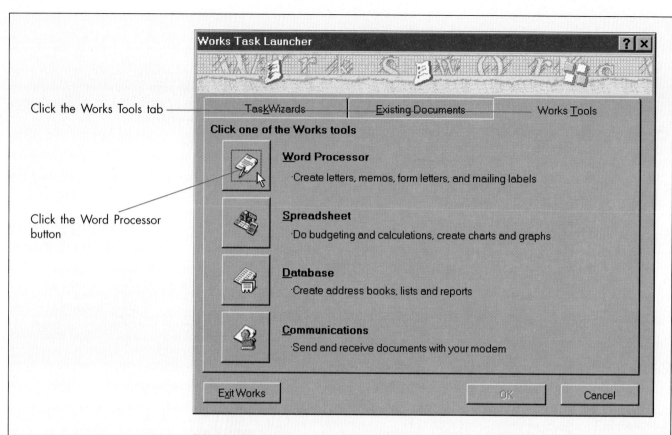

Click the Works Tools tab ──

Click the Word Processor
button

FIGURE 3.22   To create a new word processing document, click the Word Processor button on the Works Tools folder.

Set the All Characters Option

To make sure you will see everything as it is discussed in this tutorial, you will need to use the **Normal view** and turn on the **All Characters** and **Ruler** options. These options are on the View menu shown in Figure 3.23.

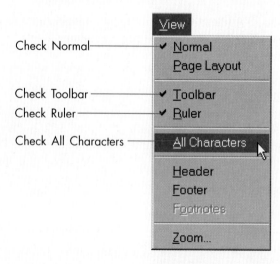

Check Normal ──

Check Toolbar ──
Check Ruler ──

Check All Characters ──

FIGURE 3.23   Set the screen options using the View menu.

1. Click View on the Menu bar.
2. Click the Normal option if it is not checked.
3. Click View on the Menu Bar.
4. Click the All Characters option if it is not checked.
5. Click View on the Menu Bar.
6. Click the Ruler option if it is not checked. If all options are checked press the ESC key twice.

The screen's work area should now have a paragraph symbol (¶) displayed. If this symbol is not displayed, check to be sure the All Characters option is turned on.

Enter Text

To begin the tutorial, enter the following three lines. Since you will want each line to be treated as a paragraph, press the Enter key at the end of each line. On the last line, enter your full name.

1. Type: Using Microsoft Works. Press Enter.
2. Type: Chapter 3 Tutorial. Press Enter.
3. Type: (Your full name). Press Enter.

Notice that each time you press the space bar, a small dot appears. This is so you can see the number of spaces you have entered. Also notice that the paragraph symbol appears at the end of each line. Each line is now a paragraph because you pressed the Enter key at the end of the line.

Now enter the following paragraph. This time, do not press the Enter key at the end of each line; let the word processor's **word-wrap** feature force the text to the next line. Before beginning the paragraph, press the Enter key once to insert a blank line between your name and the new paragraph you are about to enter. Also press the Tab key to indent the paragraph.

4. Press the Enter key.
5. Press the Tab key.
6. Type the following paragraph:

Microsoft Windows 95 is an operating system sold by the Microsoft Corporation. This version of Windows is an upgrade of Windows. Earlier versions of Windows were not operating systems. In order to use these versions you also needed an operating system. Unlike the earlier versions, Windows 95 is also an operating system. This means you do not need an operating system such as MS-DOS or PC-DOS.

7. Press the Enter key.

When you have completed entering these lines, the document should look similar to Figure 3.24.

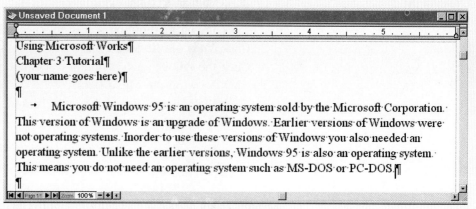

Using Microsoft Works¶
Chapter 3 Tutorial¶
(your name goes here)¶
¶
→   Microsoft Windows 95 is an operating system sold by the Microsoft Corporation. This version of Windows is an upgrade of Windows. Earlier versions of Windows were not operating systems. In order to use these versions of Windows you also needed an operating system. Unlike the earlier versions, Windows 95 is also an operating system. This means you do not need an operating system such as MS-DOS or PC-DOS.¶
¶

FIGURE 3.24   Your document after entering the first paragraph.

INSERT AND DELETE TEXT

Characters can be inserted in the text anywhere they are needed. The word-wrap feature will force existing text onto new lines to accommodate the new text. Before inserting text, make sure you are in insert mode. To see this, do the following.

1. Check the lower right side of the screen. If the letters OVR are displayed, you are in overstrike mode. Press the Insert key to change to insert mode.
2. Use the arrow keys or mouse to move the cursor to the left of the word Windows the second time it occurs in the second line of the paragraph.
3. Type: "earlier versions of" so the sentence reads: This version of Windows is an upgrade of earlier versions of Windows.

Now suppose you want to delete the words "Unlike the earlier versions" at the beginning of the fifth sentence. Use the Delete key to do this.

4. Move the cursor to the beginning of the fifth sentence.
5. Press the Delete key until the words "Unlike the earlier versions" have been deleted. Also delete the comma and space in front of the word Windows.

FORMAT PARAGRAPHS

Set Paragraph Alignment

Notice that the first three lines are aligned to the left of the document. Suppose you wanted these lines centered. Each of the lines is considered an individual paragraph, so to align all three paragraphs at once they must be selected as a block.

1. Move the mouse pointer to the word "Using," the first word in the first line of the document.
2. Hold down the mouse button and drag the mouse so the first three lines are highlighted.

Once the text is selected, the toolbar can be used to center the paragraphs.

3. Click the Center align tool. This tool is toward the right side of the toolbar.
4. Press the right arrow key to deselect the text.

Remember that the Left and Right align tools can be used to set other alignments.

Your document should now look like the one shown in Figure 3.25.

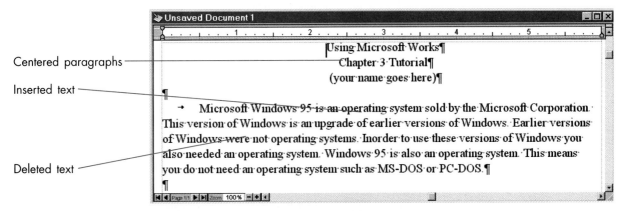

Centered paragraphs

Inserted text

Deleted text

FIGURE 3.25 Your document after centering the first three lines and making typing corrections.

One alignment option cannot be accessed from the toolbar. This is the **justified alignment**. It must be set using the Paragraph option on the Format menu. Use this option to justify align the remaining paragraph in the document. Refer to Figure 3.26.

1. Move the cursor anywhere inside the paragraph beginning "Microsoft Windows 95."
2. Click the Format menu.
3. Click the Paragraph option.
4. Click the Indents and Alignment tab of the Format Paragraph folder to bring it forward.
5. Click the Justified alignment option.
6. Click the OK button.

Click Format ———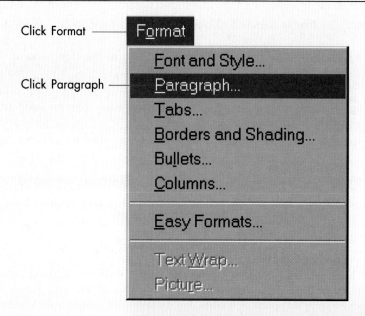

Click Paragraph ———

Click OK ———

Click Justified ———

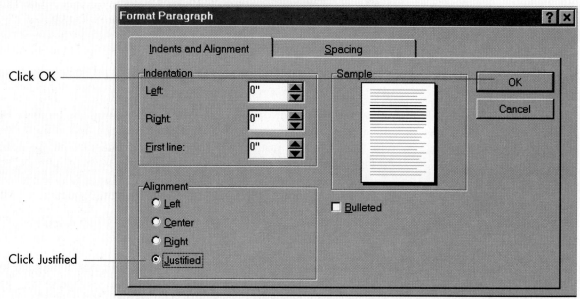

FIGURE 3.26 To select a justified paragraph alignment you must use the Indents and Alignment Folder on the Format Paragraph window.

Change Line Spacing

Line spacing for a paragraph can also be changed. This is done using the Spacing Folder of the Paragraph option on the Format menu. Make sure the cursor is still somewhere within the paragraph beginning "Microsoft Windows" and set the paragraph to space 1 1/2 lines. See Figure 3.27.

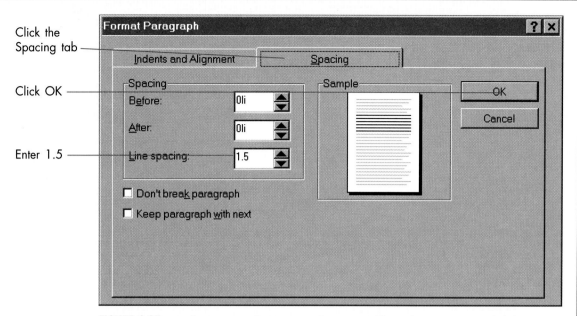

Click the
Spacing tab

Click OK

Enter 1.5

FIGURE 3.27 To change paragraph spacing, use the Spacing Folder on the Format Paragraph dialog.

1. Click the Format menu
2. Click the Paragraph option.
3. Click the Spacing tab of the Format Paragraph folder.
4. Enter 1.5 in the Line Spacing area.
5. Click the OK button.

The document should now look like the one shown in Figure 3.28.

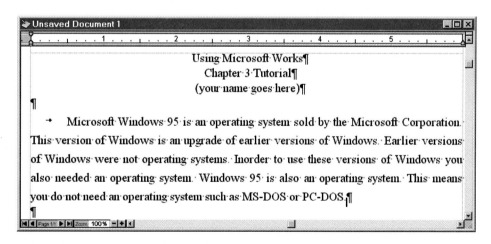

FIGURE 3.28 Your document after aligning the paragraph and setting the paragraph spacing.

ASSIGN TEXT ATTRIBUTES

The Toolbar can be used to specify underlined, bold, and italic text attributes. If these attributes are set before text is entered, the attributes will be applied to the text as it is being entered. We will now enter several lines with text attributes applied.

1. Press Ctrl/End to move to the bottom of the document.
2. Press the Enter key to leave a blank line between the last paragraph and the new line.
3. Click the B tool (for Bold) on the toolbar.
4. Type the following sentences: The Bold attribute is used to highlight important text. Use this attribute to draw the reader's attention.

This line should be displayed in bold print (on some screens it may be displayed in color). Remember that attributes must be turned on and then turned off. If more text is entered, the new text will also have the bold attribute. To turn the bold attribute off, click the Bold tool again. These attribute tools are toggles. Do this now.

5. Click the B attribute tool on the toolbar to turn off bold.

Now try one yourself. Use the toolbar to set italics on, enter the following sentence, and set italics off.

1. Turn the Italics attribute on.
2. Type: Italics are also used to indicate important text.
3. Turn the Italics attribute off.

Control keys can also be used to set attributes on and off. Control keys work as toggles just like the toolbar tools. The control keys to set the formats are:

Ctrl + B	Turns the bold attribute on and off.
Ctrl + I	Turns the italics attribute on and off.
Ctrl + U	Turns the underline attribute on and off.
Ctrl + Space	Turns all attributes off.

Attributes can be combined by having more than one attribute turned on at one time. To try this, enter the following control keys:

1. Press **Ctrl/B**.
2. Press **Ctrl /I**.
3. Press **Ctrl/U**.
4. Type: Multiple attributes can be used together by turning on each desired attribute.
5. Press the Enter key.

Now enter Ctrl/Spacebar to turn all format attributes off.

6. Press **Ctrl/Spacebar**.

Figure 3.29 shows how the document should look with the new formatted lines.

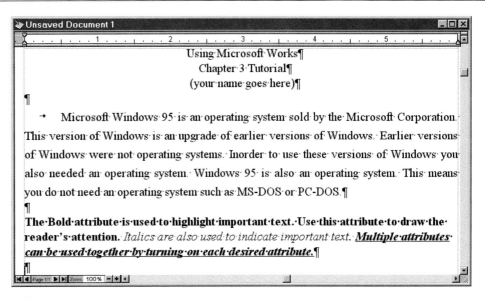

FIGURE 3.29   Your document after entering the formatted lines.

APPLY FORMATS TO BLOCKS OF TEXT

Formats can be applied to text that has already been entered. To do this, the text must be selected as a block first. There are several ways to select a block. You have already used the mouse when you centered the first three lines of the document. Another way to select a block is to use the shift and arrow keys.

To try this technique we will make the words "Microsoft Windows 95" bold in the first line of the first paragraph.

1. Place the cursor to the left of the first letter in the first full sentence of the document.
2. Hold down the Shift key.
3. Use the Right arrow key to highlight the words "Microsoft Windows 95."
4. Click the B (Bold) tool on the toolbar.
5. Press any arrow key to cancel the selected block.

The same process can be used to remove attributes from text. Select the text, then click the attribute tool for the attribute you want to remove.

USE THE UNDO OPTION

There are times when you may make a mistake and perform an operation that you did not mean to perform. You can use the **Undo** option in the Edit menu to correct the mistake. This option may read differently depending upon the last operation performed, but it will always start with the word Undo.

To see how the Undo option works, delete the first three lines in the document and use the Undo option to recover them. Follow the next few steps carefully or you may lose the lines permanently.

1. Move the cursor to the beginning of your first line.
2. Hold down the Shift key.
3. Press the Down arrow key three times to select the first three lines. Release the keys.
4. Press the Delete key to delete the block.

The lines should now be deleted. Before performing any other operation, pull down the Edit menu and select the Undo option.

5. Click the Edit menu.
6. Click the Undo Editing option.

The lines are now restored to the document.

You can undo almost any operation, but remember that only the last operation can be undone. As you learn Microsoft Works, keep this option in mind. When a mistake is made, try the Undo to correct it.

COPY TEXT

Now assume you want to make a copy of the first three lines and place the copy at the bottom of the document. The first step is to copy the lines to the **clipboard**. Next, paste the contents of the clipboard into the new location. This operation is shown in Figure 3.30.

4. Click the Paste tool

2. Click the Copy tool

1. Select the text to copy

3. Move the cursor

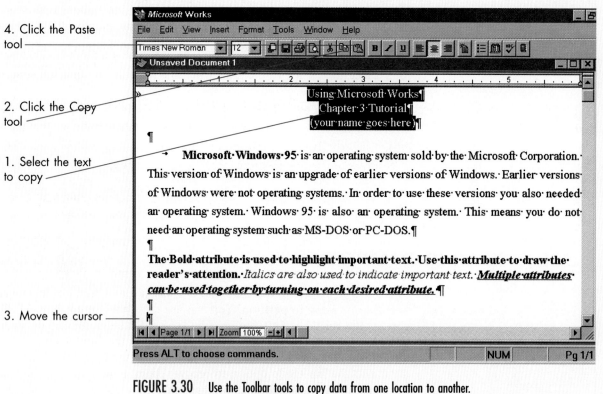

FIGURE 3.30   Use the Toolbar tools to copy data from one location to another.

1. Move the cursor to the first line of the document.
2. Hold down the Shift key.
3. Press the Down arrow key three times to select the block.
4. Click the Copy tool on the tool bar.

This copies the selected lines to the clipboard. Now, paste the lines in the new location.

5. Press Ctrl/End to move to the end of your document.
6. Press the Enter key to insert a blank line.
7. Click the Paste tool on the tool bar.

The text should now be copied to its new location. Remember, text can be moved using the same approach by clicking the **Cut tool** rather than the **Copy tool**.

We will use a different approach to move a line of text. This approach is referred to as **drag and drop**. To try the drag and drop technique, move your name so that it is above the first line you just copied.

1. Select the last line of the document. This is the line with your name. Make sure you also select the paragraph mark.
2. Move the mouse's pointer over the selected text. The cursor should change to an arrow with the word "drag" below the arrow.
3. Hold down the left mouse button. The word "move" replaces the word "drag." Move the mouse until the vertical bar is in front of the "U" in "Using Microsoft Works" two lines above the selected line.
4. Release the mouse button.

The lower portion of the document should look like the one shown in Figure 3.31.

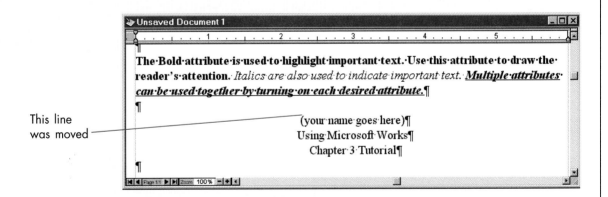

FIGURE 3.31   Your document after copying the top three lines and moving the last line.

SAVE THE DOCUMENT

It is now time to save the document to your disk. Since this is a new document, use the **Save As** option from the File menu.

1. Pull down the File menu.
2. Click the Save As option.

A window similar to the one shown in Figure 3.32 is displayed. Type a name for the document in the File Name text area. If you want the file saved on any disk or in any directory other than the ones shown in the **Save In**, you will need to select the new directory and drive or specify the drive letter and name when you enter the file name.

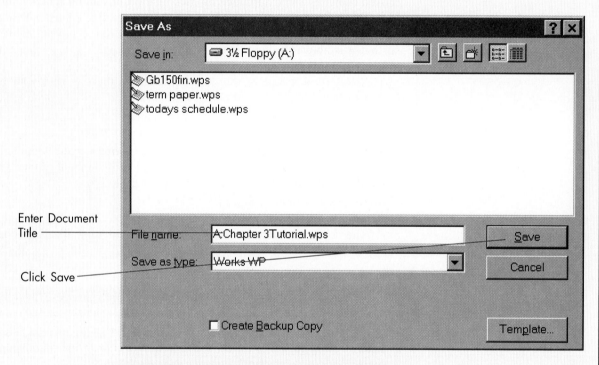

FIGURE 3.32   Use the Save As dialog to save your document.

3. Enter **A:Chapter 3 Tutorial** as the file name. (If you are saving to a drive other than A drive, enter its letter in place of A:.)
4. Click the OK button.

The file should now be saved.

PRINT THE DOCUMENT

Before printing the document, preview it to ensure it looks correct. To do this, click the **magnifying glass** in the center of the toolbar. The screen should look like the one in Figure 3.33.

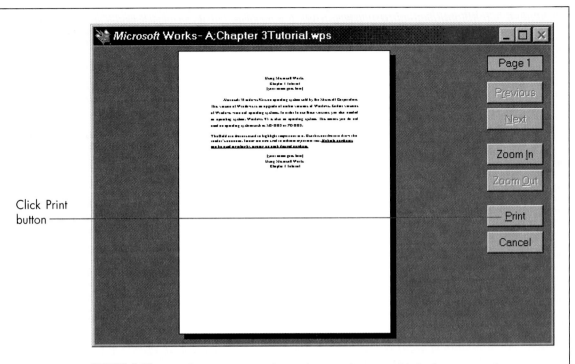

FIGURE 3.33 Use the Print Preview tool to see how your doucment will look when it is printed.

1. Click the magnifying glass tool on the toolbar.

After examining the screen, print the document. Before printing the document, make sure your printer is turned on and set on-line. Next, click the **Print** button on the print preview screen.

2. Make sure your printer is on-line.
3. Click the Print button.

It is not always necessary to preview a document before printing, but it is a good habit to develop. If you decide to print a document without previewing it, choose the **Printer tool** to the left of the magnifying glass. Neither the **Print Preview** or the Printer tool provide access to the Print window discussed in the earlier part of this chapter. To access the Print window, choose Print from the File menu.

EXIT MICROSOFT WORKS

The last step to complete this exercise is to exit Works. To do this, select the **Exit Works** option from the File menu.

1. Pull down the File menu.
2. Click the Exit Works option.

If you need to make corrections to the file at a later time, you can open the file and edit it. To open the file, click the **Existing Documents** tab from the **Task Launcher**. If your document is shown in the list of documents, click on the file name, then click the OK button.

If the file is not listed, click the **Open a document not listed here** button. This button is below the list of documents. An Open window similar to the Save As window show in Figure 3.32 is displayed. Enter the name of the file in the File Name entry at the bottom of the window, then click the Open button.

You have just completed the first Works word processing tutorial. The purpose of the tutorial was for you to become familiar with some of the elementary functions in the Word Processing module of Microsoft Works. As you work through this text, you will gain more expertise with the word processing module.

If you had trouble with the tutorial, work through it again. The information in the tutorial is necessary for the remainder of the text. The only way to be efficient with a software package is to be so comfortable with it that the operations of the package are second nature.

You should now remove any disks from the drives, turn the machine and monitor off, and remove the document from the printer.

HANDS-ON PRACTICE

Exercise 3-1

Using Microsoft Works Word Processing module, write a one-page letter that introduces you to your instructor. Describe yourself, state your major, explain any special interest, or say anything else that will make the instructor remember you. In the letter, make sure you use the following requirements:

1. Right align the date on the first line and format it as bold text.
2. Center your name and course title at the top of the letter. Print these two lines as bold underlined text.
3. Use bold, italic, and underlined text somewhere within the body of the letter.
4. Justify margins in the body of the text.
5. Double space the body of the letter.
6. Save and print the letter.

Exercise 3-2

Using Microsoft Works Word Processing module, create, save, and print the document in Figure 3.34. Make sure you format the text as it is shown in the figure. After you have entered the document, proofread it and make any necessary corrections. Double space the entire document. Enter your full name and the current date on the second and third lines. The document may not look exactly like the one shown here because your lines will not be the same width as these.

Exercise 3-2
(Your Name)
(Today's Date)

Microsoft Works 4.0 for Windows 95 combines word processor, spreadsheet, database, and communications tools into a single, integrated package. This package takes advantage of many of the most interesting features of Windows 95. As a package for the occasional user, Works 4.0 stands as the most powerful package currently available.

Some of the features available in the word processor include automatic bullets, automatic table formatting, smart text, quick paragraph formatting, multiple columns, spell checking, and a thesaurus. Works also includes a variety of clip art images that can be used to dress up a document.

The help facility in Works 4.0 is excellent. The Help window can be displayed beside a document so both can be seen at the same time. Step-by-step help can be used to guide a user through any task, from the simplest to the most complex.

The program requires a 386 or higher processor, 6 megabytes of RAM, 20 megabytes of hard drive space, and Windows 95.

As a package for the home, student, or occasional user, Microsoft Works 4.0 cannot be beat for the price.

FIGURE 3.34   Document for Exercise 3-2.

Exercise 3-3A

Using Microsoft Works Word Processing module, create, save and print the document in Figure 3.35. Make sure you format the text the way it is shown here. After you have entered the document, proofread it and make any necessary corrections. Enter your full name and the current date on the second and third lines. Your document will not look exactly like the one shown here because your lines will not be the same width as these.

Exercise 3-3A
(Your Name)
(Today's Date)

<u>Microcomputers</u> are becoming as common place as TVs and micro-waves. It is estimated that by the year 2000, two out of three households in the United States will own a microcomputer.

A microcomputer system consists of both hardware and software. The hardware are the physical devices of the system. The software are the programs that are used to make the computer run or solve specific types of problems.

A normal microcomputer system consists of a processor, a monitor, a mouse, a keyboard, disk drives, and a printer. In addition, most of today's microcomputers have a <u>modem</u> that can perform communications with other computer systems. Each of these devices are considered hardware.

There are two classes of software used by microcomputer systems. The first class is known as **system software**. This type of software controls the operation of the computer's hardware. Windows 95 is an example of system software. The second class of software is known as **applications software**. This type of software is used to solve specific types of personal and business problems. Microsoft Works 4.0 is an example of applications software.

FIGURE 3.35   Document for Exercise 3-3A.

Exercise 3-3B

Use the document in Exercise 3-3A. Make the following changes and print the document.

1. Format the first three lines (exercise number, name, and date) so that they are bold. Align these three lines on the right margin.
2. Add the following line as a document title. Place the line after the date. Format the line in bold italics and center the line.

    Microcomputer Systems: Hardware and Software

3. Remove the italic and underline attributes from the word "Microcomputers" in the first paragraph.
4. Change the attributes for the word "<u>modem</u>" from underlined to bold and italic.
5. Move the second sentence in the third paragraph (the sentence that refers to the modem) so that it is the last sentence in the paragraph.
6. Set the alignment of all four paragraphs to justified.
7. Double space all four paragraphs.
8. Copy your name and date to the end of the document. Change the alignment to left for the copied paragraphs.

4

WORKING WITH DOCUMENTS

LEARNING OBJECTIVES

When you've completed this chapter, you will be able to:

- Change margins for a document or part of a document.
- Insert, change, and delete different types of tabs and tab leaders in a document.
- Use Easy Formats.
- Create tables.
- Use borders in a document.
- Change fonts and font sizes.
- Create headers and footers for a document.
- Insert special characters into a document.
- Insert footnotes into a document.
- Use Works spell-checking feature.

USING PAGE SETUP

To have more control over the way a document is printed, the setup of the page can be changed. **Page setup** refers to the size of the page and the amount of the page that is to be used for margins. Standard typing paper is 11 inches long and 8 1/2 inches wide. Wide computer paper is 11 inches long and 17 inches wide. Once you have specified page size and margins, Microsoft Works determines how to set up the document work area.

Works uses six margins. As we explain these margins, examine the diagram of a page in Figure 4.1.

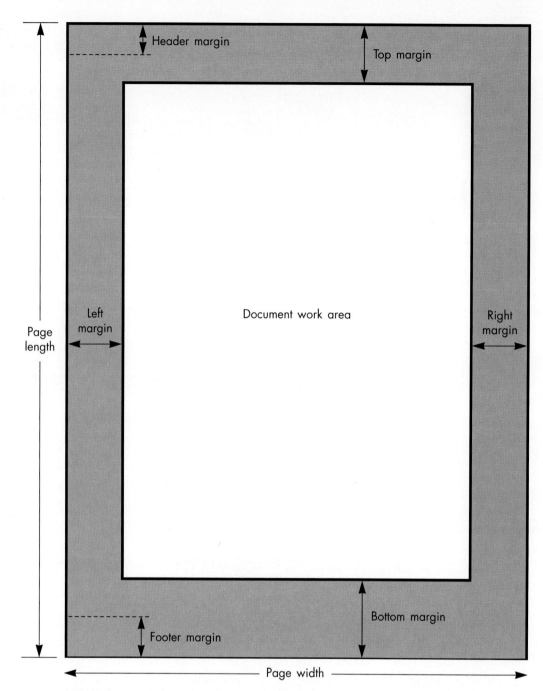

FIGURE 4.1 A sample page with margins indicated.

Top and bottom margins: The **top margin** refers to the distance from the top edge of the paper to the top edge of the first line of the work area. The **bottom margin** refers to the distance from the bottom edge of the paper to the bottom of the last line of the work area.

Left and right margins: The **left margin** refers to the distance between the leftmost edge of the paper and the leftmost character. The **right margin** refers to the distance between the rightmost edge of the paper and the rightmost character in the work area.

Header and footer margins: **Headers** are text that appear across the top of each page such as page numbers and section or chapter titles. **Footers** are text that appears across the bottom of each page. Header and footer margins refer to the distance between the top or bottom of the header or footer and the edge of the page.

To set the page size and the margins, choose the **Page Setup** option from the File menu. This option will provide the window shown in Figure 4.2.

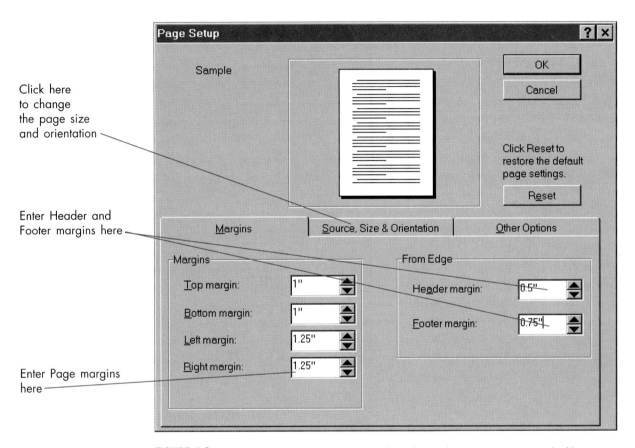

FIGURE 4.2   Page, header, and footer margins are changed using the Page Setup option on the file menu.

To set the margins, click in the appropriate Margins text area and enter a measurement. Specify all measurements for margins in inches.

To set the page size, click the **Source, Size & Orientation** tab of the middle folder. This will bring that folder forward so you can set the page size. This folder has entries to set the width and height of the page. You will normally want to use 8.5″ as the width and 11″ as the height, although this may need to be changed if you use special paper such as post cards or index cards.

The Orientation of the page determines how the text is printed on the page. The **Portrait orientation** prints a page normally, with top of the paper as the top of the page. **Landscape orientation** rotates the paper and prints the page sideways. In this orientation the right side of the page becomes the top and the top of the page becomes the left side. This difference can be seen if you examine the sample pages in Figures 4.2 and 4.3. Figure 4.2 shows a page in portrait orientation. The sample page shown in Figure 4.3 uses landscape orientation.

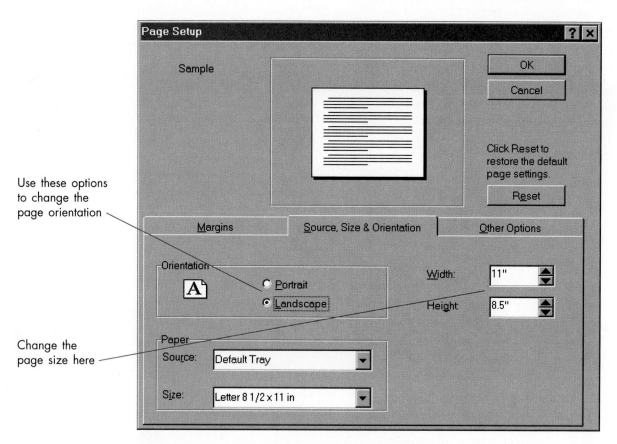

Use these options
to change the
page orientation

Change the
page size here

FIGURE 4.3   Use the Source, Size, & Orientation folder to change the page size and orientation.

USING THE RIGHT MOUSE BUTTON

The right mouse button can be used to access many of the options available to certain objects. In Microsoft Works, an object is a paragraph, picture, drawing, or other item that has been created in Works or inserted using some other Windows program.

The advantage of using the **right mouse button** is that Works will examine the type of object you are working with and provide access to options that apply only to that type of object. For example, if the cursor is in a paragraph and you click the right mouse button, the menu shown in Figure 4.4 is displayed.

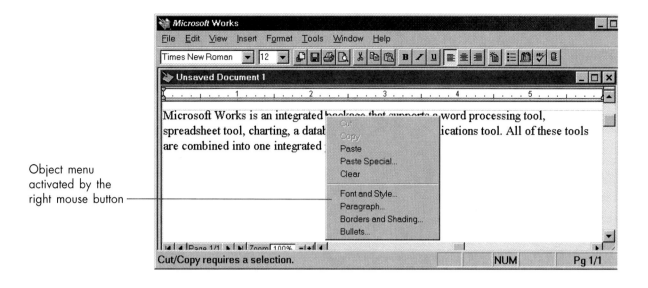

Object menu activated by the right mouse button

FIGURE 4.4 The right mouse button provides a menu of available options for the object you are currently working with.

INDENTING PARAGRAPHS

There are times when you want to change margins for part of a document. This may be necessary for special comments, notes, or quotes to separate them from other parts of the document. The simplest way to change a margin in this case is to drag the ruler's indent marker.

Examine Figure 4.5. The **ruler** has a marker for both the left and right margins. The left margin marker consists of two parts. The top part controls the first line of the paragraph and the bottom part controls the remaining lines in the paragraph.

Left margin   Left margin   First line   Right margin   Right margin
                indent   indent   indent

FIGURE 4.5 The document ruler can be used to indent the first line of a paragraph and the left and right margins.

You can change the margins for a block of text by selecting the text and dragging the **margin markers**. To change the margins for a single paragraph, place the cursor anywhere in the paragraph and drag the margin markers.

The margins may also be changed by clicking the right mouse button while working with a paragraph, choosing the Paragraph option, and using the Indents and Alignment folder. This folder is shown in Figure 4.6. To set margins using this approach, type a measurement in the appropriate text area.

Use these text areas to change margin indents

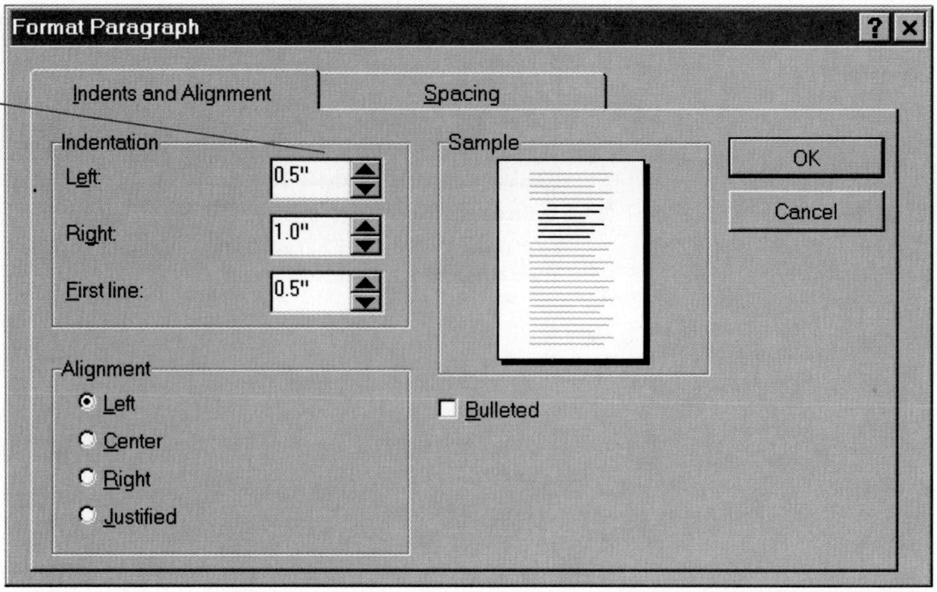

FIGURE 4.6   Paragraph margins can also be changed using the Indents and Alignment folder of the Format Paragraph option.

The left margin and first line indent can be used to create **numbered lists** with **hanging indents**. For example, suppose you want to number a set of questions and you want the number to extend past the left margin of the questions as shown below:

1. This is an example of a numbered list using a hanging indent. Notice that the number used in this paragraph extends to the left of the left margin for the paragraph. The paragraph text has a smooth left margin.

To create the hanging indent format, use the Indents and Alignments folder and set the left margin to .5 inches. Set the First line indent option to -.5. This will place the first line ½ inch to the left of the left margin. To enter a question, type the question number. This will be placed ½ inch to the left of the left margin. Press the tab key to move to the left margin and enter the text for the question. The remainder of the paragraph will be aligned on the left margin.

USING TAB STOPS

First line indent, left margin marker, and right margin marker are all displayed on the document ruler. Tab stops are also positions marked on the document ruler and are used to specify the horizontal position of text on a line and the alignment of text. **Tab stops** can be used to create multiple columns and tables.

When tab stops are inserted into a document, each tab stop is indicated on the document ruler. Each time the Tab key is pressed, the cursor moves to the next tab position. The text that is typed when the cursor is positioned at a tab stop is aligned by the tab.

Microsoft Works has several types of tabs. Each type of tab is indicated on the ruler by a different tab marker. The tab types are left, right, center, and decimal. An example of each type of tab stop is shown in Figure 4.7.

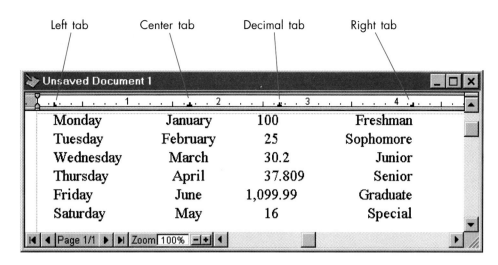

FIGURE 4.7   Tab markers and alignments.

Left tab: Specifies that the text begins at the tab position. As the text is entered, it will flow to the right of the tab mark. This provides a smooth, even left edge, but may make a ragged right edge.

Right tab: Aligns the text by the rightmost character. The text will flow to the left as it is entered. This type of tab mark will provide a smooth right edge, but it will provide an uneven left edge for a column of data.

Center tab: Forces the text placed on the tab mark to flow both to the left and to the right of the tab mark. This will align the text in the middle of the tab position, but may cause uneven edges on both the right and the left of a column.

Decimal tab: Used to enter a column of numbers. As numbers are entered, they will flow to the left until a decimal point is entered. Once the decimal point is entered, the numbers will flow to the right of the decimal.

Tab Leaders

A **tab leader** can be assigned to each tab. A tab leader is a set of characters that will be printed in all blank spaces that precede the tab. For example, leaders are used for tables of contents. Leaders help guide the reader's eye to the data at the other end of the tab. Figure 4.8 shows each of the leaders available in Works.

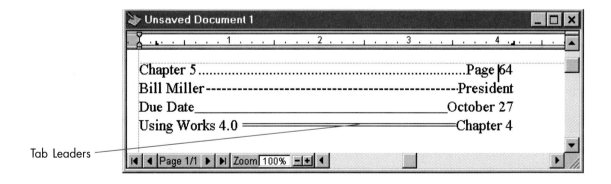

FIGURE 4.8   Four tab leaders are available in Works.

Tabs can be placed anywhere on the ruler. Tabs are used by all text below a tab mark or until a new tab setting is encountered. To assign tab settings to existing text, the existing text must be selected as a block before the tab is set. The tabs will remain on the ruler until they are replaced by other tabs or they are deleted.

To insert tab stops, choose the **Tabs** option from the Format menu. This will present the Format Tabs window in Figure 4.9.

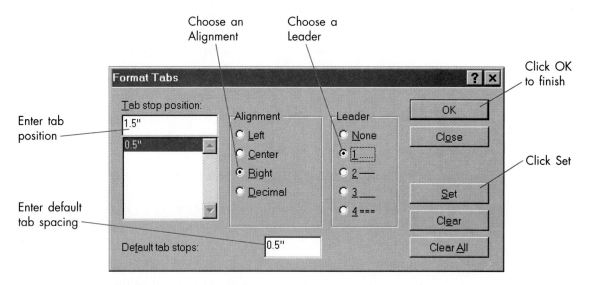

FIGURE 4.9 The Tabs dialog box can be used to insert, change, and clear tab stops.

When a document is created in Microsoft Works, a default tab is placed every ½ inch. This is shown in the **Default tab stops** text area. To change the default setting, type a new tab setting in the text area.

Custom tabs can also be entered. To specify a custom tab location, enter the location of the tab in the Tab stop position text area of the Format Tabs window. For example, to place a tab 1½ inches from the left margin, enter 1.5, then click the desired Alignment. Next, specify the Leader by clicking the appropriate leader option. The last step is to click the Set button. This button must be used to store the tab. After all tabs have been specified, click the OK button.

To change a tab stop, select the tab by clicking on its location in the Position area in the Format Tabs window. Next, change the alignment or leader for the tab. Finally, choose the Set and OK buttons to complete the change. To delete a tab, select the tab's position in the Tab stop position list and click the Clear button. To clear all tabs, choose the Clear All button.

Tab positions can be changed while working with the document by clicking the tab marker in the ruler and dragging the marker along the ruler to the new location. To remove a tab from the ruler, click the tab mark and drag it off the ruler. A left tab can be inserted while working within the document by simply clicking the appropriate location on the ruler.

CREATING TABLES

Tab stops can be used to create **tables** within a document. To use this approach you would need to insert an appropriate tab stop for each column in the table. When entering the text for the table, enter the text for the first column of the first line in the table and use the Tab key to move to the next column. At the end of each row in the table, press the Enter key to make each row a paragraph. Any formatting of the table would need to be set using several of the formatting options for text.

Microsoft Works provides an easier way to create a table. To use this easy approach, choose Table from the Insert menu. The window shown in Figure 4.10 is displayed.

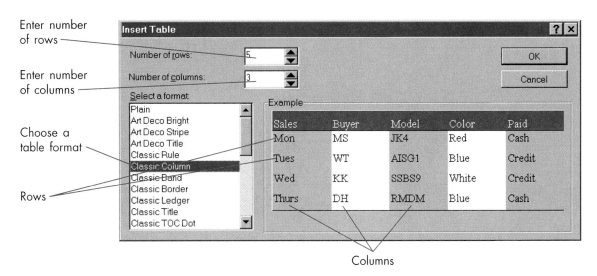

Enter number of rows

Enter number of columns

Choose a table format

Rows

Columns

FIGURE 4.10   Use the Insert Table window to create a table in a document.

The first steps to creating the table is to specify the number of rows and columns needed for the table. This is done in the first two text boxes. Next, choose a format for the table from the "Select a format" list box. Each time you click on a style, the example table on the right displays what the table would look like. When you have the style you want, click the OK button. The table with the appropriate number of rows, columns, and format is inserted into the document.

To enter text or other data into the table, click on the table row and column where the data should be placed and type the data. Use the Tab or arrow keys to move from column to column and from row to row.

At this point it is important to note that the table is actually an electronic spreadsheet table. Changes to the table are performed using the menus and options for the spreadsheet tool of Microsoft Works. When you choose a menu, the spreadsheet menu appears. Since electronic spreadsheets are covered in Chapters 6, 7, and 8, we will not discuss all the options here. The tutorial of this chapter leads you through some steps required to change the table format. You are referred to the spreadsheet chapter for more details.

CHANGING PRINT FONTS AND SIZES

There are two characteristics of print styles: **font** and size. A character font determines the shape of the character. Notice that this text uses characters having different shapes. The section titles have one shape, and the reading text has another shape. This is because they are printed in different fonts.

The second characteristic of a print style is its size. A font's size is normally measured in **points**, ½ of an inch. The greater the number of points, the larger the character. This text uses different font sizes. Several different fonts and point sizes are shown in the following lines:

This is 10 point Times.

This is 12 point Arial.

This is 14 point AvantGarde.

This is 16 point Impact.

This is 20 point Mistral.

These are 16 point Wingdings:

◻ ✗ ℯ ☜ ♑ ✍ ☾ ♌ ☒ ⌨ ✉ ✌

The Toolbar can be used to change the font and the font size. The toolbar for these options is shown in Figure 4.11. These areas display the font applied to selected text or to the right of the cursor. The fonts and the font sizes available from the toolbar depend upon which fonts are installed under the Windows program.

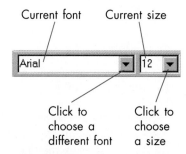

FIGURE 4.11   Toolbar Font and Size tools.

To apply a font or a font size to text, first select the text as a block, then click the down arrow next to the font or the font size area on the toolbar. This will pull down the available choices. To choose a font or size, click the desired font name or size. If the font size is not displayed in the list, enter the desired font size in the size area of the Toolbar. Figure 4.12 shows the Font tool and the Size tool pulled down.

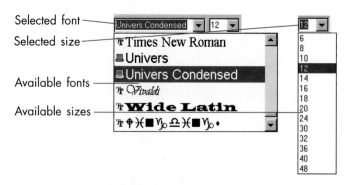

FIGURE 4.12   To change fonts and sizes, pull down the menus and select the font or size from the available options.

USING EASY FORMATS

Several paragraph formats are commonly used in documents. These have been pre-defined in Microsoft Works as **Easy Formats**. These Easy Formats can be accessed by using the Easy Formats option on the Format menu or clicking the Easy Formats tool on the toolbar. The Easy Formats window is shown in Figure 4.13.

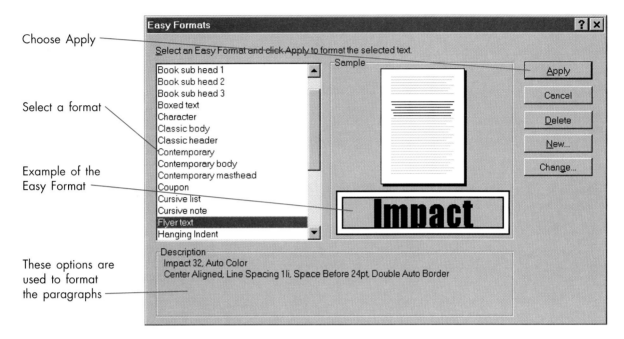

FIGURE 4.13 Easy Formats apply several formatting options at one time.

To use an Easy Format, select the desired format from the list displayed on the left of the window. The exact format specifications are displayed in the Description area at the bottom of the window and an example is displayed in the Sample area. To apply the format, click the Apply button. You can apply a format to several paragraphs at one time if you selected the paragraphs before applying the format. If you make a mistake or do not want the format selected, immediately choose the Undo option from the Edit menu.

Easy formats simply change the formatting options for the selected paragraphs. If there are some options you do not want, change them individually by resetting the undesired formatting options. You can even create your own Easy Formats. Creating Easy Formats is discussed in Chapter 5, Advanced Word Processing Features.

A **bullet** is a small symbol placed on the first line of a paragraph. A bulleted format is commonly used for lists. The symbol is aligned with the left margin and the text of the paragraph is indented from the symbol. An example of a bulleted list is shown below.

- A bullet is a small symbol placed on the first line of a paragraph.
- Several types of bullets can be used.
- When the hanging indent option is used, the left margin of the text is indented and the bullet is placed ¼ inch to the left of the left margin. This creates a margin for the text, but leaves the bullet to the left of the text margin.

   To apply bullets to a list, make each item in the list a paragraph. Next, select all the paragraphs for the list and click the right mouse button. Choose the Bullets option from the object menu. The window shown in Figure 4.14 will be displayed.

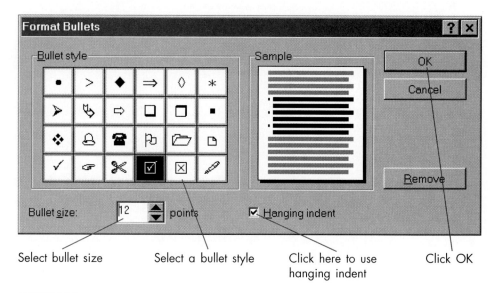

Select bullet size   Select a bullet style   Click here to use hanging indent   Click OK

FIGURE 4.14   The Format Bullets window.

   The first step is to click the bullet to be used as the symbol. Next, enter the point size to use for the bullet. Next, determine if you want to use hanging indents on the list. A hanging indent moves the left margin of the text to the right ¼ inch and the bullet is placed ¼ inch to the left of the left margin. This creates a margin for the text of a paragraph, but leaves the bullet to the left of the text margin. Check the **Hanging Indent** option if hanging indents are desired. Finally, click the OK button.

   You can also use the **Bullets tool** on the Toolbar to assign a bullet format. If no bullet symbol has been selected prior to using the bullet tool, the window in Figure 4.14 is displayed. If a bullet symbol has been selected earlier, the bullet options are applied to the selected paragraphs.

   To remove a bullet, select the paragraphs that have a bullet and click the Bullets tool on the Toolbar. This will toggle the bullets off.

Works will allow a paragraph to be assigned borders and shadings. **Borders** are used to outline a paragraph or mark the top, bottom, left, or right of the paragraph. **Shading** is used to change the background of the paragraph. These formatting options are assigned using the Borders and Shading option on the object menu displayed by the right mouse button, or this option can be selected from the Format menu. The Borders folder is shown in Figure 4.15.

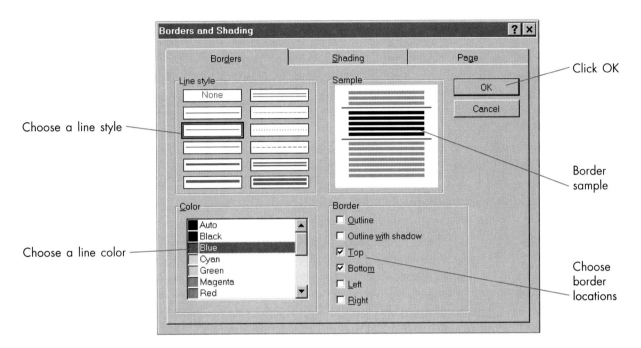

FIGURE 4.15 The Borders folder.

The first step to assigning a border is to select the line style. Once the style is selected, the Sample area displays the border in that style. Next, select the locations of the border. If the Outline option or Outline with Shadow is used, the border is placed around the entire paragraph. Combinations of Top, Bottom, Left, and Right can be selected to set a paragraph off from the body of a document. For example, the paragraph below is created using the Top and Bottom border location options and the second line style.

Combinations of paragraph borders can be used to set one paragraph off from other paragraphs.

Next, select a color for the border. You will normally want to use a black border but if you have a color printer you may want to use a special color. Finally choose the OK button to apply the border.

Shading is also used to highlight text and is applied to an entire paragraph. To assign a shading, select the paragraph to be shaded and use the Shadings folder of the Borders and Shading window. This folder is shown in Figure 4.16.

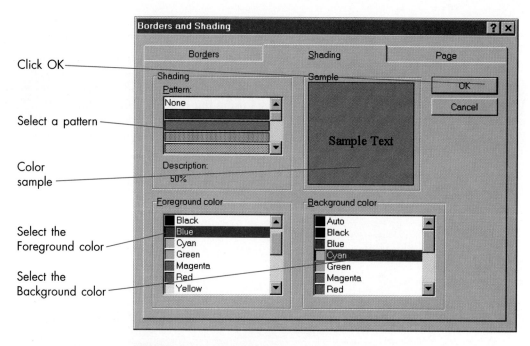

Click OK

Select a pattern

Color
sample

Select the
Foreground color

Select the
Background color

FIGURE 4.16 The Shadings folder.

The first option to set for the shading folder is the shading Pattern. The pattern list box can be scrolled using the scroll bar to select from fifteen different patterns. The second option is the foreground color. This is the major color for the shading. The next option is the background color. This is the minor color for the shading. The combination of pattern, foreground, and background colors can be used to mix almost any color you desire. Once the pattern and colors have been set, click the OK button to apply the color.

To apply borders and shading to a single paragraph, place the cursor anywhere in the paragraph and set the appropriate options. If several paragraphs are selected, the options are assigned to the entire group of paragraphs. For example, if three paragraphs are selected and the Outline border is assigned, the box is drawn around all three paragraphs, not each paragraph individually.

To remove a border or shading, select the paragraphs and use the Borders or Shading folder. To remove all formatting, select the None line style or pattern. To remove only part of the formatting, click on the checked options until the check box is clear, then click the OK button.

When borders or shading are assigned, they are drawn from the paragraph's left margin to the right margin. To create a narrower border, change the margins by indenting the paragraph. This indenting can be done using the **Indents and Alignment** folder of the Paragraph option or by dragging the ruler's margin markers.

The last folder for the Borders and Shading window is the Page folder. This folder will apply a bolder to the entire page and is commonly used to create title pages or one page brochures.

INSERTING SPECIAL TEXT

There are times when special text may need to be inserted into a document. For example, you may want the name of a file placed in a document, or you may want the current date placed in a letter or memo. The Insert menu can be used to place this special text in a document. This menu is shown on the left in Figure 4.17.

Page Break: This option inserts an end-of-page mark in a document. Use this when you want to force the following text onto a new page.

Page Number: This places the current page number in a document. Use this option in a header or footer to have page numbers printed.

Document Name: This places the name of the file in the document. This is commonly used in a header or footer.

When these options are inserted, a special **field marker** is placed in the document. For example, if you insert a Page Number, the field marker *page* is placed in the document. When the document is printed or is displayed using the Preview option, the field marker is replaced by the actual page number.

Date and Time

When the **Date and Time** option is selected from the Insert menu, the window shown on the right in Figure 4.17 is displayed.

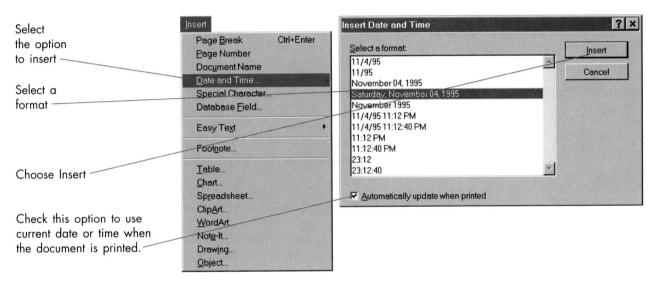

Select the option to insert

Select a format

Choose Insert

Check this option to use current date or time when the document is printed.

FIGURE 4.17 Use the Date and Time option on the Inset menu to place the date and time field markers into a document.

To insert a date or time, choose the format desired from the window. Next, set the check box at the bottom of the window to determine how the date or time is inserted. If the "Automatically update when printed" option is checked, the current date and time is used each time the document is printed. If this option is not checked, the current date or time is placed in the document and that time does not change when the document is printed. Finally, click the Insert button.

Special Characters

There are times when special types of characters are needed in a document. For example, you might want a **nonbreaking hyphen** or a **nonbreaking space**. For example, if you were to enter a date as 4-19-96, Works would interpret this as a hyphenated word and might break it on two lines. Special characters like nonbreaking hyphens and nonbreaking spaces can be used to prevent this.

These special characters can be inserted using the Special Character option on the Insert menu. This option presents a window used to select one of the special characters.

End-of-line: Creates a new line, but does not create a new paragraph.

Optional hyphen: Indicates hyphenation for a word when the word must be broken onto two lines.

Nonbreaking hyphen: Keeps two words separated by a hyphen from being broken onto two lines.

Nonbreaking space: Keeps two words that need to be separated by a space from being broken onto two lines.

These options insert a special symbol into the document to indicate their function. You can see these special characters only if you turn the **All Characters** option on using the View menu discussed in Chapter 3.

USING HEADERS AND FOOTERS

Headers are lines of text that appear at the top of each page of a document. **Footers** are lines of text that appear at the bottom of each page. The way the header and footer lines are displayed depends on whether you are using Normal view or Page Layout view. In Normal view, both the Header and the Footer lines are displayed at the top of the page. The header lines are marked with a **H** and the footer lines are marked with a **F**. In **Page Layout** view, header and footer areas are shown as outlines at the top and bottom of each page.

To create a header or footer, simply enter the header or footer text in the appropriate area. You can use any of the formatting options, such as bold, italic, or font and size options to change the appearance of the text. Special characters, covered earlier in this chapter, can also be placed in the headers and footers.

If the lines in either the header or the footer do not fit between the top or bottom margins defined in the Page Setup (discussed earlier), these margins are automatically changed to accommodate the headers and footers.

Before finishing the discussion of headers and footers, we need to note one other item. It is common not to have headers printed on the first page of a document. For example, the first page might be a title page. To prevent the header from printing on the first page, use the Page Setup option on the File menu. Click on the **Other Options** tab and the folder shown in Figure 4.18 will be displayed. Check the **No header on first page** or **No footer on first page** options to prevent headers and footers from printing on the first page.

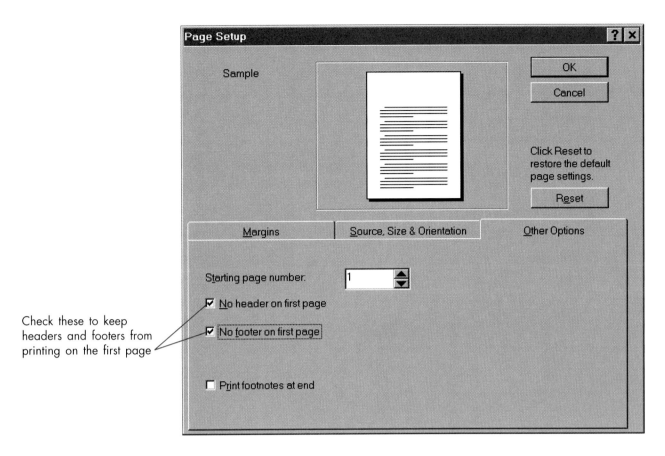

FIGURE 4.18   Use the Other Options dialog box to set printing of headers and footers for the first page.

INSERTING FOOTNOTES

Works allows **footnotes** to be inserted into a document. When the document is printed, footnote marks are printed in the body of the document where the footnote was inserted. The text that accompanies the footnote can be printed at the bottom of the page or at the end of the document.

To insert a footnote, choose the Footnote option from the Insert menu. This will provide a window like the one in Figure 4.19. This window is used to define the footnote mark. Choose the Numbered option to get numbered footnotes, or choose the **Special mark** option to specify your own footnote mark. If the Special mark option is chosen, a footnote mark will need to be entered in the Mark area. Finally, choose the Insert button.

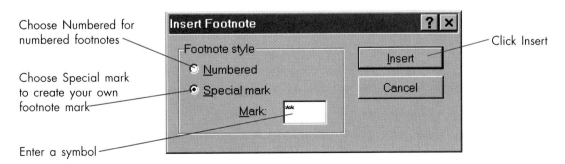

FIGURE 4.19   Use the Insert Footnote window to determine how the footnote will be marked.

If you are working in Normal view, a footnote pane is displayed. An example of a footnote pane is shown in Figure 4.20. The cursor will be in the footnote pane where the text for the footnote is entered. After completing the footnote, press the **F6 function key** or click inside the document pane to move the cursor out of the footnote pane and into the document. To remove the footnote pane from the screen, click Footnotes on the View menu.

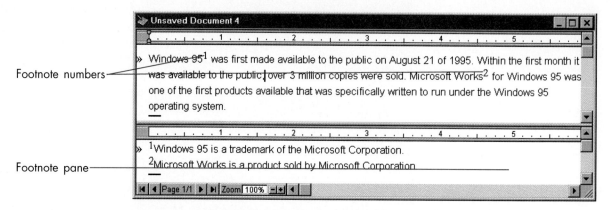

Footnote numbers

Footnote pane

FIGURE 4.20   When working in Normal view, footnotes are displayed in their own pane.

If you are working in Page Layout view, the cursor will be placed at the bottom of the current page. You can enter the text for the footnote beside the footnote number or mark.

A footnote can be changed at any time. If you are using normal view and the footnote pane is not displayed, turn Footnotes on using the View menu. To edit footnotes, use the F6 function key to move into the footnote pane. Edit the footnote as if it were normal text and use the F6 key to move back to the document. To move a footnote, select the footnote marker and cut the marker to the clipboard, then paste it into its new location. A footnote can also be copied using the clipboard. To delete a footnote, delete the footnote marker.

The **Other Options** folder of the Page Setup window accessed from the File menu is used to determine where the footnotes print. This folder is shown in Figure 4.18. To print footnotes at the bottom of a page, turn the "Print footnotes at end" option off. To print footnotes at the end of the document, turn this option on.

USING THE SPELLING CHECK

Microsoft Works includes a built-in dictionary that contains more than 120,000 words. This dictionary is used by the spell-checking feature. Works will not only check the spelling of words, it will also check for irregular capitalization and double words. A double word error occurs any time the same word occurs two or more times consecutively.

To spell check a document, choose the **Spelling** option from the Tools menu or click the **Spell tool** on the Toolbar. When the spell checker finds a word that is not in its dictionary, Works will show the word and allow you to correct the spelling. Works will also provide suggestions for the correct spelling of the word.

The Spelling window is shown in Figure 4.21. This window has several areas. In the upper left the misspelled word is shown. The "Change to" text box will contain suggested spelling of the word. The Suggestions area lists a number of possible spellings for the word. Click one of the suggested spellings, then click the Change button to change the misspelled word to the selected spelling.

Misspelled word

Suggested spellings

Buttons

Spell checking options

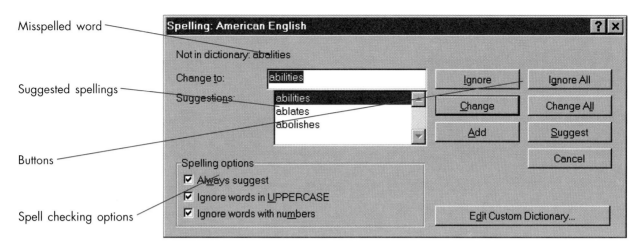

FIGURE 4.21 The Spelling window.

Each button in the window has a different function. Their functions are:

Ignore: Ignores the spelling of the word in this case, but will continue to catch the spelling in the remainder of the document.

Ignore All: Ignores this word and treats it as a correctly spelled word for the remainder of the document.

Change: Substitutes the misspelled word with the word in the Change To text box.

Change All: Correct the spelling of this word in the remainder of the document.

Suggest: Provides a list of suggested spellings.

Add: Adds the word to a personal dictionary. Do this only for commonly used words.

Cancel: Terminates the spell checker.

Although spell checkers appear to be the ultimate saving grace for poor typists and poor spellers, you cannot rely on them as a proofreading tool. The spell checker checks spelling, but it does not check grammar and punctuation.

You can have a perfectly spelled paragraph, but the paragraph may not make sense. Read the following paragraph:

> Win you use a spell checking, your should be very carefully. Spell checking is a very god tool however they cannot displace spoof reading. There design is for correct spelling only. Since your can spell wording correct but use they wrong words, ewe can right documents that makes absolutely know cents at awl.

The preceding paragraph would pass through your spell checker with no errors. This should prove to you that there is no replacement for good proofreading skills.

CHAPTER 4 SELF-TEST

1. List the six margins that can be set for a document.
2. The left margin marker on the ruler is divided into two parts. What is the function of the top part? What is the function of the bottom part?
3. What is the advantage of using the right mouse button to access menu options
4. List the four types of tab alignments available in Works.
5. What is a tab leader? How are tab leaders set?
6. What is a bullet?
7. What is a character font?
8. What does Works do when an Easy Format is applied to a paragraph?
9. What is the difference between a header and a footer?
10. When you insert a table into a document, what type of table is inserted?
11. How can you insert the current date into a document?
12. How do you use a special character as a footnote mark?
13. List three types of errors that the spell checker can find.
14. Why should you not rely on a spell checker to proofread a document?

TUTORIAL

START THE TUTORIAL

The document for this tutorial is stored on your tutorial's files disk. You should have this disk available before starting the tutorial. This document has several misspelled words and other errors. Ignore these errors until the document spelling is checked.

1. Boot your computer system.
2. Start Microsoft Works.

Open an Existing Document

Use the Existing Files folder on the Task Launcher to open the file named Chapter 4 Tutorial.

1. Click the Existing Files tab on the Task Launcher.
2. Click the "Open a document not listed here" button at the bottom of this window.
3. Enter A:Chapter 4 Tutorial.wps in the File name area. Remember, if your tutorial disk is in a different drive, you will need to use that drive letter in the file name.
4. Click the Open button.

After the file has been loaded, the screen should look similar to Figure 4.22.

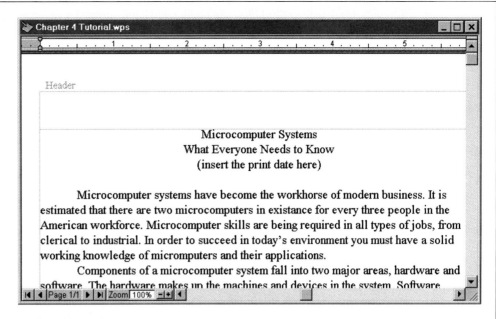

FIGURE 4.22   The tutorial document for Chapter 4.

Format the Title

The first step in the tutorial is to change the character **font** and size for the first two lines in the document. To change fonts for existing text, the text must be selected before choosing the font and size.

1. Select the first two lines of the document. These are the Microcomputer Systems and the What Everyone Needs to Know lines.

The next step is to choose the font and the size for the text. These can be chosen using the font and size boxes on the Toolbar. Refer to Figure 4.23.

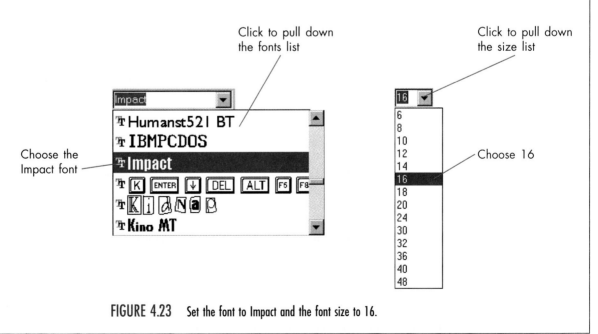

FIGURE 4.23   Set the font to Impact and the font size to 16.

1. Click the arrow on the right side of the font box on the toolbar to pull down the font menu.
2. Click the Impact font.
3. Click the arrow on the right side of the font size box on the toolbar to pull down the font size menu.
4. Click 16 for the font size.

The first two lines should now be shown larger than the other text and the shape of the characters should be different from the rest of the document.

Insert the Print Date

The next step is to replace the third line (insert the print date here) with the date the document is printed. To do this, use the **Date and Time** option on the Insert menu. See Figure 4.24.

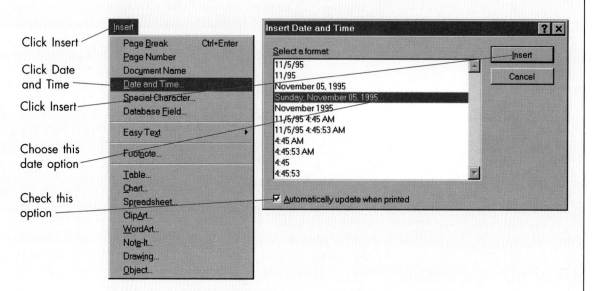

FIGURE 4.24   Insert the print date.

1. Select the third line of the document (insert the print date here).
2. Choose Date and Time on the Insert menu.
3. Click the fourth option on the format list.
4. Make sure the "Automatically update when printed" option is checked.
5. Click the Insert button.
6. If the date is not centered on the page, click the center alignment icon on the Toolbar.

The current date should now be placed on the third line. Your document should look like the one shown in Figure 4.25.

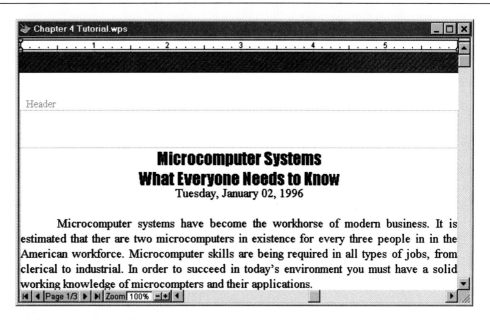

FIGURE 4.25 The tutorial document after inserting the date. Note: your date will be different.

Format Section Titles

Following the first two paragraphs, you will find the word Hardware on a line by itself. This line starts a discussion of hardware components of microcomputers. Since it is the beginning of a section of the document, assign it a Book sub head 1 **Easy Format**. Refer to Figure 4.26.

Choose this easy format

Click the apply button

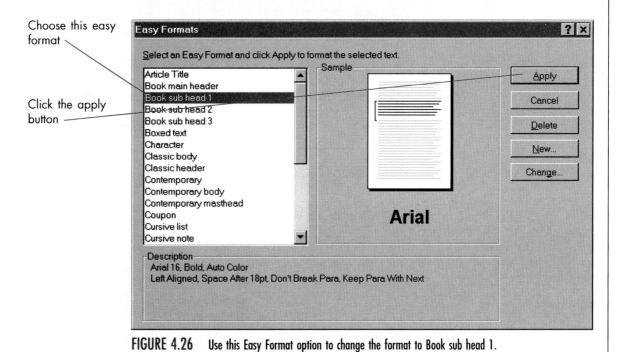

FIGURE 4.26 Use this Easy Format option to change the format to Book sub head 1.

1. Move the cursor to the line that reads Hardware. This should be below the second full paragraph.
2. Click the Easy Formats option on the Format menu.
3. Click the Book sub head 1 format.
4. Click the Apply button.

The word Hardware should now be in a 16 point Arial font.

Create Bulleted Paragraphs

Below the first paragraph under the Hardware section is a list of hardware components. Now assume you want to assign a bullet to each item and indent the list one inch from the left margin. We will start by assigning the **bullets**.

1. Select the seven lines that read Keyboard, Mouse, Monitor, Printer, Processor, Memory, and Disk drives.
2. Make sure the cursor is over the selected area and click the right mouse button.
3. Click the Bullets menu option.

The Format Bullets window shown in Figure 4.27 should now be displayed. Select a bullet symbol for the list.

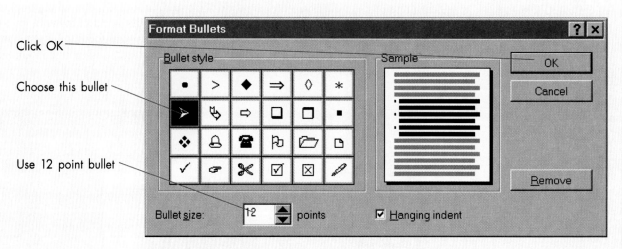

FIGURE 4.27   The Bullets window.

4. Click the arrow head shown in Figure 4.27.
5. Click OK.

The bullets should now be in front of each line. If you have the wrong bullet, try steps 4 and 5 again.

Now use the **Indents and Alignments** folder of the Paragraph option to indent the paragraphs. Refer to Figure 4.28.

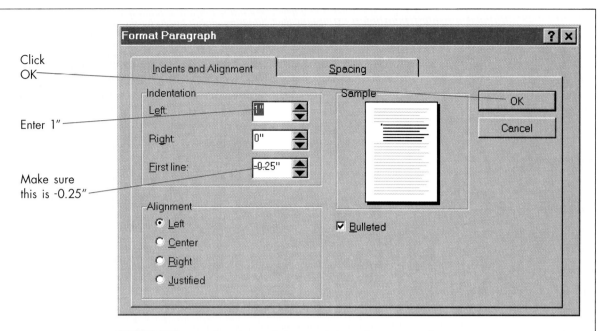

Click OK

Enter 1"

Make sure this is -0.25"

FIGURE 4.28   Use the Indents and Alignment dialog to change paragraph margins.

1. Make sure the seven lines are still selected.
2. Click the right mouse button.
3. Click the Paragraph option.
4. Enter 1 in the Left entry on the Indentation area.
5. Click OK.

The text in the lines should now be indented one inch from the left margin. Note that the bullet is only 3/4 inch from the left margin. This is because the first line indent was set to -.25 when the bullets were assigned. You can see these locations by looking at the margin markers on the ruler.

Your document should now look like the one shown in Figure 4.29.

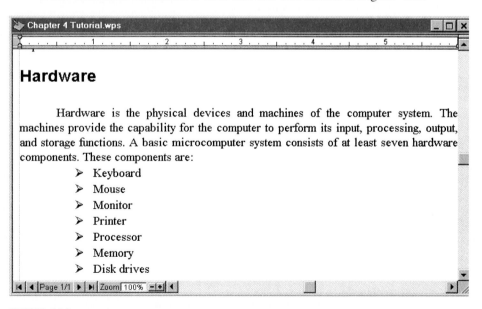

FIGURE 4.29   Your document after creating bullets for the hardware list.

Create a Table with Tabs and Leaders

The next step is to create a **table** that associates each of the seven hardware components listed earlier with one of the four basic functions of the computer. To do this we will use **tabs** and **tab leaders**. First, locate the line that reads Software and apply a Book sub head 1 to the line.

1. Locate the line that reads Software. It should be near the top of the second page.
2. Click the Easy Formats icon on the Toolbar.
3. Click the Book sub head 1 format.

Now find the location for the table.

1. Move the cursor to the beginning of the line that reads USE LEADERS HERE. This should be close to the top of your second page, just above the Software sub head 1.
2. Press the Delete key until you have deleted all the letters in the line. Make sure you are on a blank line.

Now, create the tabs for the table. You need a left tab at 1 inch and a right tab with a leader at 5.5 inches. Refer to Figure 4.30 for setting the 5.5 inch tab.

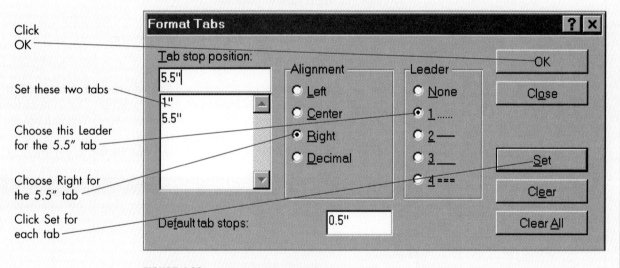

FIGURE 4.30   The Format Tabs dialog box.

CREATE THE TABS

1. Click Format on the top line menu.
2. Click tabs.
3. Enter 1" in the Tab stop position.
4. Click Left for the Alignment.
5. Click None for the Leader.
6. Click the Set button.

7. Enter 5.5 for the second tab.
8. Click Right for the Alignment.
9. Click the 1.... Leader option.
10. Click the Set button.
11. Click the OK button.

ENTER THE TABLE TEXT   The tab marks should appear placed on the ruler. The next step is to enter the text for the table. Remember, to reach a tab position press the tab key. Press Enter at the end of each line so that each line is a paragraph. We will step you through the first line.

1. Press the Tab key.
2. Enter *Keyboard*.
3. Press the Tab key. The leader should appear and the cursor should be on the right side of the screen.
4. Enter *Input function*.
5. Press the Enter key.

The first table entry should now be displayed as shown below.

Keyboard .... Input function

Now enter the next six lines.

6. Enter the six lines below.

Mouse .... Input function

Monitor .... Output function

Printer .... Output function

Processor .... Processing function

Memory .... Storage function

Disk drives .... Storage function

CHANGE THE TABLE FONT   Now change the font and size for the table to make it stand out. Assign an Arial font of 10 points.

1. Select all seven lines in the table.
2. Click the arrow on the right side of the fonts entry on the Toolbar. The font should currently show a Times New Roman font.
3. Click the Arial font name.
4. Click the arrow to the right of the font size entry on the Toolbar. The current size should be 12 points.
5. Click 10 to change the font size.

The table should now be displayed in a 10 point Arial font. Your document should look like the one shown in Figure 4.31.

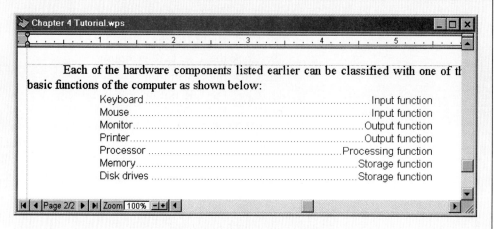

FIGURE 4.31   The tutorial document after entering each line of the table.

Insert A Table Using The Insert Table Option

The next step in the tutorial is to use the **Table** option on the Insert menu to create a table. Before you begin, remember that the table will be a spreadsheet table, so some of the menu options will change. We will step you through creation of the table slowly. Be careful with the steps or you may need to recreate the table.

INSERT THE TABLE

1. Find the line that reads INSERT A TABLE HERE. This should be about the middle of the second page.
2. Use your Delete key to remove the text in the line. Make sure you are on a blank line.
3. Click the Insert option on the top line menu.
4. Click the Table option.

You should now have the insert table window shown in Figure 4.32.

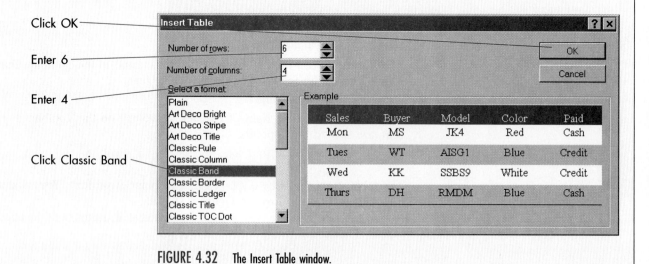

FIGURE 4.32   The Insert Table window.

You will need six rows and four columns in the table, as well as the Classic Band format.

5. Enter 6 in the Number of rows entry.
6. Enter 4 in the Number of columns entry.
7. Click the Classic Band entry in the Select a format area.
8. Click OK.

ENTER THE TABLE DATA   You should now have a blank table displayed on the screen with an outline around the first column of the top row. This row will be used to enter the table headings.

1. Enter Software and press the Tab key.
2. Enter Application and press the Tab key.
3. Enter Memory Required and press the Tab key.
4. Enter Price and press the press the Tab key.

This completes the Title. Now enter the following rows. Remember to press the Tab key between each entry. Also remember to press the Tab key at the end of a row rather than the Enter key.

5. Enter the following rows:

Microsoft Word	Word Processing	8 Megabytes	259
Microsoft Excel	Spreadsheet	8 Megabytes	329.95
Page Maker	Desktop Publishing	16 Megabytes	399
Paradox	Database	8 Megabytes	219
Corel Draw	Graphics	16 Megabytes	429.99

Your table should look like the one shown in Figure 4.33.

Click here to select a column

Software	Function	Memory Required	Price
Microsoft Word	Word Processing	8 Megabytes	259
Microsoft Excel	Spreadsheet	8 Megabytes	329.95
Page Maker	Desk Top Publishing	16 Megabytes	399
Paradox	Database	8 Megabytes	219
Corel Draw	Graphics	16 Megabytes	429.99

FIGURE 4.33   The Table after choosing the format and entering data.

FORMAT THE COLUMNS   The next step is to change some of the formatting of the columns. Remember this is a spreadsheet, so the approach and the menus will be somewhat different than the word processor.

1. Click the small gray band above the word Software in the table. This will select the entire column. See Figure 4.33.
2. Click the left alignment icon on the Toolbar.
3. Click the small gray band above the word Price.

4. Click the Format option on the top line menu.
5. Click the Number option.
6. Click the Currency option.
7. Click the OK button.

This will complete the table. If you have any incorrect entries in the table, click on the entry and make the correction. When the table appears correct, click anywhere outside the table to return to the word processing document.

8. Click any area outside the table.

This table is now complete. If you need to make further changes to the table, simply double click on any area of the table. This will return you to the spreadsheet tool of Works where you can make the changes.

If you want to delete the table, click on the table one time. The table will be outlined with a dotted line box. This selects the table. Now press the Delete key and the table will be deleted.

Format A Quote

The next step is to format a quote that is near the top of the third page of the document. We will use an **Easy Format** to change the quote margins, then place some borders around the quote and change the font size.

APPLY AN EASY FORMAT Locate the paragraph that begins: Today's micro-computers and their accompanying software... This paragraph should be near the top of the third page.

1. Place the cursor anywhere within the quote and click the Easy Formats icon on the toolbar.
2. Click the More Easy Formats option on the Easy Formats menu.
3. Click the Quotation format and click the Apply button.

The **Quotation format** should have changed the left and right margins so that they are now indented ½ inch from the document margin.

APPLY BORDERS The next step is to apply a top and bottom border to the paragraph.

1. Make sure the cursor is inside the quotation paragraph.
2. Click the right mouse button.
3. Click the Borders and Shading option.

The Borders folder should now be displayed. Set a line border for the top and bottom of the paragraph. Refer to Figure 4.34.

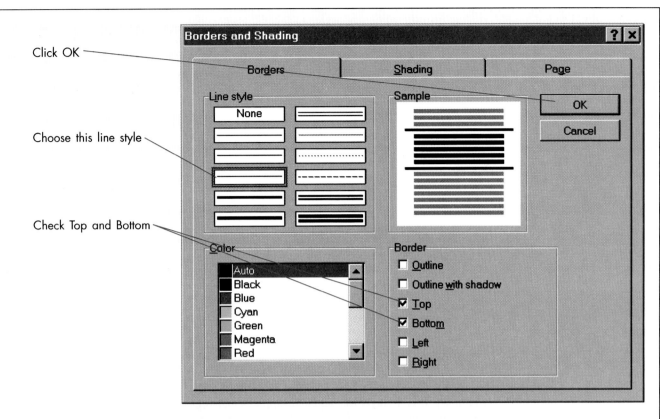

Click OK

Choose this line style

Check Top and Bottom

FIGURE 4.34 The Borders folder of the Borders and Shading window.

4. Click on the fourth line style on the left in the Line Style area.
5. Click the Top entry in the Border area.
6. Click the Bottom entry in the Border area.
7. Click OK.

The quote should now be displayed with a line across the top and bottom of the paragraph.

CHANGE THE QUOTE'S FONT SIZE   To make the quote stand out even more, change the font size to 10 points.

1. Select the entire paragraph.
2. Click the font size entry on the Toolbar.
3. Click the 10 entry.

JUSTIFY THE QUOTE

1. Click the right mouse button.
2. Choose the Paragraph option.
3. Click the Justify alignment option on the Indents and Alignment folder.
4. Click the OK button.

Your document should now look like the one shown in Figure 4.35.

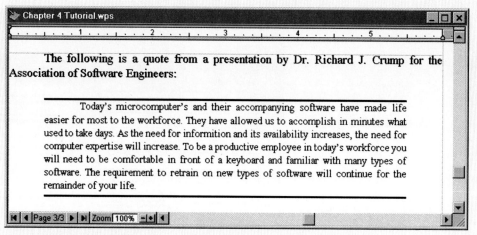

FIGURE 4.35   The formatted quote after assigning borders and changing the font size.

Insert A Footnote

Footnotes are used to add additional information or to cite references and sources of information. A footnote consists of a footnote mark and the footnote text. To insert a footnote, position the cursor at the point where you want the footnote mark placed and choose Footnote from the Insert menu. To try this, insert a footnote with a mark at the end of the paragraph that introduces the quote you just formatted.

1. Move the cursor to the end of the paragraph you just formatted.
2. Click the Insert option on the top line menu.
3. Click the Footnote option.

   You should now have the Insert Footnote window.

4. Click the Special Mark entry.
5. In the Mark text box enter two asterisks.
6. Click the Insert button.

   The cursor should have moved to the bottom of the page into the footnote area. Now enter the text for the footnote. Refer to Figure 4.36.

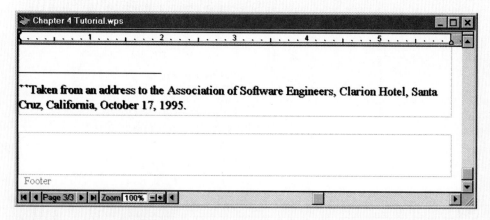

FIGURE 4.36   The completed footnote.

7. Enter: Taken from an address to the Association of Software Engineers, Clarion Hotel, Santa Cruz, California, October 17, 1995.

Create The Header and Footer

You will now enter a **header** and **footer** for the document. The header can be entered in the header area at the top of any page. The header will contain your name on the left and the name of the file on the right. You will also place a double line border under the header.

CREATE THE HEADER

1. Click in the header area at the top of the page.
2. Enter your full name.
3. Press the tab key twice to move to the right tab position.
4. Click the right mouse button.
5. Click the Insert Document Filename option.

The header should now be displayed with your name on the left and the characters *filename* on the right. Remember, the actual file name will replace the filename marker when the document is printed.

Now place a double underline border on the header line.

6. Make sure the cursor is in the header area.
7. Click the right mouse button.
8. Click the Borders and Shading option.
9. Click the thin double line line style.
10. Click the Bottom entry in the Border area.
11. Click OK.

The header area should now look like the on shown in Figure 4.37.

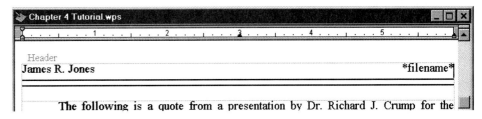

FIGURE 4.37 The completed header.

CREATE THE FOOTER

The only thing we want in the **footer** is the page number. We do, however, want **the page number** centered between the margins and the page number bracketed by dashes (-1-).

1. Move the cursor to the bottom on the page and inside the footer area.
2. Press the Tab key to move to the center tab mark.
3. Enter a hyphen and a space.
4. Click the right mouse button.
5. Click the Insert Page Number option.
6. Enter a space and a hyphen.

The footer should now show **- *page* -.**

Check The Document Spelling

The next thing to do is check the document's **spelling**. You should understand some basics about the spell checker's dictionary before checking the document.

First, realize that the spell checker uses a dictionary to check the spelling of words. Not all English words are stored in this dictionary. Many words that are seldom used or are specific to a discipline will probably not be found in the dictionary, and Works will think they are misspelled. If the spell checker cannot find a word, this does not necessarily mean that the word is misspelled. It may simply mean that the word is not in the dictionary.

Second, words that have prefixes or suffixes may not be considered correctly spelled. Possessive forms can also be missed. Many formal names will not be found in the dictionary.

The first few misspelled words you will probably find will be your name and address. If these are correct, click Ignore to skip these words.

1. First click on the last paragraph in the document, outside the Footer area, then move the cursor to the top of the document by pressing Ctrl/Home.
2. Click the Spell tool on the Toolbar.

The first misspelled word, ther, is highlighted directly above the Spelling window as shown in Figure 4.38. The suggested spellings of the word are shown in the Suggestions list. For this word the suggestions are three and there. Have the spell checker change the word to "there."

3. Click the word *there* in the Suggestions list box.
4. Click the Change button.
5. Click the Change button to correct this word.

The spell checker should have moved to the next misspelled word, existance.

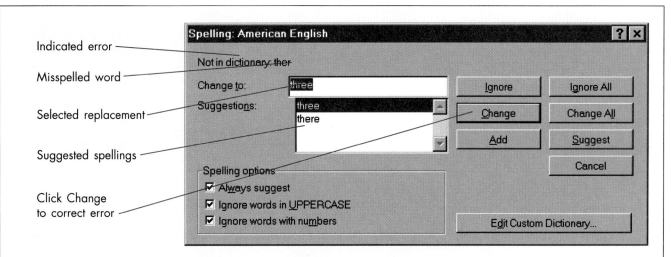

Indicated error
Misspelled word
Selected replacement
Suggested spellings
Click Change
to correct error

FIGURE 4.38   The Spelling window.

The next error should be a repeated word. This is indicated in the upper-left side of the Spelling window. The repeated word is *in*. To remove the repeated word, click the Change button.

6. Choose Change to remove the repeated word.

   Finish checking the document.

7. Continue checking the entire document. Use the Ignore button when you do not want to correct a word.
8. Click OK when the "Spelling check finished" window appears.

SAVE THE DOCUMENT

The document should now be completed. Save the document.

1. Save the document.

PRINT THE DOCUMENT

You are now ready to print the document. Before printing, set the headers so that there will be no header printed at the top of the first page. This is done using the **Page Setup** option on the File menu. Refer to Figure 4.39.

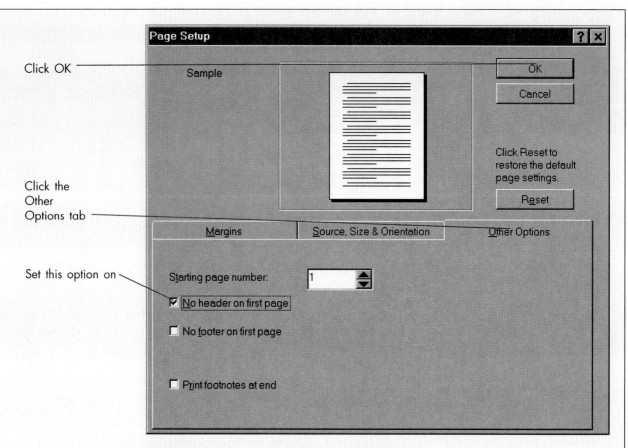

Click OK

Click the
Other
Options tab

Set this option on

FIGURE 4.39   Use the Other Options page of the Page Setup to prevent headers and footers from printing on the first page.

1. Click File on the top line menu.
2. Click the Page Setup option.
3. Click the Other Options tab.
4. Check the No Header on first page option.
5. Click the OK button.

   Now Preview and print the document.

1. Click the Preview tool on the Toolbar.
2. Use the Next and Previous buttons to examine each page of the document.
3. Click the Print button.

CONCLUSION

This completes your second word processing tutorial. Use the Exit option of the File menu to exit Microsoft Works, then turn off the computer. Remove your print-out from the printer.

If corrections are needed, you can edit the document again. Just remember to open the file with the name under which the changes were saved.

Exercise 4-1

Create a résumé for yourself. Use a résumé style similar to the one shown at the end of this assignment. Follow these requirements in the résumé:

1. Use a 12 point New Times Roman font for all text except where specified below.
2. Place your full name and address at the top of the résumé. Use a 14 point Arial bold font for your name. Use a 12 point Arial font for your street, city, state, and zip at the top of the résumé. Use a 12 point Times New Roman font for the phone number.
3. Use a 12 point Arial font for the headings for each category in the résumé. Category headings should be bold.
4. Use a bulleted list to list schools, locations, degrees, and grade point average of schools attended or those you expect to attend.
5. List several courses completed in your major. Use tabs to create two centered columns, side-by-side.
6. Use a hanging indent Easy Format for each paragraph under Work Experience. Change the first line indent and the left margin indent to hang the first line ¾ of an inch to the left of the text's left margin.
7. List several honors and activities. Use bullets on these lines.
8. Use a footnote mark by the references section. For the footnote text use "Available upon request." Use a 10 point Times New Roman font for the footnote text.
9. Adjust the top, bottom, left, and right margins to make the résumé fit on a single page.
10. Spell check, save, and print the résumé.

Your name
Street
City, State Zip
Phone

Education:

- Boomwaller High School, Boomwaller, MA. Graduated June 1992, GPA 3.5

- Tamicka Community College, Tuckersville, CA. Associate degree May 1994, GPA 3.1

- Keene University, Carson, NC. BS in Management Science, May 1996, GPA 3.2

Major Courses Completed:

Introduction to Marketing	Consumer Behavior
Simulation	Business Policy
Product Design	Production Planning

Work Experience:

1990-1991 — Brian's Department Store, Boomwaller, MA. Accepted orders from customers, filled orders, and managed the cash register.

1992-1994 — Big Mama's Soup House, Tuckersville, CA. Parked and delivered cars for patrons of Big Mama's Soup House.

1995-1996 — Marshall's Shoe Store, Carson, NC. Shoe sales agent.

Awards and Activities:

- Employee of the Month, Marshall's Shoe Store

- Accounting Society

- President of 4-H chapter in high school

- Class Senator to Student Government

References
_____

Available upon request.

Exercise 4-2

Create the survey form in Figure 4.40. The text for the survey is in the file named Exercise 4-2 on your tutorials and exercise disk. Pay particular attention to the use of different fonts and sizes. Use the following requirements:

1. Use the header area for the survey title. Format the title using the Contemporary masthead Easy Format.

2. On a second header line, use the Insert Date option to insert the month and year the document is printed. Right align the date.

3. Insert a footnote at the end of the first paragraph. Use an asterisk as the footnote mark. Use the address at the bottom of the document as the footnote text.

4. Create the outlined table using tabs and leaders, and place an outline border around the items. Use a 10 point Arial font for these items.

5. Use a bullet format for the list of check items: Microwave, Personal Computer, Second Home, Snow Blower, and Electronic Video Game. Use a 10 point Arial font for these items.

6. Create the code table using the Table option on the Insert menu. Use the Prestige Title format.

7. Create the list items below the table using tabs.

8. Format a blank line with a double border on the bottom to get the double lines under the table created in step 7 above.

9. Use bullets in the Check any statement you agree with list. Change the font to 10 point Times New Roman.

10. Place the boxed item at the bottom of the page in the page footer. Use an 8 point Arial font and outline the paragraph.

11. Save and print the document.

Market Survey

February 1996

To help us determine how to best develop products and marketing strategies in the future, please complete the following form. Return this form to the address shown at the bottom of the form.*

State.................................. ____	Age.................................... ____
Sex (M,F) .... ____	Employed .... ____
Registered Voter (Y, N)......... ____	Marital Status (S,M,D)....... ____

Check each of the following items owned by someone in your household:

- ❏ Microwave
- ❏ Personal Computer
- ❏ Second Home
- ❏ Snowblower
- ❏ Electronic Video Game

Use the following table to indicate which term most closely describes your preference:

Code Table				
Life Style	R=Rural	U=Urban	S=Suburban	X=Other
Housing	S=Single Family	A=Apartment	T=Townhouse	X=Other
Political	R=Republican	D=Democrat	I=Indpendent	X=Other
Auto	S=Subcompact	C=Compact	M=Midsize	L=Luxury
Color	R=Red	B=Blue	O=Orange	X=Other
Restaurant	A=American	I=Italian	S=Spanish	X=Other

| Life Style ____ | Housing ____ | Political ____ |
| Auto ____ | Color ____ | Restaurant ____ |

Check any statement you agree with:

- ❏ TV commercials are too violent.
- ❏ TV commercials are too long.
- ❏ Commercials that show sex and violence should not be aired between the hours of 7am and 9 p.m..
- ❏ I would boycott any company that sponsored a program I believe is too violent.
- ❏ I would boycott any company that did not have a labor union.
- ❏ Too many commercials are aimed at children.
- ❏ Most commercials fail to educate the consumer on uses of the product.
- ❏ Commercials that are geared at the holiday season are aired long before the start of the season.

*Please return to:
Market Survey Coordinators
418 W. Green Ave.
New York, NY 10578

The information provided in this survey will be kept confidential. A summary of the survey results will be provided to each respondent.

FIGURE 4.40 Completed Survey for Exercise 4.3.

The file for this exercise is on the tutorials and exercise disk. It is named Exercise 4-3.WPS and contains the text for a company newsletter. There are several misspelled words in the text. Ignore these until you spell check the document. Open the file and make the following changes. To help you locate where the changes need to be made, a number has been stored in the document that corresponds to the steps listed below. Delete the number from the document as you make the changes.

1. Center the first three lines. Change the font to Arial Black and the font size to 16. Apply the bold attribute to these lines.
2. Use the Insert menu to replace the words (place the current date here) with the current date. Use the third entry on the Date and Time window. Set the date so it will not automatically update when it is printed.
3. Use a Right align tab with a leader to format the President, Vice President, and Director lines. Place the leader tab at 6.25 inches. When this step is completed, the three lines should look like the following.

President .... May Phillips

Vice President .... Carl Thomas

Director .... Paul Miller

4. Place an outline with shadow border around the three lines in step 3 above. Also, shade the paragraphs in a 50% pattern and a color of Cyan. Now use the Indents and Spacing option to indent the right margin four inches.
5. Format the four numbered items with hanging indents. Indent the left margin .75 inches and the first line -.25 inches. After you have formatted the items, tab between the period to the right of the number and the text on the paragraph to force alignment of the paragraph's left margin.
6. Format this line using an Article Title Easy Format. Assign a thick, single line border to the bottom of this paragraph.
7. Use tab marks to format the class title, date, and cost of items into a table. Choose tab locations, but make the table look similar to the one shown below. Change the tabs on the first line so the headings are properly aligned over the columns.

Class Title	Date	Cost
Ami Pro Word Processing	January 11	55.00
Microsoft Word	January 23	5.50
Learning Windows 95	February 8	105.00
Upgrading Tips for Windows 95	March 14	125.00
Disk Doctor	March 30	275.95
Desk Top Publishing	April 3	200.00
Managing Your Hard Disk	April 25	95.50

8. Format this line using an Article Title Easy Format. Assign a thick, single line border to the bottom of this paragraph.
9. Use the insert table option to place the following table into the document. Use a Contemporary Simple format. Use the Borders folder to place the double line border around the table.

Item	Manufacturer	Price
LC1000 Laser Printer	Epson Manufacturing	$595.00
Bocca Tape Backup, 250 Meg	Bocca Memory Systems	$195.00
1 Meg, 80NS SIMMS	Intel Corporation	$49.00
Nautral Keyboard	Microsoft Corporation	$89.95
10 PK, HD Diskettes	Maxell Memory Systems	$4.90

10. Insert a footnote at the end of the paragraph beginning "We have plenty of items". Use a numbered footnote. Use your full name as the contact person. The footnote should read:

    Contact (your full name) for frequent customer discounts.

11. Format this line using an Article Title Easy Format. Assign a thick, single line border to the bottom of this paragraph.

12. Select the six paragraphs that follow this number and assign a bullet to each paragraph. Use the check mark as the bullet symbol.

13. Insert a footnote in place of this number. Use a numbered footnote. The footnote should read:

    Windows 95 is a registered trademark of the Microsoft Corporation.

14. Set the margins to a 1.5″ top margin and 1″ bottom margin. Set the left margin to 1.25″ and the right margin to 1″. Use a 1″ header margin and a .5″ footer margin.

15. Create a header for the newsletter. Insert the file name on the left of the header. Insert your full name on the right side. You will need to insert a right align tab to get your name on the right. Place a page number at the right margin of the footer.

16. Spell check the entire document. After checking the spelling, proofread the document and make any other necessary corrections.

17. Set the footnotes to print at the end of the document. Save and print the document.

ADVANCED WORD PROCESSING FEATURES

When you've completed this chapter, you will be able to:

- Find and replace text.
- Control paragraph spacing and printing.
- Create Easy Formats.
- Create Easy text.
- Create subscript, superscript, and strike-through text.
- Use bookmarks.
- Use the Works thesaurus.
- Create multicolumn documents.
- Hyphenate a document.
- Print in landscape orientation.
- Insert clipart images into a document and change their size.
- Use Word Count.

This chapter will complete the word processing section of this text. Advanced techniques used to create and edit documents will be discussed. Word processing features will be revisited in Chapter 13, Integrating Works Applications, where data are combined with other modules of Microsoft Works.

Finding Text

There are times, especially in long documents, when certain words, terms, or phrases need to be located. Rather than reading the entire document searching for the word, you can have Microsoft Works find the word, term, or phrase. This is much faster and much more accurate.

To perform a search, use the **Find** option from the Edit menu. This option provides the window shown in Figure 5.1.

Text to find

Find a Tab mark

Find a paragraph mark

These options restrict the search

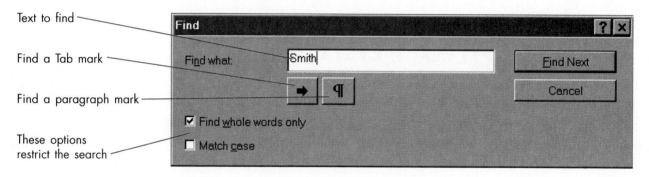

FIGURE 5.1   Use the Find option on the Edit menu to locate a word, term or phrase.

In this example, we are searching for the name *Smith*. This word is entered in the "Find what" area. Since we do not want to find the words Smithsonian, Smithfield, blacksmith, etc., we marked the **Find whole words only** option. This option forces a match on entire words. If this option were not on, words such as Smithsonian and blacksmith would be found since they contain the letters s-m-i-t-h.

The other option is **Match case**. This forces the search to check upper and lowercase characters for an exact match. This option is not activated since we want to find the name "smith" in case it is in the text, but not correctly capitalized.

Click the OK button to find the first occurrence of the word Smith. The word will be located and highlighted. Press the **F7 function key** or click the **Find Next** button to search for the next occurrence of the same word.

Finding Special Characters

Other special characters such as page breaks, and white space can also be found. To search for these special characters, a code must be used in the "Find what" text area. These character codes are listed in Figure 5.2.

Two of the special characters shown in Figure 5.2 can be placed in the Find text box by clicking the buttons on the Find window. These are the **Tab** and the **Paragraph** buttons. When these buttons are clicked, the appropriate special character is inserted. For example, if you wanted to find the name Smith only if it was at the beginning of a paragraph, click the paragraph button, then enter Smith. The text in the box would read $^\wedge pSmith$.

SPECIAL CHARACTER CODES

Character	Code	Character	Code
Any single character	?	**Paragraph mark**	$^\wedge$p
Caret	$^\wedge\wedge$	**Question mark**	$^\wedge$?
End-of-line mark	$^\wedge$n	**Tab mark**	$^\wedge$t
Manual page break	$^\wedge$d	**White space**	$^\wedge$w
Nonbreaking space	$^\wedge$s		

FIGURE 5.2   Codes used to find special characters in a document.

Finding Text Using Wild Cards

Wild cards also can be used to find text. Wild cards are used here in the same way they are used in Windows file names. The **asterisk** (*) is substituted for any number of characters. For example, using Lab* in the "Find what" text area finds LAB1, Laboratory, Label, etc. When the **question mark** is used as a wild card, it is substituted for only one character. For example, Lab? finds Lab1, LabA, laba, etc., but would not find Label or Laboratory.

Replacing Text

There may be times when it is desirable to replace one word or phrase with a different word or phrase. For example, suppose a company changes its name from First Federal Bank to Second National Bank. Also suppose the original name occurred in a document several times. The name would need to be changed in each place. The **Replace** option can be used to accomplish this task.

Replacing text is similar to finding text. In fact, a Replace actually performs a Find before replacing the text. The primary difference is that replacement text must be entered. When the original text is found, you are given an option to replace the text or ignore the replacement. An example of the Replace window is shown in Figure 5.3.

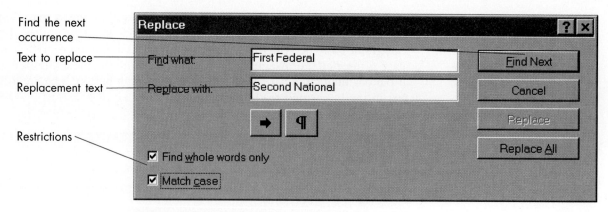

Find the next occurrence —

Text to replace —

Replacement text —

Restrictions —

Replace

| Find what: | First Federal |
| Replace with: | Second National |

→ ¶

☑ Find whole words only

☑ Match case

Find Next

Cancel

Replace

Replace All

FIGURE 5.3 The Replace window.

To use the Replace option, enter the original text in the "Find what" area, then enter the new text in the **Replace with** text area. In Figure 5.3, First Federal is entered in the "Find what" text box and Second National is entered in the "Replace with" text box to accomplish the replacement.

The "Match whole words only" and "Match case" options work the same as for the Find option.

The four buttons in the Replace window are used to execute the option. The **Find Next** button is used to find the first occurrence of the "Find what" text. When the text is found, the **Replace button** becomes available. To replace the occurrence found, click the Replace button. The occurrence of the text is replaced and the next occurrence is found.

To find the next occurrence without replacing the current occurrence, choose the Find Next button. To replace all occurrences in the document, choose the **Replace All** button. To close the Find window and quit searching, choose the Cancel button.

When the text is found and replaced, the following rules apply:

1. If the original text has attributes (underline, bold, or italics), the new replacement text will also have these attributes.
2. Capitalization of the new text will match original text. For example, if you search for the word "some" and replace it with the word "most" and Works finds "Some", it will replace "Some" with "Most".

CREATING EASY TEXT

If a large string of text is often used, such as a company name, disclaimer, or address, you can create the text one time and store it as **Easy Text**. When the text needs to be inserted into the document, enter the name of the Easy Text and press the **F3 function key**. The Easy Text will be inserted in place of the Easy Text name.

For example, suppose you write a large number of business letters and you place a name and address on each letter. You could create the name and address as Easy Text. To create the Easy Text, choose the Easy Text option on the Insert menu. Choose **New Easy Text** from the pull out menu. The window shown in Figure 5.4 will be displayed.

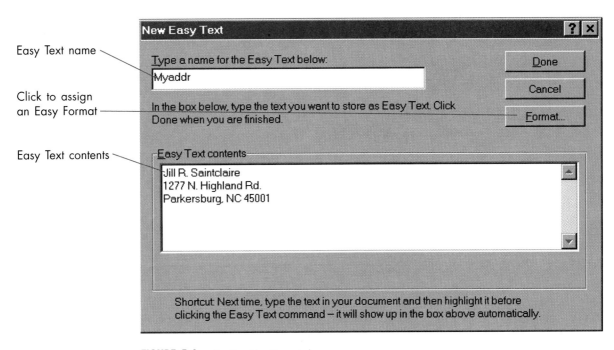

Easy Text name

Click to assign an Easy Format

Easy Text contents

FIGURE 5.4   The New Easy Text window.

The first step is to name the Easy Text using the text area at the top of the New Easy Text window. In Figure 5.4, the name of the Easy Text is *Myaddr*. The next step is to enter the Easy Text in the Easy Text contents area. The Easy Text can consist of more than one line or paragraph. To assign an **Easy Format** to the Easy Text, click the Format button. The Easy Format window discussed in Chapter 4 will be displayed. Click any Easy Format and that format will be assigned to the text. To complete the creation of the Easy Text, click the Done button.

To use the Easy Text, type its name in a document. The case of the Easy Text name is not important and it can be entered in either upper or lower case. With the cursor anywhere in the Easy Text name, press the F3 function key. The Easy Text contents will replace the Easy Text name in the document.

You can also insert the Easy Text using the Easy Text option on the Edit menu. This option will provide a list of Easy Text names. Click the Easy Text name, then click the Insert button and the text will be inserted into the document.

To delete an Easy Text entry or change its contents, choose the Easy Text option from the Edit menu. Click the appropriate Easy Text name, then click the Delete or Change buttons. To change the format for the Easy Text, click the Format button.

Note: Easy Text is global to all Microsoft Works documents. This means that anyone using Microsoft Works has access to all Easy Text. If you share a machine with someone else or are using a network, any Easy Text created is available to other users. You also have access to Easy Text created by others. This may cause conflicts unless some type of naming convention is used to determine which Easy Text is yours and which is someone else's.

Use of **Easy Formats** was discussed in Chapter 4. They are used to assign several formatting options to a block of text. Not only can the Easy Formats provided by Microsoft Works be used, but new formats can be created. There are several ways to create a new Easy Format. We will describe the simplest approach here.

The simplest approach to creating a new Easy Format is to begin by formatting a paragraph exactly the way you would like it formatted. Once this paragraph has been formatted, select the entire paragraph. Next, click the Easy Format tool on the tool bar. From the Easy Format menu, choose the Create From Selection option. The window in Figure 5.5 will appear.

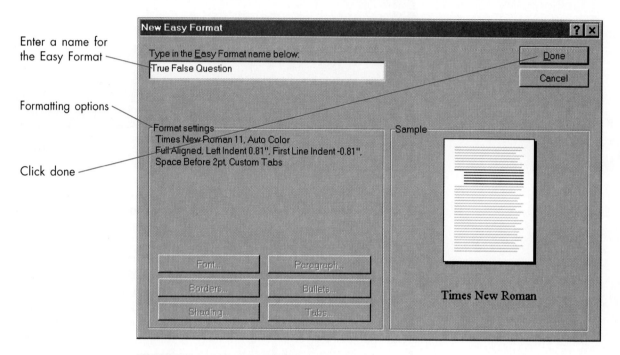

FIGURE 5.5   The New Easy Format window.

On the New Easy Format window, enter a name for the format, then click Done. The format will now be available to all Microsoft Works documents.

Note that the formatting buttons at the bottom of the New Easy Format window are not available when the format is being created. The buttons used to change the formatting options are only available when changing an existing format or creating a new format using the Format menu.

Changing Easy Formats

An Easy Format can also be changed. To change the formatting options, choose Easy Formats from the Format menu. The window shown in Figure 5.6 is displayed. Select the format to be changed, then click the Change button. The window in Figure 5.5 is displayed, but this time the buttons at the bottom are available. Use these buttons to add, change, or delete formatting options for the Easy Format.

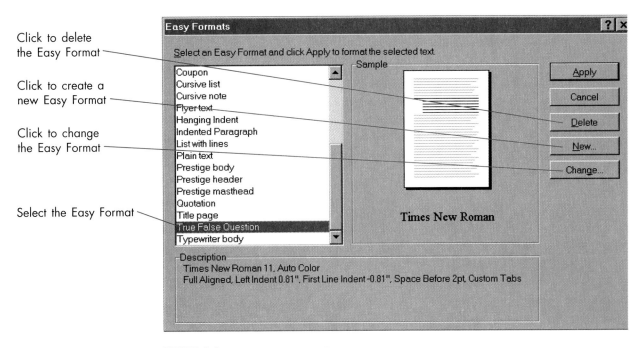

Click to delete
the Easy Format

Click to create a
new Easy Format

Click to change
the Easy Format

Select the Easy Format

FIGURE 5.6 The Easy Formats window.

You can also use the window in Figure 5.6 to delete a format or create a new format. To delete a format, select the format name and click the Delete button. To create a new format, click the New button and use the window in Figure 5.5 to name the Easy Format and set its formatting options.

CONTROLLING PARAGRAPHS

The Spacing folder of the Paragraph option on the Format menu can be used to control how lines of a paragraph are spaced and how consecutive paragraphs print. This folder is shown in Figure 5.7.

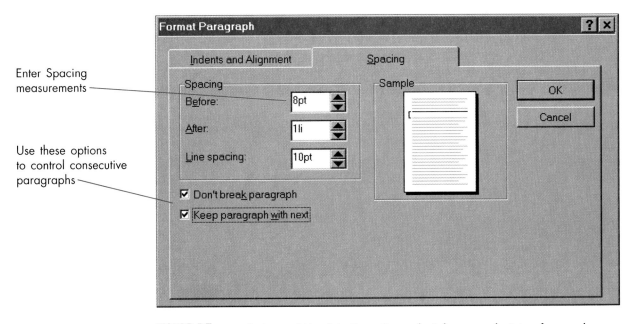

Enter Spacing
measurements

Use these options
to control consecutive
paragraphs

FIGURE 5.7 Use the Spacing folder of the Format Paragraph window to control printing of paragraphs.

The **Line Spacing** option is used to control line spacing for the paragraph. Spacing can be specified as points or lines. If a number is entered followed by the letters **li**, the distance between lines will be measured based upon the current height of the line. To change the spacing, enter a number in this entry. For example, you would enter 1.5 for line-and-a-half spacing.

To specify spacing in **points**, follow the number with the letters **pt**. Remember, a point is $\frac{1}{72}$ of an inch. In Figure 5.7 the spacing has been set to 10 points.

The **Before** and **After** entries specify the amount of space before and after a paragraph. These options can be used to provide white space between paragraphs. Measurements for these options can also be specified as either lines or points.

If the **Don't break paragraph** option is marked, Microsoft Works will keep the entire paragraph on one page. Use this option on short, two- or three-line paragraphs or for special paragraphs that need to be together.

The **Keep paragraph with next option** is used to keep the marked paragraph on the same page as the paragraph that follows it. This option can be used to keep all lines in a table on the same page, since each line in a table is normally treated as a separate paragraph. To keep table lines together, select each line of the table, except for the last line, and set this option on.

SUBSCRIPTS, SUPERSCRIPTS, AND STRIKETHROUGHS

Superscript, **subscript**, and **strikethrough** formats are set in the Format **Font and Style** window.

Subscripts are characters that are printed lower than the normal characters on the line and are often several points smaller than normal text. In this sentence, the word $_{Subscript}$ is lowered and printed as a subscript. Superscripts are raised higher than the normal characters and are often several points smaller than normal text. In this sentence, the word ^{Superscript} is printed as a superscript. Subscripts and superscripts are often used when writing formulas like the following:

$$X_i = (Y_1...Y_n)\ Z^m...Z^n$$

Subscript and superscript formatting is controlled by the Font and Style option on the Format menu. The Format Font and Style window is shown in Figure 5.8.

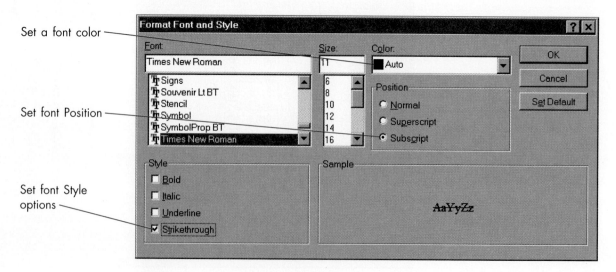

FIGURE 5.8   The Format Font and Style window.

To format text as a superscript or subscript, select the text, choose Font and Style from the Format menu or choose Font and Style from the menu provided by the right mouse button, then click the appropriate option in the Format Font and Style window.

Another style that is available from the Font and Style window is the **Strikethrough** style. If this style is chosen, the selected text will be printed with a line through each character, ~~like this~~.

Also notice that the Format Font and Style window has an option to set the **color** of the font. To change a font's color, click on the arrow at the right of the color list, then click the desired color.

> Note: When color fonts are printed on black and white printers, some colors will print as grays while other colors print as black or white. If the colored text is printed as a white color, it will not show on the paper. It will appear as if the colored text did not print.

USING BOOKMARKS

Bookmarks are special characters in a document that mark a location. Think of this as folding down the corner of a page. When the page needs to be referenced, you simply look for the folded corner. In Works, a bookmark is placed in a document and given a name. Bookmarks are created using the Bookmark option on the Edit menu. In the Bookmark Name window, enter a name for the bookmark and click the OK button. The Bookmark Name window is shown in Figure 5.9.

Enter a name
for the bookmark

Click OK

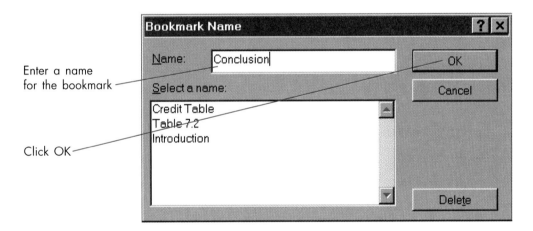

FIGURE 5.9   The Bookmark Name window.

To delete a bookmark, choose the Bookmark option from the Edit menu. On the Bookmark Name window, select the name to be deleted and click the Delete button.

Once a bookmark has been created, the **Go To** option of the Edit menu can be used to move directly to the bookmark. When the Go To window is displayed, click the bookmark name, then click the OK button and the cursor will move to that location. The Go To window is shown in Figure 5.10.

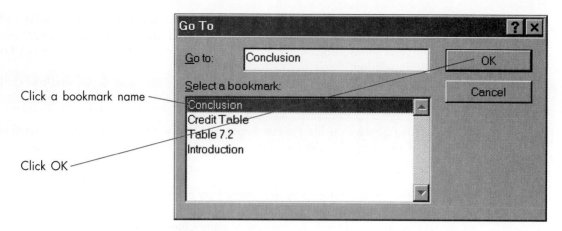

Click a bookmark name

Click OK

FIGURE 5.10   The Go To window.

The Go To option can also be used to move to a specific page within a document. To go to a specific page, enter the page number in the text area of the Go To window and click OK.

USING THE THESAURUS

The **thesaurus** in Microsoft Works can be used to find alternate words that have the same or similar meaning as an existing word. The alternate word is a **synonym**. Using the thesaurus can improve your writing style by helping to eliminate words or phrases that are overused or by finding the right word to express a thought.

To use the thesaurus, place the cursor anywhere in the word and choose Thesaurus from the Tools menu. A window like the one in Figure 5.11 will be displayed. At the top of the window is the word being used by the thesaurus. On the left side of the window, in the Meanings area, several words are listed. Each meaning is marked with an indication of the use of the word, (a) adjective, (n) noun, (v) verb, etc. On the right side of the window is a list of synonyms for the word selected in the Meanings box. If a different word in the Meanings box is selected, the list of synonyms is changed to represent synonyms for the newly selected word. To substitute the word in the document with one of the words in the thesaurus, select the word to be substituted and choose the Replace button. This will substitute the selected word with the chosen synonym.

Selected word

New word

Available synonyms

Synonyms for the selected synonym

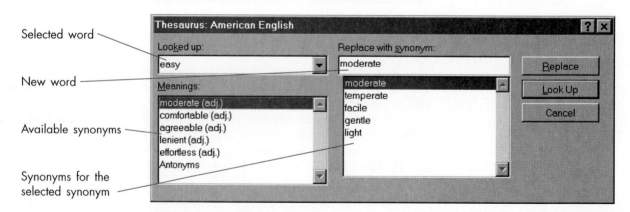

FIGURE 5.11   The Thesaurus window.

Works will also display synonyms for a synonym. To get these displayed, select one of the words in the synonyms area and click the Look Up button. A new list of synonyms will appear in both the Meanings area and in the Synonyms area.

USING MULTIPLE COLUMNS

Multiple-column documents like those in newspapers and magazines can be created using the Columns option of the Format menu. An example of a **multiple-column document** is shown in Figure 5.12.

Earth Watch News

Global Warming Questioned

Global warming has been a hotly contested issue over the last several decades. Experts cannot agree on the degree to which the earth has warmed and some experts claim there has been no global warming. A study sponsored by the **Friends of Earth** and written by Jane Doe announced last week that unless carbon dioxide emissions were reduced over the next decade, catastrophic changes in regional temperatures would occur. According to the report, there is a direct relation between warming and the amount of carbon dioxide produced. The formula provided in the report is:

$$CO^2 * T_{(1-v)} + T^3$$

Whether the experts agree or not, global warming will be a hot subject for years to come. Improvements made over the past several years continue for several decades to reverse a warming trend.

Economic Indicators Up for Third Straight Month

Jane Doe, chief spokesperson for the President's Economic Advisors, announced that several key economic indicators were up again this month. This marks the third straight month that these indicators have been on the positive side. According to Jane Doe, "The Federal Reserve deserves credit for maintaining a strong consistent monetary policy over the past several years". Among the indicators that lead the way were:

- Housing starts up by 15 %
- Unemployment decreased to 8.7%
- Inflation remained unchanged
- Prime interest rate declined by 1/4 point

Intel Announces 32 Bit Chip

Jane Doe, president of the Intel Corporation, announced this week that the new 32 bit Pentium processor is available to the public. A nameless reference from inside Intel says there will be ample supply to keep the price of the chip affordable. The new chip is expected to double speeds of the today's fastest desktop computers. Many software companies have already begun developing programs for the new chip.

The lighter Side

On the lighter side, Jane Doe of the American Heart Association, announced that most Americans are eating less and enjoying it more. The average American meal has been reduced by over 150 calories. Jane Doe claims that this improvement in eating habits will save over 2,000 lives each year.

Stock Market Tops the 4200 Mark

The Dow Jones Industrial Average climbed to a record high today with active trading. After an initial drop of 15 points in the early trading hours, the DOW recovered shortly before lunch and climbed to a record 4205 high before closing. Gainers outweighed losers by 2-to-1. Investment analyst, Jane Doe, of the Beeker and Beeker accounting firm said today that the end is not in sight.

Volume V   January 1996

FIGURE 5.12   A sample document printed using three columns.

To format a document into multiple columns, choose the **Columns** option from the Format menu. The window shown in Figure 5.13 will be displayed.

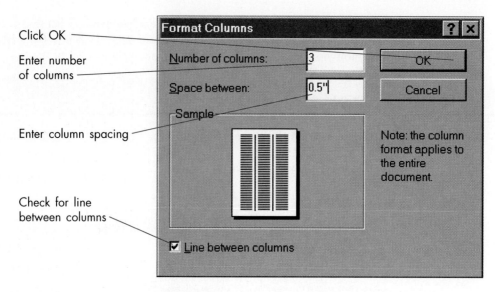

Click OK

Enter number
of columns

Enter column spacing

Check for line
between columns

FIGURE 5.13 The Format Columns window.

The number of columns for the document is entered in the **Number of columns** area. The **Space between** is used to specify the distance from the right margin of the left-hand column to the left margin of the right-hand column. The distance between columns will be the same for all columns in the document. The **Line Between** option is used to specify that a vertical bar is to be placed between the columns. This option was used for the document in Figure 5.12.

Works will only display multiple columns in **Page Layout view**. If this view is not being used when the columns are specified, Works asks if you would like to switch to this view. If you choose not to switch to Page Layout view, the document will be displayed as only one column.

Also note that the multiple columns will apply to the entire body of the document. Only the **header** and **footer** lines will be exempt from the multiple column format. Header and footer lines can be used to create a banner for a newsletter or advertisement as shown in Figure 5.12.

USING HYPHENATION

Hyphenating words can be used to improve the appearance of a document with right-aligned and justified margins. This is especially desirable with multi-column documents where the columns are narrow. When Works hyphenates words, optional hyphens are placed only in words at the end of a line. If the hyphenated word is moved, the optional hyphen is removed.

To hyphenate a document, choose the **Hyphenation** option from the Tools menu. The Hyphenation window is shown in Figure 5.14.

When the hyphenation process begins, Works scans each line in the document looking for words at the beginning of the line to see if the word can be broken on two lines. The options in the Hyphenation window specify how the hyphenation occurs. If the **Hyphenate CAPS** option is on, Works will check words that are in all capitals. If this option is off, Works will skip capitalized words.

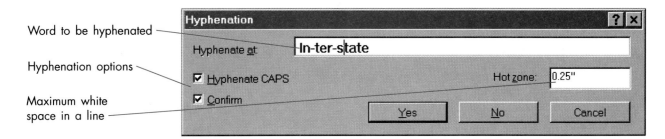

Word to be hyphenated

Hyphenation options

Maximum white
space in a line

FIGURE 5.14 The Hyphenation window.

If the Confirm option is on, Works displays each word in the Hyphenate at area showing possible hyphenation points. Using this option, you can specify where the optional hyphen is inserted.

The **Hot zone** text box is used to define the maximum distance between the last letter on a line and the right margin. If the Hot zone is small, the right margin will be smoother, but there will be many hyphenated words. Larger Hot zones create fewer hyphenated words, but a more ragged right-hand margin.

USING WORD COUNT

The **Word Count** option on the Tools menu counts the number of words in a document. The number of words will be displayed in a box when this option is used. The word count will include words in the body of the text, the headers and footers, and all footnotes.

USING LANDSCAPE ORIENTATION

Documents can be created using either **portrait** or **landscape orientation**. Portrait is the normal orientation of a page. This orientation is taller than it is wide. Landscape orientation flips the page sideways. It uses the height of the page as the width and the width of the page as the height. Figure 5.15 shows a document in both orientations.

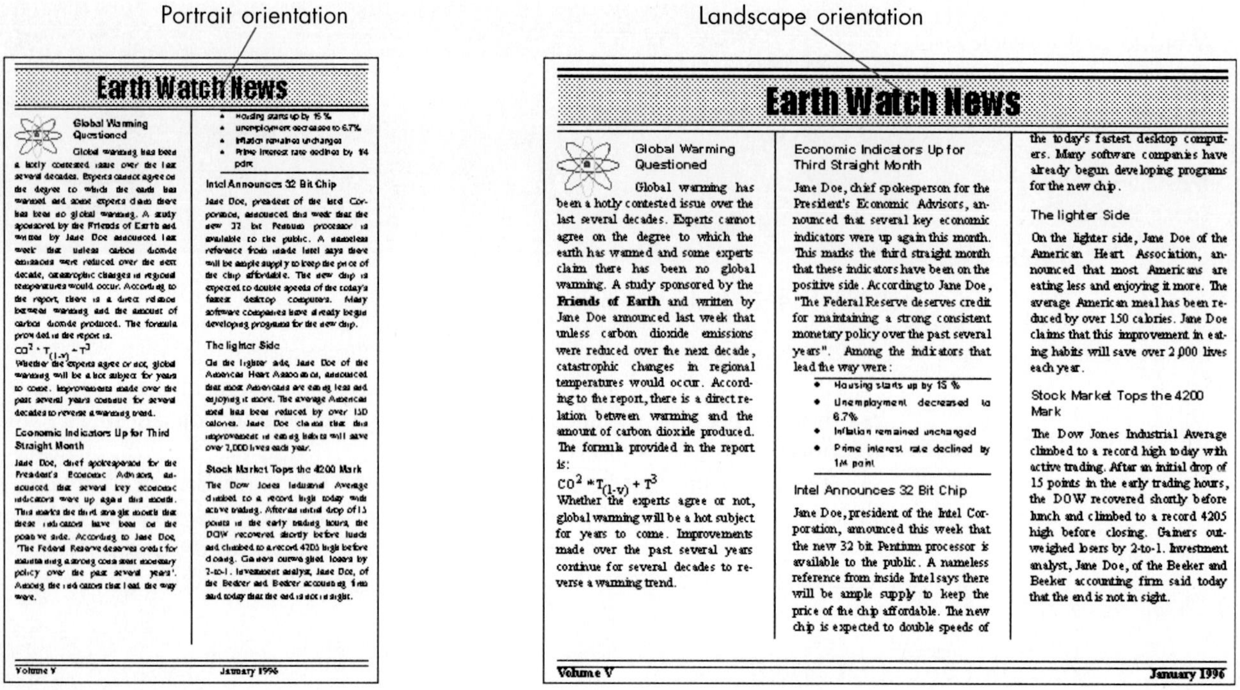

Portrait orientation   Landscape orientation

FIGURE 5.15 Examples of Portrait and Landscape orientations.

The orientation is set using the Source, Size & Orientation folder of the Page Setup window. This window is shown in Figure 5.16. To choose an orientation, click the desired entry in the Orientation area and click the OK button. Works will change the work area of the document to the orientation selected. When a document is printed in landscape orientation, it is turned sideways to print correctly on the printer.

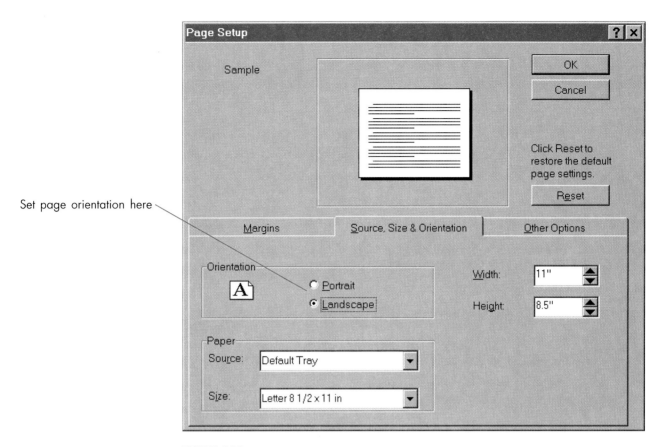

Set page orientation here

FIGURE 5.16 Source, Size & Orientation Folder.

INSERTING CLIPART

Clipart contains small picture images used to illustrate a point, visually show an object, or otherwise dress up a document. Microsoft Works will allow you to insert clipart images into a word processing document. This feature provides a limited amount of desktop publishing capability. The clipart images themselves must be created by some other application program. For example, a painting could be created with Microsoft Paint or Microsoft Draw. There is also a picture gallery provided with the Microsoft Works program.

There are several ways to insert clipart images into a document. The technique described here is only one method.

To insert a picture into a document, position the cursor where the picture is to be placed and choose the **ClipArt** option on the Insert menu. This will start the **Microsoft ClipArt Gallery** program provided with Microsoft Works. When the program starts, a screen similar to the one in Figure 5.17 will appear.

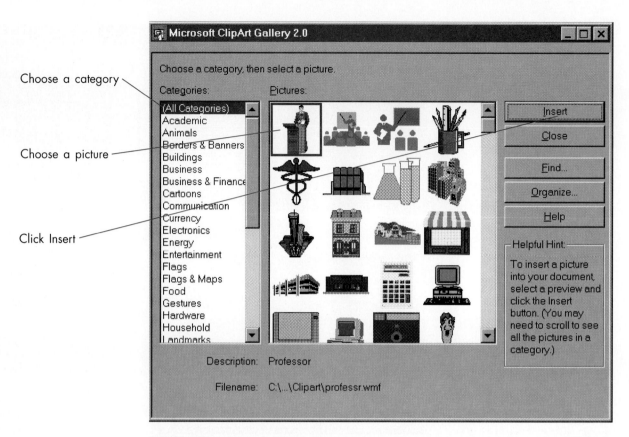

Choose a category

Choose a picture

Click Insert

FIGURE 5.17 The Microsoft ClipArt Gallery screen.

When the Gallery is first started, all pictures in the current gallery are displayed as thumbnails. A **thumbnail** is simply a reduced view of the picture. To select a picture for the document, click the desired picture's thumbnail, then click the OK button. The selected picture will be inserted into the document to the right of the cursor.

Each picture in the gallery is assigned to a category. These categories are listed at the left of the screen in the categories area. To restrict the pictures to a specific category, click the category name.

The other buttons on the screen are used to add, change, and delete pictures from the gallery. To use these buttons, we refer you to the Microsoft Works documentation.

Setting the Text Wrap

The text wrap is specified using the Text Wrap option of the Format menu. This window is shown in Figure 5.18. To choose a wrapping option, select the picture by clicking it, choose **Text Wrap** from the Format menu, then click the appropriate option's symbol. This window can also be used to specify a picture's location on a page and the page of the document upon which the picture is to be printed.

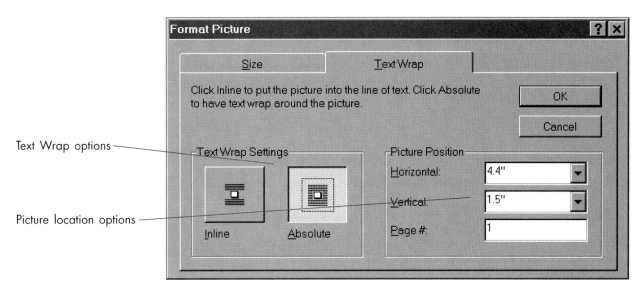

Text Wrap options ——————

Picture location options ——————

FIGURE 5.18 The picture Text Wrap options window.

There are two options for **text wrapping** in relation to a picture. The first option is to have the object **In-line** with the text. When this option is chosen, the spacing above and below the line the picture is on is increased, if necessary, to accommodate the picture. When new text is inserted above the picture, the picture is moved so that it stays in the same position relative to the surrounding text. The picture is always on a line by itself.

The second option is **Absolute**. If the text wrap is set to absolute, the picture stays in one position on the page and the surrounding text wraps around the picture. Several lines of text may be on the same line as the picture and text may be on both the left and right sides of the picture. As new text is entered, the picture does not move. The folder in Figure 5.18 shows the difference between the In-line and Absolute options.

Moving and Sizing a Picture

To move a picture or change its size, the picture must first be selected. To select a picture, click anywhere on the picture. When the picture is selected it is surrounded by a dotted frame with six squares. These squares are referred to as the picture's **handles**. Figure 5.19 shows a selected picture with its handles.

Use the handles to
change a picture's size ——————

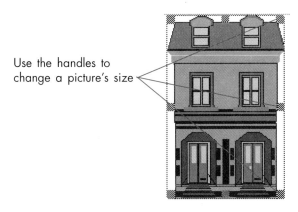

FIGURE 5.19 A clipart picture
with handles displayed.

To change a **picture's size**, drag one of the handles. To make a picture shorter or taller, use the center handle on the top or bottom lines of the frame. To make a picture narrower or wider, use the handles in the center of the left or right frame sides. To reduce or enlarge the picture while keeping the width and height proportional, use the left or right corner handles. When the handles are used to change the size of a picture, the scaling percentage is displayed on the left side of the status bar.

The picture can also be sized using the **Size** folder of the Picture option on the Format menu. This folder is shown in Figure 5.20. The picture must be selected before this option is available. Using this folder, the exact size of the picture can be specified in the Width and Height size box. You can also specify picture sizing in percentages in the Height and Width Scaling areas.

Set Size in inches

Set Scaling as percent of original

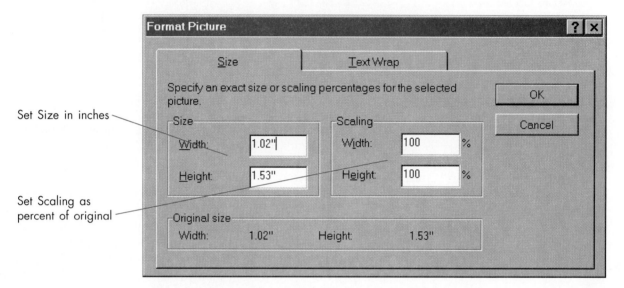

FIGURE 5.20 Size window.

To move a picture, select the picture, click anywhere inside the picture's frame, and drag the mouse. If the picture's text wrap is set to In-line, drag the insertion bar to the new location. When the mouse button is released, the picture will be moved. If the picture's text wrap is set to Absolute, the picture's outline will move as the mouse is dragged.

CHAPTER 5 SELF-TEST

1. Which find option on the Find window will keep Works from finding characters that occur in the middle of a word?
2. If you were to perform a search for the letters t-h-e and you did not select the "Match whole word only" option but you did select the "Match Case" option, which of the following would be found?
   the   The   Theater   therefore   another   GATHER   WeaTher
3. What is the equivalent of 16 points in inches?
4. Explain how you could force Microsoft Works to place three consecutive paragraphs on the same page.
5. Explain how you create Easy Text.
6. What is the difference between a subscript and a superscript?
7. What is a bookmark used for?
8. Why would you use the thesaurus?
9. What does the Hot zone specify in the Hyphenation window?
10. What view will display multiple columns of a document?
11. Explain the difference between landscape and portrait orientation.
12. List the steps taken to insert a graphic image into a document.
13. How would you stretch a graphic image to make it wider?
14. What is the difference between In-line and Absolute text wrap for a picture?

CHAPTER 5 TUTORIAL

In this tutorial, you will use the file Chapter 5 Tutorial.WPS on the tutorials and exercises disk.

START THE TUTORIAL

Start Microsoft Works and open the document Chapter 5 Tutorial.WPS on the tutorials and exercises disk.

1. Start Microsoft Works and open the Chapter 5 Tutorial.WPS file.

REPLACE TEXT

The name Jane Doe is stored several times in the document. For this step, you want to change each occurrence of the name Jane Doe to your first and last name. Use the **Replace option** to do this.

1. Make sure the cursor is at the beginning of the document.
2. Choose the Replace option from the Edit menu.

A replace window like the one in Figure 5.21 should be displayed. Fill in the window and find the first occurrence of the name Jane Doe.

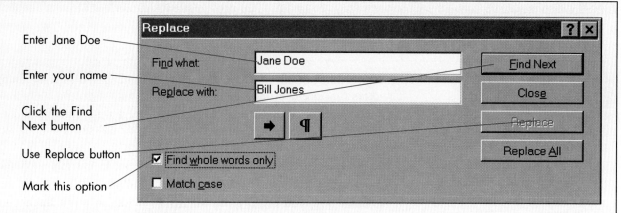

Enter Jane Doe

Enter your name

Click the Find
Next button

Use Replace button

Mark this option

FIGURE 5.21 The filled-in Replace window.

3. Enter Jane Doe in the "Find what" text box.
4. Enter your first and last name in the "Replace with" text box.
5. Set the "Find whole word only" option on and set the "Match case" option off.
6. Click the Find Next button.

Works has located the first usage of Jane Doe. Use the Replace button to replace this occurrence. Then find the remaining occurrences and replace each occurrence.

7. Choose the Replace button to replace this occurrence.
8. Continue replacing each occurrence of the name Jane Doe with your name. There should be seven occurrences in the document.

USE THE FIND OPTION

The word *source* is somewhere in the document. Rather than reading the entire document to find the word, use the **Find option** on the Edit menu. The Find window is shown in Figure 5.22.

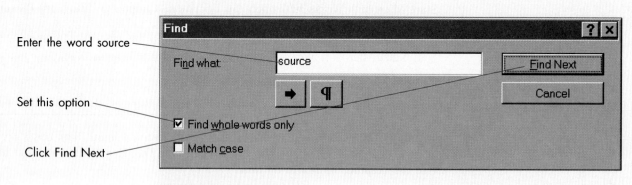

Enter the word source

Set this option

Click Find Next

FIGURE 5.22 Filled-in Find window.

1. Enter Ctrl/Home to move to the beginning of the document.
2. Choose Find on the Edit menu.
3. Enter "source" in the "Find what" area.
4. Set the "Find whole word only" option on and the "Match case" option off.
5. Click the Find Next button.

   The word *source* should now be highlighted. Close the Find window.

6. Click the Cancel button.

USE THE THESAURUS

Now suppose you wanted to use a word other than *source*. The **thesaurus** can be used to find a synonym. Since the word "source" has been selected by the Find command, it is highlighted and will be the word used by the thesaurus.

1. Choose Thesaurus from the Tools menu.

   Notice the Meanings box at the left side of the window. The synonyms listed are origin, expert, and spring. The words listed in the synonyms box on the right-hand side of the window are for the word "origin" since it is the word currently selected. The best synonym for source is expert, but assume you do not like this synonym. To get synonyms for expert, click the word. Refer to the Thesaurus window shown in Figure 5.23.

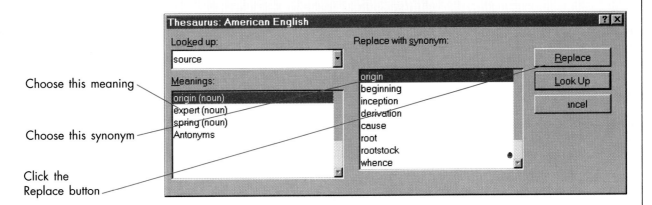

FIGURE 5.23 Thesaurus window.

2. Click the word "expert" in the Meanings list.

   The Synonyms list now contains synonyms for the word "expert." The word reference will work well, so choose that word.

3. Click the word "reference" in the synonyms list.
4. Click the Replace button.

   The word reference has now replaced the word source.

FORMAT A TITLE

There is a title for each article in the document. Normally, titles are set off by white space above and below the title. To provide this white space, the spacing before and after the paragraph needs to be changed. This can be done using the **Spacing** folder for paragraph formatting.

1. Press Ctrl/Home to move to the beginning of the document, which is a title.
2. Make sure the mouse pointer is on the first line and click the right mouse button.
3. Click Paragraph.
4. Click the Spacing folder's tab.

A folder similar to the one in Figure 5.24 is displayed. To provide spacing for the title, enter a spacing measure in the Before and the After areas. To prevent the title and the following text from being broken onto different pages, set the **Don't break paragraph** and the **Keep paragraph with next** options on.

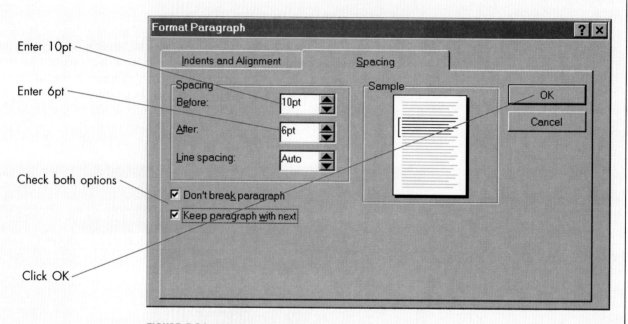

FIGURE 5.24 Filled-in Spacing folder.

5. Enter 10 pt in the Before area.
6. Enter 6 pt in the After area.
7. Click the "Don't break paragraph" option.
8. Click the "Keep paragraph with next" option.
9. Click the OK button

Now change the font and style for the paragraph.

10. Select the entire line.
11. Assign the Arial font.
12. Click the Bold tool on the Toolbar.

This completes the formatting for the first article title.

CREATE AN EASY FORMAT

Once a paragraph has been formatted, the format can be used to create an **Easy Format**. This technique allows you to work with one paragraph, get it correct, then quickly apply its format to other paragraphs. We will do this with the remaining titles in the document.

First, create the Easy Format.

1. Select the line you just formatted.
2. Click the Easy Format tool on the toolbar.
3. Click the Create From Selection option on the Easy Formats menu.

You should now have the window shown in Figure 5.25.

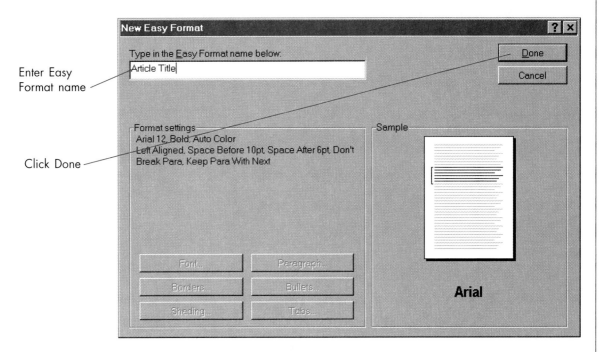

Enter Easy Format name

Click Done

FIGURE 5.25 The New Easy Format window.

4. Enter a name for the Easy Format. Enter "Article Title" as the name.
5. Click the Done button. (Note: If you get a message that says the Easy Format already exists, Do you want to replace it? Choose the YES button.)

Apply the Easy Format

Now, assign the Easy Format to the next article title.

1. Move the cursor to the next article title. It's the line reading Economic Indicators Up for Third Straight Month.
2. Click the Easy Format tool on the Toolbar.
3. Click the Article Title format.

The second title is now formatted. There are three more titles in the document. Use the Easy Format option to format the remaining three titles.

4. Apply the Easy Format to the remaining three titles. They are the lines that read Intel Announces 32 Bit Chip, The Lighter Side, and Stock Market Tops 6000 Mark.

USE A BOOKMARK

To complete the next task you need to find a bookmark that has been stored in the document. Use the Go To option to move to the Formula **bookmark**.

1. Click the Go To option on the Edit menu.

A Go To window like the one in Figure 5.26 is displayed. To move to the bookmark location, select the bookmark name and click the OK button.

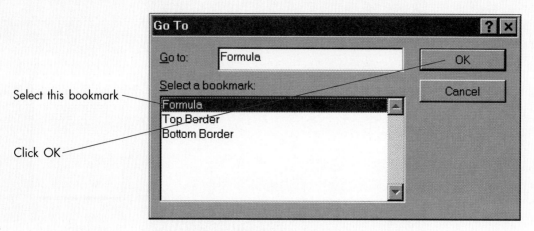

Select this bookmark

Click OK

FIGURE 5.26 The Go To window.

2. Choose the Formula bookmark.
3. Click the OK button.

The cursor should now be on a blank line below a line that reads "The formula provided in the report is:".

CREATE SUBSCRIPTS AND SUPERSCRIPTS

The Font and Style window accessed using the right mouse button can be used to create **subscripts** and **superscripts**. Figure 5.27 shows this window. The next step in the tutorial is to enter a formula in the document. The complete formula looks like the following:

$$Temp = CO^2 * T_{(1-v)} + T3$$

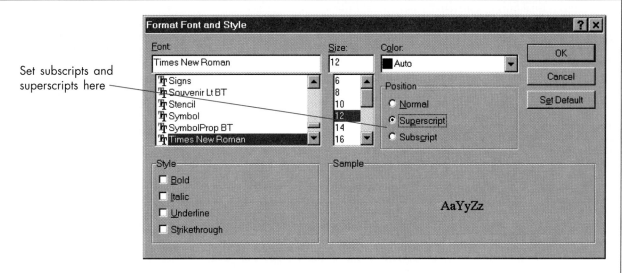

Set subscripts and superscripts here

FIGURE 5.27 Font and Style window.

Enter the formula by doing the following:

1. Type the entire formula as Temp = CO2 * T(1-v) + T3
2. Select the number 2 in the formula.
3. Choose Font and Style from the Format menu.
4. Click the Superscript option in the Position box and choose the OK button.
5. Select the characters (1-v) in the formula.
6. Choose Font and Style from the Format menu.
7. Click the Subscript option in the Position box and choose the OK button.
8. Select the number 3 in the formula.
9. Choose Font and Style from the Format menu.
10. Click the Superscript option in the Position box and choose the OK button.
11. Use the Spacing window of the Paragraph option on the Format menu to place 6 pts before and after the formula paragraph.

The formula should now be displayed with the appropriate subscripts and superscripts:

$$\text{Temp} = CO^2 * T_{(1-v)} + T3$$

INSERT A CLIPART IMAGE

To insert a clipart image into the document, use the **ClipArt** option on the Insert menu. This will start the ClipArt Gallery program and display available pictures. The first step will be to insert a picture for the first article.

1. Press Ctrl/Home to move to the top of the document.
2. Choose ClipArt from the insert menu.

The ClipArt Gallery like the one in Figure 5.28 is displayed. To insert a picture, double-click the picture.

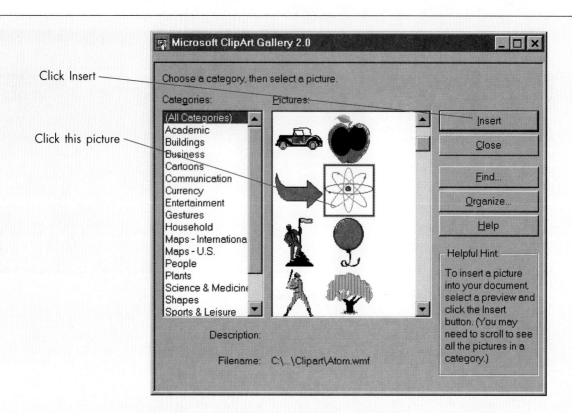

Click Insert

Click this picture

FIGURE 5.28 The ClipArt Gallery screen.

3. Use the scroll bar to scroll until a picture of the atomic symbol is in view.
4. Click the atomic symbol (see Figure 5.28).
5. Click the Insert button.

The picture should now be inserted in the document.

Change the Picture's Size

To change the size of the **picture**, click anywhere on the picture. This will display the handles. Drag the handles until the picture is the correct size. Watch the left side of the status bar to see the percentage of reduction for the picture.

1. Click the atomic symbol picture.
2. Click the lower right corner handle (see Figure 5.29) and drag the handle up and to the left, toward the upper left corner. Watch the left side of the status bar. Drag the handle until the scaling is 50% high and 50% wide.

Handles

Drag this handle

Scaling of selected picture

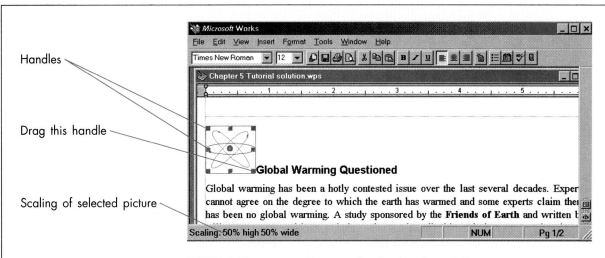

FIGURE 5.29 Document with picture selected and handles available.

The picture should now be scaled to the correct size. Remember, the scaling can also be set in the Size folder of the format Picture menu.

Set Text Wrap for the Picture

The last step for setting up this picture is to set the **Text Wrap** option. To allow the text to wrap beside the picture, set the wrap to automatic. The folder to use is shown in Figure 5.30.

Click OK

Click Absolute

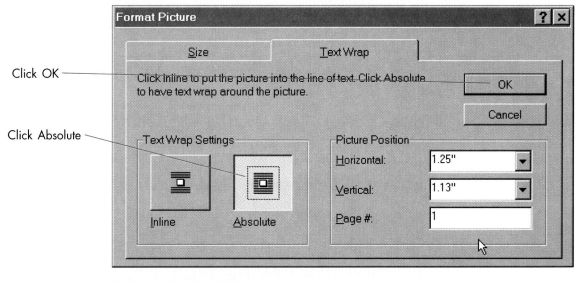

FIGURE 5.30 Text Wrap folder.

1. Select the picture.
2. Click the right mouse button and choose the Format Picture option.
3. Click the Text Wrap folder's tab.
4. Click the Absolute option.
5. Click the OK button.
6. If you get a window recommending that you switch to Page Layout view, click the Yes button.

CREATE TWO COLUMNS

Two-column documents are common for newsletters like the one you are creating. To format the document as two columns, use the **Columns** option on the Format menu. The window is shown in Figure 5.31.

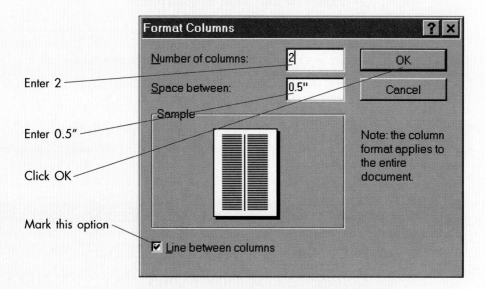

FIGURE 5.31 The completed Format columns window.

1. Choose Columns from the Format menu.
2. Enter 2 in the Number of columns area.
3. Enter .5 in the Space between area.
4. Mark the Line between option.
5. Click the OK button.

The document is now displayed as two columns. Use the Print Preview option to see the entire document.

6. Click the Print Preview tool on the Toolbar.

Your document should look similar to the one shown in Figure 5.32.

7. Cancel the Preview.

FIGURE 5.32 The document formatted as two columns.

CREATE AN EASY TEXT ENTRY

We will create an **Easy Text** entry and then use that entry to create a banner for the document. The step will be performed without much explanation, but think about what you are doing and it should be simple.

1. Click on any of the text to deselect the picture, then choose Easy Text from the Insert menu.
2. Choose New Easy Text from the pull out menu.
3. Enter EN for the name of the Easy Text. (See Figure 5.33).
4. Enter Earth Watch News as the Easy Text contents.
5. Click the Format button.
6. Click the Flyer text Easy Format.
7. Click the Apply button.
8. Click the Done button. (If you get a message that says the Easy Text already exists, Do you want to replace it?, click the Yes button.)

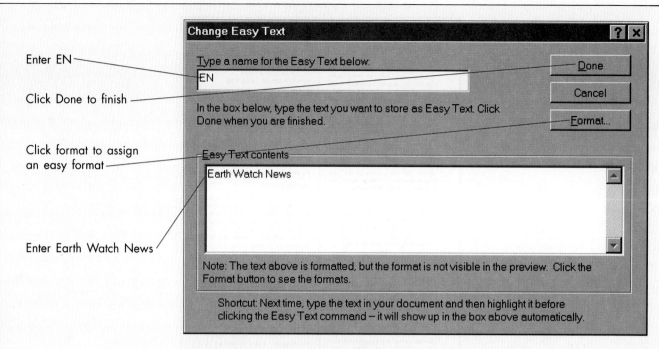

Enter EN

Click Done to finish

Click format to assign
an easy format

Enter Earth Watch News

Change Easy Text

Type a name for the Easy Text below:

EN

In the box below, type the text you want to store as Easy Text. Click Done when you are finished.

Easy Text contents

Earth Watch News

Note: The text above is formatted, but the format is not visible in the preview. Click the Format button to see the formats.

Shortcut: Next time, type the text in your document and then highlight it before clicking the Easy Text command — it will show up in the box above automatically.

Done

Cancel

Format...

FIGURE 5.33 The completed Easy Text window.

CREATE THE BANNER

Remember that the columns option will format the entire document as multiple columns. Only the **header**s and **footer**s are exempt from the multiple column format. To create a **banner** for the newsletter, the banner will need to be placed in a header.

Create the Banner Title

The first step is to create the banner title using the Easy Text just created.

1. Click inside the Header area.
2. Enter EN (the name of the Easy Text).
3. Press the F3 function key.

The banner title should now be in the document.

Format the Banner

Now shade the banner and place double lines above and below the title.

1. Click the Center tool on the Toolbar.
2. Click the right mouse button.
3. Click Borders and Shading.
4. Click the double underline at the top right side of the lines area.
5. Click the top and bottom Border choices.
6. Click the Shading tab.
7. Click the lightest shading option (20%). It should be the fourth on the shading bar.
8. Click OK.

The Banner should now be formatted with both shading and borders. If the border and shading does not flow all the way to the left margin, click the atomic symbol clipart image and drag it down so it is completely below the header area.

CREATE THE FOOTER

To format the bottom of the document, place a volume number, date, and border in the footer.

1. Move the cursor to the footer area.
2. Enter: Volume V.
3. Press the Tab key twice to move to the right-hand footer tab.
4. Choose the Date and Time option from the Insert menu.
5. Double-click the month and year date option.
6. Select the entire footer paragraph and click the Bold tool on the toolbar.
7. Format the paragraph as a 12 point Arial font.
8. Use the Border option to set a double line border along the top of the footer paragraph.
9. Preview the document.

Your Preview should look like the one in Figure 5.34.

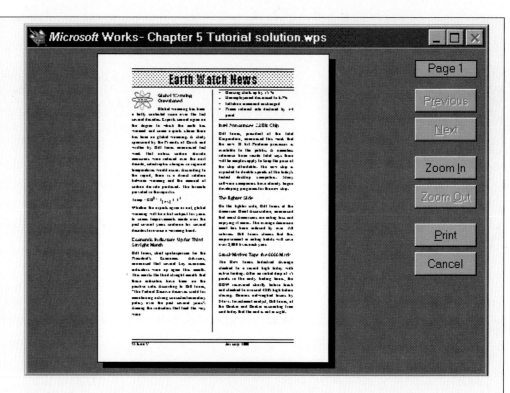

FIGURE 5.34   Completed document in Portrait orientation.

SAVE AND PRINT THE DOCUMENT

Now save and print the document.

1. Save the document with the name Chapter 5 TutorialP.WPS.
2. Print the document.

USE LANDSCAPE ORIENTATION

This document could also be formatted with three columns. In the current portrait orientation of the document, three columns would probably be too many for the width of the page. The **landscape orientation** would work better in that case. Format the document as three columns and change to landscape orientation.

1. Choose the Columns option from the Format menu.
2. Enter 3 in the Number of columns text box.
3. Enter .3 in the Space between text box.
4. Choose the OK button.

The next step is to switch the document to Landscape orientation. This is done using the **Source, Size, & Orientation** folder.

1. Click Page Setup on the Format menu.
2. Click the tab on the Source, Size, & Orientation folder.
3. Click Landscape in the Orientation area and click the OK button.
4. Click the Preview tool on the toolbar.

Complete the Landscape Layout

Two final touches need to be performed on this document. Notice that the date is no longer on the right margin of the Footer. To correct this, drag the tab marks on the header and footer ruler.

1. Cancel the Print Preview.
2. Place the cursor in the footer paragraph.
3. Scroll with the horizontal scroll bar until you can see the right margin marker and drag the right tab mark to the right margin marker.
4. Click the Preview tool.

The document should look like the one in Figure 5.35.

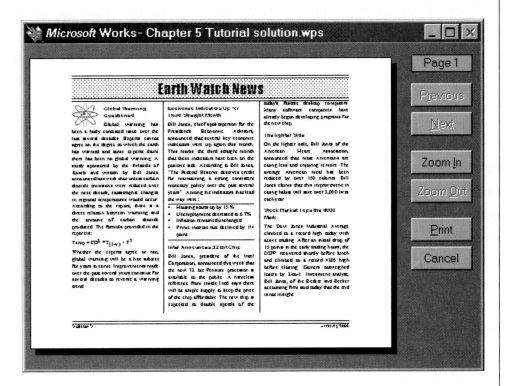

FIGURE 5.35 Completed document in Landscape orientation.

HYPHENATE THE DOCUMENT

One final step will complete the document. Because the columns have a justified alignment, the words on some of the lines are far apart. To improve the appearance of these lines, **hyphenate** the document. This will allow some words to be broken on two lines and thus place more text on the lines where the words are far apart.

1. Cancel Print Preview.
2. Move the cursor to the left of the first article title.
3. Choose Hyphenation from the Tools menu.
4. Set the Confirm option on and the Hyphenate CAPS option off.
5. Click the OK button.

A Hyphenation window like the one in Figure 5.36 is displayed.

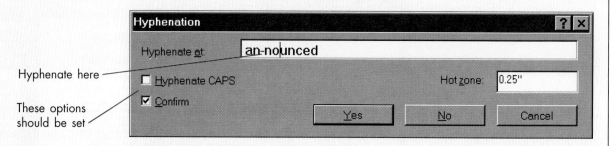

Hyphenate here ⟶

These options
should be set ⟶

FIGURE 5.36 The Hyphenation window

The word "announced" should now be in the **Hyphenation** text box. The hyphenation will occur between the two "n"s. This is acceptable, so choose Yes for this word. Continue to hyphenate the remainder of the document. Hyphenate all words except words in titles.

1. Choose the Yes button.
2. Hyphenate the remainder of the document. Do not hyphenate words in the article titles.

COMPLETE THE TUTORIAL

This completes the tutorial for this chapter. Save the document. Use the Save As option and save the file under the name Chapter 5 TutorialL.WPS. Also print the document.

1. Use the Save As option to save the file with the name TUTOR5L.WPS
2. Print the document.
3. Exit Works.

CONCLUSION

This is the final chapter on the Works word processor. By now you should be fairly proficient with its use. Remember that a word processor is a tool to help you improve written communications. You should make frequent use of this tool.

HANDS ON PRACTICE

Exercise 5-1

Review the clipart in the Works ClipArt Gallery. Write a story or article, create an advertisement or announcement, or create a newsletter that uses clipart. Use the following guidelines when creating the story.

1. Use at least two clipart images in the document.
2. Use borders to draw lines or an outline for at least one paragraph.
3. Use the Spacing between paragraphs option to separate paragraphs in the document.
4. Use multiple columns in the document.
5. Use a header banner and a footer.
6. Use the thesaurus to find the best words for the article.
7. Print the document in both portrait and landscape orientations.

Exercise 5-2

Create the questionnaire in Figure 5.37. Pay particular attention to the use of different fonts and sizes. Match the fonts and sizes as closely as you can. The text for this questionnaire is in the file Exercise 5-2.WPS on your tutorials and data disk. You will need to format the text from this file to create the questionnaire. (Hint: Lines can be drawn if you border a blank line. The location of the line can be adjusted with the left and right margins. Work with "Space before" and "Space after" to space paragraphs.)

National Survey Service

Computer Usage Survey
Developed by: Jane Doe

Education Level ...._____   Age.. _____

Salary ...._____   Sex.. _____

Own Home......................................._____   Nationality .... _____

Married ...._____   Single.. _____

Please check each statement that applies to you:

_____   I own my own computer system, or I use a computer system on my job at least one time every day.

_____   I would consider myself computer literate. (literacy means that you can use a computer system to accomplish routine tasks such as word processing, spreadsheets, and database processing)

_____   I do not own a computer system but have access to one either at work or from a neighbor.

_____   I am totally computer illiterate and have never used a computer in either my personal or professional life.

_____   I have obtained most of the information I know about computers from formal education course work.

_____   I have obtained most of the information I know about computers from on-the-job training, trial and error, informal training from friends, or from television programs.

Please return to:
**National Survey Service
109 E. Market Street
Jamestown, VA 29099**

The information given on this survey will be kept private and confidential. A summary of the results of this survey will be distributed to the department of higher education.

FIGURE 5.37   Completed Exercise 5.2.

Exercise 5-3

For this exercise, you will be using the file Exercise 5-3.WPS on your tutorials disk. Make the changes listed below. Use Figure 5.38 to see where to make your changes.

1. Place your name to the right of the word "By:" in the first line.
2. Use the Replace option to replace every occurrence of the letters PC with the word microcomputer. Replace only cases where the letters PC are in capital letters.
3. Insert the diskettes clipart images as shown.
4. Create an Easy Format to format the numbered items as hanging indents. Change the paragraph indents so the paragraph is indented 1/4 inch to the right of the left margin. Space 4 pts after the paragraph. Change the font to 10 point Arial. Apply the Easy Format to all four numbered items.
5. Use bullets on these lines. Place a border around all four paragraphs. Use the Paragraph Spacing folder to keep these paragraphs together.
6. Enter the following formula here: $CR_Y = AR^{(y-1..yn)}P_Y$. Space 4 points before and after the formula.
7. There are three bookmarks in the text. Each bookmark is in front of a word. Use the Go To option to find each bookmark, then use the thesaurus to find a synonym for the word that follows the bookmark.
8. Insert the trophy picture above the heading Be A Winner. Assign the Book sub head 1 Easy Format to this title.
9. Create the banner shown. Insert the checkmark clipart image. Assign the Flyer Text Easy format to the title. Assign a superscript position to the banner's title so it will be in the center of the banner.
10. Create the Footer shown. Place the current date on the left side of the footer. Place the current time on the right side of the footer.
11. Format the document in two columns with a line between columns. Use a Portrait orientation.
12. Use the Page folder of the Borders and Shading option to place a shadowed border around the entire page.
13. Experiment with different sizes for the pictures, top, left, right, and bottom margins to get the document to print on one page.
14. Check the spelling and hyphenate the document. Perform any other adjustment to make it look like Figure 5.38.
15. Save and print the document.

Evaluating Computer Software

By: (place your name here)

Software selection is one of the most critical components of a personal computer system. If the software is poorly designed it cannot take advantage of the advanced capabilities of newer PCs. If the software is clumsy to use, it costs the user in time and errors. If the software is too limited, there are too many things that must be performed by hand.

When evaluating software, ask the following questions concerning the overall operation of the system and the user interface:

1. Does the system use control codes, menus, or a combination of the two? Menus provide a shorter learning curve, however accomplished users prefer to use control codes. The codes are faster once you have mastered their pattern and know which ones to use.

2. Does the software use the disk as a work area? Systems that use only memory to store data usually have a limited size for their documents.

3. Does the vendor provide a 240-hour help line to answer questions? This is especially important for beginners.

4. How well is the documentation written? Too much documentation is written assuming that you already know the software.

Since word processing is a common application, special consideration should be paid to this software. When evaluating a word processor for a personal computer, you should consider the following.

- What is its maximum document size?
- Does it have a spelling checker?
- Is it a WYSISWYG system?
- What is the upgrade policy?

Speed of the text searching is also a consequence for word processors. When evaluating the speed of the total system you should use the following formula:

$$CR_Y = AR^{(y-1..yn)}P_Y$$

 Be a Winner

Since desk top publishing is becoming a major use for the personal computer, you should also consider the capabilities of the word processor to handle colors. Some word processors will not allow colors to be assigned to the text.

The word processor should also allow clipart and other pictures to be inserted in the document. If pictures can be used in a document, it should be easy to move the pictures and change their size.

The ability to produce multiple columns will be the last thing to check. With the advent of desk top publishing, the multiple column capability is a must.

Finally, make sure the word processor will allow you to create styles. A style will allow you to create a format for text and assign to format to many different paragraphs. This technique is similar to an Easy Format is Microsoft Works.

Finally, don't hesitate to experiment. With a creative mind and a little experience you can create very sophisticated documents.

Friday, February 02, 1996   3:17 PM

FIGURE 5.38   Completed Exercise 5.3.

6

AN INTRODUCTION TO COMPUTER SPREADSHEETS

LEARNING OBJECTIVES

When you've completed this chapter, you will be able to:

- Describe the components of the Works spreadsheet.
- Differentiate among labels, values, and formulas.
- Understand how to navigate around a spreadsheet using the mouse and the keyboard.
- Enter, edit, and format data in a spreadsheet.
- Change the appearance of the data in cells.
- Write simple formulas that use cell references.
- Copy formulas from one cell to other cells in the spreadsheet.
- Edit and delete data in cells.

SPREADSHEET CONCEPTS

The **electronic spreadsheet** is one of the most popular applications for personal computers. These spreadsheets, which allow you to calculate quickly and compare all sorts of data, are based on the manual accounting ledger sheet, or worksheet. The original paper worksheet provided a neat and accurate method in which to record columns of information. The computerized spreadsheet dramatically extends the power of the paper worksheet, yet at the same time, makes it much easier to use. Since the spreadsheet program uses a computer, you can change numbers and values and see the results instantly on the screen. Further, you can use the power of the computer to transform numbers into powerful charts that convey information at a glance. Finally, the electronic spreadsheet provides you with easy-to-use formulas to find answers to sophisticated problems such as calculating loan payments and finding the average of a group of numbers.

Manual Worksheet Basics

Since computer-based spreadsheets have their origins in the paper worksheet, it is a good idea to develop the basic concepts within that framework. Manual spreadsheets used a grid format comprised of horizontal rows and vertical columns. This format allowed you to work with a related column of numbers to sum them, find an average, or look for errors. Each row usually consisted of information about some given object, such as an item or a person. Each column contained related values for each object. An example of this relationship is shown in the worksheet in Figure 6.1, where each row contains information about a given product such as disks or pens, and each column contains a value, such as unit cost or net cost, for each row entry.

Clair's Aquatic Pets

Item Description	Unit Cost	Quantity Purchased	Total Cost	5% Discount	Net Cost
Balanced feed	$8.50	130	$1,105.00	$55.25	$1049.75
Air pumps	21.25	100	2,125.00	106.25	2,018.75
20 gal. tank	38.49	20	769.80	38.49	731.31
Fin Aide	4.75	250	1,187.50	59.38	1,128.12
Totals			$5,187.30	$259.37	$4,927.94

FIGURE 6.1   A paper worksheet using manual data entry and calculations.

Figure 6.1 illustrates how some entries will be computed using information contained above them or to the side. For example, total cost can be calculated as unit cost times quantity purchased. The table format, which has served well in manual systems for many years, forms the foundation for the automated spreadsheet in Microsoft Works 4.0 for Windows 95.

ELECTRONIC SPREADSHEET BASICS

The spreadsheet in Microsoft Works 4.0 gives you the power and computing capabilities of the computer's processor in place of the paper worksheet, pencil, and calculator used in old manual systems.

With the electronic spreadsheet, the pencil is replaced by the keyboard. This change allows you to copy repeated data instantly, use auto repeat keys for faster entry, and save the file to disk so your work can be recalled later without reentry. Even the traditional eraser is still available in the form of the Delete key.

In addition, the old calculator is replaced by the computer, which allows you to enter a long string of numbers. With the calculator, if you made an entry mistake, you had to reenter all the numbers. With the computer, you can just correct the error. Further, the electronic spreadsheet can store and recall literally millions of entries quickly and accurately. By design, calculators are used with manual worksheets and perform simple functions. Computers, on the other hand, are used with spreadsheets that can be as simple or as complex as you need to make them.

Rows, Columns, and Cells

Like the manual worksheet, the Microsoft Works spreadsheet is composed of rows and columns. Rows run horizontally across the screen and columns run vertically down the screen. Each row is assigned a number and each column has a letter. In the Microsoft Works spreadsheet, the row numbers run consecutively from 1 to 16,384 and the columns are identified by capital letters, which start with A. When the number of columns reaches Z (26 columns), an additional letter is placed in front so the column is labeled AA, AB, AC, and so forth. Works provides 256 columns ending with the label IV.

The intersection of a row and a column is called a cell. The cell is a box in which you can enter numbers or other information you want the spreadsheet to keep track of and manipulate. Works provides an ample number of cells for you to enter data into, with a maximum of 16,384 x 256 = 4,194,304 cells available!

Using Rows and Columns in the Spreadsheet

Normally, you will store information about a particular item in a row. For example, in Figure 6.2, row 7 contains information about balanced pet feed. This information includes the unit cost, quantity that was purchased, total cost, discount, and net cost. Row 8 contains the same information about air pumps, and so forth.

Columns normally contain information that pertains to the item in the row. In the sample spreadsheet, column A contains an item description, column B holds the unit cost, column C the quantity purchased, and so forth.

Clairs pets						
	A	B	C	D	E	F
1						
2			Clair's Aquatic Pets			
3						
4	Item	Unit	Quantity	Total	5%	Net
5	Description	Cost	Purchased	Cost	Discount	Cost
6						
7	Balanced feed	$8.50	130	$1,105.00	$55.25	$1,049.75
8	Air pumps	21.25	100	2125.00	106.25	2018.75
9	20 gal. tank	38.49	20	769.80	38.49	731.31
10	Fin Aide	4.75	250	1187.50	59.38	1128.13
11		TOTALS		$5,187.30	$259.37	$4,927.94
12						

FIGURE 6.2   A sample Works 4.0 spreadsheet containing data from the manual spreadsheet in Figure 6.1.

Defining the Cell Coordinates

Individual cells, formed by the intersection of the rows and columns, represent the fundamental building blocks of the electronic spreadsheet. Think of a cell as a holding area for data, much the same as a mailbox holds letters. Each cell is referenced by both the letter of its column and the number of its intersecting row.

This combination of a letter and a number is referred to as the cell coordinate. For example, for the cell highlighted in Figure 6.3, the cursor (the highlighted box) is at the intersection of column D and row 6. Thus, the cell coordinates are D6. When specifying a cell coordinate, specify the letter of the column followed by the number of the row. Finally, remember that the cell coordinate refers to a location in a spreadsheet, and a given cell is a special area that contains data.

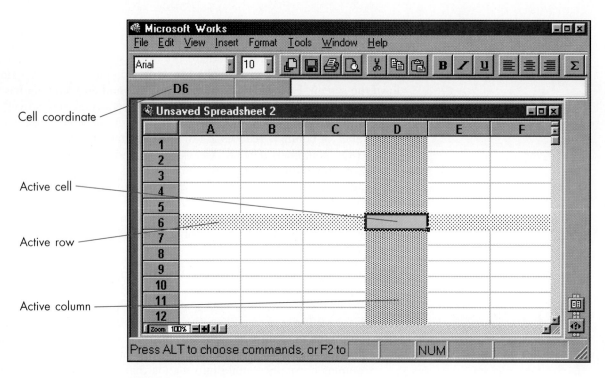

Cell coordinate

Active cell

Active row

Active column

FIGURE 6.3   The active cell is formed by the intersection of the active row and active column.

The highlighted cell in Figure 6.3 is called the **active cell** and shows which cell is currently in use. The row in which the active cell is located is called the **active row** and the column is referred to as the **active column**. When the cursor or highlight is moved on the spreadsheet, the active cell will be the one on which the highlight is placed.

CELL CONTENTS

A cell can contain **labels**, **values**, **formulas**, or a combination of all three. Labels are usually names or a description. A label can be made up of alphabetic, numeric, or alphanumeric (a combination of both alphabetic and numeric characters) data. Labels, by their nature, cannot be used in any kind of arithmetic function or formula.

Values consist of numbers and special numeric characters such as dollar signs, commas, and decimal points. Since values are numbers, they can be used in any type of arithmetic function and in formulas.

Formulas are numeric operations performed on values. Formulas can contain cell coordinates, numbers, or a combination of both. For example, you could write the formula shown in cell A4 of Figure 6.4 which appears as =A3*5. This formula takes the contents of cell A3 and multiplies it by 5. When the formula is completed, the cell will display 500. We will learn later that formulas often begin with an equals sign to ensure that Works knows the entry is a formula and not a label.

To help you understand the differences between these three types of data, consider the following example: if you entered 5*100 as a label, the characters 5*100 would be displayed as in cell A2 of Figure 6.4. If you instead entered 5*100 as a formula, 500 would be displayed.

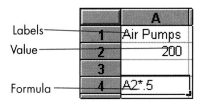

Labels
Value
Formula

FIGURE 6.4
You can enter labels,
values, or formulas into
a spreadsheet cell.

SPREADSHEET FORMULA CONCEPTS

Spreadsheet cells often contain formulas that perform some mathematical operation, such as adding two numbers or finding the average of a range of numbers. When you enter a formula into a cell, you only see the answer on the computer screen. Thus, you can think of the formula as being behind the screen with only the answer displayed for your use. This important concept is illustrated in Figure 6.5.

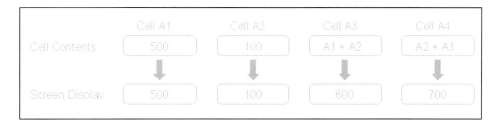

FIGURE 6.5   The contents of the cell shown in the upper row will appear on the screen as shown in the lower row.

Figure 6.5 shows that the formula entered into cell A3 is A1+A2. The formula will take whatever value is stored in cell A1 (500 in this case) and add it to the value in A2 (which is 100). The result of the formula (600) will be displayed in cell A3. This displayed answer, 600, would now be considered the value of cell A3. This value can be referenced by other cells, such as cell A4, which uses cell A3 in its formula.

This ability to reference the contents of a cell is handy, since a change in referenced cell A2 would automatically update the result displayed in cell A3. Such a change is shown in Figure 6.6. This ability to update data quickly provides the electronic spreadsheet with much of its power.

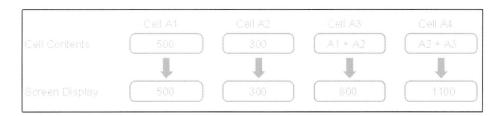

FIGURE 6.6   When cell A2 is changed to 300, notice how the other cells are updated.

Formula Development

A formula consists of two or more values, cell coordinates, or functions (discussed in Chapter 7, *Using Spreadsheet Functions*) separated by an arithmetic operator. When you use cell coordinates in a formula, the contents of that cell must be either a numeric value or another formula. The cell cannot contain a label even if the label is a number.

Formulas are written as algebraic equations and follow the same rules for evaluation as does algebra. One difference between standard algebraic operations and spreadsheet operations is that implied operations are not supported in spreadsheets. Therefore, to multiply 2 by 12, you would have to enter 2 * 12, not 2(12) as you might in standard algebra.

FORMULA EVALUATION SYMBOLS

( )	Parentheses; these must always be used in pairs.
+	Addition
-	Subtraction
*	Multiplication
/	Division
^	Exponents

FORMULA EVALUATION ORDER

1. Parentheses first, from innermost set to outermost set.
2. Exponents next, from left to right.
3. Multiplication and division next, from left to right.
4. Addition and subtraction next, from left to right.

WORKS SPREADSHEET SCREEN

Microsoft Works spreadsheet screen is similar to the Works word processor screen with the exception of the rows and columns. A labeled spreadsheet screen is shown in Figure 6.7. The parts of a spreadsheet are as follows:

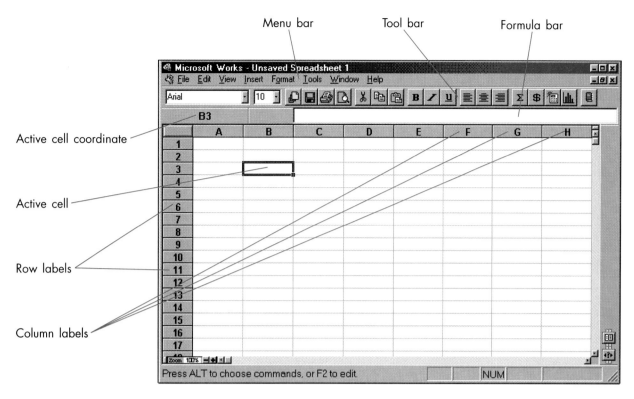

Menu bar   Tool bar   Formula bar

Active cell coordinate

Active cell

Row labels

Column labels

FIGURE 6.7   The Works 4.0 spreadsheet screen

Menu bar: Allows you to access the menus like in the word processor, using the Alt key or by dragging the mouse.

Toolbar: Used for quick access to common font, format, and style selections.

Formula bar: Displays the contents of the active spreadsheet cell, which is highlighted by the cursor.

Column labels: Letters used to identify the columns.

Row labels: Numbers used to identify the rows.

Active cell: The active cell highlight shows where data can be entered or changed.

Active Cell Coordinate: The active cell coordinates also show where the highlight is located.

SPREADSHEET NAVIGATION

The Works spreadsheet has millions of cells available for use; however, it is quickly apparent that only a few cells will fit on the computer screen at one time. Therefore, you need to be able to move around the spreadsheet, or navigate, using the methods provided by Works. Some of these methods may be familiar to you from the word processing module and include the use of the mouse, arrow keys, and special keys such as the Ctrl, PgUp, and PgDn keys. The following are the spreadsheet navigation commands.

Arrow keys: The four arrow keys move the highlighted cursor one cell in the direction of the arrow. Works will automatically move the spreadsheet and keep the cursor in view. If, for example, you move from cell A19 to A20, you will see row 20 appear at the bottom of the screen and row 1 disappear from the top. To move the cursor rapidly in one direction, hold down an arrow key.

PgUp/PgDn: The PgUp and PgDn keys will move the spreadsheet up or down a screen at a time. These keys are handy when you need to move many rows up or down.

Ctrl/PgUp Ctrl/PgDn: The PgUp and PgDn keys are helpful when you want to move up or down, but how do you move sideways across columns? To move right a screen at a time, hold the Ctrl key down and press the PgDn key. This will move you from column A to column H instantly. Similarly, the Ctrl/PgUp combination will move you one screen to the left. The highlighted cursor will stay in the same relative position on the screen as the spreadsheet moves behind it.

NOTE: Some keyboards require that the Num Lock indicator be off before this key combination will work (press Num Lock once to turn it off).

Home: The Home key will move the cursor horizontally to the A column, staying in the same row.

Ctrl/Home: The Ctrl/Home key combination will move the cursor to cell A1 in the upper-left corner of the spreadsheet. This navigation command is used when you want to get to the top of your spreadsheet quickly.

End: The End key works a bit differently than the other navigation keys in that it works in an "active" area of your spreadsheet. The active area of your spreadsheet is the part of the sheet in which you entered information into cells. For example, if you entered information into columns A through G, and pressed the End key, the cursor will move in column G, which has the last active cell. Like the Home key, the End key moves the cursor horizontally in the same row in which it was in when you pressed the key. This key is useful when you return to a spreadsheet and want to move near the place where you last entered data.

Ctrl/End: The Ctrl/End combination will move the cursor to the active cell in the bottom-right corner of the spreadsheet.

Ctrl/Arrow: The Ctrl/Arrow key combination will move the cursor to a "boundary" cell in the direction of the arrow key that was pressed. The boundary cell is the last occupied cell before a blank cell is encountered. For example, if you wanted to move down a long column of numbers to the last number in the list, use the Ctrl/Down arrow key combination.

GoTo (F5): The GoTo, or F5, key gives you the ability to move instantly to a given cell coordinate. Press F5, enter the cell coordinate (A6 as an example), and press the Enter key. The cursor will instantly move to the desired cell.

ENTERING DATA INTO A SPREADSHEET

You will find that entering data into a spreadsheet is easy if you remember a few simple rules. Works will determine if the data you enter into a cell is a label, a value, or a formula.

Label: If the first character you enter into a cell is a letter, or if the data contain nonnumeric characters, the data are assumed to be a label. Labels can contain any type of character, but you cannot perform arithmetic functions with labels. To enter a number as a label, precede the number with a quotation mark as shown in Figure 6.8. Works will not display the quotation mark in the cell, but you will be able to see it in the formula line. Labels are aligned to the left of the cell by default.

Works inserts a quotation mark to indicate labels

There are no quotation marks with values

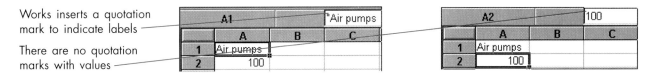

FIGURE 6.8   Label and value cell entries.

Value: If the first character you enter is a number or a numeric symbol, such as a dollar sign or decimal point, Works will infer that you are dealing with numeric data as seen in Figure 6.8. Numeric data are aligned to the right of the cell by default.

Formula: If the first character you enter is an equals sign (=), Works treats the data as a formula as shown in Figure 6.9. The equals sign alerts Works that the characters after the sign are part of a formula, not text. Works evaluates formulas as you enter them and displays the results in the cell when you press the Enter key.

Enter a formula by first typing an equals sign

	A	B	C
B1		X ✓ ? =A1+A2	
1	10	=A1+A2	
2	20		

FIGURE 6.9   Formulas are
entered starting with an equals sign.

To enter information, just position the cursor over the cell desired, type the label, data, or formula, and press Enter. Pressing Enter will finalize the entry into the cell, but will not move the cursor from the cell it is on. Frequently, you will find that you wish to enter data into a cell and move directly to another cell to enter additional information. This can be done by pressing any arrow key after you have completed the data entry in the cell. The arrow key will both enter the data and move to the next adjacent cell.

CHANGING THE CONTENTS OF A CELL

Frequently, you will want to alter the contents of a given cell. One way to do this is to enter new data into the cell by moving the cursor to the cell and typing the new data. The new data will replace the original data, which are erased. Other ways to change the contents of a cell are to edit the contents or delete the contents.

Editing cells: To edit the contents of a cell, position the cursor on the cell and press the F2 Edit key. The contents of the cell, such as a formula or a label, is displayed on the formula bar as seen in Figure 6.10. Then use the arrow keys, Backspace key, or Delete key to move the cursor and edit the contents of the cell. You can also use the mouse to click the formula bar and edit the cell.

Deleting cells: To delete the contents of a cell, position the cursor on the desired cell and press the Delete key. This will erase the contents of the cell so that you can enter new data. If you want to leave the cell blank, press the Enter key after you press the Delete key.

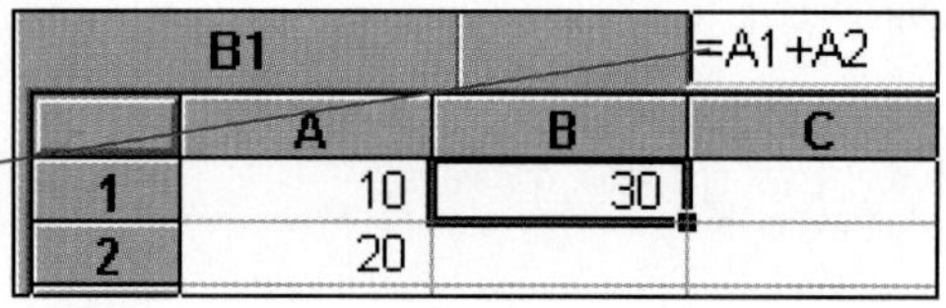

Click the Formula bar or press F2 to edit a formula

	A	B	C
1	10	30	
2	20		

B1 =A1+A2

FIGURE 6.10 Edit the contents of a cell by clicking on the Formula bar or pressing F2

Selecting a Block of Cells

Occasionally, you want to perform some operation on several cells at once. Some examples of such changes include changing the format of a group of cells, copying a group of cells, or deleting a group of cells. Before you can work with several cells at once, you must first identify the group of cells as a **block**. In the Works spreadsheet, a block must be a square or a rectangular group of cells as illustrated in Figure 6.11. There are two ways to select a block.

Mouse: Use the mouse to move the cursor to the first cell in the block. Then hold down the left mouse button and drag the mouse to highlight the block. When all cells in the block are highlighted, release the button. This is the quickest way to select a block.

Extend key: First, position the cursor on the first cell of the block to be selected and press the F8 **Extend key**. Next, use the arrow keys to extend the highlighted block.

Whichever method you use, you will highlight a block of cells similar to the block shown in Figure 6.11.

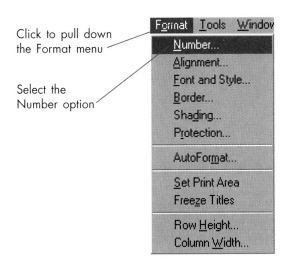

	A	B
4	Item	Unit
5	Description	Cost
6		
7	Balanced feed	$8.50
8	Air pumps	21.25
9	20 gal. tank	38.49
10	Fin Aide	4.75
11		TOTALS

Select a block of cells by highlighting them

FIGURE 6.11   Use the F8 Extend key or the mouse to select a block of cells. Blocks can be formatted, copied, moved or deleted.

Formatting the Cell Contents

You will often find that when you enter data into a cell, you will want to format, or display, the data so that they include dollar signs, a specific number of decimal positions, commas, and the like. The formatting process in the Works spreadsheet allows you to customize the appearance of your spreadsheet much like the character formatting process in the word processor.

You can specify the format for a cell either before or after you enter data in the cell. Position the cursor on the cell and pull down the Format menu, displayed in Figure 6.12, either by using the mouse or by pressing the Alt/O key combination. The Format menu works exactly like the Format menu in the word processor, except that the format options differ slightly. The Number option under the Format menu provides you with the Number window listing all the possible formatting options. It is shown in Figure 6.13. Notice that you can access other format options directly from the Number option window by clicking the tab at the top of the box as illustrated in Figure 6.13.

Click to pull down the Format menu

Select the Number option

Format	Tools	Window
Number...		
Alignment...		
Font and Style...		
Border...		
Shading...		
Protection...		
AutoFormat...		
Set Print Area		
Freeze Titles		
Row Height...		
Column Width...		

FIGURE 6.12
The Spreadsheet Format menu

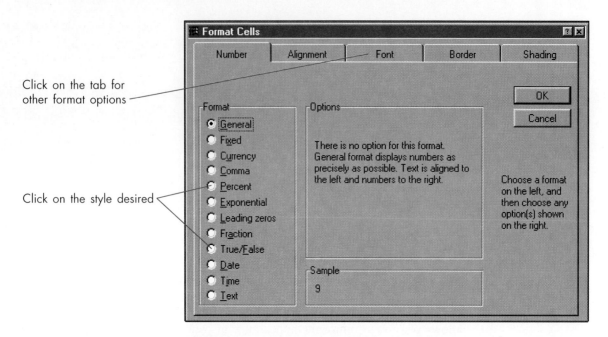

Click on the tab for
other format options

Click on the style desired

FIGURE 6.13 The Number options allow you to alter the appearance of one or more cells in
a spreadsheet.

Since spreadsheets typically deal with numbers, the majority of the options
on the Number window allow you to determine the way in which numeric data
will be displayed. Some of these options require that you specify the number of
decimal positions to be displayed to the right of the decimal point.

The following descriptions and Figure 6.14 show you how the formats on the
Number window will display the values of the numbers .889 and 13.632 in spreadsheet cells.

	A	B	C
1	General	0.889	13.632
2	Fixed	0.89	13.63
3	Currency	$0.89	$13.63
4	Comma	0.89	13.63
5	Percent	88.90%	1363.20%
6	Exponential	8.89E-01	1.36E+01
7	Leading Zeros	00001	00014
8	Fraction	0 8/9	13 79/125
9	True/False	TRUE	TRUE
10	Date	Invalid Date	1/13/00
11	Time	9:20 PM	3:10 PM
12	Text	0.889	13.632

Must contain a number
>1 for a valid date

FIGURE 6.14 The Works spreadsheet supports many different number formats.

General: The General format is the default. It will display only those decimal positions to the right of the decimal point that are significant. This format is sufficient for most numeric information and displays the numbers as 0.889 and 13.632.

Fixed: The Fixed format allows you to instruct Works to display a given number of decimal positions. The number in the cell being formatted is rounded to the nearest displayed decimal. Notice that the sample numbers are displayed as .89 and 13.63 and that Works has rounded the numbers to fit into two (the default) decimal positions.

Currency: The Currency format is the same as Fixed, except that it also displays a dollar sign adjacent to the leftmost digit and commas. The sample numbers are also rounded as with the Fixed format and appear as $0.89 and $13.63. Naturally, you would want to use this format option when dealing with dollar amounts.

Comma: The Comma format is the same as the Currency format, except that no dollar sign is displayed. This format is helpful when you want to display a column of currency amounts, but want a dollar sign included only with the first number.

Percent: The Percent format is used to display percentages. You will be asked to specify the number of decimal places to be displayed. Remember that percentages are based on the number one as equal to 100%. This means, for example, to yield a display of 10%, enter 0.1 and format it with the Percent option and 0 decimals. Similarly, 10 formatted with the Percent option and 0 decimals yields 1000%. The sample numbers will display as 88.90% and 1363.20%.

Exponential: The Exponential format is used for scientific notation. It is normally used for very large or very small numbers that would be difficult to use in the spreadsheet. To determine the actual number of an exponential number, move the decimal; if the number that follows the E is negative, move the decimal to the left. For example, 5.056E-03 is actually 0.005056. If the number following the E is positive, move the decimal to the right. For example, 5.67E+5 is 5,670,000. The sample numbers in Figure 6.14 display as 8.89E-01 and 1.36E+01.

Leading Zeros: If you enter a number with leading zeros like a postal Zip code, choose this format. This keeps the zeros at the beginning of the number from being dropped. This format will also round the number to the nearest whole number and cause the sample numbers to display as 00001 and 00014.

Fraction: The Fraction format allows you to display numbers as common fractions instead of decimal notation. This is useful when dealing in stock prices which are priced in fraction form rather than decimals. The Fraction format will display the sample numbers as 0 8/9 and 13 79/125.

True/False: The True/False format is a logical function, and is usually used with a special IF statement based on the value in the cell. An example of this use might be to determine if a payment had been received from a customer with the cell showing TRUE if an entry is made and FALSE otherwise.

Time: The Time format allows you to enter and work with times in the spreadsheet. You can enter time values in the normal HH:MM format using hours and minutes separated by a colon.

Date: The Date option is similar to the Time option. The use of Time and Date format options is covered in Chapter 7, *Using Spreadsheet Functions*.

Text: The Text option allows text to be stored in the spreadsheet. This is useful when using special characters such as a hyphen in a phone number (so it is not considered a minus function).

Setting Cell Alignment

The Works spreadsheet **cell alignment** options allow you to specify where the contents of a cell will be displayed in a spreadsheet. To choose a cell alignment, select the Alignment option from the Format menu. This will display the Alignment window like the one in Figure 6.15. The options in the Alignment window perform as follows:

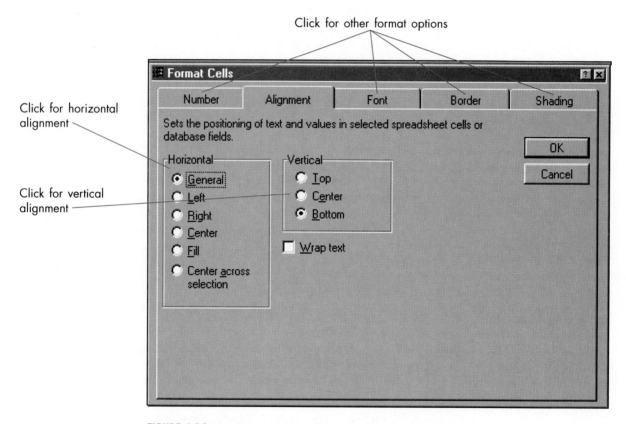

FIGURE 6.15 The Alignment window allows you to align the contents of a cell.

General: The General, or default, alignment automatically right aligns values and left aligns labels. If no Alignment option is specified, you will automatically get the General style.

Left: Positions all data starting at the left border of the cell.

Right: Positions all data starting at the right side of the cell.

Center: Centers data in the cell.

Center across Selection: Centers data across several adjoining, highlighted cells. This alignment is useful for creating a title or heading.

Wrap text: Allows text to appear on several lines within a cell rather than across adjoining cells.

Vertical: Allows you to select where a cell entry appears vertically in a cell. This alignment allows you to position an entry at the top, center, or bottom of a cell.

If you need only basic alignment for a cell, use the **Toolbar** shown in Figure 6.16. These buttons work in the same manner as in the word processing section. Figure 6.17 shows how the cell contents are displayed with each of the various alignment options.

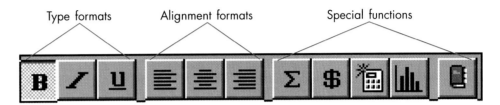

FIGURE 6.16 The spreadsheet toolbar

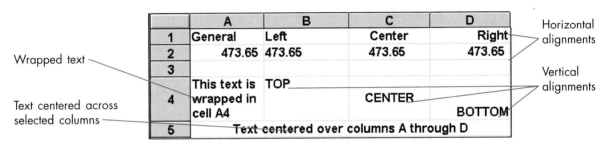

FIGURE 6.17 Alignment options determine how the contents in a cell are displayed.

Selecting Cell Fonts and Styles

To alter other cell appearances, select the **Font and Style** option from the Format menu. Works will display the Font and Style window seen in Figure 6.18. The Bold, Italic, and Underline commands are used the same way as they are in the Works word processor. You can use them to alter the appearance of any data in any cell. You will find these commands helpful for setting off titles, column headings, and the like.

Choose the cell font

Change the font size and color

Click to change the cell appearance

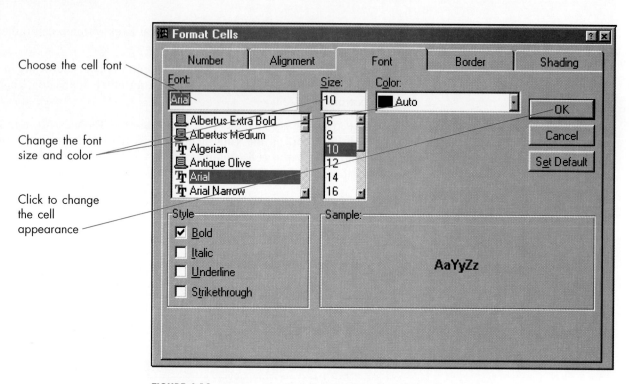

FIGURE 6.18 The Font and Style window changes the type font of the cell contents.

Fonts are applied as they were in the Works word processor and can be assigned to a given cell, group of cells, or the entire spreadsheet. This means you can have one font for column headings and another for the column entries, providing great flexibility in formatting your spreadsheet.

You can also change the text appearance and font using the Toolbar seen in Figure 6.16 and mouse in the same manner as in the Works word processor.

Border Option

The **Border** option on the Format menu provides the Border window shown in Figure 6.19. It allows you to create a border around a cell or group of cells. Use the Outline option to draw a border around a block of cells. Use the other options to draw a border around part of the block or single cell.

To remove a border, highlight the cells containing the border, choose the Border option on the Format menu, and select the first line style (no line) option. Next, click each border option you want to remove (Top, Bottom, Left, Right). Finally, click OK. To remove an Outline border, click all the options (Top, Bottom, Left, Right), then OK.

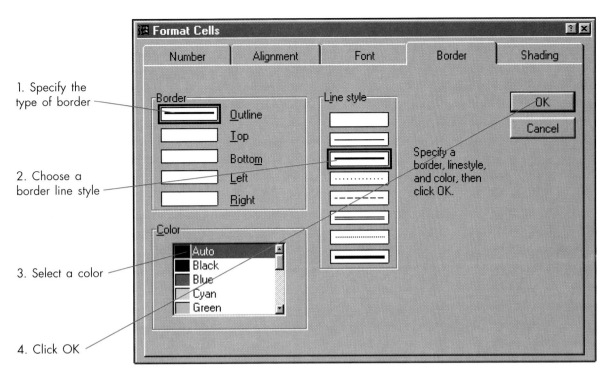

1. Specify the type of border

2. Choose a border line style

3. Select a color

4. Click OK

FIGURE 6.19   Use the Border window to put borders around a group of cells.

Setting Column Width and Row Height

The **Column Width** option in the Format menu is used to change the width of columns. It is important to realize that when you alter the width of a column, you affect the width of all cells in the column. Therefore, the minimum width of the column should be at least as wide as the largest cell entry.

The **Row Height** option in the Format menu is used to adjust the height of each row. By increasing the height for a given row, you can add space between rows to make the spreadsheet easier to read.

To set the width of a column, position the cursor on any cell in the column and select the Column Width option from the Format menu. To set the height of a row, position the cursor on any cell in the row and select the Row Height option from the Format menu. The Column Width or Row Height window is displayed, with the current column width or row height setting in the box. If you have not changed the width or height, the default column width of 10 or row height of 12 will be in the box, as shown in Figure 6.20.

Enter the desired width

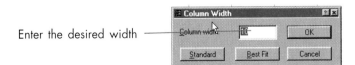

FIGURE 6.20   The Column Width window allows you to change the width of the cells. A similar window appears for Row Height.

Works allows you to specify a given width or height or to choose a Best Fit option, in which case Works automatically sets the width and height as needed. It is important to note that the Best Fit option will only size the row or column to data currently in the spreadsheet. If you later enter a longer entry, you will have to resize the row or column. You can assign the Best Fit option to any row or column by double clicking the mouse on the column label.

Figure 6.21 illustrates another shortcut to change the column width or row height. Position the mouse pointer between the column or row labels of the column or row you want to change. Notice that the pointer changes shape and that the word ADJUST appears. Hold down the mouse pointer and move the mouse to set the width or height as desired. Release the mouse button; the width or height will be set.

Position mouse pointer here to change column width

Position mouse pointer here to change row height

FIGURE 6.21   Use the mouse pointer to change the column width quickly.

Cell Display Concepts

Cells actually have two widths: the width of their contents and the width of what is displayed. Although this may seem a bit confusing at first, remember that what is displayed in a cell (such as a sum) and what is actually entered in the cell (such as a formula) may be different. When you alter the column width, you are actually changing the width of the *display*, not the width of the cell contents. The content width is system set and can accommodate up to 256 characters, which is usually more than enough. You might think of the cursor as being a window which allows you to look into the cell. The width of the cursor can be thought of as the width of the cell window, a concept illustrated in Figure 6.22.

Expand the cell width

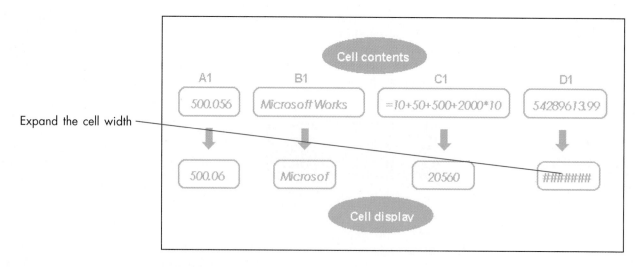

FIGURE 6.22   Comparing the contents of a cell with the display of a cell.

In Figure 6.22, the top blocks show the actual contents of the cells, and the lower blocks show what is displayed in the cell. In cell A1, the decimal places have been set to two, so the rightmost decimal is truncated. Cell B1 shows what happens when a label display width is smaller than the cell's contents. The rightmost characters are not displayed; however, the data are still in the cell. You could make the column wider to see the entire contents of the cell. Cell C1 illustrates the display when a cell contains a formula. The formula is larger than the display window; however, the result of the formula, the cell's value, is not, so the entire number is displayed. Cell D1 displays number signs (#) instead of the number, which indicates the cell width is too narrow to display the entire number; widen the column to correct this.

CONCLUSION

You are now familiar with many of the basic spreadsheet concepts required to use the Microsoft Works spreadsheet and have learned the basic concepts of data entry, displayed contents of cells, formula use, and general formatting. Complete the chapter review to be sure of your understanding as these concepts form a foundation for later spreadsheet use.

CHAPTER 6 SELF-TEST

1. In a spreadsheet, rows run _____ and use _____ for their labels. Columns run _____ and use _____ for their labels.
2. What is a coordinate in a spreadsheet?
3. What would be the coordinate of the ninth cell in the sixth row?
4. What is the difference between a label and a value?
5. What is the difference between the contents and the value of a cell?
6. Write formulas to carry out the following operations:
   a. Multiply the contents of cell A3 by the contents of cell B4 and subtract the contents of cell C2.
   b. Divide the contents of cell C5 by the sum of cells D2 and E2.
   c. Add cells A2, D2, and F2, and subtract the contents of cell A4.
7. How would you type the formula A3*L4+B2 into a cell?
8. Explain what is meant by referencing a formula from another cell.
9. How can you change the formula in a cell without retyping it?
10. Describe two ways to select a block of cells.
11. If cell C7 contained the value 3792.3983, how would it be displayed for each of the following formats? (Assume the format is set for two decimals.)

   General_____
   Fixed   _____
   Currency_____
   Comma _____
   Percent _____
   Exponential _____

12. How would you make all cells from A2 through G12 bold by using the Tool-bar and the mouse?
13. What happens when the width of a column's display is smaller than the contents of the cell and the cell contains a label? What happens when the cell contains a number?
14. How can you quickly set the width of a column to accommodate all entries presently in the column?

CHAPTER 6 TUTORIAL

In this tutorial, you will create a small business spreadsheet that will calculate total profit as shown in the completed spreadsheet displayed in Figure 6.23.

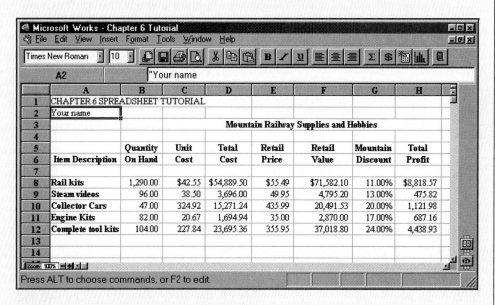

FIGURE 6.23   The finished Chapter 6 Tutorial spreadsheet.

CREATING A NEW SPREADSHEET

To create a new spreadsheet, follow these steps:

1. Start Microsoft Works 4.0 and wait until the Task Launcher appears.
2. Click the Works Tools tab shown in Figure 6.24.
3. Click the Spreadsheet box or press the S key to open a new spreadsheet.
4. You will see an empty spreadsheet screen like that in Figure 6.25.

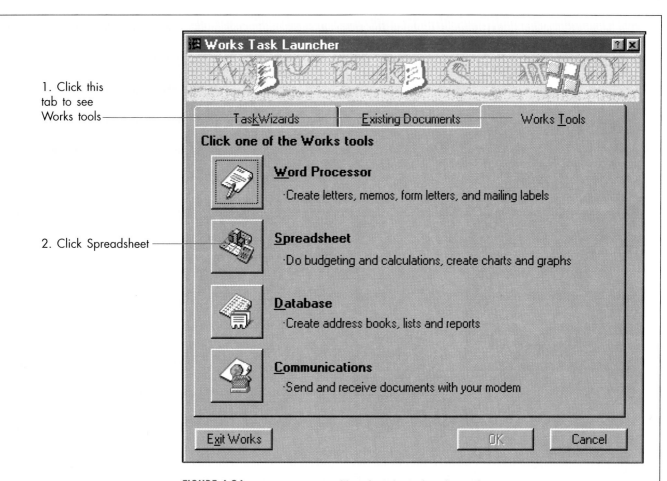

1. Click this tab to see Works tools

2. Click Spreadsheet

FIGURE 6.24   Create a new spreadsheet from the Works Task Launcher.

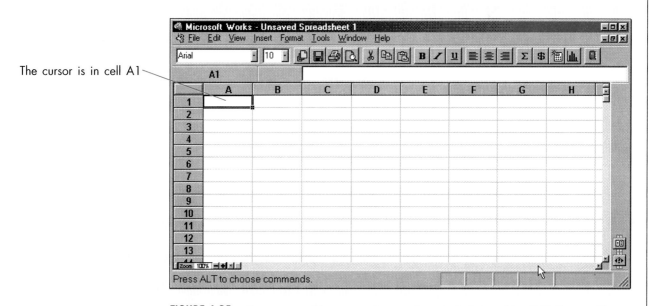

The cursor is in cell A1

FIGURE 6.25   On a new spreadsheet screen, the cursor is automatically located in cell A1. The spreadsheet is called Unsaved Spreadsheet 1 until you save it and give it a name.

SOME QUICK PRACTICE ON NAVIGATION

Before entering data into the spreadsheet, take a moment to try some of the navigation commands mentioned earlier. As you move through the spreadsheet, notice that the current position of the cursor is shown at the upper-left corner of the screen. Also, take special note of the position of the scroll bars on the right side and bottom of your screen. These bars can give you an idea of where you are in the spreadsheet. Now, try these steps:

1. Use the arrow keys to move the cursor to cell G14.
2. Press the Home key to move back to cell A14.
3. Now try the PgDn and PgUp keys to move up and down one screen at a time.
4. Be sure the Num Lock indicator is off. Then use the Ctrl/PgDn key to move one screen to the right and the Ctrl/PgUp key to move one screen to the left.
5. Hold the Ctrl key down and press the Down arrow key to move to row 16384, the very bottom of the spreadsheet. Next, use the Ctrl/Right arrow to move the cursor to cell IV16384, which is the bottom-right corner of the spreadsheet.
6. Use the Ctrl/Home key combination to instantly return to cell A1, the home cell.
7. To move instantly to cell GZ2088, press the F5 key and enter the cell coordinates GZ2088, then press the Enter key. Finally, use the Ctrl/Home key combination to return to cell A1.

ENTERING TITLE AND COLUMN HEADINGS

1. Be sure the cursor is positioned on cell coordinates A1 (use Ctrl/Home if it is anywhere other than cell A1).
2. Type **CHAPTER 6 SPREADSHEET TUTORIAL** in cell A1 and press the Down arrow key. (The characters above are in bold, italic type to indicate the letters you should type. You do not need to format these entries as bold italic, so simply type them into the cell in plain format.)
3. Enter **your name** (type your full name) in cell A2 and press Enter.
4. Move the cursor to cell C3 and type the heading **Mountain Railway Supplies and Hobbies**. Press Enter. The spreadsheet should now look like Figure 6.26.
5. Enter the column headings by moving the cursor to cell A6, typing **Item Description,** and pressing the Right arrow key.
6. Type **On Hand** in cell B6 and press Enter. When you have completed the entry of these cells, the spreadsheet should look like Figure 6.27.
7. Take a look at cell A6 where it appears as though you have lost the last characters in the word *Description*. Don't worry, everything is fine. Recall that a cell's contents can be wider than the cell width. We will adjust the column width later.

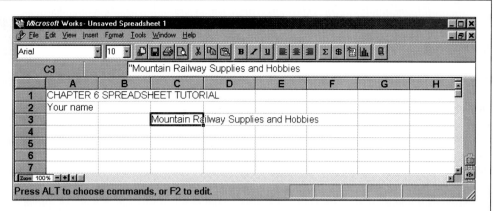

FIGURE 6.26   The initial entries in the spreadsheet. Enter the data, then press Enter or the Down arrow after each entry.

We will adjust this later on

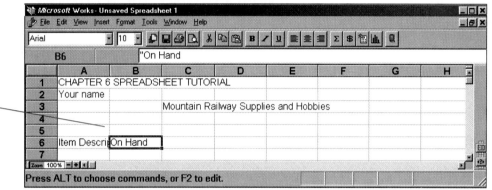

FIGURE 6.27   When the titles are entered, do not be alarmed that they run together. This indicates that the column is not wide enough to hold the data.

Enter the Remaining Row 5 Titles

1. Move the cursor to cell B5, type **Quantity** and press the Right arrow key.
2. Type **Unit** in cell C5, and press the Right arrow key.
3. Continue to type the titles in row 5 and to use the Right arrow key to enter the titles and move to the next cell. Follow this procedure until all row 5 titles are entered as shown in Figure 6.28.
4. Next, enter the row 6 titles shown in Figure 6.29. Move the cursor to cell C6, type **Cost**, and press the Right arrow key to move the cursor. Follow this procedure until all row 6 titles are entered. Press Enter after you type **Profit**.
5. Be sure that the spreadsheet looks like Figure 6.29, correcting any errors you might find.

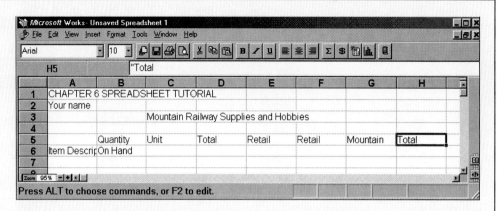

FIGURE 6.28   Enter the additional titles and press the Right arrow after each entry.

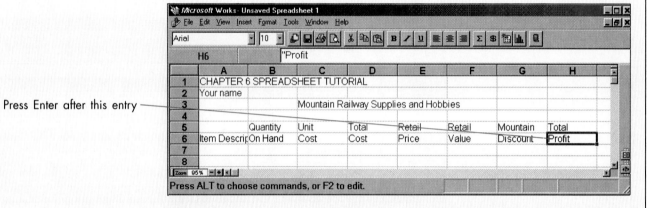

Press Enter after this entry

FIGURE 6.29   Enter the row 6 titles and press the Right arrow after each entry.

Setting the Column Width

Now you need to adjust the width of column A so that it will be wide enough to display all the item descriptions and titles.

1. Press the Home key to move the cursor to cell A6.
2. Pull down the Format menu with the mouse.
3. Select the Column Width option.
4. Click the Best Fit button on the Column Width window as seen in Figure 6.30.
5. The entire Item Description entry is now visible.

Click here for best fit

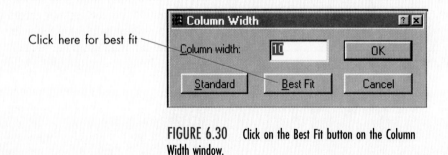

FIGURE 6.30   Click on the Best Fit button on the Column Width window.

The next step is to enter the data for columns A, B, and C in rows 8, 9, 10, 11, and 12 using the information in Figure 6.31. DO NOT include any commas when you enter numbers such as 1264. The spreadsheet program will do this for you automatically when you format the entries.

	A	B	C
5		Quantity	Unit
6	Item Description	On Hand	Cost
7			
8	Rail kits	1290	42.55
9	Steam videos	96	38.5
10	Collector cars	47	324.92
11	Engine kits	82	20.67
12	Complete tool kits	104	227.84
13			

FIGURE 6.31 Enter the spreadsheet data in columns A, B, and C.

1. Move the cursor to cell A8, type **Rail kits**, and press the Right arrow key.
2. Enter **1290**, the Quantity On Hand, in cell B8 and press the Right arrow key.
3. Enter **42.55** the Unit Cost, in cell C8 and press Enter. Be sure to type the decimal point.
4. Enter the rest of the item descriptions, quantities, and costs shown in Figure 6.31.
5. Check the width of cell A12 to be sure the words "Complete tool kits" appears. If part of it is hidden, position the cursor on cell A12 and select the Best Fit option for Column Width as shown earlier in Figure 6.30.

Formatting the Cells in a Column

Now that some of the data are entered into the spreadsheet, you will need to format them. Notice that some entries in column B need commas and items in column C require a dollar sign and a comma.

The first step to format several cells at once is to select them as a block. The second step is to format them using the Number window in the Format menu. In the Number window illustrated in Figure 6.32, we will use the Comma format and specify the number of decimal positions to the right of the decimal.

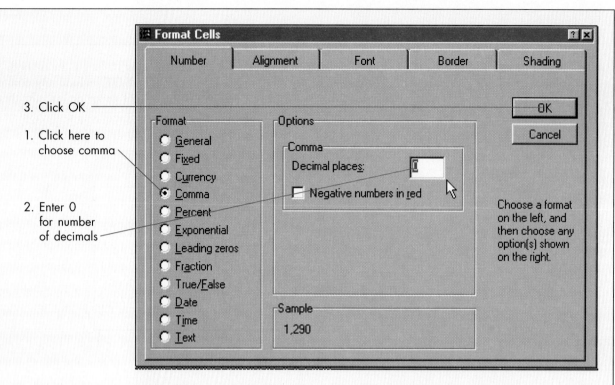

3. Click OK

1. Click here to choose comma

2. Enter 0 for number of decimals

FIGURE 6.32 Use the Number window to select the Comma format with zero decimals.

Format the cells in column B by following these steps:

1. Move the cursor to cell B8.
2. Use the mouse, or press the F8 (Extend) key and the Down arrow key, to highlight cells B8 through B12.
3. Select the Number option from the Format menu.
4. Select the Comma format, enter *0* for the Number of decimals, and click OK.
5. To format the entries in column C, move the cursor to cell C8.
6. Click Currency on the Toolbar as shown in Figure 6.33.
7. Select the block consisting of cells C9 through C12 using the mouse or the F8 and Down arrow keys.
8. Select the Comma format from the Number option under the Format menu. Format the block with two decimal positions and click OK.
9. The spreadsheet should look like Figure 6.34.

Click here for
Currency format

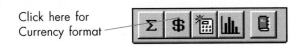

FIGURE 6.33   Use the Toolbar
to set the Currency format with two
decimal places.

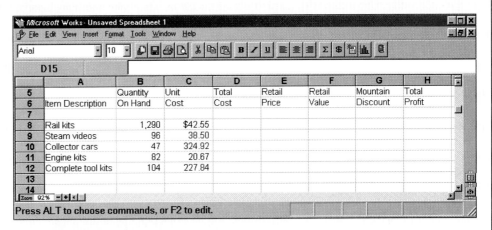

	A	B	C	D	E	F	G	H
5		Quantity	Unit	Total	Retail	Retail	Mountain	Total
6	Item Description	On Hand	Cost	Cost	Price	Value	Discount	Profit
7								
8	Rail kits	1,290	$42.55					
9	Steam videos	96	38.50					
10	Collector cars	47	324.92					
11	Engine kits	82	20.67					
12	Complete tool kits	104	227.84					
13								
14								

FIGURE 6.34   The spreadsheet with initial formatting.

Entering the Total Cost

Now that you have entered most of the labels and data, you can use the power of
the spreadsheet to compute some values, such as the total cost for each product.
The total cost value can be calculated by multiplying the item's unit cost by the
quantity on hand. This calculation can best be done by using a formula in the
spreadsheet. For example, in cell D8, the formula would be B8*C8. Remember,
when entering a formula, you must start the formula with the equals sign (=).

Start the formula
with an equals sign (=)

D8	X ✓ ? =B8*C8				
	A	B	C	D	E
5		Quantity	Unit	Total	Retail
6	Item Description	On Hand	Cost	Cost	Price
7					
8	Rail kits	1,290	$42.55	=B8*C8	
9	Steam videos	96	38.50		
10	Collector cars	47	324.92		
11	Engine kits	82	20.67		
12	Complete tool kits	104	227.84		
13					

FIGURE 6.35   Create a formula to calculate total cost.

1. Move to cell D8.
2. Enter **=B8*C8** as shown in Figure 6.35.
3. Press Enter. The cell should now display the value 54889.5.

Using the Fill Down Option

To compute the value for the other total costs, you could type the same formula in cells D9 through D12; however, Microsoft Works has a feature that will perform this process for you. It's called the **Fill Down** feature (found in the Edit menu) and will copy the contents of the first cell in a block to all the cells below it in the same block. Further, when formulas that contain cell coordinates are copied, it increases by one each cell-row coordinate in the formula. This feature enables you to perform what is called a **relative copy**, or fill. This powerful feature, shown in Figure 6.36, will copy the formula you specify and make changes relative to the rows where you copy it. To see how this feature is used and to format the cell contents after they are copied, follow these steps:

Select the block and choose Fill Down from the Edit Menu

Notice the formula increments when filled down

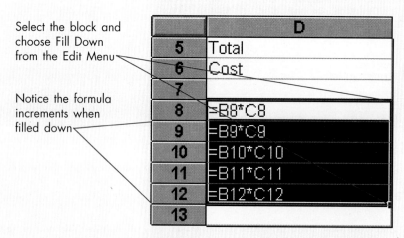

FIGURE 6.36 Use the Fill Down feature to perform a relative copy. Note: your spreadsheet will not display the formulas on the screen. Instead, the result of the formula will be displayed.

1. Select cells D8 through D12 as a block.
2. Pull down the Edit menu and select the Fill Down option.
3. Use the Toolbar to format cell D8 in Currency format.
4. Use the Number option under the Format menu to format the cells D9 through D12 as Comma and two decimals.

Entering the Retail Price

The next step in the construction of the spreadsheet is to enter the retail price for each product.

1. Enter the retail price figures shown in Figure 6.37 for cells E8 through E12.
2. Format cell E8 as Currency.
3. Format cells E9 through E12 using Comma format with two decimal places.
4. The spreadsheet should now look like Figure 6.38.

		A	B	C	D	E
	5		Quantity	Unit	Total	Retail
	6	Item Description	On Hand	Cost	Cost	Price
	7					
	8	Rail kits	1,290	$42.55	$54,889.50	55.49
	9	Steam videos	96	38.50	3,696.00	49.95
	10	Collector cars	47	324.92	15,271.24	435.99
	11	Engine kits	82	20.67	1,694.94	35
	12	Complete tool kits	104	227.84	23,695.36	355.95
	13					

Enter these Figures in column E →

FIGURE 6.37   Type the retail price informatiom from column E.

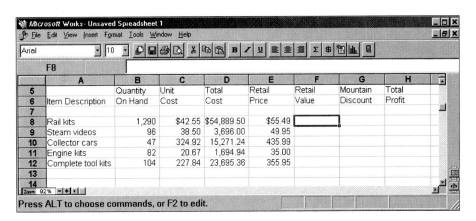

FIGURE 6.38   The tutorial spreadsheet with columns A through E entered.

Entering the Retail Value

You now need to develop and enter the formula that will calculate the retail value. This value shows the total value of all the items in stock and is found by multiplying the cell contents in the Quantity On Hand column by the contents in the Retail Price column. For row 8, this would be =B8*E8. Follow these steps to enter this formula in cell F8 as shown in Figure 6.39, and use the Fill Down function to copy the formula into cells F9 through F12.

Use Fill Down to copy the formula in cell F8 to cells F9 through F12 →

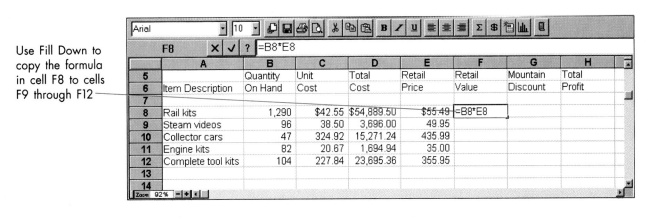

FIGURE 6.39   Use a formula and Fill Down to enter the retail value.

1. Enter = **B8*E8** in cell F8. The result should be 71582.1.
2. Select cells F8 through F12 as a block.
3. Use Fill Down from the Edit menu to copy the formula.
4. Format cell F8 using Currency, and format cells F9 through F12 using Comma format with two decimal places.
5. You may notice that cell F8 now contains number signs (##########) rather than the value of the total retail. The number characters indicate the width of the cell must be increased. Do not be concerned if you do not need to increase the width. If you do not see the ##### figures, do not worry and continue.
6. Be sure that the cursor is in column F, then select the Column Width option from the Format menu.
7. Enter **12** for the width.
8. Press Enter.

Entering the Mountain Discount

1. Enter the Mountain discount information shown in Figure 6.40.
2. Format the data as percentages with two decimal positions using the Number option under the Format menu so the data appear as shown in Figure 6.41.

	A	B	C	D	E	F	G
5		Quantity	Unit	Total	Retail	Retail	Mountain
6	Item Description	On Hand	Cost	Cost	Price	Value	Discount
7							
8	Rail kits	1,290	$42.55	$54,889.50	$55.49	$71,582.10	0.11
9	Steam videos	96	38.50	3,696.00	49.95	4,795.20	0.13
10	Collector cars	47	324.92	15,271.24	435.99	20,491.53	0.2
11	Engine kits	82	20.67	1,694.94	35.00	2,870.00	0.17
12	Complete tool kits	104	227.84	23,695.36	355.95	37,018.80	0.24
13							

Enter these values —

FIGURE 6.40 Enter the values for the Mountain Discount, then format as percent. After entering, highlight and format as percent with 2 decimals.

Computing the Total Profit

To compute the total profit, subtract the sum of the total cost and the discount amount from the retail value (this is found by multiplying the Mountain discount by the retail value).

First, develop the formula in English using parentheses to identify which procedure should be done first. The formula looks like this:

Retail value - (total cost + (retail value * Mountain discount))

Next, convert this formula to a spreadsheet formula using the appropriate cell coordinates in place of the English descriptions. Type the formula in cell H8 and use Fill Down to copy the formula into the other cells. Finally, apply the appropriate format and widen the column width as required.

1. Develop and enter the spreadsheet formula in cell H8.
2. Use Fill Down to copy the formula into cells H9 through H12.
3. Format the cell H8 in the Currency format and cells H9 through H12 in the Comma format. All cells use two decimal places.
4. Adjust the column width, if needed, so all entries are displayed. The spreadsheet will now look like Figure 6.41.

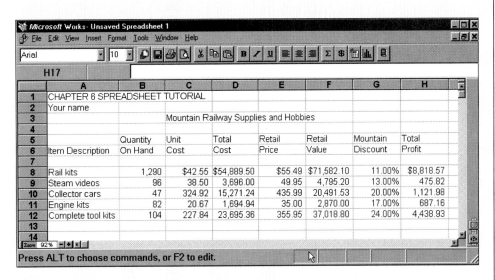

FIGURE 6.41   The tutorial spreadsheet with all data entry complete.

SAVING THE SPREADSHEET

Now that all the basic data entry is complete, it is a good idea to save the spreadsheet to your disk. After it is saved, you will be able to reload it should you make an error. It is a good idea to save to the disk as you proceed and thus minimize the possibility of losing data.

Save the completed spreadsheet to your disk after checking to be sure a diskette is in drive A: or in another appropriate drive, then follow these procedures.

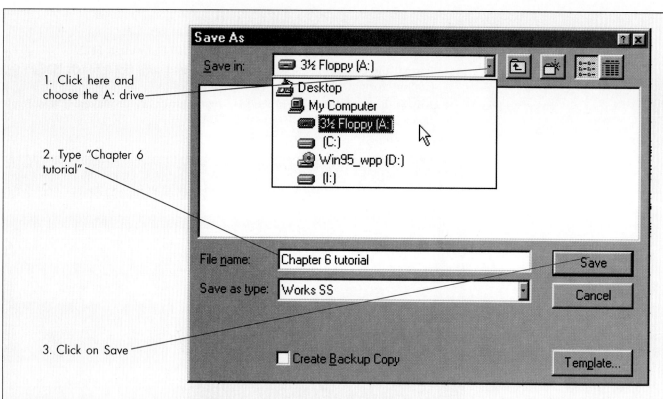

1. Click here and choose the A: drive

2. Type "Chapter 6 tutorial"

3. Click on Save

FIGURE 6.42   Save the file with the Save window.

1. Pull down the File menu and select the Save option.
2. Click the Drives arrow.
3. Use the mouse to highlight the drive (A: or B:) you want to use (be sure a disk is in the drive first).
4. Click in the File name box and type ***Chapter 6 tutorial*** as shown in Figure 6.42, and click Save. Works will automatically add the file type icon to indicate that the file is a spreadsheet.

ALIGNING AND STYLING THE COLUMN HEADINGS

You have probably noticed that the column headings do not line up very well with the data in the columns. This is because Works aligns labels (like the column headings) on the left side of the cell and aligns data and formulas on the right side. To align the headings with the numeric data, use the Toolbar buttons shown in Figure 6.43 or the Alignment option from the Format menu.

Click for bold   Click to center headings

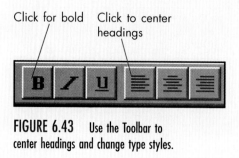

FIGURE 6.43   Use the Toolbar to center headings and change type styles.

1. Select cells A5 through H6 as a block.
2. Click the Center align button on the Toolbar, or choose the Alignment option from the Format menu, select Center from the Alignment window, and click OK.
3. Click the Bold button on the Toolbar to make the headings boldface.
4. Use the mouse and Toolbar to make the product descriptions in column A boldface. Adjust the column width as needed.
5. Highlight cells A3 through H3 and select the Alignment option from the Format menu. Choose the Center across selection option and click OK.

PRINTING THE SPREADSHEET

The spreadsheet is now complete, and you are ready to print it. The finished spreadsheet may, however, be too wide to fit on a standard page. There are several methods to adjust the spreadsheet to fit on one page, including adjusting the margins, printing in landscape mode (sideways on the page), or changing the type font and size. We will change the font and size in this tutorial and make the other changes in later chapters.

Fonts are used in the Works spreadsheet in the same way they are used in the word processing section of Works. To change fonts, click the arrow next to the Font option of the Toolbar. That displays fonts as shown in Figure 6.44.

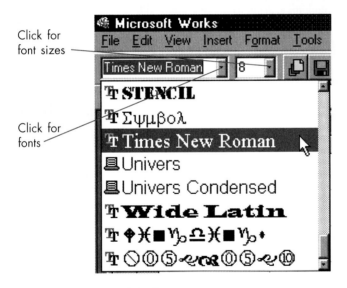

Click for font sizes

Click for fonts

FIGURE 6.44   Change the font by using the Toolbar.

The actual print fonts and sizes that are available will depend on the printer you are using, but the process is the same regardless of printer and available type fonts.

1. Choose the Select All option from the Edit menu so the entire spreadsheet is highlighted.
2. With the Toolbar, set the font to Times New Roman and set the size to 8.
3. Use the Print Preview option from the File menu to see how the spreadsheet will print, as shown in Figure 6.45.
4. Check to be sure the spreadsheet will fit on one page. If it does not, change the left and right margins to .5″ on the Page Setup window under the Page Setup option on the File menu.
5. Select Print from the Preview screen.
6. Click OK in the Print window.

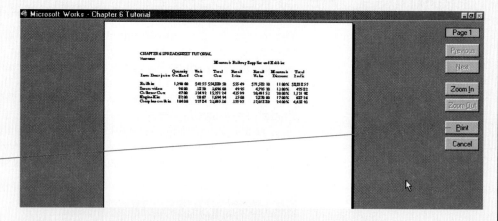

Click here to print

FIGURE 6.45   Use Print Preview to see how the spreadsheet will print.

HANDS-ON PRACTICE

Exercise 6-1

Using the Spreadsheet module of Microsoft Works, create the spreadsheet illustrated in Figure 6.46 by entering the information in the figure into the cells as shown. You will have the opportunity to format the data later, so just enter them as shown for now.

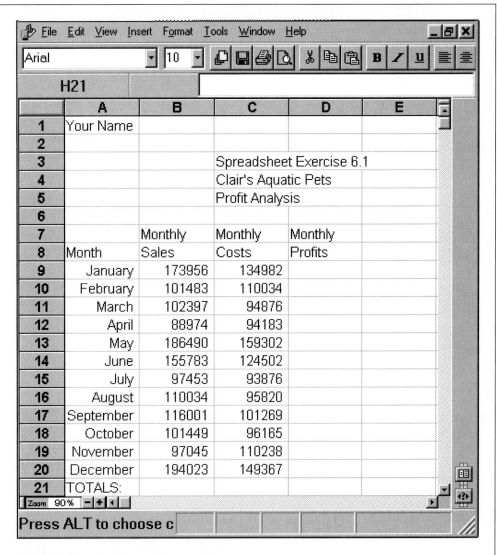

FIGURE 6.46 The initial data for Exercise 6-1.

NOTE: As a shortcut for entering months, just type the first three letters of the month and press the Down arrow key. Works has a special date function that will fill in the full name of the month.

Begin the exercise by typing in the data as shown in Figure 6.46. Be sure to type each entry into the cell shown in Figure 6.46. When you have completed the basic data entry, adjust the spreadsheet as follows:

1. Use the Toolbar to boldface your name. Also use it to boldface and underline the titles (Spreadsheet Exercise 6.1, Clair's Aquatic Pets, and Profit Analysis). Finally, change the style for TOTALS: to bold type.

2. Alter the style for the names of the months so they align with the left side of the cell instead of the right.

3. Use the Border option (under the Format menu) to place a box around the headings in cells A7 through D8 (highlight these cells as a block first).

4. Use a formula with cell references to calculate profits for January (sales minus costs), then use Fill Down to copy the formulas for the other months.

FIGURE 6.47 Use the Autosum button to sum
a column of numbers quickly.

5. Position the cursor in cell B21 and click the Autosum button on the Toolbar as in Figure 6.47. This will automatically sum all the numbers directly above giving a sum of total sales. Complete the sum by pressing Enter. Then use the Fill Right command to copy the formula to the totals cells for costs and profits. The Fill Right command is found under the Edit menu and works just like the Fill Down command except cells to the right are filled with the copied information.

6. Use the Number window to format the numeric cells with the Comma format with two decimal positions. Also check the Negative numbers in red option. Underline the last sales, costs, and profits entry just above the Totals row.

7. Adjust the column width as needed to display all the numeric entries. A good way to do this is to use the Best Fit option in the Column Width window.

8. Save the file on your work disk under the name *Exercise 6-1 Clair's Pets* and print the completed spreadsheet. If your printout displays the ### characters, widen the columns with the Best Fit option and print the spreadsheet again.

9. Close the spreadsheet and exit the Works program.

Exercise 6-2A

Enter the information for Sunny Hills Wholesale as shown in Figure 6.48 into a new Works spreadsheet. You will format it later.

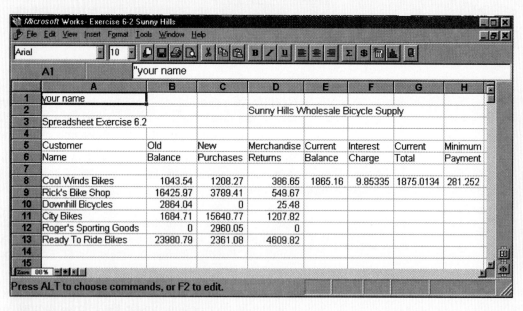

FIGURE 6.48 Sunny Hills initial data for Exercise 6-2.

Be sure to enter the data in the first three columns as values and to use formulas to compute the data in the last four columns. The numbers in the last four columns of row 8 are for you to use to check your formulas. Do not enter these numbers as values; use formulas.

1. Sunny Hills Wholesale figures the current balance as follows:

    Current balance = (Old balance + new purchases) - merchandise returns

    Develop a spreadsheet formula for cell E8 and make sure your results agree with those shown in Figure 6.48. Use the Fill Down feature to copy the formula to cells E9 through E13.

2. Complete column F by computing the interest charge at 1.5% (entered as .015) of the old balance minus returns.
3. Compute the current total as equal to the current balance plus the interest charge.
4. Compute the minimum payment so that it equals 15% of the Current Total.
5. In row 15, add up all the cells in the Old Balance, New Purchases, Merchandise Returns, Current Balance, Interest Charge, and Current Total columns to arrive at a total amount owed to the firm in each of these categories.
6. Format the spreadsheet so the first numeric entry and the totals in each column of data are in the Currency format with two decimal positions. Format all other numeric entries with the Comma format and two decimals.
7. Adjust the column width as required to display all the data in each column.
8. Center align and boldface all the titles in rows 5 and 6. Boldface customer names and align them to the right.
9. Save the spreadsheet as *Exercise 6-2 Sunny Hills* on your work disk.
10. Adjust the print font as required to print the spreadsheet on one page, and print the spreadsheet. When you are done, close the spreadsheet.

Exercise 6-2B

1. Update the spreadsheet to reflect the changes in steps 2 and 3. If you used formulas correctly, all you will need to do is change the values given in those steps.
2. Sunny Hills has just learned that the current merchandise return figures for two customers should be replaced by these that have just been received. You should be able to enter these figures into cells D8 and D9 and the spreadsheet will be updated automatically.
    Cool Winds: $250.65
    Roger's Sporting Goods: $215.98
3. The president of Sunny Hills Wholesale has decided to recalculate the interest charge based on the new rate of 1.25% to reflect lower interest costs. Don't forget to use the Fill Down feature to make sure all accounts are adjusted.
4. Change the title of the spreadsheet to *Exercise 6-2 PART B*, and print the spreadsheet. You do not need to save these changes.

Spreadsheets are often used to keep track of financial information. One common example of this is to develop a spreadsheet to track investment performance for an investment portfolio.

Use the spreadsheet module of Works to create a spreadsheet like the one in Figure 6.49. Enter the data as values and change the column width, style, and format as required. Be sure to use Fill Down to copy formulas to other cells. Complete the spreadsheet as follows:

	A	B	C	D	E	F	G
1	your name						
2							
3	Spreadsheet Exercise 6-3		Stock Portfolio				
4							
5	Stock	Purchase	Number	Broker	Current	Percent	Amount
6	Name	Price per Share	of Shares	Fee	Price per Share	Change	Profit or Loss
7	Micro Systems	$2.25	2000		$5.75		
8	Northern Gas	72.5	100		68.12		
9	Cress Financial	25.12	1100		26.25		
10	Micro Devices	44.50	500		30.75		
11	Wilson Controls	8.75	1800		14.12		
12	Diamond Rental	6.25	250		7.25		
13	EasternFloral	9.50	600		12.50		
14							
15	TOTAL:						
16							

FIGURE 6.49   Exercise 6-3 data.

1. Develop a formula and complete column D. The broker fee is computed as 2.73% of the total cost of the stock (total cost = number of shares*purchase price per share). Format this value as currency with two decimals for the first entry and comma with two decimals for the rest.

2. Compute the percent change, which is calculated as

$$\text{Percent Change} = \frac{\text{(Current price per share - Purchase Price per share)}}{\text{Purchase Price per share}}$$

Format this column as Percent with two decimal positions.

3. Compute the amount profit or loss by calculating the total current value of the stock minus the sum of the broker fee and the purchase price initially paid.

4. Format the amount profit or loss column the same way as the broker fee column.

5. Center the labels (column titles) over all of the columns. Place a bottom border under the second row of labels.

6. Use Bold format for the stock names.

7. Develop a formula in cell G15 to find the total for the amount profit or loss column. Underline the total.

8. Print the spreadsheet on one page, changing the print font and column width if needed.

9. Save the spreadsheet under the name *Exercise 6-3 Stock Portfolio*, close Works, and turn off the computer.

USING SPREADSHEET FUNCTIONS

When you've completed this chapter, you will be able to:

- Insert single or multiple rows and columns into a spreadsheet.
- Delete single or multiple rows or columns from a spreadsheet.
- Describe how information is cut or copied from, or pasted between cells.
- Explain relative and absolute cell addresses.
- Understand relative and absolute cell copying.
- Know how to create and use cell ranges with the mouse.
- Describe the concept of a spreadsheet function.
- Understand how to sort rows of information.
- Show the correct format of the IF function.
- Develop a nested IF statement.

SPECIAL SPREADSHEET FUNCTIONS

The Works spreadsheet provides special features that increase its power and ease of use. Some features enable you to answer complex financial questions with ease, whereas others let you perform tedious mathematical equations quickly and accurately. The spreadsheet also gives you the ability to insert, move, and delete columns or rows of information. You will find that these special capabilities will make using the spreadsheet much easier.

INSERTING/DELETING ROWS AND COLUMNS

Frequently, you will find you need to add an extra row or column in a spreadsheet that already contains data. Works allows you to do this by using the Row or Column options from the Insert menu. Notice that each option allows you to insert or delete rows and columns as shown in Figure 7.1. Works will assist here in that if a column is highlighted, the row options are unavailable from the menu. Similarly, column options are unavailable when working with rows.

Click to insert or delete rows

Click to insert or delete columns

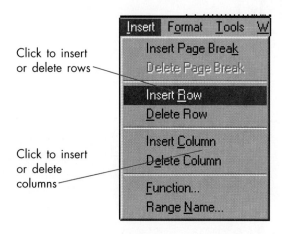

FIGURE 7.1   Use the Insert menu to insert or delete rows and colomns

Inserting Rows

To insert a new row as illustrated in Figure 7.2, select the row immediately *below* where you want the new row inserted. Open the Insert menu and choose Insert Row. The new row will then be inserted directly *above* the highlighted row. Therefore, if you want a new row between rows 1 and 2, highlight row 2 by clicking the row 2 label. Then select Insert Row from the Insert menu.

Click here to highlight row 2

Notice row is inserted above the highlighted row

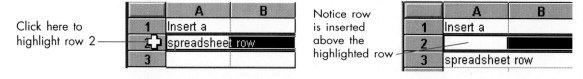

FIGURE 7.2   Select the Insert Row option from the Insert menu to insert row.

You can also insert multiple rows at one time by selecting (as a block) the number of rows to be inserted. For example, to insert five new rows between rows 1 and 2, select rows 2, 3, 4, 5, and 6. Then choose the Insert Row option from the Insert menu. The new rows are inserted above row 7 and data in row 2 are now in row 7. You should also be aware that Works knows that rows have been inserted and will adjust any formulas accordingly.

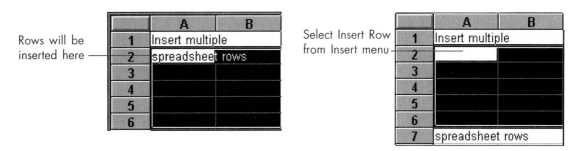

Rows will be inserted here

Select Insert Row from Insert menu

FIGURE 7.3   Insert multiple rows by first highlighting rows

Inserting Columns

Inserting new columns is accomplished in the same manner as inserting of new rows. To insert a single column, click the column label to the *right* of where you want the new column inserted. Then use the Insert Column option from the Insert menu. For example, to insert a new column between columns A and B, highlight column B and select the Insert Column option from the Insert menu. A new column is inserted between the old columns A and B (and will be labeled column B) as seen in Figure 7.4.

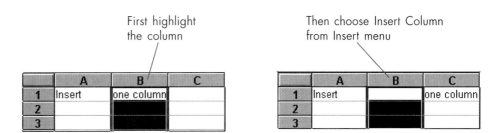

First highlight the column

Then choose Insert Column from Insert menu

FIGURE 7.4   Insert columns with the Insert Column option from the Insert menu.

To insert multiple columns, use the same approach as for inserting multiple rows, but highlight multiple columns instead of rows. Should you wish to insert three new columns between columns A and B, for example, select columns B, C, and D as a block. Then use the Insert Column option from the Insert menu. When the new columns are inserted, all existing columns are relabeled appropriately.

Formula Adjustment when Adding Rows and Columns

Recall that when you enter formulas in a spreadsheet, cell references are used to denote which cells to add, multiply, and so forth. When new rows and columns are inserted, Works automatically updates the cell address for the new cell position.

Deleting Rows and Columns

To delete rows and columns, use the same approach used to insert rows and columns. Highlight the rows or columns to be deleted. Then use the Delete Row or Delete Column option from the Insert menu. Works will delete the highlighted row or column. You can also highlight rows or columns and use the Ctrl/X (Cut) key combination to delete them.

COPYING, CUTTING, AND PASTING
CELLS

Recall the Fill Down and Fill Right commands from Chapter 6. Although they are powerful, they have some inherent limitations, including the inability to copy up or to the left. Further, they require cells to be adjacent to each other. When these conditions are not met, you can use the Copy command from the Edit menu as shown in Figure 7.5.

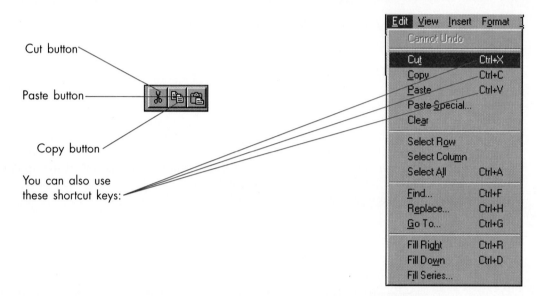

FIGURE 7.5   Use the Cut, Copy and Paste commands from the Toolbar or menu.

The copy procedure for the spreadsheet is similar to the copy procedure used for the word processing section. First, highlight a cell or block of cells you want to copy. Next, select the Copy option (or use the Ctrl/C key combination) from the Edit menu. Now move the cursor to the target cell where the data will be copied, and choose the Paste option from the Edit menu (or use the Ctrl/V keys).

If you are copying a block of data, position the cursor in the upper-left cell of the target range (the cells into which the block will be copied) before using the Paste option. The data will be copied to its new location. When formulas are copied from one location to another, cell coordinates are automatically adjusted.

You can also move cells from one location to another. First, select the cells as a block, then choose Cut from the Edit menu (or use the Ctrl/X keys). Next, position the cursor on the new location and use the Paste option from the Edit menu (or use the Ctrl/V keys).

Finally, instead of the menu commands, you can also use the toolbar for cut, copy, and paste as seen in Figure 7.5.

Using Drag and Drop with the Mouse

You can accomplish many copy and move operations using only the mouse and the drag and drop feature. To use this feature, position the mouse pointer at the border of the cell you wish to move. You will see the drag symbol appear as in Figure 7.6. Holding down the mouse button, move the mouse pointer to the new location in the spreadsheet. You will see the move symbol appear and the cell will move along with the mouse pointer. Once you are at the desired location, release the mouse button, and the cell will be repositioned.

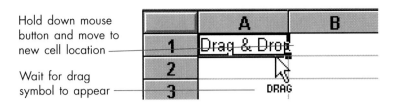

Hold down mouse button and move to new cell location

Wait for drag symbol to appear

FIGURE 7.6   Use the drag and drop feature to move cells with the mouse.

Relative Cell Addresses

Formulas used in cells usually refer to the relative positions of other cells. These positions are called **relative addresses**. For example, if a relative address in cell B3 refers to the contents in cell C2, the spreadsheet understands that the cell to reference is located one column to the right and one row up as seen in Figure 7.7.

Cell B3 refers to the contents of cell C2

	B	C
1		
2		100
3	=C2	
4		

FIGURE 7.7   The relative address in cell B3 refers to the contents of cell C2

If cell B3 is copied to cell B4, the formula inside cell B3 will be changed so that it still refers to a cell one row up and one column to the right. This is cell C3 as seen in Figure 7.8. Notice that the formula is incremented even though cell C3 is empty.

Notice cell B4 now refers to cell C3

Cell B3 is copied to cell B4

	B	C
1		
2		100
3	=C2	
4	=C3	

FIGURE 7.8   Cell addresses are updated when they are copied.

Similar changes occur when you use a Fill Down or Fill Right operation. Each row coordinate is increased by one (1), from B3 to B4, B4 to B5, and so forth. Each column coordinate is increased by one letter from B2 to C2, C2 to D2, and so forth. You can see in Figure 7.9 that when the contents of cell B3 are copied to cells B4 through B7, the formula references are changed. This is called a relative copy since the cell address changes to reflect the relative position of the cells in the formula.

As cell B3 is filled down, notice how the formula changes

	B	C	D
1			
2		100	50
3	=C2+D2		
4	=C3+D3		
5	=C4+D4		
6	=C5+D5		
7	=C6+D6		

FIGURE 7.9   When Fill Down is used, formulas are incremented.

Caution: When you delete rows or columns, be aware that the deletion may affect formulas referencing the deleted cells. When this situation occurs, you will see the notation ERR in the affected cell. Immediately choose the Undo option under the Edit menu to put back any rows or columns deleted by mistake.

Using Absolute Cell References

What happens when you do *not* want the automatic adjustment of formulas to happen when you copy a cell to a new location? For instance, assume you had an interest rate value stored in one cell and want to use that rate to compute the payments for several loans. Since all payments are computed using the same formula, you enter the formula into one cell and use the Fill Down procedure to copy it into all the other cells. If the Fill Down procedure automatically adjusted the cell coordinates in the formula by adding 1 to the current interest rate cell position, the copied payment formulas would no longer refer to the correct cell. Figure 7.10 shows how this could happen. To avoid this problem, the formula should always refer to cell B2, the interest rate, even after it has been copied.

Cell B2 is needed in all formulas

But after Fill Down, formula no longer refers to B2

	A	B
1		
2		0.1
3	=PMT(C2,B2,D2)	
4	=PMT(C3,B3,D3)	
5	=PMT(C4,B4,D4)	

FIGURE 7.10   When the payment formula in cell A3 is filled down, the formula is incremented even though errors will be made.

To allow you to control when you want the cell reference to change, the Works spreadsheet allows the use of both **relative** and **absolute addressing** to define the coordinates of a given cell. When you use **relative coordinates** in a formula and the formula is copied or moved, the coordinates are adjusted automatically. When you use **absolute coordinates** in a formula and the formula is copied or moved, no adjustment takes place.

Since Works uses the relative coordinate type as its default, you must specify if you want a cell coordinate treated as an absolute, or nonmoving, coordinate. This specification is accomplished by placing a dollar sign ($) in front of the coordinate you want to make absolute. Recall that each cell has both a row coordinate and a column coordinate; you can control each of these separately with an absolute notation. This means you can use up to four combinations of coordinate control as follows (the shaded areas of Figures 7.11 through 7.14 indicate where the cell coordinates will be adjusted):

A1: Both the column A and row 1 are treated as relative. When the coordinate is copied left or right, the column coordinate is adjusted. When a coordinate is copied up or down, the row coordinate is adjusted. This is the default setting for Microsoft Works. Formulas will increment throughout the shaded area in Figure 7.11.

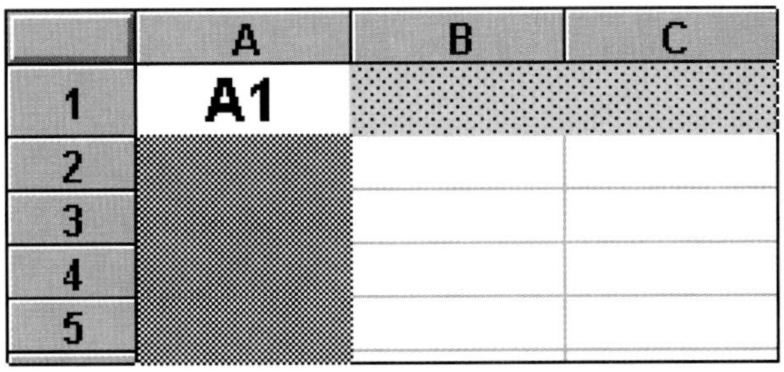

FIGURE 7.11 Formulas increment horizontally in rows and vertically in columns.

$A1: The dollar sign causes column A to be treated in an absolute manner as seen in Figure 7.12. Row 1 remains relative. When the coordinate is copied to different columns (left or right), it will not change. When the coordinate is copied between rows (up or down), it is adjusted.

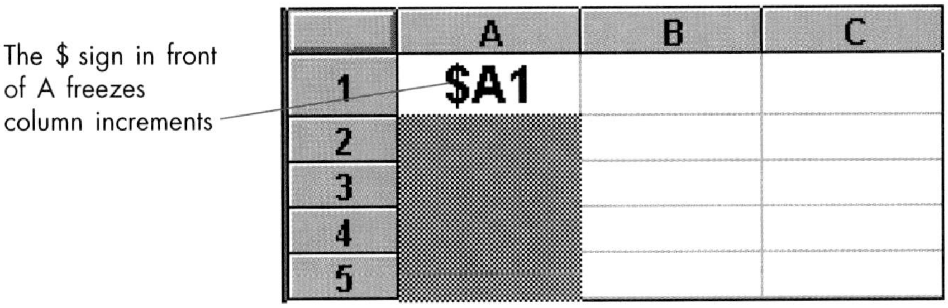

The $ sign in front of A freezes column increments

FIGURE 7.12 Formulas increment only vertically in rows. Columns will not increment.

A$1: This case illustrates that column A will adjust, but row 1 will remain as an absolute coordinate. Therefore, when the cell is copied between columns, the coordinate is adjusted. When the cell is copied between rows, it will not change. This is illustrated in Figure 7.13.

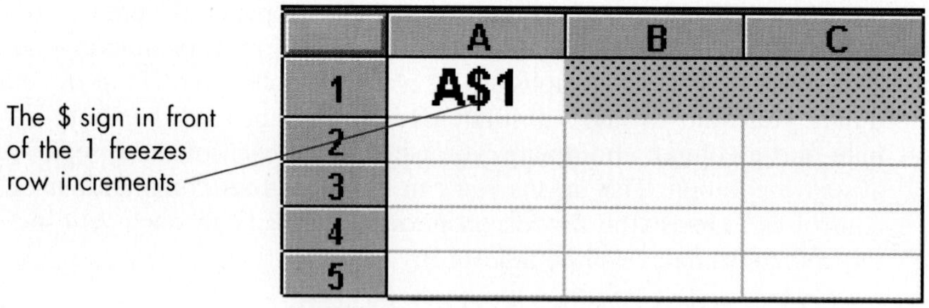

The $ sign in front of the 1 freezes row increments

	A	B	C
1	A$1		
2			
3			
4			
5			

FIGURE 7.13   Formulas increment only horizontally across columns. Rows will not increment.

$A$1: The final case involves absolute references for both the column A and row 1 as seen in Figure 7.14. Here, the cell coordinates will not change regardless of the copy direction. This specification is often used as illustrated in Figure 7.15.

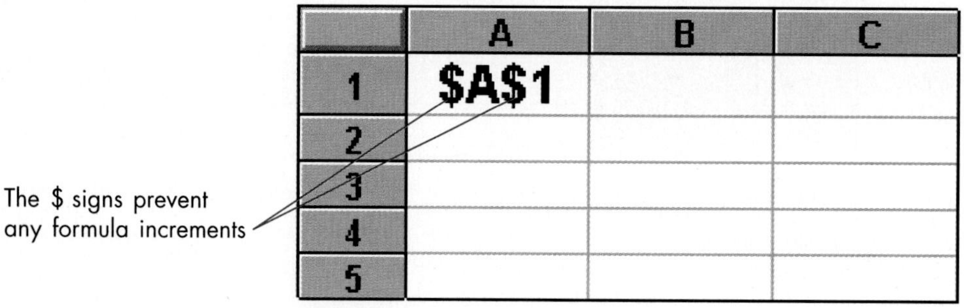

The $ signs prevent any formula increments

	A	B	C
1	$A$1		
2			
3			
4			
5			

FIGURE 7.14   Formulas will not increment.

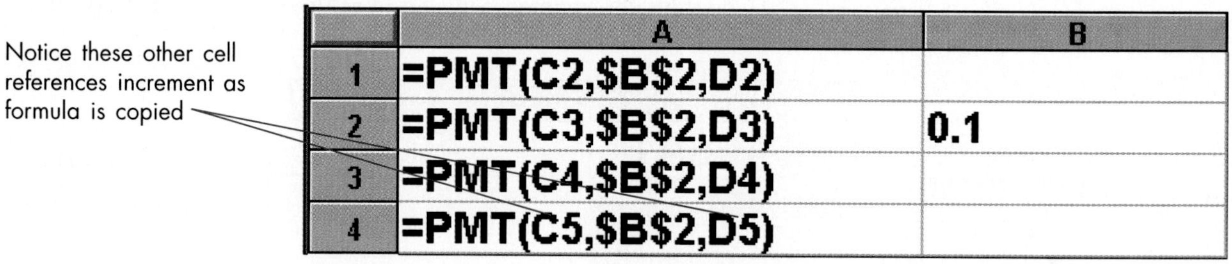

Notice these other cell references increment as formula is copied

	A	B
1	=PMT(C2,$B$2,D2)	
2	=PMT(C3,$B$2,D3)	0.1
3	=PMT(C4,$B$2,D4)	
4	=PMT(C5,$B$2,D5)	

FIGURE 7.15   The $ signs keep cell B2 from incrementing as this formula is filled down.

Functions are special mathematical routines defined in the spreadsheet software that allow you to perform operations without writing complex formulas. Functions used by the Works spreadsheet typically have the following general format:

=function name(argument1, argument2, . . . argumentn)

This general format indicates that the first thing to appear in any function is the equals (=) sign that informs Works that the characters following are part of a formula and not a label. The next thing is a special function name that tells Works what to do. The last items are arguments enclosed in parentheses. These arguments provide the working data for the function in the form of literal values, formulas, cell coordinates, or even other functions. Although the number and order of the arguments will vary from one function to another, all the required arguments must be specified in the correct order.

Cell Ranges and Range Names

Many functions are designed to determine answers based on a selected block of cells in a spreadsheet. These blocks of cells are referred to as cell ranges. Specify ranges as cell coordinates by typing the starting cell and the ending cell separated by a colon (:). For example, to select a range of cells from cell J4 to J18, type J4:J18.

You can also assign a special name to a range of cells. For example, you might want to call a block of cells containing test scores by the word Results. If you wanted to use these scores in a formula or chart later on, you could simply enter the range name, Results, instead of the cell addresses. This feature makes it easy to remember what the cells mean in a formula.

Functions Used in Microsoft Works

The following are the most commonly used Works spreadsheet functions. Other common functions are included at the end of this chapter. For all possible functions, see the Works documentation.

=SUM(range)   This function computes the sum of all cells in the given range. If you wanted to find the sum of all the cells from A5 to A20, for example, the Sum function would be =SUM(A5:A20). Works will insert a value of 0 for any blank cell or label in the range of cells being summed. Further, if you insert or delete any rows in a range, Works will automatically adjust the range to reflect the new range of cells.

=AVG(range)   This function computes the arithmetic mean, or average, of the cells in the range. The same rules apply to inserting and deleting rows that apply to the SUM function. If cells are blank, the average function excludes them from the computation. If cells contain labels, the average function interprets them as 0 and includes them in the calculation of the average.

=MAX(range)   This function identifies the largest value in a range of cells. Again, blank cells in the range are ignored, and cells containing labels are considered to be 0. As an example of the MAX function, suppose you want to find the highest test score for a group of students, and the test scores are stored in cells D5 through D40. You would use the function =MAX(D5:D40).

=MIN(range)   The MIN function works just like the MAX function, except it finds the minimum value in a specified range. The rules for the MIN function are the same as for the MAX function.

=PMT(principal,rate,term)   The PMT function computes the amount of a payment given the principal of a loan, interest rate per period, and number of periods. To compute the monthly payment for a loan of $10,000 at 9.5 percent annually for four years, for example, you would use =PMT(10000,.095/12,4*12). The answer is $251.23.

Describing a Range by Cursor Pointing

You can identify a range by using the mouse or the arrow keys in the same way you select a block of cells. To identify a range as illustrated in Figure 7.16, enter the equals sign, function name, and left parenthesis. Next, press one of the arrow keys. You will see the cell coordinate for the cursor position in the function area. Continue to press the arrow key until the cursor is on the first cell you want in the function range. Now, press the colon (:) key to inform Works you want to start the range at that point. Use the arrow keys to extend the highlight until the entire desired range is covered. Type the right parenthesis, press Enter, and the function is complete.

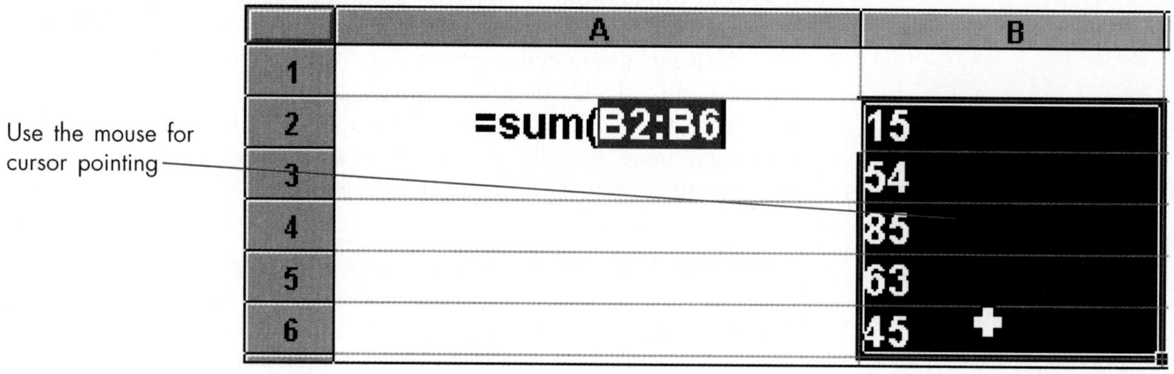

Use the mouse for cursor pointing

FIGURE 7.16   Cursor pointing can quickly establish a cell range.

Range selection using the cursor pointing method with the mouse is easier than with the keyboard. Enter the equals sign, function name, and left parenthesis. Then use the mouse to highlight the cells you want to include. Finally, type the right parenthesis and press Enter to complete the function.

Once you try either of these methods of range selection, you will find it is fast and accurate because you can visually confirm that the range is correct.

IF FUNCTION

The IF function is a logical function used to test a given condition and perform certain operations depending on whether the result of the test is true or false. The general format of the IF function is

=IF(condition,True,False).

The IF function consists of four components. The first is the IF function name. The second component is the condition that tests the relationship between two cells or values. For example, the IF function can test the condition A5 > 100 (that is, if the contents of cell A5 are greater than 100).

The condition being tested can be simple, with a single coordinate or value on each side (A2 > 10). Or it could be complex, with other functions being evaluated as part of the IF condition. Regardless of its complexity, each condition must be made up of two coordinates or values separated by a relational operator, such as those listed.

Operator	Meaning	Example
=	Is equal to	A1 = 100
>	Is greater than	A1 > 100
<	Is less than	A1 <100
< >	Is not equal to	A1 < >100
>=	Is greater than or equal to	A1 >= 100
<=	Is less than or equal to	A1 <= 100

As an example of the IF function, suppose you were developing a payroll and needed to establish whether employees worked more than 40 hours per week to see if they qualified for overtime. The hours worked are stored in cell A5. Therefore, you need to test the content of cell A5 to see if it is greater than 40. If it is greater than 40, the condition is true, and you multiply the pay rate in cell A6 by 1.5 and display the total pay in cell A7. If the test is false (cell A5 is less than or equal to 40), you multiply cell A6 by 1 (the normal rate) and display the answer in cell A7.

To develop the payroll, place the following formula in cell A7:

=IF(A5>40,A6*1.5,A6*1)

Note that the result of the IF statement appears in the same cell occupied by the IF statement.

Nested IF Statements

Frequently, you will encounter a situation in which the IF statement must choose between three or more conditions. For example, income taxes might be assessed at 25% for incomes under $30,000, 28% for incomes between $30,000 and $50,000, and 30% for incomes over $50,000. A single IF statement can evaluate only two conditions, however, by combining two IF statements, we can evaluate all three conditions presented here. This is called nesting IF statements. The easiest way to learn this concept is to look at an example. The nested IF statement for the income tax problem (assume the income figure is in cell B9) would appear as Figure 7.17.

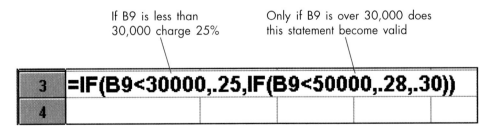

FIGURE 7.17   A nested IF statement.

The IF statement in Figure 7.17 first determines if cell B9 is less than 30,000. If it is, the function returns the value .25. If, however, B9 is greater than 30,000, the next IF statement is applied. That IF statement then evaluates B9 to see if it is less than 50,000. If it is and since the second IF statement was activated, the IF statement recognizes that B9 is a value between 30,000 and 49,999 and returns a value of .28. Finally, if the second IF statement recognizes that B9 is greater than 50,000 it returns a value of .30.

Nested IF statements offer considerable flexibility to spreadsheet development. While they appear complex at first, they are actually quite easy to use. The key to successful use is to first write out in English what you want the IF statement to do. Then it is a simple matter to develop it.

USING WORKING FIGURES

One of the most powerful features of any electronic spreadsheet is the ability to make a change in one cell and have that change update the contents in a large block of cells. This ability to use working figures allows you to use the spreadsheet to find answers quickly to "what if" questions based on various changes in the spreadsheet data.

To understand how this powerful feature can assist you, suppose you create a spreadsheet that used the payment function, =PMT(principal,rate,term), to determine the payment to purchase a new car. If the loan amount was for $10,000 borrowed at 8.75% per year (.0875/12 for monthly rate) over 48 months, you could type this function as =PMT(10000,.0875/12,48). The PMT function would work fine for these specific values, but it would also be nice to see how your payment changed for different time periods or amounts. To see the impact of these changes without rewriting the formula, you can use working figures.

The concept of working figures is based on the creation of four cells used by the PMT function. The first cell stores the principal, the second the interest rate, and the third the term. The last cell contains the PMT function, but you use the coordinates of the first three cells rather than the actual values as shown in Figure 7.18.

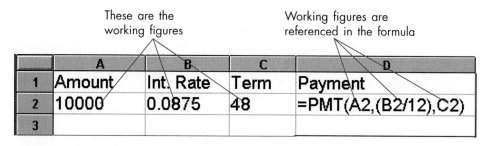

FIGURE 7.18   Using Working figures in a payment function.

Now, to find the new payment for a loan of $15,000, all you have to do is change the value of cell A2. The formula will automatically recalculate and display the answer based on the new information. Similarly, to adjust the term to 60 months, you would change only the value in cell C2. These changes are shown in Figure 7.19.

Original payment amount ─

	A	B	C	D
1	Amount	Int. Rate	Term	Payment
2	$10,000.00	0.0875	48	$247.67
3				

Payment is updated after
amount and term working
figures are changed ─

	A	B	C	D
1	Amount	Int. Rate	Term	Payment
2	$15,000.00	0.0875	60	$309.56
3				

FIGURE 7.19   Working figures allow you to change the cell entries, not the formula.

This concept saves some time even in this small example, but what if you were dealing with values in many cells? If the formulas in ten cells had the interest rate entered as a value and the rate changed, you would need to change ten formulas. If these same ten cells used the coordinate of a working figure, you would need to make only one change.

SORTING SPREADSHEET DATA

The Works spreadsheet allows you to sort data so you can quickly arrange them to see various patterns and trends. For example, you might want to sort an expense spreadsheet from the largest expense item to the smallest. This type of sort is called a descending sort. Or you might want to sort a list of grades from the lowest to the highest. This type of sort is called an ascending sort.

To sort data in the spreadsheet, first select a block of cells containing the information you want to sort. Next, pull down the Tools menu and choose the Sort option as shown in Figure 7.20. Next, select the information you want the sort on and in which column it is contained. This is called the Sort By column. Finally, choose the sort order (Ascend or Descend) from the Sort window and click Sort. The data are then sorted.

NOTE: When you sort spreadsheet data, *all* the cells in the selected range will be sorted, even the blank cells. If the sort does not perform as you expected, be sure to use the Undo option found in the Edit menu to return the spreadsheet to its presort form.

1. Click Sort from
   the Tools menu ─

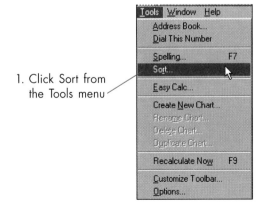

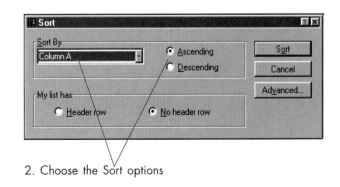

2. Choose the Sort options

FIGURE 7.20   Use the Sort option from the Tools menu to sort the spreadsheet rows.

CHAPTER 7 SELF-TEST

1. How would you insert three new rows between row 8 and row 9?
2. How would you delete columns C, D, and E?
3. If you copied the formula =A1+B1 from cell B3 to cell C3, what formula would be in cell C3?
4. Explain the difference between relative and absolute coordinates.
5. Write the coordinates for the following:
    a. Column E absolute, row 7 relative.
    b. Column B absolute, row 2 absolute.
    c. Column C relative, row 106 absolute.
    d. Column AG relative, row 1008 relative.
6. Write the function to find the average of all cells from A45 through C100.
7. Write the function to find the largest number in the range of cells from G12 through J99.
8. Write the IF function to test cell A7 given the following: If the value in cell A7 is less than 115.5, display cell A7's value multiplied by 5.5. If the value in cell A7 is equal to or greater than 115.5, display cell A7's value divided by 2.5.
9. Develop a nested IF statement to test cell A4 as follows:
    If A4 is less than 500, display a 3.
    If A4 is greater than or equal to 500, but less than 1,000, display a 4.
    If A4 is greater than or equal to 1,000 display a 5.
10. Write the IF function to display the average of cells A2 through A20 if the value in cell B3 is less than zero. If the value in cell B3 is equal to or greater than zero, display the sum of cells A2 through A20.
11. How would you sort cells A7 through G26?

In this tutorial, you will practice the procedures discussed earlier by loading a partially completed spreadsheet from your data disk and completing most of the column entries. The completed spreadsheet will look like Figure 7.21.

	A	B	C	D	E	F	G	H	I	J
1	Chapter 7 Tutorial									
2	Author:	Your Name								
3					*Blue Ridge Hardware*					
4										
5	Invoice	Invoice	Invoice	Number of	First	Payment	Discount	Discount	Net	Net
6	Number	Date	Amount	Payments	Payment	Due	Date	Amount	Date	Amount
7										
8	1634	8/13/95	12,347.33	24	9/12/95	572.62	August 23, 1995	12,100.38	9/12/95	0.00
9	1635	8/15/95	921.08		9/14/95	0.00	August 25, 1995	902.66	9/14/95	921.08
10	1636	8/15/95	624.65		9/14/95	0.00	August 25, 1995	612.16	9/14/95	624.65
11	1637	8/17/95	7,724.50	24	9/16/95	358.23	August 27, 1995	7,570.01	9/16/95	0.00
12	1638	8/23/95	8,734.40	48	9/22/95	223.63	September 02, 1995	8,559.71	9/22/95	0.00
13	1639	8/24/95	14,456.50	36	9/23/95	469.87	September 03, 1995	14,167.37	9/23/95	0.00
14	1640	8/25/95	10,224.50	48	9/24/95	261.78	September 04, 1995	10,020.01	9/24/95	0.00
15	1641	8/26/95	8,069.90	42	9/25/95	230.43	September 05, 1995	7,908.50	9/25/95	0.00
16	1642	9/2/95	570.10		10/2/95	0.00	September 12, 1995	558.70	10/2/95	570.10
17	1643	9/2/95	9,125.50	60	10/2/95	196.14	September 12, 1995	8,942.99	10/2/95	0.00
18	1644	9/3/95	4,759.37	24	10/3/95	220.72	September 13, 1995	4,664.18	10/3/95	0.00
19	1645	9/3/95	3,675.50	36	10/3/95	119.46	September 13, 1995	3,601.99	10/3/95	0.00
20	1646	9/6/95	878.85		10/6/95	0.00	September 16, 1995	861.27	10/6/95	878.85
21	1647	9/11/95	924.50	12	10/11/95	81.49	September 21, 1995	906.01	10/11/95	0.00
22	1648	9/15/95	1,424.50		10/15/95	0.00	September 25, 1995	1,396.01	10/15/95	1,424.50
23	1649	9/17/95	1,524.50	24	10/17/95	70.70	September 27, 1995	1,494.01	10/17/95	0.00
24	1650	9/22/95	6,116.49	48	10/22/95	156.60	October 02, 1995	5,994.16	10/22/95	0.00
25	1651	10/7/95	3,574.50	18	11/6/95	215.50	October 17, 1995	3,503.01	11/6/95	0.00
26	1652	10/12/95	4,724.50	36	11/11/95	153.56	October 22, 1995	4,630.01	11/11/95	0.00
27	1653	10/13/95	1,514.00	24	11/12/95	70.21	October 23, 1995	1,483.72	11/12/95	0.00
28	1654	10/20/95	565.50	12	11/19/95	49.85	October 30, 1995	554.19	11/19/95	0.00
29	1655	11/12/95	724.50		12/12/95	0.00	November 22, 1995	710.01	12/12/95	724.50
30	1656	11/15/95	359.17		12/15/95	0.00	November 25, 1995	351.99	12/15/95	359.17
31	1657	12/4/95	380.70		1/3/96	0.00	December 14, 1995	373.09	1/3/96	380.70
32	1658	12/15/95	481.30	12	1/14/96	42.43	December 25, 1995	471.67	1/14/96	0.00
33	1659	12/22/95	45,899.50	60	1/21/96	986.56	January 01, 1996	44,981.51	1/21/96	0.00
34	1660	1/4/96	424.50	12	2/3/96	37.42	January 14, 1996	416.01	2/3/96	0.00
35	1661	1/11/96	570.49		2/10/96	0.00	January 21, 1996	559.08	2/10/96	570.49
36	1662	1/12/96	1,859.00	33	2/11/96	65.10	January 22, 1996	1,821.82	2/11/96	0.00
37	1664	1/15/96	279.50		2/14/96	0.00	January 25, 1996	273.91	2/14/96	279.50
38	1665	2/1/96	237.50		3/2/96	0.00	February 11, 1996	232.75	3/2/96	237.50
39										
40	Interest Rate:		10.5%		Total of Invoices:		$153,696.83			
41	Days to Due Date:		30		Average Invoice:		$4,957.96			
42	Discount Days:		10		Total Due Payments:		$4,582.32			
43	Discount Rate:		2.0%		Total Due Discount:		$150,622.89			
44	Days to Net:		30		Total Due Net:		$6,971.04			

FIGURE 7.21   The completed Chapter 7 tutorial worksheet.

PROBLEM DESCRIPTION

You are in charge of the credit department of the Blue Ridge Hardware Company, and it is your job to keep track of the accounts receivable (money owed to your firm by customers) for your company. The former accounts receivable manager tried to develop a spreadsheet to handle this application, but was unable to complete it. Your task is to take up where the former manager left off and develop a spreadsheet similar to the one in Figure 7.21.

When customers place orders with your company, the order is filled and shipped, and an invoice is created. This invoice contains an invoice number, invoice date, invoice amount, and information concerning how payment will be made. If the invoiced items are to be charged, an entry is made showing the number of monthly payments the customer wants to make. For items that are not charged, your company gives a discount if the invoice is paid within 10 days; otherwise, the net value of the invoice is due within 30 days. This is a 2/10, Net/30 payment schedule (2 percent discount in 10 days, net due in 30 days).

	A	B	C	D	E	F	G	H	I	
1	Chapter 7 Tutorial									
2	Author:	Your Name								
3				Blue Ridge Hardware						
4										
5	Invoice	Invoice	Invoice	Number of	First	Payment	Discount	Discount	Net	
6	Number	Date	Amount	Payments	Payment	Due	Date	Amount	Date	A
7										
8	1638	8/23/95	8,734.40	48						
9	1645	9/3/95	3,675.50	36						
10	1637	8/17/95	7,724.50	24						
11	1639	8/24/95	14,456.50	36						
12	1641	8/26/95	8,069.90	42						
13	1653	10/13/95	1,514.00	24						
14	1634	8/13/95	12,347.33	24						
15	1642	9/2/95	570.10							
16	1643	9/2/95	9,125.50	60						
17	1635	8/15/95	921.08							
18	1644	9/3/95	4,759.37	⛶						
19	1647	9/11/95	924.50	12						
20	1636	8/15/95	624.65							
21	1656	11/15/95	359.17							
22	1640	8/25/95	10,224.50	48						
39										
40	Interest Rate:		10.5%		Total of Invoices:					
41	Days to Due Date:		30		Average Invoice:					
42	Discount Days:		10		Total Due Payments:					
43	Discount Rate:		2.0%		Total Due Discount:					
44	Days to Net:		30		Total Due Net:					

Your file will have 44 rows

FIGURE 7.22 The Chapter 7 tutorial after you load it from disk.

Start Works and Load the Chapter 7 Tutorial File

1. Start Microsoft Windows and start the Works program.
2. Select Open An Existing Document.
3. Select the file named Chapter 7 tutorial. Your spreadsheet will look like Figure 7.22, but will contain 44 rows.

Enter Your Name and Look at the Working Figures

1. Enter *your name* in cell B2.
2. Press the F5 (GoTo key), type the cell address A44, and press Enter to move down to view cells A40 through C44.
3. Notice there is a entry in cell C41 (30). Our firm uses this as a working figure to show the number of days until the due date of the first payment. We use this as a working figure since the figure may need to be changed when we offer a No Payment for 90 Days special. Because of this requirement, when you need to calculate Payment Due Dates in the spreadsheet, you will want to use the number of days as the absolute coordinates of cell C41, or $C$41.
4. Use the Ctrl/Home key combination to move to cell A1.

Sort the Rows into Invoice Number Order

1. Click the row 8 label (the number 8) so the entire row is highlighted.
2. Use the scroll bar to move down until row 38 is visible on your screen.
3. Position the mouse pointer over the row 38 label (the number 38) then hold down the Shift key and click the mouse button. Rows 8 through 38 are highlighted. This will be the part of the spreadsheet you will sort.
4. Pull down the Tools menu and choose the Sort option.
5. The Sort window shown in Figure 7.23 is displayed, with column A appearing in the Sort By box. This means you will sort the rows based on the contents of column A, which contains the invoice number. Notice also that the rows will be sorted in ascending order (smallest to largest).
6. Since we are happy with the defaults presented in the Sort window, click Sort to start.
7. Press the Up arrow key to cancel the block and move to row 8. The invoices and related information appear in ascending order, beginning with number 1634 and ending with 1665.

These default values are okay for our sort

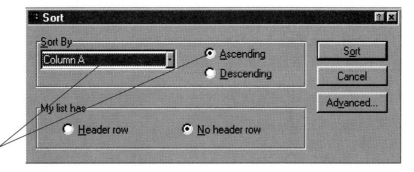

FIGURE 7.23   The Sort dialog box appears after selecting Sort from the Tools menu.

Completing the Date of First Payment Column

The formula for the date of the first payment expressed in English is

First Payment = Invoice Date + Days to Due Date

Notice that the first Invoice Date is in cell B8 and the days to due date value is in cell C41. Therefore, the spreadsheet formula is =B8+$C$41.

Take special note that cell C41 has been specified as an absolute reference so that when the formula is copied into the other rows, this coordinate will not change.

1. Using arrow keys or the mouse, move the cursor to cell E8.
2. Enter **=B8+$C$41** into cell E8 and press Enter.
3. The value in the cell is 34954, which represents the Julian date or simply the number of days since January 1, 1900. This is seen in Figure 7.24.

Enter this
formula into
cell E8

E8			=B8+$C$41		
	A	**B**	**C**	**D**	**E**
5	Invoice	Invoice	Invoice	Number of	First
6	Number	Date	Amount	Payments	Payment
7					
8	1634	8/13/95	12,347.33	24	34954
9	1635	8/15/95	921.08		

FIGURE 7.24   The date for the first payment appears as a Julian date before formatting.

Change the Cell Format to MM/DD/YY

1. Select Number from the Format menu. The Number window appears as in Figure 7.25.
2. Select the Date option from the left side of the window.
3. Select the Month/Day/Year format (the default setting) from the Date box.
4. Press Enter. Cell E8 will now display 9/12/95.

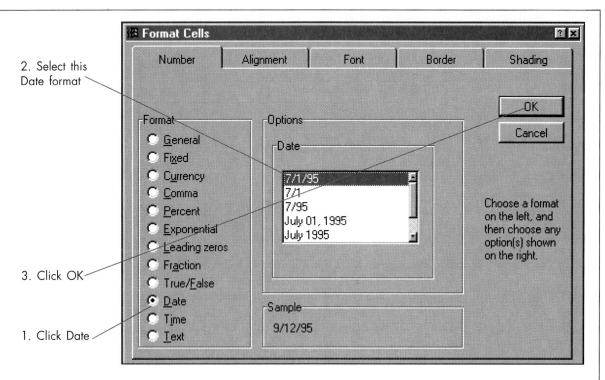

2. Select this
Date format

3. Click OK

1. Click Date

FIGURE 7.25   Select the Date option from the Number dialog box from the Format menu.

Use Fill Down to Copy the Formula to Other Cells

1. Select cells E8 through E38 as a block.
2. Select Fill Down from the Edit menu.
3. Press the Right arrow key to move to cell F8.

Completing the Payment Due Column

Use the payment function to calculate the monthly payment. The format of the PMT function is

$$=PMT(principal,rate,term)$$

principal   The amount of the loan (this is the *amount* of the invoice).

rate   The interest rate. Since the annual rate is stored as a working figure in cell C40 and customers make monthly payments, you will need to divide the annual rate in cell C40 by 12 to convert to monthly interest.

term   The number of payments stored in column D.

1. Click cell F8 and type *=PMT(C8,$C$40/12,D8)*. Press Enter. Note that you are replacing the PMT function variables with working figures from the spreadsheet.
2. Format the cell using the Comma format with two decimals. Cell F8 should contain the value 572.62.
3. Select cells F8 through F38 as a block.
4. Select the Fill Down option from the Edit menu.
5. Press the Up arrow key to cancel the block.

I Get an Error (ERR) in Some Cells!

The ERR entry indicates that the formula cannot be computed.

The formula references cell D9

The ERR results because D9 is empty

	F9		=PMT(C9,$C$40/12,D9)			
	A	B	C	D	E	F
7						
8	1634	8/13/95	12,347.33	24	9/12/95	572.62
9	1635	8/15/95	921.08		9/14/95	ERR
10	1636	8/15/95	624.65		9/14/95	ERR

FIGURE 7.26 The ERR in cell F9 alerts you to an error in the formula.

1. Move the cursor to the first ERR, cell F9, and notice that in the formula bar the term of the payment refers to cell D9.
2. Observe that cell D9 is empty, as seen in Figure 7.26. This blank cell occurred because the customer did not want to charge the invoice and hence has no Number of Payments entry. This same situation is true of all the other cells that contain ERR.

Develop an IF Statement to Correct the Error Condition

To avoid the ERR condition, test each cell in the Number of Payments column to determine if it has an entry or is blank. If a cell in the column is blank, the payment is zero. If the cell has an entry, the payment is computed normally.

This relationship can be described in English as follows:

If the Number of Payments is blank, the payment is zero; otherwise, compute the payment.

This relationship can be converted to a spreadsheet IF function as seen in Figure 7.27.

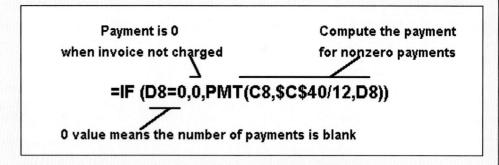

Payment is 0 when invoice not charged

Compute the payment for nonzero payments

=IF (D8=0,0,PMT(C8,$C$40/12,D8))

0 value means the number of payments is blank

FIGURE 7.27 Development of the IF statement to correct the ERR condition.

Entering the IF Statement

1. Move the cursor to cell F8 and press the F2 edit key.
2. Edit the formula in cell F8 to read:

$$=IF(D8=0,0,PMT(C8,\$C\$40/12,D8))$$

Note: You must delete the = in front of PMT.

3. Press Enter.
4. Select cells F8 through F38 as a block.
5. Select Fill Down from the Edit menu.
6. Press the Right arrow key to cancel the block. The spreadsheet should look like Figure 7.28.

The ERR entry is now corrected to show 0.00 ——

	A	B	C	D	E	F
5	Invoice	Invoice	Invoice	Number of	First	Payment
6	Number	Date	Amount	Payments	Payment	Due
7						
8	1634	8/13/95	12,347.33	24	9/12/95	572.62
9	1635	8/15/95	921.08		9/14/95	0.00
10	1636	8/15/95	624.65		9/14/95	0.00
11	1637	8/17/95	7,724.50	24	9/16/95	358.23
12	1638	8/23/95	8,734.40	48	9/22/95	223.63
13	1639	8/24/95	14,456.50	36	9/23/95	469.87

FIGURE 7.28   The interim spreadsheet after the payment formula error is corrected.

Entering The Discount Date Column

Customers can receive a discount of 2% (a working figure in cell C43) by paying their balance by the discount date. This date is computed by adding the invoice date and the working figure in cell C42, which is currently 10 days. To use the working figure, develop a formula using absolute coordinates.

1. Move the cursor to cell G8 and type **= B8+$C$42**. Press Enter.
2. Format cell G8 as a date (found in the Number option under the Format menu). Choose the date option so the entry in cell G8 appears as **August 23, 1995**.
3. Use Fill Down to copy the formula and format to rows G9 to G38.
4. Widen column G using the Best Fit option to display all the dates. Press the Right arrow key to cancel the block.

The Discount Amount Column

If the invoice is paid before the discount date, the customer is eligible for the discount. This is calculated using the percentage stored at cell C43. The English computation of the discount amount is

Invoice Amount * (100%- Discount rate%)

1. Go to cell H8 and enter **=C8*(1-$C$43).** (Recall that the 1 in the formula represents 100%). Press Enter.
2. Format the cell as the Comma format with two decimal places.
3. Select cells H8 to H38 and use the Fill Down option to copy the formula. Then press the Right arrow key to cancel the block.
4. Compare your spreadsheet with Figure 7.29 and correct any entries if necessary.

	A	B	C	D	E	F	G	H	I
5	Invoice	Invoice	Invoice	Number of	First	Payment	Discount	Discount	Net
6	Number	Date	Amount	Payments	Payment	Due	Date	Amount	Date
7									
8	1634	8/13/95	12,347.33	24	9/12/95	572.62	August 23, 1995	12,100.38	
9	1635	8/15/95	921.08		9/14/95	0.00	August 25, 1995	902.66	
10	1636	8/15/95	624.65		9/14/95	0.00	August 25, 1995	612.16	
11	1637	8/17/95	7,724.50	24	9/16/95	358.23	August 27, 1995	7,570.01	
12	1638	8/23/95	8,734.40	48	9/22/95	223.63	September 02, 1995	8,559.71	
13	1639	8/24/95	14,456.50	36	9/23/95	469.87	September 03, 1995	14,167.37	
14	1640	8/25/95	10,224.50	48	9/24/95	261.78	September 04, 1995	10,020.01	
15	1641	8/26/95	8,069.90	42	9/25/95	230.43	September 05, 1995	7,908.50	
16	1642	9/2/95	570.10		10/2/95	0.00	September 12, 1995	558.70	

FIGURE 7.29   The completion of the Discount Date and Discount Amount columns.

Completing the Net Date and Net Amount Columns

The last two columns are completed just like columns E through H. To see how familiar you are with the concepts, complete these last two columns yourself.

The net date consists of a specified number of days after the invoice date, which is stored in cell C44 as a working figure. Don't forget absolute referencing where needed. Format this column in the MM/DD/YY date format.

The net amount is the same as the invoice amount unless the customer has set up a monthly payment. Therefore, you have a net amount only if there are no payments (the cell for the number of payments is equal to zero), so an IF statement might be helpful. This column should be formatted in the Comma format with two decimal positions.

1. Complete columns I and J and check the figures against those in Figure 7.30.

	A	B	C	D	E	F	G	H	I	J
5	Invoice	Invoice	Invoice	Number of	First	Payment	Discount	Discount	Net	Net
6	Number	Date	Amount	Payments	Payment	Due	Date	Amount	Date	Amount
7										
8	1634	8/13/95	12,347.33	24	9/12/95	572.62	August 23, 1995	12,100.38	9/12/95	0.00
9	1635	8/15/95	921.08		9/14/95	0.00	August 25, 1995	902.66	9/14/95	921.08
10	1636	8/15/95	624.65		9/14/95	0.00	August 25, 1995	612.16	9/14/95	624.65
11	1637	8/17/95	7,724.50	24	9/16/95	358.23	August 27, 1995	7,570.01	9/16/95	0.00
12	1638	8/23/95	8,734.40	48	9/22/95	223.63	September 02, 1995	8,559.71	9/22/95	0.00
13	1639	8/24/95	14,456.50	36	9/23/95	469.87	September 03, 1995	14,167.37	9/23/95	0.00
14	1640	8/25/95	10,224.50	48	9/24/95	261.78	September 04, 1995	10,020.01	9/24/95	0.00
15	1641	8/26/95	8,069.90	42	9/25/95	230.43	September 05, 1995	7,908.50	9/25/95	0.00
16	1642	9/2/95	570.10		10/2/95	0.00	September 12, 1995	558.70	10/2/95	570.10
17	1643	9/2/95	9,125.50	60	10/2/95	196.14	September 12, 1995	8,942.99	10/2/95	0.00
18	1644	9/3/95	4,759.37	24	10/3/95	220.72	September 13, 1995	4,664.18	10/3/95	0.00
19	1645	9/3/95	3,675.50	36	10/3/95	119.46	September 13, 1995	3,601.99	10/3/95	0.00
20	1646	9/6/95	878.85		10/6/95	0.00	September 16, 1995	861.27	10/6/95	878.85
21	1647	9/11/95	924.50	12	10/11/95	81.49	September 21, 1995	906.01	10/11/95	0.00

FIGURE 7.30   The spreadsheet with the Net Date and Net Amount columns completed.

Using Cursor Pointing to Complete Cell G40

1. Move the cursor to cell G40 by pressing the F5 key, entering G40, and pressing Enter.

This cell should contain the sum of all Invoice Amounts computed with the SUM function. The format of the SUM function is SUM(range), where range will be all invoice amounts or cells C8 through C38, written as C8:C38.

Notice the formula still appears even though cell G40 is hidden

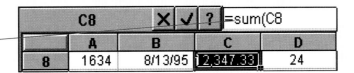

FIGURE 7.31   Watch the Formula bar for the cells included in cursor pointing.

2. In cell G40, enter **=SUM(**, but DO NOT PRESS Enter.
3. Move the cursor up to cell C8 with the arrow keys. The formula line should show =SUM(C8 as seen in Figure 7.31.
4. Enter a colon (:) after C8 so the formula line reads =SUM(C8:C8 .
5. Move the cursor to cell C38 with the arrow keys. The formula bar should now show =SUM(C8:C38.
6. Enter the closing parenthesis).
7. Press the Enter key.
8. Cell G40 should now show 153696.83, which is the sum of all cells from C8 through C38.

Enter the Average Invoice Amount in Cell G41

The format of the AVG function is the same as for the SUM function: AVG(range). Follow the same approach used to enter the SUM function in cell G40 to compute the average of cells C8 to C38.

1. Use cursor pointing to enter the AVG function in cell G41.
2. Be sure the value in cell G41 is 4957.962258.

Use Cursor Pointing to Complete Cells G42, G43, and G44

1. Complete cells G42, G43, and G44.
   Cell G42, the Total Due Payment, is the sum of cells F8 through F38.
   Cell G43, the Total Due Discount, is the sum of cells H8 through H38.
   Cell G44, the Total Due Net, is the sum of cells J8 through J38.
2. Format cells G40 through G44 using Currency format with two decimals. The totals should look like those in Figure 7.32.

	A	B	C	D	E	F	G
40	Interest Rate:		10.5%		Total of Invoices:		$153,696.83
41	Days to Due Date:		30		Average Invoice:		$4,957.96
42	Discount Days:		10		Total Due Payments:		$4,582.32
43	Discount Rate:		2.0%		Total Due Discount:		$150,622.89
44	Days to Net:		30		Total Due Net:		$6,971.04

FIGURE 7.32   The completed working figures and totals entries.

SAVE THE COMPLETED TUTORIAL

1. Adjust the font characteristics to set the titles as Bold face, and place a border under the row 6 titles as shown in Figure 7.21.
2. Change the font for the Blue Ridge Hardware title to size 16 type and use the Bold and italics font characteristics.
3. Change the remaining font sizes as needed to print the spreadsheet on one page.
4. Save the spreadsheet as *Chapter 7 Finished tutorial* on your disk.

TESTING THE FINISHED SPREADSHEET

You have completed the spreadsheet, but before you quit the Works program, take a moment to see the real value of what you have created. Assume you had the following questions:

Q1 If the interest rate were changed to 12 percent, what would be the payment due for invoice 1662? What about for the total due in payments?

To answer this question, note the payment amount in cell F36 is 65.10. To see what happens at the higher interest rate, follow this step:

1. Enter *.12* in cell C40. Not only did the Total Due Payments change to $4,688.93, but all payments have been recalculated. The payment in cell F36 should now be 66.42.

Q2 *If the discount days value is changed to 20 days, what is the new discount date for invoice 1665?*

1. Enter *20* in cell C42.
2. Examine cell G38. The date is February 21, 1996.
3. Close the spreadsheet and do not save these changes to the tutorial.

HANDS-ON PRACTICE

Exercise 7-1A

You have been asked to develop a grade-recording spreadsheet. You can use the spreadsheet to enter, sort, and update grades. Begin by loading the spreadsheet **Chapter 7 Exercise 1** from your exercise disk. The spreadsheet will appear as shown in Figure 7.33. Complete these tasks to finish the exercise:

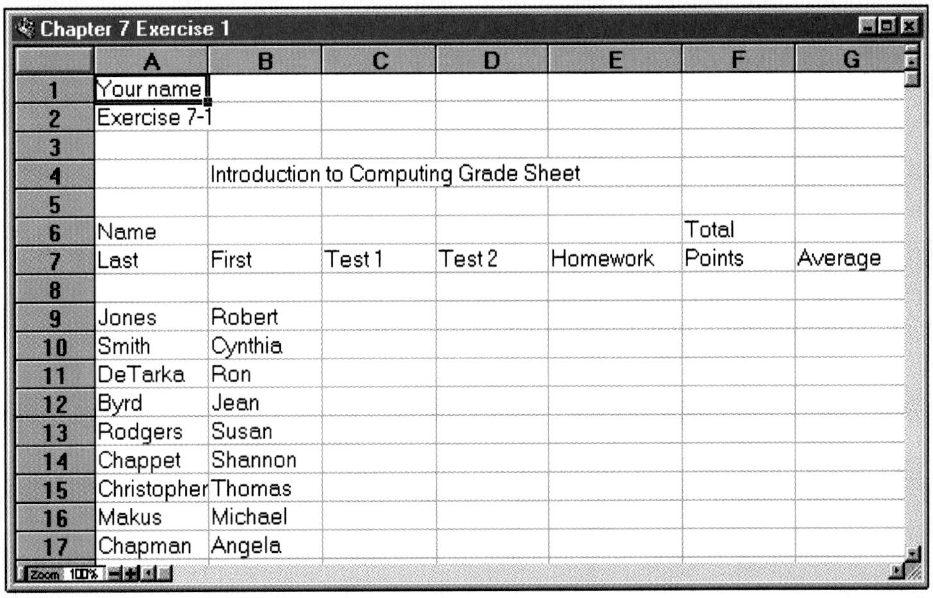

	A	B	C	D	E	F	G
1	Your name						
2	Exercise 7-1						
3							
4		Introduction to Computing Grade Sheet					
5							
6	Name					Total	
7	Last	First	Test 1	Test 2	Homework	Points	Average
8							
9	Jones	Robert					
10	Smith	Cynthia					
11	DeTarka	Ron					
12	Byrd	Jean					
13	Rodgers	Susan					
14	Chappet	Shannon					
15	Christopher	Thomas					
16	Makus	Michael					
17	Chapman	Angela					

Chapter 7 Exercise 1

Zoom 100%

FIGURE 7.33   The initial Chapter 7 Exercise 1 spreadsheet.

1. Type your name in cell A1.
2. Delete row 8.
3. Insert two rows between the current rows 1 and 2.
4. Set all titles to Bold type and place a border under the row 7 titles.
5. Enter the following grades:

NAME	TEST 1	TEST 2	HOMEWORK
Jones	71	89	100
Smith	42	74	88
DeTarka	100	93	93
Byrd	43	64	66
Rodgers	94	98	95
Chappet	84	94	84
Christopher	81	63	72
Makus	81	91	92
Chapman	93	98	97

6. Compute the total points for each student. Each test score is worth 200 points, so multiply each test score by 2. The homework score is worth 150, so multiply that score by 1.5 points. The English version of the formula is

$$((Test1 + Test2)*2) + (Homework*1.5) = Total\ Points$$

In cell F10, create a spreadsheet formula that will compute the total points for Jones entries. After entering the formula for Jones, use the Fill Down option to complete the entry for the other students.

7. Fill in the Average column by dividing the total points earned by a possible 550 points. Again, first complete the entry for Jones, then use the Fill Down for the other students. Format the averages as percent with two decimals.

8. Highlight all of the student information as a block of cells, and sort by the student's last name in ascending order. Your spreadsheet should look like Figure 7.34.

Chapter 7 Exercise 1

	A	B	C	D	E	F	G
1	Your name						
2							
3							
4	**Exercise 7-1**						
5							
6		**Introduction to Computing Grade Sheet**					
7							
8	**Name**					**Total**	
9	**Last**	**First**	**Test 1**	**Test 2**	**Homework**	**Points**	**Average**
10	Byrd	Jean	43	64	66	313	56.91%
11	Chapman	Angela	93	98	97	527.5	95.91%
12	Chappet	Shannon	84	94	84	482	87.64%
13	Christopher	Thomas	81	63	72	396	72.00%
14	DeTarka	Ron	100	93	93	525.5	95.55%
15	Jones	Robert	71	89	100	470	85.45%
16	Makus	Michael	81	91	92	482	87.64%
17	Rodgers	Susan	94	98	95	526.5	95.73%
18	Smith	Cynthia	42	74	88	364	66.18%
19							

FIGURE 7.34 The completed exercise 7-1A spreadsheet.

9. Save the spreadsheet using the Save As command. Name the spreadsheet **Exercise 7-1A Complete** and save it on your data disk.
10. Print the spreadsheet.

Exercise 7-1B

After completing Exercise 7-1A, you find that you need to enhance your spreadsheet to enable it to track class attendance and participation. Complete the following steps to accomplish this:

1. Insert five columns between the current columns B and C.
2. Label and format the new columns as shown in Figure 7.35.

	A	B	C	D	E	F	G	H
7								
8	**Name**					**Total**	**Attendance**	
9	**Last**	**First**	**Week 1**	**Week 2**	**Week 3**	**Absences**	**Points**	**Test 1**
10	Byrd	Jean						43

FIGURE 7.35 The new column headings after five rows are inserted.

3. Enter the absences for Weeks 1 through 3 as shown in Figure 7.36.

	A	B	C	D
7				
8	Name			
9	Last	Week 1	Week 2	Week 3
10	Byrd	1	0	0
11	Chapman	0	0	2
12	Chappet	1	2	1
13	Christopher	2	0	2
14	DeTarka	1	1	1
15	Jones	1	0	0
16	Makus	0	0	0
17	Rodgers	0	0	1
18	Smith	1	0	1

FIGURE 7.36   Enter these absence figures.

4. Use the SUM function to total all absences for Byrd in cell F10.
5. Use the Fill Down Function to complete the entries in column F.
6. Enter the following nested IF statement in cell G10 and fill down as needed to award attendance points based on these criteria:

   0 to 1 absence = 100 points

   2 to 3 absences = 50 points

   4 or more absences = 0 points

   Use this IF statement: =IF(F10<2,100,IF(F10<4,50,0))

7. Insert a new column between the existing columns B and C. Label it Participation. Format it to be bold and underlined, and adjust the column width to Best Fit.
8. Enter the participation points as displayed in Figure 7.37.

	A	B	C
8	**Name**		
9	**Last**	**First**	**Participation**
10	Byrd	Jean	82
11	Chapman	Angela	93
12	Chappet	Shannon	55
13	Christopher	Thomas	65
14	DeTarka	Ron	60
15	Jones	Robert	95
16	Makus	Michael	98
17	Rodgers	Susan	85
18	Smith	Cynthia	85

FIGURE 7.37   Enter these participation points in the new column.

9. Revise the Total Points formula in cell L10 to reflect the attendance and participation points. Attendance points in cell H10 are simply added to the total, and Participation points in cell C10 are multiplied by 1.5, then added. Use Fill Down to enter the revised formula in column L.
10. Recompute the Average in cell M9 based on a maximum of 800 points. Use Fill Down to enter the revised formula in column M.
11. Print the finished spreadsheet on two pages.
12. Use the Save As feature to save it as Exercise 7-1B Complete.
13. Close the spreadsheet and exit Works.

Exercise 7-2A: Developing a Payroll

Your firm uses the Works spreadsheet to calculate the payroll. The former payroll manager started to develop a spreadsheet to calculate the payroll, but left the company. Your job is to develop a spreadsheet similar to Figure 7.38 to accomplish this task.

	A	B	C	D	E	F	G	H
1	Your name							
2								
3			*Cody Construction Company*					
4								
5								
6	Employee	Hourly	Hours	Overtime	Gross	State	Federal	Net
7	Name	Rate	Worked	Hours	Pay	Tax	Tax	Pay
8	Jones, Ralp	6.85	28					
9	Setier, Shar	15.02	46					
10	Angus, Willi	11.38	40					
11	Carouso, Jo	9.52	40.5					
12	Bakuss, Sh	8.56	54.5					
13	Harrison, R	5.45	38					
14	Christopher	8.65	35					
15	Suetter, And	17.05	41					
16	Williamson,	6.48	51.5					
17	Chacel, Ste	11.23	41.25					

FIGURE 7.38   The initial spreadsheet for Exercise 7-2.

1. Load the spreadsheet *Exercise 7-2* from your data disk. It will appear as shown in Figure 7.38.

2. Type your name in cell A1.

3. Center and boldface the titles in rows 6 and 7. Set each column to a width that will display all data in the column. Create a border around cells A6 through H7.

4. Develop an IF statement in cell D8 to compute the number of Overtime hours. Overtime hours equal 0 if the employee works 40 hours or less, and total hours minus 40 if the employee works more than 40 hours. Use Fill Down to enter overtime hours for the other employees.

5. Compute gross pay in cell E8. Develop a formula to multiply the hourly rate times hours for the first 40 hours worked and the hourly rate times 1.5 for overtime hours. Use Fill Down as appropriate.

6. Compute taxes on the gross pay based on a rate of 5.5% for state tax and 32% for Federal tax.

7. Complete the Net Pay column.

8. Format all entries to comma format with two decimal positions. Format all entries in row 8 to currency with two decimals.

9. Save the spreadsheet as Exercise 7-2 Complete.

10. Print the spreadsheet changing the font and type size to print on one page.

Exercise 7-2B

Use the spreadsheet developed in Exercise 7-2A and make the following changes:

1. Change the hours Sharon Setier worked to 45.5.
2. Adjust Stephen Chacel's hourly rate to $7.95.
3. Sort the spreadsheet in alphabetical order by employee last name. Also, adjust the numeric formatting so that only the first row entry is in the Currency format.
4. Develop an IF statement to compute Federal taxes. The rate is 25% for the first $200 of earnings, and 31% for everything over $200.
5. Type PART B next to your name, and print the spreadsheet.
6. Save the spreadsheet as Exercise 7-2B Complete.
7. Close Works and exit Windows.

Exercise 7-2C

1. Replace the IF statement developed in part B above with a nested IF statement to compute Federal taxes. The rate is 20% for the first $300 of earnings, 25% for earnings of $300.01 to $500.00 and 35% for everything over $500.
2. Save the spreadsheet under the name Exercise 7-2B Nested.

ADVANCED SPREADSHEET OPERATIONS

ADVANCED FEATURES IN THE SPREADSHEET

The Works spreadsheet offers you great power and flexibility in a variety of situations. To get the maximum benefit from this powerful tool, however, you must learn to recognize how different problems can best be handled in the spreadsheet environment.

Works provides some helpful features for some of the difficult situations you will encounter when working with spreadsheets. These features, which are commonly found in most spreadsheet packages, include the use of table-based lookups, freezing spreadsheet titles, and altering the way in which recalculations occur on the values in the spreadsheet. Learning when and how to use these advanced features will allow you to reap the maximum reward from the Works spreadsheet package.

Using a table to look up information is often used in our everyday lives. For example, when you go to a store to make a purchase, you often find that you must pay a sales tax based on the amount of the purchase. Typically, the tax is calculated as a percentage of your purchase amount; however, you have probably noticed that a straight percentage will often not work correctly because of rounding problems. For example, at a tax rate of 5% on a purchase of 51¢, the tax is 2.55¢, but you are charged 3¢. Therefore, to provide consistency, tax tables let the sales clerk look up the exact tax amount. An example of a tax table is seen in Figure 8.1.

Sales Tax Table	
Sales Amount	*Tax*
.00 - .10	.00
.11 - .30	.01
.31 - .50	.02
.51 - .70	.03
.71 - .90	.04
.91 - 1.10	.05

FIGURE 8.1   A sales tax table created without using a computer.

This straightforward table method, widely used in many manual systems, forms the basis for spreadsheet functions that use tables. To use the table, a Works spreadsheet Lookup function, is available that can match a value in a given cell with a value in the table. When the values match, the spreadsheet selects a second value from the table in the same fashion a sales clerk selects the sales tax.

Since the value you wish to find will seldom match a value in the table exactly, the spreadsheet needs a process to determine when to stop searching for a match. The Works spreadsheet accomplishes this by arranging table data in a specific order, either ascending or descending. Then, when the table is searched, the spreadsheet can determine the appropriate range of values that contains the amount in question.

The Works spreadsheet contains two Lookup functions that work in the same way, but differ in the actual layout of the data table.

VLookup-Vertical Lookup Function

Perhaps the most common table lookup involves looking down a list of numbers until a match is found, as in the sales tax table in Figure 8.1. Works can do this same operation with the VLookup function. The general format of the VLookup function is similar to functions that you have already used and appears as:

=VLookup(LookupValue, RangeReference, ColumnNumber)

The LookupValue is the value you are looking for and must be a numeric value or a cell coordinate that contains a numeric value. This value is from the working spreadsheet and is the value that you are trying to match in the table. The lookup value for the sales tax example would be the sales amount.

The RangeReference describes the area of the spreadsheet that will be searched. The range reference describes a block of cells in the spreadsheet that contains all the cells used by the lookup function. The range will always consist of multiple rows and multiple columns. For example, if your table started in cell A2 and had entries to B6, the range would be A2:B6. This is illustrated in Figure 8.2.

The RangeReference ——

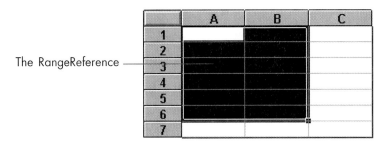

FIGURE 8.2 The VLookup RangeReference is the highlighted area.

The ColumnNumber informs the spreadsheet how you will look for a value in the table. This variable represents the number of columns to the right of the lookup value that the spreadsheet will search to find the value you want to retrieve. The column number in the sales tax example would be 1, since you read down the sales amount until you find the amount of the sale, then move one column to the right to find the amount of the tax. This idea may be better understood by referring to Figure 8.3.

The VLookup function entered in cell C1

Column number informs function to look at this column (one column to the right)

The value returned from the lookup function

C1		=VLOOKUP(0.48,A1:B6,1)		

Unsaved Spreadsheet 1

	A	B	C	D
1		0	0.02	
2	0.11	0.01		
3	0.31	0.02		
4	0.51	0.03		
5	0.71	0.04		
6	0.91	0.05		

FIGURE 8.3 The VLookup function in cell C1 automatically finds the tax on a 48 cent purchase. The table lookup returns a value of 0.02.

The function in Figure 8.3 specifies the RangeReference as cells A1 through B6. Notice that the table is set up as two columns, with the first column containing the values you wish to compare to the value you are seeking. The first column of values (column A) contains the *Lookup* values. The second column contains the values that will be returned from the VLookup function.

For example, to find how much tax will be assessed on a given purchase, look down the first column of Figure 8.3 until you find a number that is equal to or greater than the amount of your purchase. Assume you are looking for the tax on 48¢. If the number in the lookup value column (column A) matches the number you are looking for, the tax will be in the column directly to the right, which would be equivalent to a column number of 1. If the number you are looking for is less than the number in the table, the tax will be in the row to the right and immediately above, which is also a column number of 1. In this case, 48¢ is less than 51¢, so you should stop when you get to 51¢ in the first column and move up one row, and to the right finding the tax of 2¢.

Summarizing the Lookup Value in VLookup

Works uses the lookup value in the VLookup function to determine which row contains the function result. To do this, Works searches the first column of the table for the first value that *matches or exceeds* the function's key value. If the spreadsheet finds a match, the result of the function will be found in the row that contains the match. If Works finds a value that exceeds the key value, it uses the row immediately above, which is the largest value that does not exceed the key value. This selection is automatic and is not something you have to specify.

HLookup Horizontal Lookup Function

The horizontal lookup function works generally the same as the vertical lookup function, except that the data table is constructed horizontally. A horizontal table is illustrated in Figure 8.4.

The HLookup function entered in cell B4

The value returned from the lookup function

	B4		=HLOOKUP(0.48,A1:F2,1)			
Unsaved Spreadsheet 1						
	A	B	C	D	E	F
1		0.11	0.31	0.51	0.74	0.91
2	0	0.01	0.02	0.03	0.04	0.05
3						
4		0.02				

FIGURE 8.4   The HLookup function works well for information found in rows instead of columns.

This approach places the lookup values in a row rather than a column, with the lookup values being found in the first row and the values to be returned in the second row. The Works spreadsheet will use this table by comparing values across the first row (row 1 in Figure 8.4) until a value is found that is equal to or greater than the lookup value. If the table value is equal to the lookup value, the function returns the value immediately below the lookup value. If the lookup value is less than the number in the spreadsheet, the function returns the value to the left of the spreadsheet entry, which is the largest value not exceeding the lookup value.

The choice to use the vertical VLookup function or the horizontal HLookup function is usually determined by the kind of data that you need to include. When you are working with a table of data that is vertical in nature (like sales tax), use the VLookup function. When you are working with data laid out in a horizontal or row format, the HLookup will be easier to use. Normally, most users find they will use the VLookup function more frequently.

Finally, in both the VLookup and HLookup functions presented, the tables are shown as single dimensional because there is only one row or column used to store results. Both functions can easily be expanded by increasing the offset value to accommodate multiple rows and columns of results.

USING THE WORKS EASY CALC FEATURE

The Microsoft Works 4.0 spreadsheet offers many powerful functions like the Lookup functions we have just covered. It can, however, be difficult to recall how the functions work and where each function component must be entered to make the function work correctly. Works offers you a powerful assistant to help with the use of functions in the form of the Easy Calc feature shown in Figure 8.5.

Click here to use other functions in Works

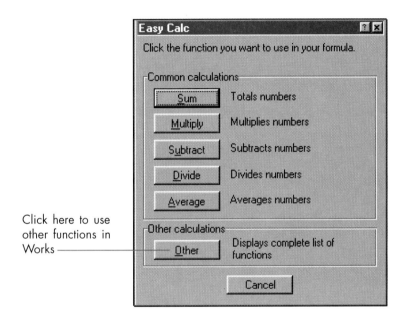

FIGURE 8.5 The Easy Calc window assists you with the development of formulas and functions and can be accessed from the Tools menu.

The Easy Calc window is accessed from the Tools menu of the spreadsheet and initially displays the most commonly used functions as seen in Figure 8.5. To access other functions available in Works, such as the Lookup functions, click the mouse on the Other button in the Easy Calc window. Figure 8.6 displays the categories of functions available in Works. Select the category you require, then click on the specific function you want to use. Finally, click on Insert to use the function. After you click the Insert button, Easy Calc will display a window similar to Figure 8.7 where you are prompted to enter the function variables. When all the variables are entered, click Next to inform Works where you want the finished function inserted in the spreadsheet.

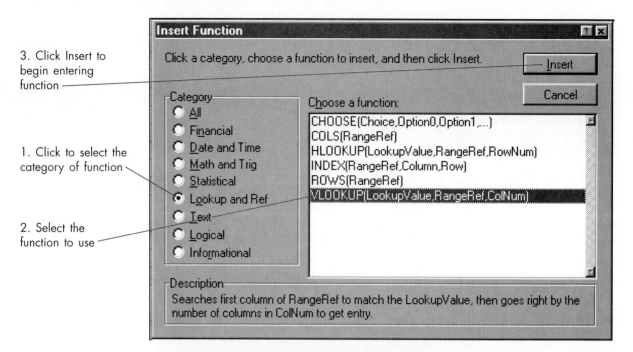

3. Click Insert to begin entering function

1. Click to select the category of function

2. Select the function to use

FIGURE 8.6 All Works functions can be accessed by clicking the Other button on the Easy Calc window.

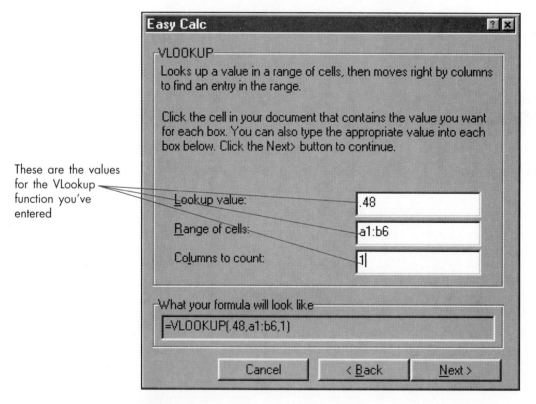

These are the values for the VLookup function you've entered

FIGURE 8.7 The window for the function you've selected appears. Fill in the boxes to complete the function.

Easy Calc is a great way to access the power of the Works functions without having to remember the details of how each one works. We suggest you routinely use the Easy Calc feature for any function you do not use regularly.

FREEZING TITLES IN ROWS AND COLUMNS

You have probably noticed it can be difficult to keep track of which row or column you are working in when a spreadsheet scrolls down or to the right. Although Works displays the current cell location on the cell coordinate line, you cannot be sure what the column title is after the column titles scroll off the screen. This same problem occurs when the cursor is moved to the right and the row labels and other information to the left scroll out of view. This situation occurs because the computer screen acts as a window to the spreadsheet and is much too small to display all the cells at one time.

Fortunately, Works provides a method for you to stop certain rows or columns from scrolling off the screen by locking them in place. This useful function is activated from the Format menu and is called the Freeze Titles option. The Format menu is shown in Figure 8.8.

Click here to freeze titles

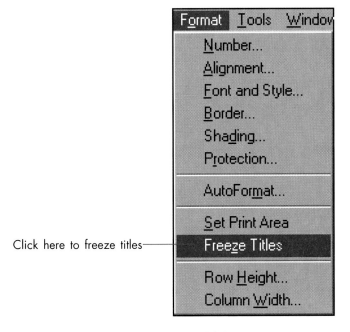

FIGURE 8.8   Pull down the Format menu to select the Freeze Titles option.

When the Freeze Titles option is selected, rows *above* and columns *to the left* of the cursor position will be frozen, or locked, in their current position on the screen. When the cursor is then moved off the screen, titles will stay in their frozen position. This is an excellent way to be sure you are entering data in the correct column or row, since you can always see the titles on the screen.

The Freeze Titles option also provides an easy method to view columns, located in different positions of the spreadsheet, side by side. If you wanted to compare column A with column E, you could freeze column A, then move the cursor to the right until column E scrolls to a position next to column A.

To unfreeze the titles, select the Freeze Titles option again from the Format menu since this option works as a toggle. The cursor can be any place in the spreadsheet to unfreeze titles.

USING A SPLIT SCREEN

Although the Freeze Titles option can be used to hold a given portion of the screen in view at all times, there are times when it is easier to split the screen into sections and see different parts of the spreadsheet in each window. The Split screen option can be used to do this and actually allows you to view up to four different portions of the spreadsheet at the same time.

Within each smaller window pane that results from the screen split, you can access the entire spreadsheet. Therefore, by moving around in different window panes, you can have different parts of the same spreadsheet visible in different panes.

Splitting the Screen into Windows with the Mouse

The easiest way to split the screen into window panes is with the mouse. First select the Split command from the Window menu. Special split bars and the word ADJUST appear on the spreadsheet screen as shown in Figure 8.9. Move the mouse, and the split bars will follow the mouse movement. When the windows are the desired size, click the left mouse button. This will cause the bars to become fixed and the screen to be split. Should you want only two panes, move the bar that is not needed off the screen, then click the mouse button. Any bar not on the screen when the mouse button is clicked is removed.

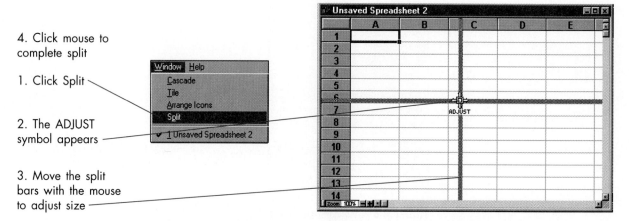

4. Click mouse to complete split

1. Click Split

2. The ADJUST symbol appears

3. Move the split bars with the mouse to adjust size

FIGURE 8.9 Choose the Split option under the Window menu, then use the mouse to adjust the sizes of the windows.

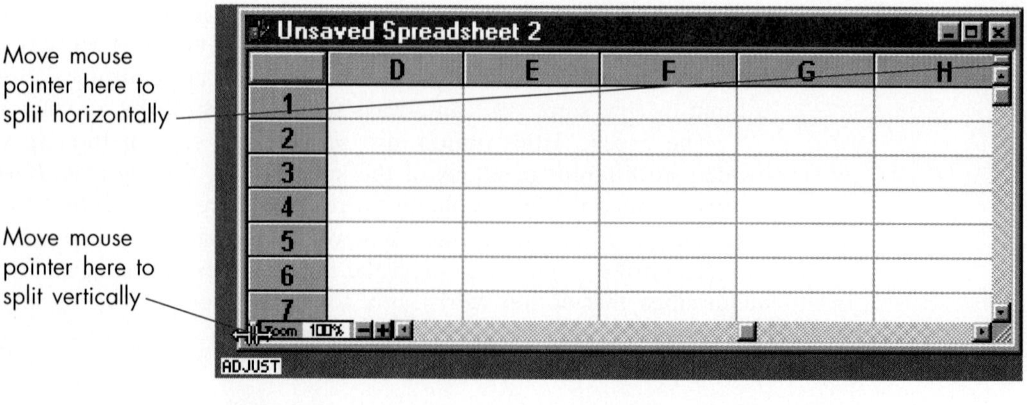

Move mouse pointer here to split horizontally

Move mouse pointer here to split vertically

FIGURE 8.10 You can also split the screen with the mouse and the split bars.

Figure 8.10 shows another method of splitting the screen using the mouse. Move the mouse pointer to the split bar located in the lower-left corner of the screen or the upper-right corner of the screen. You will see the word ADJUST appear when the pointer is over the split bar. Holding the mouse button down, move the bar to the desired location, then release the button. Repeat for the other split bar if desired.

Splitting the Screen with the Arrow Keys

You can also split the screen into multiple window panes with the keyboard. Select the Split option from the Window menu as shown in Figure 8.9, then use the arrow keys to move the split bars to the desired location. The Up and Down arrow keys move the horizontal line; the Left and Right arrow keys move the vertical line. Press the Enter key to complete the window split.

To remove a bar, use the arrow keys to move the bar completely off the screen at the left side or top, then press Enter. To change the size of the windows after they have been created, choose the Split window option again and move the bars to the location desired.

Moving Between Windows

Once the screen is split into windows by using either the arrow keys or the mouse, you will want to move from one window to another. To use the mouse, just click the pointer on the desired window and the cursor will be repositioned. To use the keyboard, press the F6 (Next Window) key. Each time the F6 key is pressed, the cursor will move clockwise to the next window. This process is illustrated in Figure 8.11. If there are only two horizontal windows, the cursor will move up and down between the windows. If there are only vertical windows, the cursor will move back and forth. The Shift/F6 (Previous Window) key combination will move the cursor in a counterclockwise direction.

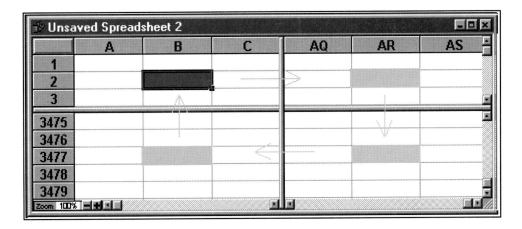

FIGURE 8.11   Move between windows with the mouse or the F6 key.

Notice that you can display several different parts of the same spreadsheet on one screen as seen in Figure 8.11. Here, you can see cells B2 and AR3477 on the same screen. This makes working with large spreadsheets much easier.

Closing the Windows

To close the windows and return to the standard screen, choose the Split window option and move the window separator bars off the screen with either the arrow keys or the mouse. This will close the windows and leave the screen as it was before windows were opened.

Remember, you have only one copy of the spreadsheet active, even though you may have multiple window panes. This means that any change to the spreadsheet from any pane is immediately reflected in all window panes.

MANUAL AND AUTOMATIC CALCULATION

Whenever a change is made to any part of a spreadsheet, Works will automatically update all the entries that are affected. This automatic recalculation feature of the spreadsheet is very handy and is the default setting for the Works spreadsheet. When large spreadsheets with many complex formulas are being used, however, the constant recalculation can be time-consuming even on a fast computer. This constant need to stop entering data and wait for the computer can be avoided by turning off the automatic recalculation feature and having Works recalculate only when you tell it to do so.

Selecting Manual Recalculation Mode

Automatic recalculation can be turned off by selecting the Options selection from the Tools menu. The Options window, as shown in Figure 8.12, will appear. Select the Use manual calculation option, then click on OK.

Click for manual calculation

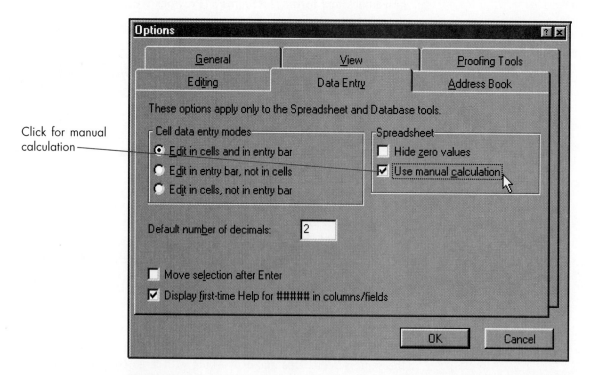

FIGURE 8.12   Activate manual calculation from the Options window selected by clicking the Options item under the Tools menu.

When the spreadsheet is operating in Manual Calculation mode and formulas have been altered but not recalculated, the word CALC will appear on the bottom right corner of the message line to let you know that a recalculation is needed. To instruct Works to recalculate, press the CALC Now (F9) key or select the Recalculate Now option from the Tools menu. To avoid errors caused by not recalculating after making changes, watch for the CALC indicator in the bottom right corner of the spreadsheet.

To return to the automatic calculation mode, select the Tools menu, choose the Options selection, then click on the Use manual calculation option again to remove the check mark from the box, and click OK.

DISPLAYING AND PRINTING FORMULAS

Once data and formulas have been entered into a spreadsheet, only the values are displayed on the screen. Whereas this is usually what you will be interested in, it can lead to a false sense of security, since any possible errors in the formulas are out of sight and out of mind. To avoid potential problems, experienced spreadsheet users will often display or print the spreadsheet formulas and examine them for both typographical and logic errors. The best way to do this is to display the formulas on the screen.

Displaying Formulas on the Screen

Formulas are displayed by using the Formulas option from the View menu, as shown in Figure 8.13. This option also operates as a toggle. Select it once and the formulas are displayed; select it a second time and the cell values resulting from the formula are displayed.

The checkmark indicates the formula display is on

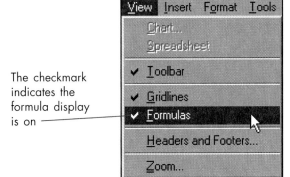

FIGURE 8.13   The Formulas option allows the diplay and printing of all formulas in the spreadsheet.

Printing Formulas

Spreadsheet formulas can be printed by selecting the Formulas option on the View menu before printing the spreadsheet. When formulas are printed, the printed columns become wider to accommodate the longer width of the formulas. As a result, it is likely that several pages will be needed to print all formulas in the spreadsheet. Use the Print Preview option under the File menu to check.

PRINTING PART OF A SPREADSHEET

Occasionally, only part of a spreadsheet needs to be printed. To do this, first select the area of the spreadsheet to be printed as a block, then choose the Set Print Area option from the Format menu as shown in Figure 8.14. Only the highlighted area will print. Should you then want to print the entire spreadsheet, reselect the full spreadsheet and use the Set Print Area option again. To select the entire spreadsheet quickly, use the Select All option found under the Edit menu.

Highlight the part of the spreadsheet to print, then click here

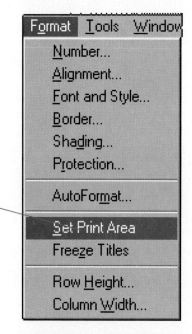

FIGURE 8.14   Print a selected part of the spreadsheet by using the Set Print Area option under the Format menu.

PRINTING TITLES ON EACH PAGE

The first few rows and the leftmost column usually contain titles or other information that help identify the contents of the columns and rows. You will generally want this information included on each printed page. When a spreadsheet is printed that requires more than one page, however, titles normally print only on the first page. To force these titles to print on all pages of the spreadsheet, use the Freeze Titles option from the Format menu to freeze the desired information before you print. The Freeze Titles option is another example of a toggled option, and when it is selected, frozen titles will be printed on each page. When Freeze Titles is selected again, title printing is turned off.

Printing Row and Column Headers and Gridlines

The row and column headers are the numbers down the left-hand side of the screen and the letters across the top of the screen. They are usually not included in a Works spreadsheet printout. Occasionally when you are testing a spreadsheet or checking it for errors, you will want these headers included on the printout. This feature is activated by choosing the Page Setup option from the File menu, then selecting the Other Options folder and turning on the Print row and column headers option. The window shown in Figure 8.15 is displayed when you choose the Page Setup selection from the File menu. To display the Other Options area, click the folder's tab in the Page Setup window as seen in Figure 8.15.

The printing of Gridlines is also activated on the Other Options folder in the Page Setup window. When the Gridline option is selected, Works will place a box or border around all the active cells in the spreadsheet.

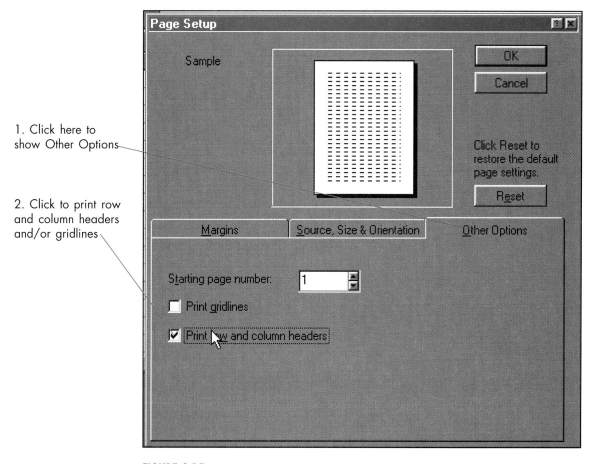

FIGURE 8.15   Print row and column headers using the Other Options folder of the Page Setup window.

The real value of an electronic spreadsheet is its ability to manipulate data in ways that can provide information to aid decision-makers. It is important to remember that the spreadsheet cannot reach a decision independently and the information in the spreadsheet is only as good as the data and formulas used in its development. This important concept can easily be forgotten when working with tools as powerful as the Works spreadsheet, and probably represents the spreadsheet's biggest weakness.

Problems well-suited to spreadsheet analysis are often referred to as "what if" questions. Some examples are as follows:

- If inflation increased by 2% a year for three years, what would happen to my average business expenses?
- If the new warehouse were financed for twelve years rather than eight, what would be the additional finance charges?
- If production were increased by 20%, what would be the additional labor costs?

Assuming that the spreadsheet is formulated correctly, the answers to these and similar questions can be found quickly and easily. Similar questions and techniques used to answer them are covered in this chapter's tutorial.

CHAPTER 8 SELF-TEST

1. Set up a table to locate a monthly commission rate for the sales representatives of a firm. If a salesperson sells more than $100,000, a 6% sales commission is paid. If sales are more than $250,000, an 8% commission on sales is earned. For sales more than $500,000, 9% is paid.
2. What is the difference between an HLookup and a VLookup function?
3. How would you set up the table lookup in question 1 in a spreadsheet? Assume that the table will start in cell A1.
4. What steps would you use to develop an HLookup function using the Easy Calc feature or Works?
5. If you wanted to freeze the first three rows and the first two columns of a spreadsheet as titles, what cell should the cursor be on when you set the Freeze Titles option?
6. Explain two ways to split a spreadsheet screen into multiple windows.
7. What is the difference between automatic and manual recalculation in a spreadsheet? How can you change from one method to the other?
8. You are working with a large spreadsheet in manual recalculation mode. How do you know when you should force the spreadsheet to recalculate? How do you instruct the spreadsheet to update its calculations?
9. You want to print only rows 1 through 5 and columns A through D of a large spreadsheet. What procedure should you follow to do this?
10. How can you print titles on each page of a printout?

For this tutorial you will modify an existing spreadsheet stored on disk. The modifications include changing one row of formulas, adding a lookup table, and using advanced concepts to manipulate the spreadsheet in Figure 8.16.

Chapter 8 Tutorial

	A	B	C	D	E	F	G	H
1	Your name							
2								
3			Cashflow Projections					
4			Blue Ridge Sun and Fun T-Shirts					
5								
6								
7								Total
8	STORE	July	August	Sept.	Oct.	Nov.	Dec.	Income
9	Lakeshore	14,186.48	12,842.23	9,581.02	7,821.95	11,526.22	15,764.89	71,722.79
10	Downtown	7,865.45	6,682.15	10,895.60	8,572.33	5,002.01	6,492.52	45,510.06
11	Beachside	13,256.18	13,205.08	7,923.54	8,851.69	9,245.78	12,865.12	65,347.39
12								
13	Total Income	35,308.11	32,729.46	28,400.16	25,245.97	25,774.01	35,122.53	182,580.24
14								
15	Fixed Expenses							
16	Rent	3,500.00	3,500.00	3,500.00	3,500.00	3,500.00	3,500.00	21,000.00
17	Salaries	11,645.00	11,645.00	11,645.00	11,645.00	11,645.00	11,645.00	69,870.00
18	Telephone	238.00	238.00	238.00	238.00	238.00	238.00	1,428.00
19	Total Fixed Expenses	15,383.00	15,383.00	15,383.00	15,383.00	15,383.00	15,383.00	92,298.00
20								
21	Variable Expenses							
22	Electric	3,883.89	3,600.24	3,124.02	2,777.06	2,835.14	3,863.48	20,083.83
23	Delivery	3,001.19	2,782.00	2,414.01	2,145.91	2,190.79	2,985.42	15,519.32
24	Misc. Expenses	2,824.65	2,618.36	2,272.01	2,019.68	2,061.92	2,809.80	14,606.42
25	Waste	1,871.33	1,734.66	1,505.21	1,338.04	1,366.02	1,861.49	9,676.75
26	Total Variable Expense	11,581.06	10,735.26	9,315.25	8,280.68	8,453.88	11,520.19	59,886.32
27								
28	Total Income	35,308.11	32,729.46	28,400.16	25,245.97	25,774.01	35,122.53	182,580.24
29	Minus Total Expenses	26,964.06	26,118.26	24,698.25	23,663.68	23,836.88	26,903.19	152,184.32
30	Profit Before Taxes	8,344.05	6,611.20	3,701.91	1,582.29	1,937.13	8,219.34	30,395.92
31	Taxes	2,628.38	2,082.53	1,166.10	498.42	610.20	2,589.09	9,574.72
32	Profit After Taxes	5,715.67	4,528.67	2,535.81	1,083.87	1,326.94	5,630.25	20,821.21
33								
34	Actual Profit Margin	0.16	0.14	0.09	0.04	0.05	0.16	0.11
35	Over/Under Margin	0.04	0.02	-0.03	-0.08	-0.07	0.04	-0.01
36								
37	=================================Working Expenses=================================							
38	Fixed Expenses							
39	Tax Rate	31.5%		Variable Expenses				
40	Rent	3,500.00		Electric		11.00%		
41	Salaries	11,645.00		Delivery		8.50%		
42	Telephone	238.00		Misc. Expenses		8.00%		
43				Waste		5.30%		
44	Expected Profit Margin:	12.0%						

FIGURE 8.16 The Chapter 8 Tutorial spreadsheet as it is loaded from your disk.

Follow these steps to begin the tutorial:

1. Start Microsoft Works.
2. Open the spreadsheet called Chapter 8 Tutorial.
3. Save the spreadsheet with the Save As command to a file called **Chapter 8 Tutorial (finished)**. This will allow you to periodically save your work while you complete the tutorial.
4. The spreadsheet contains information on income, expenses, profits, losses, and taxes for the three stores of the Blue Ridge Sun and Fun T-shirt Company. Fixed expenses are assumed to be the same for each month. Variable expenses are calculated as a percent of the store's income.
5. Enter your name in cell A1.

Using a Lookup Table to Calculate Taxes

State tax calculations are based on a working figure stored in cell B39 and are computed at a fixed rate. This rate has changed, and you would like to alter the spreadsheet so that the tax rate depends on the amount of profit that is earned. Figure 8.17 shows how the taxes will be computed. For example, if the firm's profits before taxes were $22,075, the correct tax rate would be found at the fifth row of the table, which would correspond to a tax rate of 23%.

Profit More Then	But Less Then	Tax Rate
0	2,001	.10
2,001	3,501	.13
3,501	7,001	.15
7,001	15,001	.19
15,001	40,001	.23
40,001	75,001	.26
75,001		.30

FIGURE 8.17   The noncomputerized tax table you will need to enter in the spreadsheet.

HINT: Recall that the spreadsheet lookup function searches for a greater than or equal to condition when it searches a table. If the condition is equal, it uses the value to the right of the matched key. If the condition is less, it uses the lower value above the row where the matched key is. Therefore, if the value 2001 is used as the less than key, the correct percent rate should be stored in the row above this key.

Entering the Table into the Spreadsheet

1. Use the F5 key to move Cell B47. Enter *.1* in cell B47.
2. Complete the table as shown in Figure 8.18. Format the cell contents of cells A48:A53 with commas and zero decimal positions. Format the values in cells B47:B53 in the Fixed format with two decimal positions.

	A	B
47		0.1
48	2001	0.13
49	3501	0.15
50	7001	0.19
51	15001	0.23
52	40001	0.26
53	75001	0.3

FIGURE 8.18   Enter these tax table values in the spreadsheet.

Entering the VLookup Function

The Profit Before Taxes for July is stored in cell B30 and the lookup table is located in cells A47 through B53, so this is the range reference. The column number is 1, since the table values are located one column to the right of the lookup value column. The function would appear as

=VLookup(B30,A47:B53,1)

Before you enter this function, consider that you will use the Fill Down or Fill Right commands to cause the function in cell B30 to be copied into other cells. Therefore, you will need to specify the table range using absolute coordinates. This revised function will look like

=VLookup(B30,$A$47:$B$53,1)

Finally, note that the Profit Before Taxes must be multiplied by the tax rate to arrive at the total tax amount. The resulting final formula is

=B30*VLookup(B30,$A$47:$B$53,1)

1. Move to cell B31.
2. Enter *=B30*VLookup(B30,$A$47:$B$53,1)*.
3. The new value in B31 should be 1,585.37.
4. Select cells B31 through H31 as a block.
5. Use the Fill Right command from the Edit menu.
6. Press the Left arrow key to cancel the block.
7. Compare your figures with those shown in Figure 8.19.
8. Use the Save option from the File menu to save the current spreadsheet as *Chapter 8 Tutorial (finished).*

	A	B	C	D	E	F	G	H
31	Taxes	1,585.37	991.68	555.29	158.23	193.71	1,561.67	6,991.06
32	Profit After Taxes	6,758.68	5,619.52	3,146.62	1,424.06	1,743.42	6,657.67	25,349.97

FIGURE 8.19   The taxes row after the Fill Right operation.

Freezing Column and Row Titles

To prevent the titles in column A and rows 7 and 8 from scrolling off the screen, use the Freeze Titles command from the Format window.

Position cursor here to freeze titles

	A	B	C
7			
8	STORE	July	August
9	Lakeshore	14,186.48	12,842.23
10	Downtown	7,865.45	6,682.15
11	Beachside	13,256.18	13,205.08

Chapter 8 Tutorial (finished)

FIGURE 8.20   Freeze the row and column titles before scrolling through the spreadsheet.

1. Use the F5 key to move the cursor to cell A7. Then use the arrow keys to position the cursor at cell B9 as shown in Figure 8.20. Be sure the titles in rows 7 and 8 are showing.
2. Select Freeze Titles from the Format menu.
3. Use the down arrow key to scroll down in the spreadsheet until row 34 appears directly under the frozen titles in rows 7 and 8 as shown in Figure 8.21. You should be able to see the Over/Under Profit Margin figures in row 35, as well as the expected Profit Margin in row 44.

Using Manual Calculation

1. To better see the changes in the spreadsheet, change to manual recalculation by choosing the Options item from the Tools menu, then clicking the Use manual calculation box in the window.
2. Click the mouse on cell B44 (the expected profit margin).
3. Management is planning to increase the expected profit margin to 18% and wants to know in which months the stores would meet that target. To find out, enter *.18* in cell B44 and press Enter. Notice that the numbers did not change in row 35, but the word CALC appears on the bottom right corner of the screen. This indicates you must initiate manual recalculation.
4. Press the F9 (Calculate now) key and note the change in row 35. Which months actually meet such a goal today?
5. Change cell B44 back to .12, press Enter, then press F9 to recalculate.
6. Again select the Options item from the Tools menu and turn off the manual calculation option by clicking it.

	A	B	C	D	E	F	G	H	I
1	Your name								
2									
3				Cashflow Projections					
4				Blue Ridge Sun and Fun T-Shirts					
5									
6									
7								Total	
8	STORE	July	August	Sept.	Oct.	Nov.	Dec.	Income	
34	Actual Profit Margin	0.19	0.17	0.11	0.06	0.07	0.19	0.14	
35	Over/Under Margin	0.07	0.05	-0.01	-0.06	-0.05	0.07	0.02	
36									
37	==========================Working Expenses===========================								
38	Fixed Expenses								
39	Tax Rate	31.5%		Variable Expenses					
40	Rent	3,500.00		Electric		11.00%			
41	Salaries	11,645.00		Delivery		8.50%			
42	Telephone	238.00		Misc. Expenses		8.00%			
43				Waste		5.30%			
44	Expected Profit Margin:	12.0%							

FIGURE 8.21   Position the spreadsheet so that row 34 is directly under the titles in row 8.

Splitting the Screen into Multiple Windows

While freezing titles allows quite a bit of flexibility in positioning spreadsheet data under headings and the like, it does not allow two different parts of the spreadsheet to be scrolled independently. Splitting the screen into multiple window panes will allow this, as well as allow entries in different parts of the sheet to be viewed together.

Vertical split bar is moved off the screen to the left

Move horizontal bar to row 27

	A	B	C	D	E	F	G	H	I
20									
21	Variable Expenses								
22	Electric	3,883.89	3,600.24	3,124.02	2,777.06	2,835.14	3,863.48	20,083.83	
23	Delivery	3,001.19	2,782.00	2,414.01	2,145.91	2,190.79	2,985.42	15,519.32	
24	Misc. Expenses	2,824.65	2,618.36	2,272.01	2,019.68	2,061.92	2,809.80	14,606.42	
25	Waste	1,871.33	1,734.66	1,505.21	1,338.04	1,366.02	1,861.49	9,676.75	
26	Total Variable Expense	11,581.06	10,735.26	9,315.25	8,280.68	8,453.88	11,520.19	59,886.32	
28	Total Income	35,308.11	32,729.46	28,400.16	25,245.97	25,774.01	35,122.53	162,580.24	
29	Minus Total Expenses	26,964.06	26,118.26	24,698.25	23,663.68	23,836.88	26,903.19	152,184.32	
30	Profit Before Taxes	8,344.05	6,611.20	3,701.91	1,582.29	1,937.13	8,219.34	30,395.92	
31	Taxes	1,585.37	991.68	555.29	158.23	193.71	1,561.67	6,991.06	
32	Profit After Taxes	6,758.68	5,619.52	3,146.62	1,424.06	1,743.42	6,657.67	25,349.97	
33									
34	Actual Profit Margin	0.19	0.17	0.11	0.06	0.07	0.19	0.14	
35	Over/Under Margin	0.07	0.05	-0.01	-0.06	-0.05	0.07	0.02	
36									
37	==========================Working Expenses===========================								
38	Fixed Expenses								
39	Tax Rate	31.5%		Variable Expenses					

FIGURE 8.22   Split the screen into two windows to view different parts of the spreadsheet.

1. Unfreeze the titles by selecting Freeze Titles from the Format menu.
2. Use the F5 key to move the cursor to cell A39.
3. Select Split from the Window menu.
4. Move the horizontal split bar with the mouse pointer until it is on row 31. Move the vertical split bar to the left until it is off the screen as shown in Figure 8.22.
5. Click the mouse button or press Enter to complete the split.
6. Click on the upper or lower window, then use the arrow keys to move the spreadsheet until the screen display looks like Figure 8.23. Be sure you can see rows 22 through 32 in the top window and rows 39 through 44 in the bottom window. If rows 22 through 32 are not visible, use the mouse to reposition the horizontal split bar until the rows are visible.
7. Change the electric cost from 11% to 6% by typing *.06* into cell F40 as seen in Figure 8.23. Since the window is split, you will be able to see that the expense and profit information is updated immediately.
8. Change the value of cell F40 back to 11% and verify that the spreadsheet is updated.

You should be able to see rows 22 through 32 here

Electric costs change from 11% to 6%

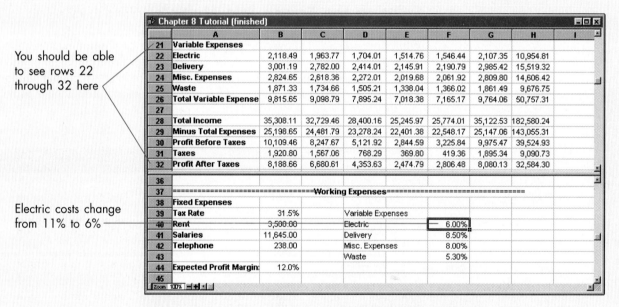

FIGURE 8.23   Observing changes to profitability based on working figure changes with the split screen.

Displaying Formulas

1. Select Split from the Window menu and use the mouse to move the horizontal split bar to the top of the screen. This will return the screen to one window.

2. Click the mouse, or press Enter, to complete the Split option and return the screen to one window.

3. Choose Select All from the Edit menu to highlight all cells.

4. Select the Font and Style option from the Format menu. Choose the Arial font, size 6, from the Font and Style window as shown in Figure 8.24. If the Arial font is not available, use the Times font instead. Click OK or press Enter. The smaller font allows you to see more of the spreadsheet on the screen.

5. Use the F5 key to move to cell A7 and cancel the block.

6. Select Formulas from the View menu.

7. The columns have automatically been made wider so that Works can display the complete formula as shown in Figure 8.25. The width will be reduced when the Formulas option is turned off.

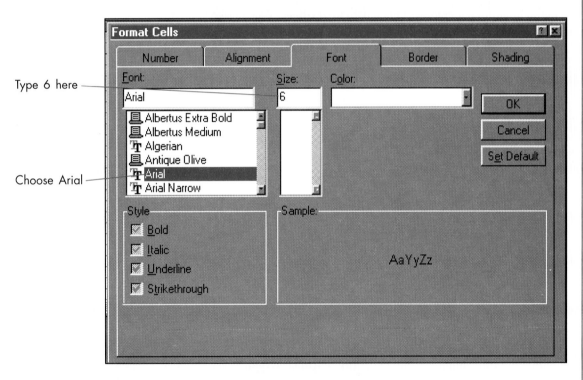

FIGURE 8.24   Use the Font and Style window to change type styles.

Note that the column width has increased

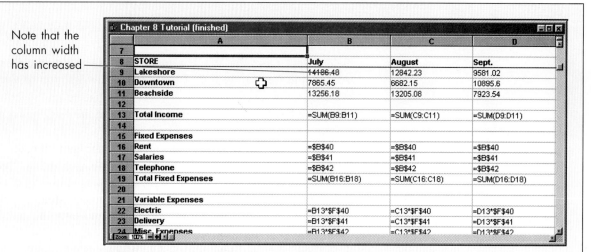

FIGURE 8.25 The Formulas option under the View menu will display cell formulas.

Printing Formulas with Row and Column Labels

1. Choose the Page Setup option from the File menu. Click the Other Options folder if necessary.
2. Select "Print row and column headers as shown" in Figure 8.26, and click OK.
3. Select Print from the File menu, choose pages 1 through 2 in the print pages options and click on OK.

Click to display other options

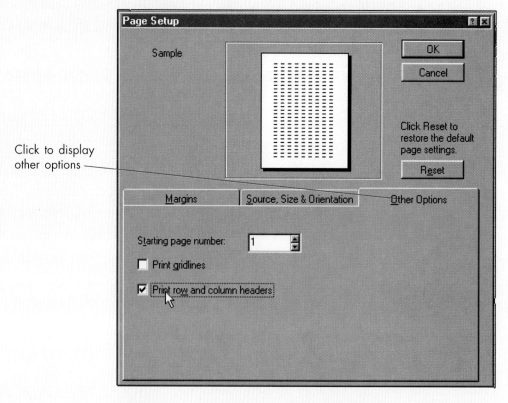

FIGURE 8.26 Select the Print row and column headers from the Page Setup window.

Returning the Spreadsheet to the Normal View

1. Select Formulas from the View menu to turn off the formula display option.
2. Choose the Select All option from the Edit menu to highlight all cells.
3. Change the font to Arial, size 8.
4. Click the mouse on cell A7 to cancel the highlighted block of cells.

USING THE SPREADSHEET TO ANSWER WHAT IF QUESTIONS

1. If rents were raised to $4,500 each month, what effect would it have on total profit after taxes? Recall different profit levels are taxed at different rates.
   a) Move the cursor to cell A7.
   b) Split the screen vertically by positioning the vertical split bar between columns B and C. Move the horizontal bar until it covers row 9. Your computer screen is now split into 4 windows.
   c) Make the bottom right window active (press the F6 key), then use the arrow keys to position the window so that cell H32 is visible and you can observe the current profits of $25,349.97.
   d) Activate the bottom left window, then use the F5 key to move to cell B40, the rent working figure.
   e) Type 4500 in cell B40 and observe cell H32 while you press the Enter key.
   f) Notice that cell H32 now shows the revised profits of $20,284.01.
2. If the change to the $4,500 rent per month were made, what effect would this have on the total six-month profit margin?
   a) After changing the rent to $4,500, the profit margin in cell H34 is 0.11 or 11%. Change the rent back to $3,500 in cell B40 to see that the original profit margin was 14%. Thus, after the change was made, the profit margin dropped 3%.
3. If waste were cut by 2%, what impact would this change have on the total waste expense?
   a) Remove the vertical window split, then split the screen horizontally by positioning the split bar about halfway down the screen. Position the windows so that both cells H25 and F43 are visible.
   b) Total waste is calculated as a percentage of total sales and is stored as a working figure in cell F43. Be sure the bottom window is active, then use F5 to move the cursor to F43.
   c) Enter 0.033 (a 2% decline) in cell F43. Press Enter and note the change in cell H25.
   d) The new waste figure is $6,025.15, a decrease of $3,651.60.
   e) Enter .053 back into F43 and remove the split bars to return the screen to the normal display.

4. If the Lakeshore store had increased its sales by $10,000 in July, what effect would that have had on the actual profit margin for the six-month period?

   a) Move the cursor to cell B9.

   b) Position the split bars on row 12, and between columns B and C. Split the screen into four windows.

   c) Click the mouse pointer on the lower-right window.

   d) Move to cell H34 (use the F5 key or the arrow keys) and notice the profit margin.

   e) Click the mouse on the upper-left window and position the cursor on cell B9.

   f) Enter 24186.48 in cell B9. Press Enter while observing the profit figure in cell H34 change.

   g) Notice that the profit value in cell H34 is instantly recalculated to show the new 16% profit level.

EXIT FROM THE WORKS PROGRAM

1. Exit Works and reply NO when asked if you want to save your recent changes to Chapter 8 Tutorial (Finished).
2. Close Windows.
3. Shut down the computer.

HANDS-ON PRACTICE

Exercise 8-1A

A common function you will use in a spreadsheet is the payment function, which can determine the payment for any length of time or amount. The payment function can also determine an amortization or loan repayment schedule, as shown in this exercise. Since these schedules tend to be rather long, it is helpful to use the Freeze Titles and/or the Split screen options when you are working on them. Be sure to read the *Hints* for the exercise.

EXERCISE DESCRIPTION

You have decided to purchase a new automobile that will require you to finance $12,500. Before you go shopping, you want to know your monthly payment on the loan and the repayment or amortization schedule of the loan. Finally, you want to see the total sum of all the payments you will make.

Assume that you can finance the car for 60 months at a rate of 8.5% per year. To develop a solution, first create a spreadsheet like the one shown in Figure 8.27.

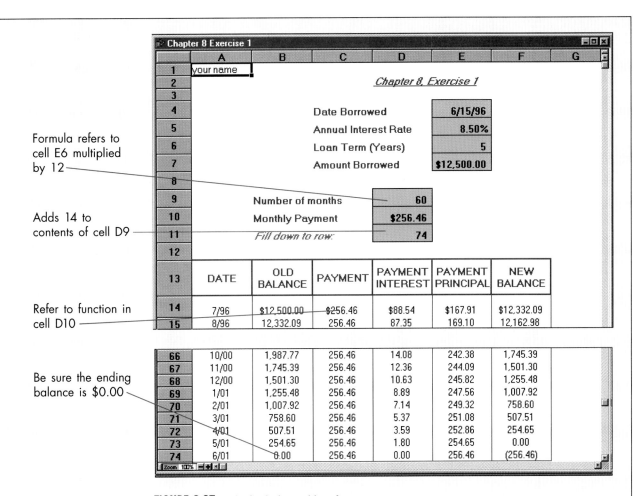

Formula refers to cell E6 multiplied by 12

Adds 14 to contents of cell D9

Refer to function in cell D10

Be sure the ending balance is $0.00

	A	B	C	D	E	F	G
1	your name						
2				*Chapter 8, Exercise 1*			
3							
4				Date Borrowed	6/15/96		
5				Annual Interest Rate	8.50%		
6				Loan Term (Years)	5		
7				Amount Borrowed	$12,500.00		
8							
9			Number of months	60			
10			Monthly Payment	$256.46			
11			*Fill down to row:*	74			
12							
13	DATE	OLD BALANCE	PAYMENT	PAYMENT INTEREST	PAYMENT PRINCIPAL	NEW BALANCE	
14	7/96	$12,500.00	$256.46	$88.54	$167.91	$12,332.09	
15	8/96	12,332.09	256.46	87.35	169.10	12,162.98	
66	10/00	1,987.77	256.46	14.08	242.38	1,745.39	
67	11/00	1,745.39	256.46	12.36	244.09	1,501.30	
68	12/00	1,501.30	256.46	10.63	245.82	1,255.48	
69	1/01	1,255.48	256.46	8.89	247.56	1,007.92	
70	2/01	1,007.92	256.46	7.14	249.32	758.60	
71	3/01	758.60	256.46	5.37	251.08	507.51	
72	4/01	507.51	256.46	3.59	252.86	254.65	
73	5/01	254.65	256.46	1.80	254.65	0.00	
74	6/01	0.00	256.46	0.00	256.46	(256.46)	

Zoom 100%

FIGURE 8.27 The finished spreadsheet for Exercise 8-1A.

HINTS FOR EXERCISE 8-1   When you enter the spreadsheet data, format the information as follows:

a) Use the Font and Style window to display all titles as boldface and dark blue (if you have a color monitor). Set the row height to 18 for rows 4 through 12. Set the row height to 36 for row 13 and 22 for row 14.

b) Use the Format menu options for Shading and Border to shade cells E4 through E7 and D9 through D11 using light Cyan (this is the Foreground color). Place a border around these cells with the border option (use the Top and Bottom options to place the border between the cells).

c) Center align the titles in row 13 both horizontally and vertically using the Alignment option. Place dark blue (use black if you do not have a color monitor) borders around all row 13 titles and between the columns as in Figure 8.27.

d) For simplicity, assume that payments are due every 30 days from the date borrowed, and use the Date format option (MM/YY) to format dates in the date column.

e) This spreadsheet makes extensive use of working figures, so *do not* type all the values in row 14 and 15. Instead, reference the working figures and use formulas to develop rows 14 and 15.

f) Be sure to use the Payment function in cell D10 (reference the working figures in E5 through E7, and cell D9). If you do not use this function, you will not end up with a zero balance at the end of the spreadsheet.

NOTE: If the value in at the end of the spreadsheet is not zero, you probably typed in the payment amount ($256.46) in cell C14, rather than referencing the payment calculation in cell D10. This will cause a small rounding error, so be sure to reference the function in cell D10.

g) Develop your formulas carefully (you will need to use absolute references), and use the Fill commands to copy them throughout the spreadsheet.

h) Pay special attention to absolute referencing (you will need to use it).

i) You will save time by formatting the first row (including the borders), then filling down since all formats will then be copied.

j) The *Fill down to row* entry simply adds 14 (the first row with formulas) to the number of months. This will inform you of how many rows to fill down.

k) Remember that the interest paid each month is charged on the new balance amount, therefore as the balance is reduced, the interest will decline.

l) Finally, use the Split screen option when examining the spreadsheet to answer questions. This makes it much easier to compare information in different cells.

Since all of row 15 in Figure 8.27 is developed with formulas, you are ready to use the Fill command. You will have 74 rows in your completed spreadsheet. When you are done, save the spreadsheet as *Chapter 8 Exercise 1A.* Then change the print font to a size that will let you print on one page (you may need to adjust the page margins), such as Arial or Times size 8 or 6.

Print the spreadsheet, including the row and column labels. Then print the spreadsheet showing the formulas.

Exercise 8-1B

You have just decided that you would really like a nicer car, so you are now planning to borrow $18,000 for 48 months. You have also learned that the interest rate will be 12% per year.

Change your spreadsheet to accommodate these new figures, and type *Part B* after your name. Set the print area to print the changed rows and print out the new spreadsheet.

NOTE: This exercise allows you to use the power of the spreadsheet to automatically recalculate information after changes are made. If you have used the formulas correctly, all you will need to change are the three new figures for amount, term, and interest rate.

The VLookup and IF functions in Works can assist in making a spreadsheet easier to use and understand. Works 4.0 allows you to not only use numbers in these functions, but also letters or comments. In this exercise, you will use this feature to modify an earlier spreadsheet.

Exercise 7-1 had you create a grade sheet for a class of students. The spreadsheet you created computed student averages based on their test scores, attendance, and other factors. It did not, however, assign a letter grade. Also, the spreadsheet did not give any comments back to the students. In this exercise, we will modify the Exercise 7-1 spreadsheet to perform these functions. Don't forget to use the Easy Calc function if you need assistance.

1. Load the completed Exercise 7-1B from your disk. If you did not complete Exercise 7-1, do so at this time.
2. Split the screen vertically between columns B and C. Move to the right window and add the title, Letter Grade in column N and Comments in column O.
3. Create a VLookup table in cells A22:B26 to return a letter grade. This table is shown in Figure 8.28. The VLookup function will be typed in cell N10 and uses the average in cell M10 lookup value.
4. Create a second VLookup table to automatically insert comments in column O. This table will appear as shown in Figure 8.29
5. Type the VLookup function in cell O10 for student comments, then fill it down. Don't forget to use absolute references for the function in the range reference.
6. Save the spreadsheet with the SAVE AS option. Name it *Exercise 8-2 Complete*.
7. Change the column width to zero (0) for columns D, E, and F. Change the paper orientation to landscape in Page Setup and modify the font size to enable the spreadsheet to print on one page. Use the Print Preview to check that the spreadsheet will fit before printing.

These are the letter grades

	A	B
22		F
23	0.6	D
24	0.7	C
25	0.8	B
26	0.9	A

FIGURE 8.28 The VLookup table for Exercise 8-2.

	L	M	N
21		See me right away.	
22	0.6	Please check with me.	
23	0.7		
24	0.8	Keep up the good work	
25	0.9	Great job!	

FIGURE 8.29 The VLookup table for comments. Note the blank next to the .7. Enter a quotation mark and press the space bar in cell M23.

Exercise 8-2B

1. Enter the following changes to the spreadsheet created in part A:

   Cynthia Smith's homework score should be 38.

   Thomas Christopher's participation should be 50.

   Jean Byrd's Test 1 score should be 75.

2. Print the spreadsheet on one page. You do not have to save these changes.

Exercise 8-3

A friend has asked you to develop a loan amortization table (similar to Exercise 8-1A) for her townhouse purchase. She will borrow $110,000 at an interest rate that is dependent on the length of the loan and wants you to determine her **monthly** payment for various periods of time. She began to develop a spreadsheet to compute these payments, but wants your help to complete it. Open the spreadsheet called Exercise 8-3 Setup on your disk. You will want to use appropriate functions to complete the spreadsheet.

Each different loan period carries with it a different interest rate with the appropriate rate and loan duration shown below. Create a Vlookup table in cells H3:I7 for this information.

Your friend also wants to find the total interest charge for each of these payment options. Do this by subtracting the amount borrowed from the Payment sum. Show this new total in cell G11 and label it Interest Paid. Print out the entire spreadsheet for the 10-year option and the first page for the 20- and 30-year options.

INTEREST RATE TABLE	
Time	**Rate (per year)**
10 years	9.00%
15 years	9.50%
20 years	10.00%
25 years	10.25%
30 years	10.50%

CREATING AND USING CHARTS

LEARNING OBJECTIVES

When you've completed this chapter, you will be able to:

- State how a chart can help convey information.
- Describe different types of charts.
- Select the best chart for a given situation.
- Explain how Works creates a chart.
- Be able to draw a chart from spreadsheet data.
- Add data labels and borders to a chart.
- Create titles for a chart and change the type fonts.
- Alter a chart's scales to represent spreadsheet data.
- Print a chart in normal and landscape modes.

GETTING STARTED IN SPREADSHEET CHARTS

This chapter will introduce you to the powerful graphing tools offered in Microsoft Works 4.0 for Windows 95. Graphing tools, or charting tools, as they are called in Works, allow you to represent complex data so they can be quickly understood. Further, the tools allow you to make professional and powerful presentations that allow your audience to focus quickly on the items you are stressing. The old saying *a picture is worth a thousand words* certainly holds true when data are presented in a chart.

CREATING CHARTS

Although many other spreadsheet programs call the graphic display of data graphs, the Works software package refers to them as charts. You will find, however, that the method that Works uses to create and display charts is virtually the same as that of other software. Works allows you to create many different types of charts and permits you to specify many variations within each chart type. Because there are so many different options available, one of the most important skills you will need to work effectively with charts is the ability to recognize which chart type to use in a given situation. Once you choose the type, you can enhance the chart by adding titles, changing fonts, and the like.

CHART CONCEPTS

When you first create a chart, Works will automatically design a bar chart as shown in Figure 9.1. You can customize this and other Works charts to fit your needs.

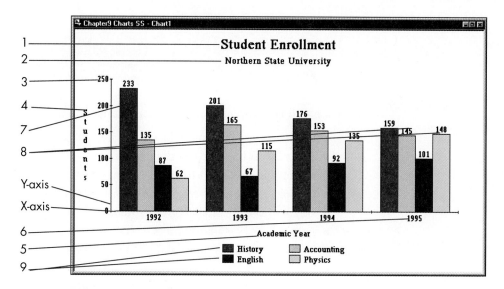

FIGURE 9.1 The components of a bar chart.

Chart Components

There are several special terms that relate to charts. Some of the most common of these are:

Y-axis: The vertical axis of the chart which runs from the top to the bottom of the chart.

X-axis: The horizontal axis of the chart, which runs left to right across the chart.

1. **Chart title:** Appears on the top line on the chart, and identifies the chart. Only one chart title per chart is allowed.

2. **Chart subtitle:** Printed on the second line of the chart directly below the title. Used to further describe the chart.

246 USING MICROSOFT WORKS 4.0 FOR WINDOWS 95

3. **Scale:** Printed along the left vertical axis (Y-axis) of the chart. Used to indicate the assigned value for each position in the chart. The values in the scale will be set automatically by the Works program, but you can assign values if you want.

4. **Y-axis titles:** Printed along the Y, or vertical, axis. Describes the unit of measure for the Y-axis.

5. **X-axis title:** Printed below the chart along the horizontal, or X-axis. Describes the data printed along this axis.

6. **X-axis labels:** Labels appear at the bottom of the chart along the X-axis. Used to identify the bars in the chart. There will be one label for each set of bars.

7. **1st Data series:** Each bar in the chart represents one data series, or group of cells, in the spreadsheet. Separate data series are represented by different shades on the chart; the Works program can support up to six data series in any given chart. Figure 9.1 has four data series.

8. **Data labels:** Labels or values printed above the bars in bar charts or with data points on line charts. In Figure 9.1, the data labels specify the actual value of a specific data series.

9. **Legend:** Displayed at the bottom of the chart. Used to identify the data represented by each bar. The legend box is the same shade as the bar it represents.

Types of Charts

Works offers a wide variety of chart formats and allows you to customize these in a variety of ways. Because there are many options, it is important to understand that each type of chart will convey different kinds of data better than others. Study the following chart types so that you will be able to choose the appropriate chart to display your data in the best manner.

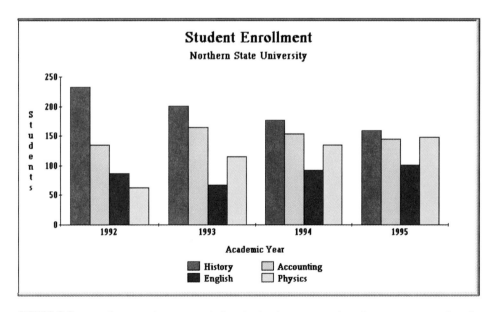

FIGURE 9.2 Bar Chart: Bar charts are used when the data being compared are distinct in nature, such as the population in different cities or the number of majors in a school. This bar chart includes four data series, each shown as a bar filled with a different pattern or color.

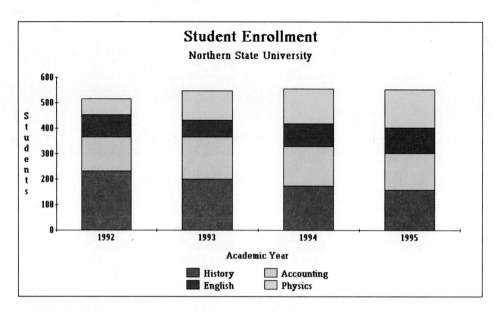

FIGURE 9.3   Stacked Bar Chart: The stacked bar is used to compare entire categories of data. It presents bars on top of each other to represent the combined total of a category. This chart shows total student enrollment for a given year, as well as chosen major. Each bar consists of one number from a different series of data.

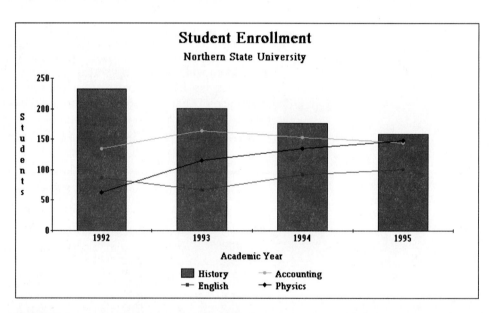

FIGURE 9.4   Combination charts: Combination charts allow you to use line and bar charts at the same time. Use these charts to make one chart category stand out.

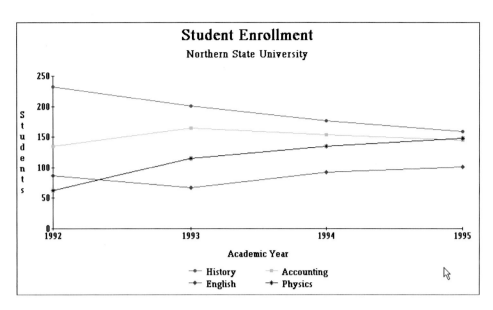

FIGURE 9.5   Line Chart: A line chart compares changes over time for each set of data. Each line represents one category, and each point represents one event or value from a data series.

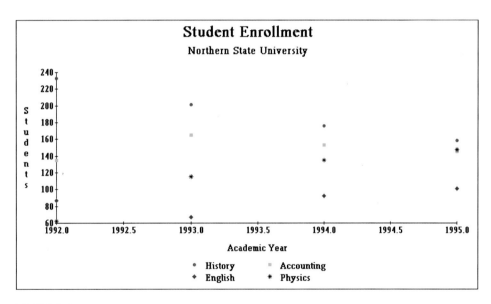

FIGURE 9.6   X-Y Scatter Chart: Often called scatter diagrams, X-Y charts plot points along the X- and Y-axes as coordinates. Data can be hard to understand with this chart type, so use it carefully.

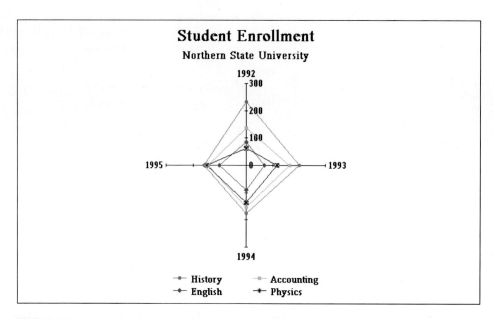

FIGURE 9.7   Radar Chart: Radar charts show a change in the data with respect to a central point (in this case, zero). Use this chart to evaluate relative differences between spreadsheet categories.

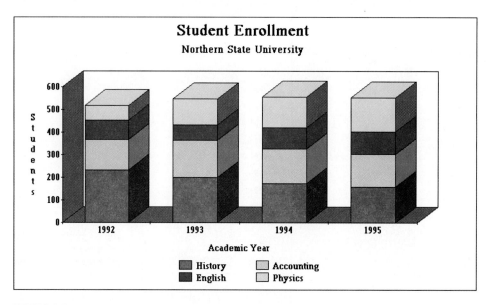

FIGURE 9.8   3-D Chart Options: Many of the Works charts can be displayed in a three-dimensional format. This allows you to develop a high-quality chart for display or printed use.

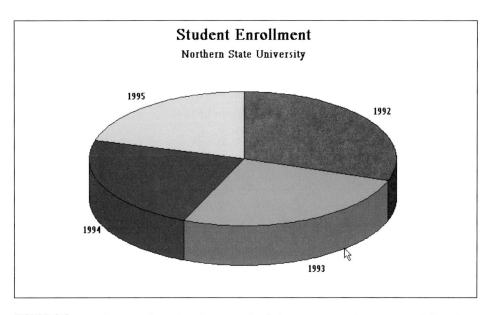

Student Enrollment
Northern State University

1995

1992

1994

1993

FIGURE 9.9   Pie Charts: Pie charts show the impact of each data component with respect to a whole. Each pie chart represents one data series and is a percent of the total.

CREATING A CHART

To create a chart, data and legends must be stored in an active spreadsheet. Figure 9.10 shows a spreadsheet used to store college enrollment levels for the years 1992 through 1995. Data are available for the English, History, Physics, and Accounting departments.

To create a chart, highlight the data

Then click the chart tool on the Toolbar to create the chart

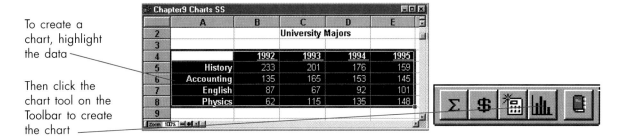

Chapter9 Charts SS					
	A	B	C	D	E
2		University Majors			
3					
4		1992	1993	1994	1995
5	History	233	201	176	159
6	Accounting	135	165	153	145
7	English	87	67	92	101
8	Physics	62	115	135	148
9					

FIGURE 9.10   Data stored in this spreadsheet were used to create the charts shown earlier.

Column A in Figure 9.10 contains the department names that will be used as the legends in the chart. Row 4 contains the year titles that will become the chart's X-axis labels. Each column contains data for that year and represents one category of data. Each row represents one data series, such as the enrollment for the Department of English. It is possible to store the actual chart titles in the spreadsheet, although it is often easier to enter the titles after the chart has been created.

The fastest way to create the new chart is to highlight the desired data in the spreadsheet, then select the new chart tool from the Toolbar, as illustrated in Figure 9.10. Works will automatically assign the information to appear on the Y-axis based on the shape of the blocked data.

Creating a Chart with More Rows Than Columns

Before you select the New chart tool, take a moment to examine the shape of the highlighted block of data. If the shape of the block is longer than it is wide (has more rows than columns), each *row* of data will be measured against the scale on the Y-axis and would become a different Y-series. For example, if you selected columns A, B, and C and the five rows in the spreadsheet shown in Figure 9.11 as a block, each row becomes a Y-series and is charted in a different color on a bar chart. This creates a chart with four sets of bars with each set consisting of two bars as shown in Figure 9.11. The data in the first cell of each Y-series (1992, 1993) become the legend and the data in the left column, which is the department name, become the X-axis labels.

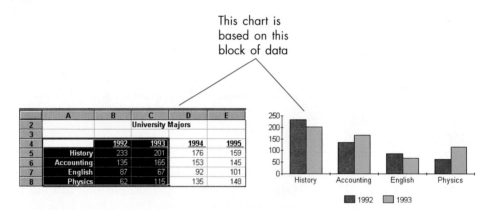

FIGURE 9.11   A chart with spreadsheet rows forming the Y-axis.

Creating a Chart with More Columns Than Rows

If the shape of the block selected in a spreadsheet is wider than it is long (more columns than rows), each *column* of data would become a different Y-series. In the spreadsheet shown in Figure 9.12, rows 4, 5, 6, 7, and 8 and columns A, B, C, D, and E are selected, with each column becoming a Y-series and displayed in a different color. This creates a chart consisting of four groups of four bars each. This time, each row or department is a different shade. The first cell in each row (cells A5, A6, A7, and A8) becomes the legend, and the first cell in each column is the X-axis label.

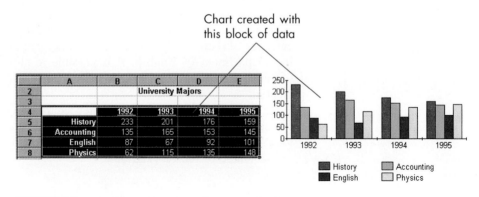

FIGURE 9.12   Spreadsheet columns form the Y-axis in this chart.

DRAWING THE CHART

Once the data are selected as a block, use the Create New Chart option from the Tools menu or use the Toolbar New Chart tool. This will display the New Chart window illustrated in Figure 9.13. The New Chart window allows you to select the type of chart you want, enter a title, and select several other features. The window displays a preview of the chart, which is updated as you add features to it. Once you are satisfied, click OK to display the finished chart.

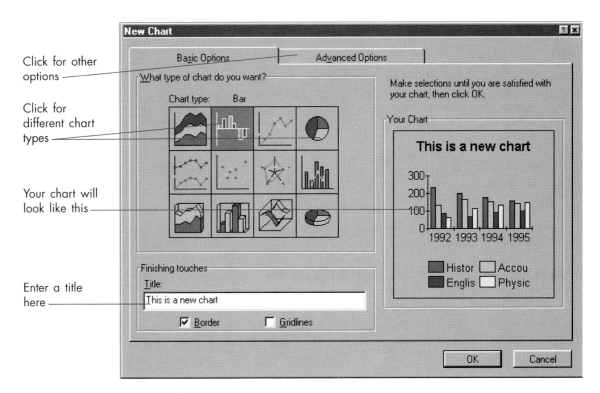

FIGURE 9.13   The New Chart window is accessed from the Tools menu or by clicking the New Chart tool on the Toolbar.

When the new chart is displayed, you are automatically moved into the Works Chart module where the options on the menus and Toolbar are changed as shown in Figure 9.14. Notice that the menu now excludes the Insert option and that the Toolbar contains a number of chart options. The menu selections in the Chart module are adjusted to provide you with a number of specific chart functions. The menu and Toolbar will change back to the standard spreadsheet display when the Chart module is canceled.

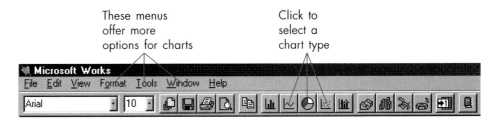

FIGURE 9.14   The Chart module menu and Toolbar.

Viewing and Exiting the Chart

When you are done viewing the chart, close it by clicking the box in the upper left corner as shown in Figure 9.15, and choosing Close. The chart is not deleted when you close it. To view it again, pull down the View menu, click Chart, and double-click the chart name. If you did not name the chart, the charts are identified as Chart1, Chart2, etc. on the View menu.

Click here
to pull down
menu, then
choose Close

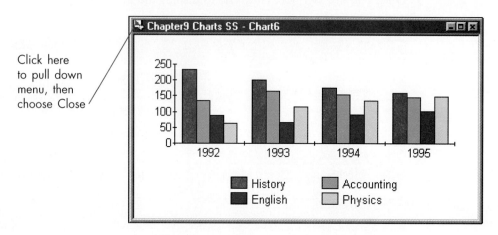

FIGURE 9.15   Close the chart by using the Close option or pressing CTRL/F4.

CHANGING THE CHART TYPE

You will want to view your chart using different chart types to determine the best-suited for your data. This can be done using the Chart Type option on the Format menu shown in Figure 9.16, or by clicking a tool on the Toolbar as shown in Figure 9.14. Remember that these options are available only when you have a chart displayed and are in the chart module.

Click to access
chart type

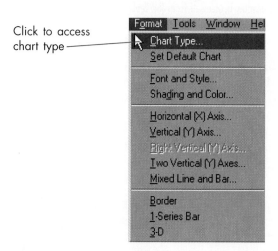

FIGURE 9.16   Change chart types
from the Format menu or the Toolbar.

When you click the Chart Type option, you will see a window similar to Figure 9.13, displaying each type of chart that is available. To choose a different chart type, simply click the chart you want, then click OK.

CREATING CHART TITLES

Titles help explain what is being shown in a chart and can be added using the Titles option from the Edit menu. The Edit Titles window, shown in Figure 9.17, provides areas to enter titles and labels.

Click here, then
type the title

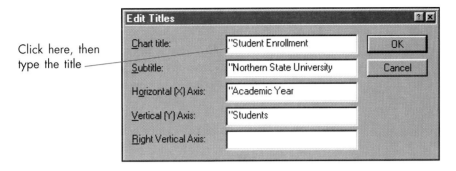

FIGURE 9.17 Use the Edit Titles window, accessed from the Edit menu, to add titles to charts.

Chart titles can be entered in either of two ways:

1. You can enter the chart titles directly into the Edit Titles window by clicking the mouse of the title area, then typing the title. Click OK when all titles are entered. Titles can be edited using the same process.

2. If the title you want to use is stored in a cell of the spreadsheet, you can enter the cell coordinate containing the title in the title area.

SPECIFYING LEGENDS

Chart legends allow you to identify important areas of the chart and provide further detail. To enter or change legend data, be sure the correct chart is displayed. Then select the Legend/Series Labels option from the Edit menu to display the Legend/Series Labels window shown in Figure 9.18. To change a legend, highlight the appropriate Value series you want to change, then enter the new legend or cell coordinate.

Enter legend here

Click to eliminate
legends

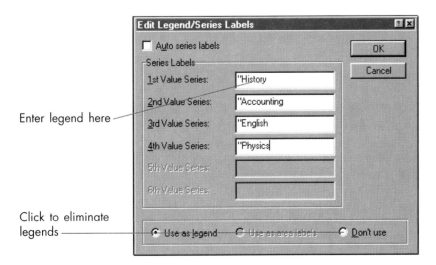

FIGURE 9.18 Adding legends helps describe the data displayed in the chart.

Creating and Deleting Data Labels

Data labels are values or text displayed above the bars on bar charts and next to the data points on line charts (data labels are not available for 3-D bar charts). To use these values, you must define them since they are not created by default. Use the Data Labels option by first selecting the cells in the spreadsheet that contain the values for the labels. Then, use the Copy command from the Edit menu (or use the Ctrl/C keys) to copy the cell information. Once these cells have been copied, activate the chart you want to use, pull down the Edit menu, and select the Data Labels option. You will then see the Edit Data Labels window seen in Figure 9.19. Click the data series to be identified by the labels and select the *Paste* button. Continue to enter the labels in this manner, then click the OK button after all labels have been assigned.

1. Highlight and copy cells that will be labels

2. Select chart and pull down Data Labels window from the Edit menu

3. Click series to be used

4. Click paste

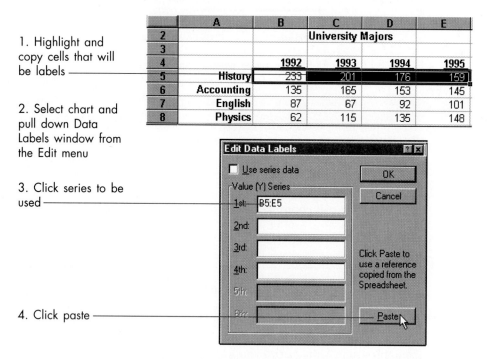

FIGURE 9.19 Add data labels by first copying the spreadsheet cells, then pasting them into the Data Labels window.

To delete existing data labels, select the Data Labels window from the Edit menu, then highlight the labels to be removed. Next, press the Delete key on the keyboard to erase the label reference. Finally, click OK to finish removing the data labels.

Using the Display As Printed Option

Microsoft Works assigns a default color, or pattern, for each Y-series of data. Since most printers cannot print color, you may want to change the chart patterns so they are easier to read when printed. The quickest way to do this is to choose the Display As Printed option from the View menu as shown in Figure 9.20. This will cause Works to change the bars, or Y-series, from color to black-and-white patterns, so that they will stand out when printed as shown in Figure 9.21.

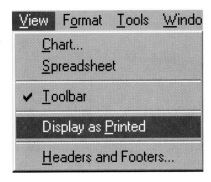

FIGURE 9.20   Selecting the Display as Printed option from the View menu.

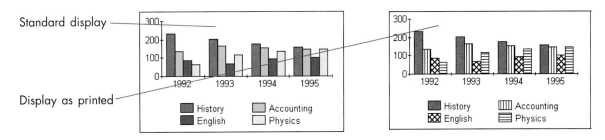

FIGURE 9.21   A chart displayed in standard and Display as Printed formats.

CHANGING THE DEFAULT DATA FORMAT

You can change each individual Y-series or bar on a bar chart manually. There is a wide variety of colors, shades, and patterns available by using the Shading and Color option from the Format menu in the Chart module. Selecting this option will display the Format Shading and Color window displayed in Figure 9.22.

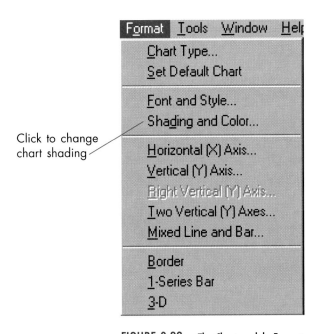

FIGURE 9.22   The Chart module Format menu is used to change chart options.

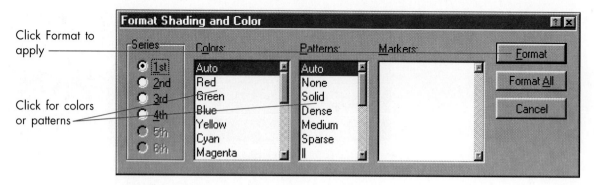

Click Format to apply ——

Click for colors or patterns ——

FIGURE 9.23   The Format Shading and Color window.

The Format Shading and Color window consists of four option boxes. The first box, Series, identifies which of the six possible (we are using four: History, English, Accounting, and Physics) data series you want to change. Before changing the chart colors or other attributes, you must select a data series in the Series box. A quick way to select a given series is to click the mouse on the bar of the chart you wish to change. Then select the Shading and Color option and the correct series will be highlighted.

The Colors option box lets you specify the color for the highlighted series.

Note: Colors are only available if you are using a color monitor.

The third option box, Patterns, is used to change the default shade or pattern of the highlighted data series. This option is especially useful when working with a bar graph, as there are many available patterns. Use the arrow keys to scroll the Patterns box to see the available patterns. To select a specific pattern, simply highlight it.

The last option box in this dialog is the Markers. The available markers will only be displayed if you have some type of a Line or an X-Y chart selected.

When you have finished selecting the options for each series, click the Format button to enter the changes. You must click the Format button each time you change a series. Continue this process until all series have been changed. When you have finished with the changes to all of the series, click the Close button (which replaces the Cancel button) after you format a series.

CHANGING THE DATA FOR THE Y-SERIES

You will encounter situations in which you want to change the data coordinates for one or more of the six Y-series into data groups to reflect a different set of data from the spreadsheet. To change these coordinates, pull down the Edit menu, select the Series option, and enter the new data series. Click OK to finish the selection. The new coordinates will then be displayed in the chart.

SETTING CHART OPTIONS

The Works Chart module includes many different options that can improve the appearance of your charts. These options are found under the Format menu as shown in Figure 9.24.

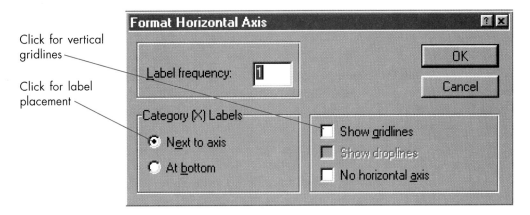

Click for vertical gridlines

Click for label placement

FIGURE 9.24　The Format Horizontal Axis window.

Setting X- and Y-axis Gridlines and Options

The Horizontal (X) Axis window shown in Figure 9.24 provides control over format options that affect the horizontal axis. The label frequency option allows you to specify the frequency of the horizontal labels. An entry of "1" prints a label for each bar grouping; "2" prints a label every second bar group; "3" every third, etc. This feature should be used when there are many groups of bars and the labels run together. The Show gridlines option specifies that vertical gridlines be included in the chart. These vertical lines help to align points from the X-axis vertically onto the chart.

　　　The Vertical (Y) Axis window, selected from the Format menu and shown in Figure 9.25, allows you to specify the scaling of the Y-axis in place of the Works automatic scaling. You can specify the starting (Minimum) point for the scale, the ending (Maximum) point, and the Interval for the scale. This window also allows you to specify horizontal gridlines.

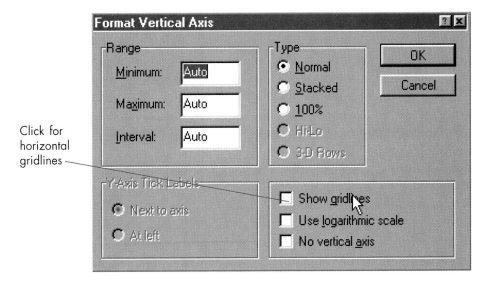

Click for horizontal gridlines

FIGURE 9.25　The Format Vertical (Y) Axis window.

The next two options, the Right Vertical (Y) Axis and Two Vertical (Y) Axes, are not commonly used. For information on these options, refer to the Microsoft Works manual or the on-line help facility.

The Mixed Line and Bar option is used to combine a bar and line chart into one chart. The window allows you to specify which Y-series will be shown in the line format and which will use the bar format. You should exercise some restraint when using this option, since too much information on a chart can become confusing.

The final options on the Format menu act as toggles (the option turns on when selected the first time and off when selected again).

Border: Use this option to draw a box around the graph.

1-Series Bar: Displays a single series in the bar chart.

3-D: Use this option to convert the active chart into a three-dimensional display.

SETTING CHART FONTS

The Works Chart module supports many special fonts. These fonts allow you to set up customized titles in your charts, and are activated through the Font and Style option on the Format menu, as shown in Figure 9.26.

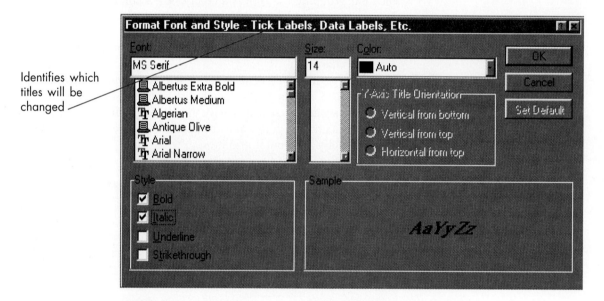

Identifies which titles will be changed

FIGURE 9.26 The Format Font and Style window is used to change chart fonts.

To alter the font or type style of the main chart title, click the mouse on the title to highlight it. Then, click the right mouse button to select the Font and Style option. You can also select the Font and Style option from the Format menu. Select the font, size, and style. Click OK. Alter the fonts and styles of other titles, legends, and labels in the same manner.

Note: when you select one axis title and change the font, the other axis title will be changed as well.

PRINTING THE CHART

Printing charts usually takes longer than printing other material because the printer is operating at maximum resolution (its best quality). This means that you will want to be sure that the chart is set up correctly before you print it.

The first thing to do is use the Page Setup option from the File menu. The options in the three-part window shown in Figure 9.27 determine how the chart will look when it is printed. The margins option allows you to adjust the page margins.

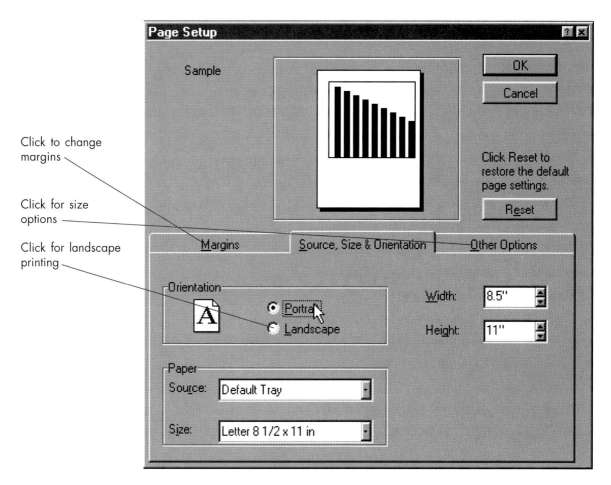

Click to change margins

Click for size options

Click for landscape printing

FIGURE 9.27   The Page Setup window allows you to control how a chart will print.

The Other Options let you determine the overall size and proportions of the chart. Usually, you will use either the Screen size option or the Full page, keep proportions option. The Screen size option will print the chart the same size as you display it on the computer screen. You can change this size by changing the chart window size with the mouse. The Full page, keep proportions option will print the chart on a full page of paper while retaining the proportions of the chart as displayed on the computer screen. The Full page option will display the chart on a full page of paper but will not automatically keep the proportions you saw on the screen. Experiment with the page margins and chart orientation to find the best chart print settings.

The Source, Size, Orientation folder of the Page Setup window allows you to print the chart sideways on the page. This is called changing the chart's orientation, and specifies whether the chart will be printed normally, across the page, or sideways, down the page. The landscape mode prints sideways; the portrait mode prints in the normal, horizontal fashion. Figure 9.27 shows these options of the Page Setup window.

With any option, be sure to use the Print Preview option from the File menu to see how the chart will look before you print it.

NAMING, SELECTING, SAVING, AND DELETING CHARTS

Each chart is automatically assigned a default chart name when it is created. These names will be Chart1, Chart2, Chart3, etc.

To change the name of a chart, choose the Rename Chart option from the Tools menu. That will cause the Rename Chart window, shown in Figure 9.28, to be displayed. Highlight the chart to be named by clicking it, then click the "Type a name below" box. Type the name you want to call the chart, then click the Rename button. The new name will appear in the Name Chart window. Click Cancel to close the window.

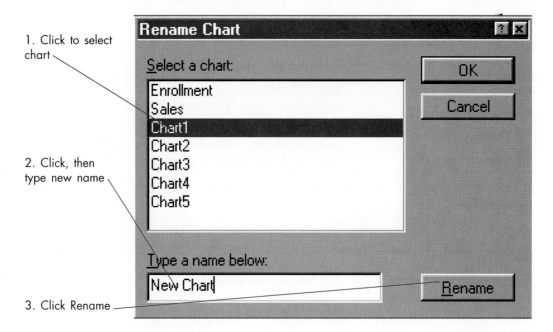

FIGURE 9.28   The Rename Chart window allows you to name or rename a chart.

When you want to work with a different chart, pull down the View menu and select Chart. You will see a list of all the charts you have defined for the spreadsheet. To make a chart active, click the chart's name.

The Tools menu allows you to Duplicate a chart. The Duplicate feature is a good way to copy a chart description then change one feature so you have two charts that are only slightly different.

You can also use the Tools menu to delete charts. First, highlight the chart to be deleted, then select the Delete option from the Tools menu. On the Delete Chart window, highlight the chart to delete, click Delete, and click OK. Works allows you to store eight charts with one spreadsheet. If you want to create additional charts after eight exist, you will need to delete an earlier chart.

Saving a chart is done automatically for you when the spreadsheet is saved. To work with a chart after it has been saved, load the spreadsheet, then enter the Chart module by selecting Chart from the View menu.

CHAPTER 9 SELF-TEST

1. Define the following chart terms:
   Horizontal (X) axis
   Vertical (Y) axis
   Scale
   Legend
   X-axis Label
   Data labels
   Data series
2. List two ways to enter chart titles.
3. How do you create a legend for a data series?
4. What is a gridline? How do you specify that you want Gridlines displayed?
5. What do each of the following chart options do?
   a. Border
   b. Display As Printed
6. How do you change the size of the printed graph?
7. What is the difference between landscape and portrait printing?
8. How do you change chart fonts?
9. How do you manually specify the Y-axis scale?
10. How do you delete a chart?

This tutorial allows you to practice charting techniques by creating several charts based on data in an existing spreadsheet named Chapter 9 Tutorial.

1. Start Microsoft Works.
2. Open spreadsheet file Chapter 9 Tutorial. You will see the spreadsheet shown in Figure 9.29. Notice that the years in row 1 are used as labels, not as numeric entries.

Chapter 9 Tutorial				
	A	**B**	**C**	**D**	**E**
1		1992	1993	1994	1995
2	Fine Arts	649	589	694	707
3	History	1,103	1,157	1,096	1,203
4	Sciences	804	944	1,076	1,233
5	Business	291	342	351	403
6					
7					

FIGURE 9.29 The Chapter 9 Tutorial spreadsheet.

Creating the Chart

1. Select the entire spreadsheet as a block by highlighting all cells A1 through E5.
2. Click the New Chart tool on the Toolbar. When the New Chart window appears, make no changes and click OK. You will see a bar chart labeled Chart1 as shown in Figure 9.30.

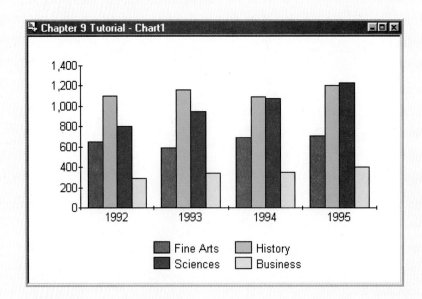

FIGURE 9.30 The new bar chart.

Adding Titles to the Chart

The new chart does a good job of comparing data, but it is difficult to understand since no titles are included. Fortunately, adding titles is an easy process using the Edit menu.

1. Be sure that the chart is still displayed.
2. Pull down the Edit menu and select the Titles option.
3. Enter the titles in the Titles window as shown in Figure 9.31. Use the Tab key to move from one title entry to the next.

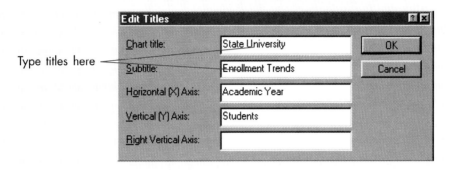

Type titles here

FIGURE 9.31   Enter these titles in the title window.

Chart Title:	**State University**
Subtitle:	**Enrollment Trends**
Horizontal (X) Axis:	**Academic Year**
Vertical (Y) Axis:	**Students**

4. Click OK or press Enter. The chart should look like the one shown in Figure 9.32. If you made a mistake, use the Titles window to reenter the titles.

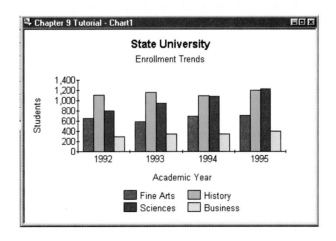

FIGURE 9.32   The new bar chart with titles added.

Special note: Depending on your computer setup, it is possible that the vertical (Y) axis title *Students* was truncated, and future graphs will how this condition. This is *not* a problem, and you will learn how to adjust this.

Adding Gridlines and Using 3-D

Gridlines help you locate a point on the chart and can be added to both the horizontal and vertical axis. When using a bar chart, horizontal gridlines help align a point on a bar with a point on the scale.

1. Select Vertical (Y) Axis from the Format menu.
2. Click the Show Gridlines box.
3. Click OK or press Enter.
4. Select the Horizontal (X) Axis option from the Format menu.
5. Click the Show Gridlines box, then choose OK.
6. Finally, click the 3-D option on the Format menu. The chart should appear as in Figure 9.33.

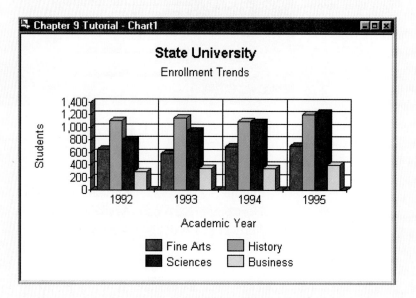

FIGURE 9.33   The chart modified with gridlines and in 3-D formats.

Setting Data Labels

Data labels in bar graphs appear over each bar of a data series and can be anything that exists in your spreadsheet. In our case, assume we are interested in knowing exactly what the enrollments are for the History department. We will use data labels to display this quickly. Data labels cannot be used in the 3-D format, so you must return the chart to the standard display. Here are the steps to change to a standard display and create the data labels.

1. With the chart displayed, pull down the Format menu and click the 3-D option. This will turn off the 3-D display and convert the chart to the standard display.
2. Return to the spreadsheet by either clicking the spreadsheet (behind the chart) or the Close option in the File menu.
3. Select cells B3 through E3 as a block.
4. Copy the cells using the Ctrl/C key combination or the Copy command from the Edit menu.
5. Make Chart1 active by clicking the Chart option on the View menu, then double clicking Chart1.
6. Select Data Labels from the Edit menu

   Note: The chart must be displayed before you do this.

7. Click the 2nd Series box since History is represented by the second bar in the chart.
8. Click the Paste option in the Data Labels window. The label values you copied from the spreadsheet will be placed in the first series in the box.
9. Click OK.
10. The chart should look like Figure 9.34.

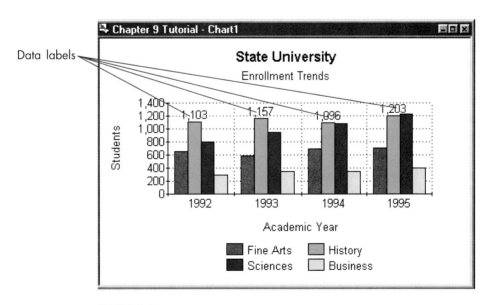

FIGURE 9.34 Data labels for history are entered in the chart.

Changing the Bar Patterns

1. With the chart displayed, pull down the Format menu and select the Shading and Color option.
2. Be sure the 1st Series is selected (the dot is filled in).
3. Click on the down arrow in the Patterns box to scroll down until you see the backslashes \\.
4. Click Format to complete the series.
5. Click on the 2nd Series.
6. Select the XX pattern in the same manner as you selected the \\ pattern.
7. Click the Format button.
8. Click the Close button.
9. The chart should now look like Figure 9.35.

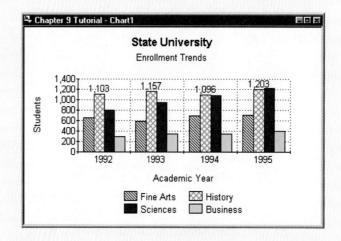

FIGURE 9.35 Change the patterns with the Shading and Colors options.

Setting Borders

1. Select Border from the Format menu.
2. Look at the chart and observe the border.

Changing the Scale of the Chart

The scale is the numeric guide that runs along the left side or Y axis of the chart. By default, Works automatically calculates this scale based on the data being charted. There are times when you will want to change the scale to show differences more clearly. Change the scale as follows:

1. Select Vertical (Y) Axis from the Folder menu.
2. Set the Minimum to 0. Press the Tab key.
3. Set the Maximum to 1200. Press Tab.
4. Set the Interval to 300.
5. Click OK.
6. Look at the chart and notice how the display was changed.

Changing Fonts

Note: Due to the differences in some computer systems, not all fonts or font sizes may be available. If a specified font is not available, choose another font and size that would approximate the size given in the tutorial.

1. Click the chart title State University to highlight it.
2. Choose the Font and Style option from the Format menu or by clicking the right mouse button.
3. Select the Times New Roman Font from the Format Font and Style window.
4. Select size 24 (substitute a similar size if you do not have 24).
5. Click OK.
6. Click the subtitle, Enrollment Trends, and change it to Times New Roman, size 16, italic type.
7. Adjust the X- and Y-axis titles to the Arial font, size 12.
8. Set all other titles to Arial size 8.
9. The chart should look like Figure 9.36.

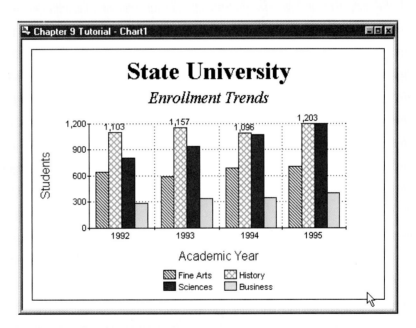

FIGURE 9.36   The chart with the title fonts adjusted.

Changing Chart Types

Once the data series have been defined as a block of cells and a New Chart created, other chart types can be quickly displayed with the same data specification using the Toolbar. Hint: If you cannot recall which tool controls which chart type, move the mouse pointer over the tool, but, do not click the mouse button. In a few seconds, Works will display the tool's definition.

1. With the chart displayed, click the Bar Chart tool on the Toolbar which will cause the Chart Type window to be displayed. Click on the Variations folder to display other types of bar charts.
2. Click on the rightmost chart type in the top row, the stacked bar chart, click OK and view the chart.
3. Select the 3-D Line chart option from the Toolbar and click OK when the Chart Type window appears.
4. Select the 3-D Area chart tool from the Toolbar and click OK on the Chart Type window.

CREATING A NEW CHART

1. Close the chart with the Close option on the File menu.
2. Select cells B2:B5 in the spreadsheet.
3. Click the New Chart tool on the Toolbar or select the Create New Chart option from the Tools menu.
4. Select the Pie option in the New Chart window and click OK. The chart should look like Figure 9.37.

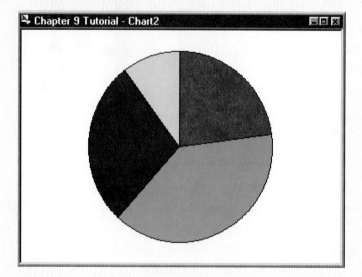

FIGURE 9.37   The new pie chart.

Notice that the pie slices are not identified by department. To identify the slices, use data labels defined as the X-axis labels.

1. Close the chart to return to the spreadsheet.
2. Highlight cells A2 through A5.
3. Copy the highlighted cells using the Copy command.
4. Select Chart2 from the Chart option under the View menu.
5. Select the Data Labels option from the Edit menu.
6. Click the Cell Range text box in the Data Labels window.
7. Click the Paste button to enter the cell range (A2:A5).
8. Click OK.
9. View the chart and notice that the labels still do not show.
10. Click the Pie option from the Toolbar to display the Chart Type window, then click on the Variations folder. Select the pie chart tool surrounded by the letters A, B, C (this is the leftmost choice in the bottom row), which will display the labels. Click OK. The chart will appear as shown in Figure 9.38.

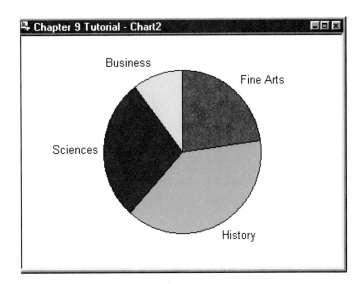

FIGURE 9.38   The pie chart with data labels.

Adding Titles to the Chart

1. Select the Titles option from the Edit menu.
2. Type **Departmental Enrollments** into the Chart Title box, then press the Tab key.
3. Type **your name** in the Subtitle box, and press Enter or click OK.
4. The titles should now appear in the pie chart.

Changing the Title Fonts

1. Highlight the main title, Departmental Enrollments, then select the Font and Styles option from the Format menu.
2. Set the Font to Times New Roman, Size 24, and click OK.
3. Click your name and set the font to Times New Roman, Size 14. Click OK.
4. Click on any of the data labels, then change the font style to italic type.
5. Choose Border from the Format menu.
6. The chart should now look like Figure 9.39.

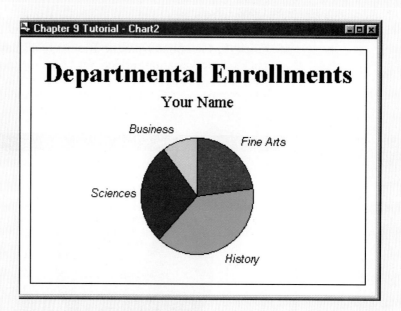

FIGURE 9.39 The completed pie chart.

Exploding a Pie Slice and Converting to 3-D

1. Assume that you want to explode or emphasize the Sciences pie slice.
2. Select the Shading and Color option from the Format menu.
3. In the Slices box of the Format Shading and Color window, highlight slice 3, which represents the Sciences spreadsheet entry.
4. Click the Explode Slice box, click the Format button, and click Close.
5. Choose the 3-D option from the Format menu. Your chart should look like Figure 9.40.

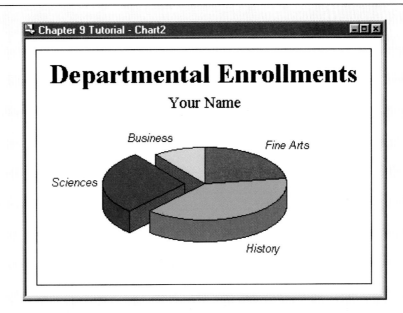

Departmental Enrollments
Your Name

Business

Fine Arts

Sciences

History

FIGURE 9.40 The exploded pie chart in 3-D format.

PRINTING THE CHART

1. Be sure the pie chart (Chart2) is displayed.
2. Select the Page Setup option from the File menu.
3. We will print the chart in landscape mode, so click the Source, Size & Orientation folder.
4. Click the landscape mode in the Setup window then click OK.
5. To see how the chart will print, use the Print Preview option from the File menu.
6. If necessary, return to normal view and make any changes.
7. Click the Print button in the preview mode to print the chart. Click OK in the Print window. You can also print the chart without previewing it by choosing the Print option from the File menu.
8. Save the spreadsheet as Chapter 9 Tutorial Charts on your disk.
9. Exit Works and Windows and turn off the computer.

Exercise 9-1

You have been asked to develop a series of charts to compare salaries paid to different company managers. Use the data on your exercise disk in the file **Exercise 9 Spreadsheet**. Include legends, chart titles, and both X- and Y-axis titles. Use your name as the subtitle for each chart.

1. Chart A: Create a bar chart that displays yearly salaries according to job title. Include years along the X-axis and job titles in the legend. Show data labels for the Operations VP only. Use horizontal gridlines. Print the chart in landscape format.

   Hint: Consider duplicating a completed chart (use the option under the Tools menu) to make the next chart if most of the information remains the same.

2. Chart B: Create a 3-D 100% bar chart using the same requirements (but without data labels) as chart A. Print the chart.

3. Chart C: Create and print a 3-D area chart that stacks the job salaries on top of each other and shows the total salaries of all categories for each year.

Exercise 9-2

1. Chart A: Create a 3-D bar chart for the Operations VP, Environmental Controller, and Insurance Mgr. salaries. Construct the chart so that the highest salaries are *behind* the lower salaries.

   Hint: The order information is entered into the Series box under the Edit menu determines the order the bars appear in the chart.

   Set the scale for a minimum of 10,000, a maximum of 80,000, and increment to 10,000. Print the chart in landscape format.

2. Chart B: Create a combination bar/line chart using the data for chart A. Represent the Operations VP salaries in the bar form and the other salaries in line form. Print the chart.

3. Chart C: Create an exploded 3-D pie chart that shows the salaries for the Environmental Controller. Show the year as a data label. Explode the pie slice for 1995, then print the chart.

Exercise 9-3

Create a line chart with one data series showing 1995 salaries for all employment categories and a second series showing the *average* for all 1995 salaries. Insert the employment categories as data labels (Operations VP, Information Officer, etc.).

Hint: You will need to use the average function in the spreadsheet to determine the average of the 1995 salaries. Remember that you need an entry for the average for each point shown on the line chart. Print the chart.

INTRODUCTION TO DATABASE

LEARNING OBJECTIVES

When you've completed this chapter, you will be able to:

- Define the database terms field, record, and cell.
- Name and format fields for a database.
- Enter data into a database in List view.
- Enter database data in Form view.
- Enter formulas for fields in a database.
- Protect database fields from editing.
- Sort database records.
- Print a database.
- Save a database.

DATABASE CONCEPTS

A **database** is an electronic filing system used to keep track of appointments, household inventory, customer records, mailing lists, and other types of information. Once the data are stored in the database records, records can be added, modified, deleted, sorted, and filtered; reports can also be generated. With the mail merge feature of the Word Processing module, the database can be used to create customized form letters.

Perhaps the best example of a database is a telephone book. The telephone book stores information about people who have telephones. It is used to retrieve information, such as a person's address or phone number. A database serves much the same purpose — storage and retrieval of information — but it is in an electronic form. This provides better, faster retrieval and more efficient ways to keep the data current.

With an electronic database you can also maintain both the structure of, and the information in, the database.

Records, Fields, and Cells

Figure 10.1 shows the basic components of data in a database. Databases are organized much like spreadsheets. Each database is made up of a number of **rows** or **records**. A record is a compilation of information used to describe one particular object stored in a database. For example, in a telephone book, a record would have all the information about one phone number. Each record would have the same type of data: a person's name, street, city, and phone number.

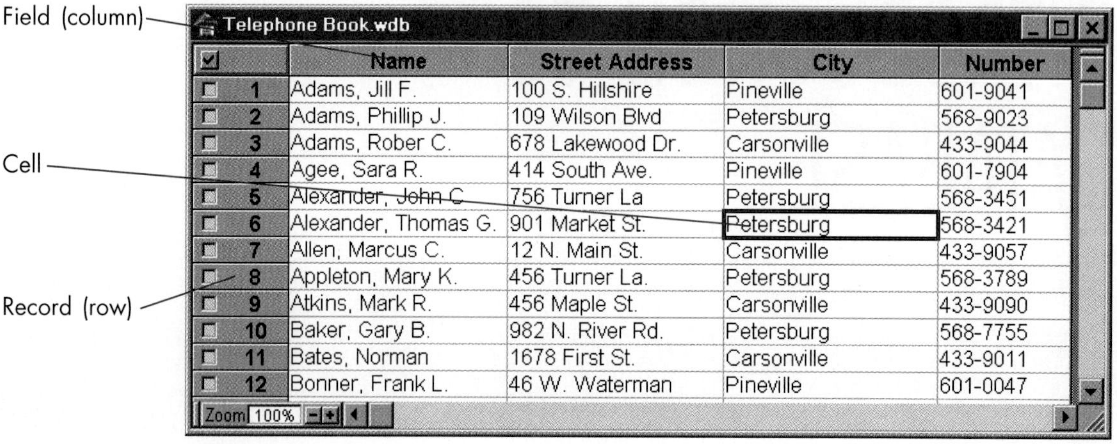

Field (column) —
Cell —
Record (row) —

		Name	Street Address	City	Number
☑		**Name**	**Street Address**	**City**	**Number**
☐	1	Adams, Jill F.	100 S. Hillshire	Pineville	601-9041
☐	2	Adams, Phillip J.	109 Wilson Blvd	Petersburg	568-9023
☐	3	Adams, Rober C.	678 Lakewood Dr.	Carsonville	433-9044
☐	4	Agee, Sara R.	414 South Ave.	Pineville	601-7904
☐	5	Alexander, John C.	756 Turner La	Petersburg	568-3451
☐	6	Alexander, Thomas G.	901 Market St.	Petersburg	568-3421
☐	7	Allen, Marcus C.	12 N. Main St.	Carsonville	433-9057
☐	8	Appleton, Mary K.	456 Turner La.	Petersburg	568-3789
☐	9	Atkins, Mark R.	456 Maple St.	Carsonville	433-9090
☐	10	Baker, Gary B.	982 N. River Rd.	Petersburg	568-7755
☐	11	Bates, Norman	1678 First St.	Carsonville	433-9011
☐	12	Bonner, Frank L.	46 W. Waterman	Pineville	601-0047

Telephone Book.wdb

Zoom 100%

FIGURE 10.1   Records, Fields, and Cells in a database.

Each record is made up of a number of **columns** or **fields**. A field is a group of cells that contain the same type of information and are referenced by the same name. For example, all phone numbers would be stored in the phone number field. In a database, a field is a column.

There are two types of fields used in a database: **source field** and **calculated field**. The data for the source field are entered from the keyboard. We say this type of field has its origin from outside the database. The values for the calculated field are derived from data within the database. We say these data's origin is from within the database.

A **cell** is an area that stores one piece of information. For example, in Figure 10.1, Thomas Alexander's city is stored in a single cell. His name is stored in a different cell of the same record, and his street in another cell. This is similar to the concept of a cell in a spreadsheet.

All cells in a field must contain the same type of information and have the same format. For example, if a column contains a phone number, then each record in the database must contain a phone number in that column, and the format must be the same for each phone number.

DATABASE VIEWS

There are several views and tools used in the database module of Microsoft Works. These views include List view, Form view, and Report view.

List View

The **List View** lets you enter, modify, and view the data in the database. The List view shows as many records as the screen can hold at one time. The records are shown as rows and columns. In this view, the entire record may not fit on the screen; you may need scroll to the left or right to see all of a record's contents. The data shown in Figure 10.1 are in List view.

Form View

In **Form view** you see one record at a time in a form format. This view is used to see records individually. The form can be designed to look like printed forms and used to enter data. The data and the form can be printed at the same time. Figure 10.2 shows a record displayed in form view.

Form view

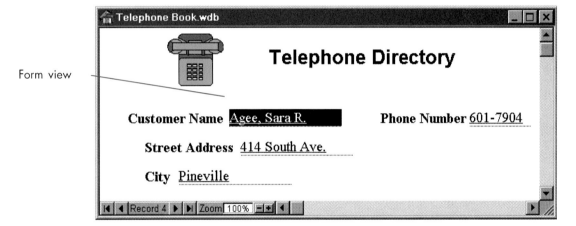

FIGURE 10.2   The form view shows only one record at a time in a form style layout.

Report View

Use the **Report View** to define the reports you need from the data in the database. You specify the fields required for the report, the order of the fields, and how the records are to be sorted. You can also request totals, subtotals, and statistics for the data in the report. Once a report is defined, it is stored with the database so you can use it at any time in the future.

Other Tools

Sometimes you will want to see only certain records. For example, you may want to see a list of students who are seniors or a list of payments that are past due. You can use a database **filter** to specify which records to view or print. To create a filter, you enter conditions or sample data in certain fields; Works then displays only those records that meet the specified conditions in the filter.

Works also has a **Form design** tool. This tool allows you to create a form used to display or edit records in the database. The form can be designed to match a printed form.

Database views and tools can be selected using the Toolbar. Figure 10.3 shows the tools used to select views and database tools along with the **Insert Record tool**.

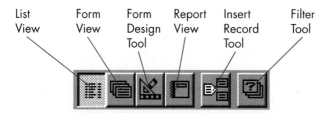

| List View | Form View | Form Design Tool | Report View | Insert Record Tool | Filter Tool |

FIGURE 10.3   The tools to select database phases and views.

DATABASE DESIGN

Before you create a database, you should spend some time determining the fields required and what type of data will be in each field. This front-end preparation can save you many hours trying to make a database that is improperly designed produce the required results. The full scope of database design is far beyond this text, but there are a few simple things that should be considered.

1. Determine what fields are needed. Remember, fields are columns in the database. During creation of the database, each field is identified and named. Use field names that indicate the type of data in the field. For example, use First Name rather than something like Name1.

2. Determine any data that can be created from other data in the database. For example, suppose you wanted the total price of a purchase. If the database contained the number of items and the unit cost of each item, the total cost could be computed using these two fields. This field could be computed using a formula.

3. Determine the format and appearance for each field. Each field will be displayed using a selected format such as currency, integer, date, etc. Also determine the appearance of the field. For example, if the format is a date, determine if the date should be displayed as 3/14/96 or March 3, 1996.

4. Determine any default value for each field. In the database, the cells in a field must contain either a value or a formula, or they must be blank. A default value is the value for the field if no value is entered by the user. For example, suppose 90% of the people in a telephone book lived in Petersburg. If a default value of Petersburg were specified for the city field, Works would place this value in each new record. The user would only need to enter the city if it were not Petersburg.

5. Determine how the database might be sorted. For example, suppose the database needed to be sorted by last name. If a single name field were created and the names were entered like James E. Jones and William B. Jones, Works would not know where the last name begins. Therefore, Works could not sort by last name. During creation of the database, each item of data that might be used to sort records should be created as an individual field.

These are only some of the things that should be considered before creating a database. As you work with databases, other considerations will become apparent. Although these considerations may appear trivial at first, you will find that there is nothing more important than preparation when creating a database.

CREATING A DATABASE

To create a new database, click the Works Tools tab on the **Task Launcher**, then click the **Database button** in the Works Tools folder as shown in Figure 10.4.

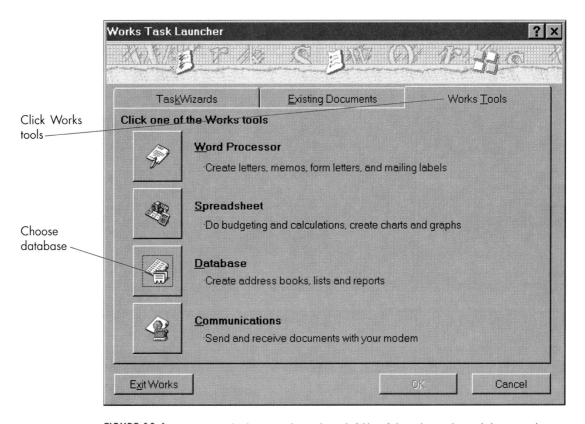

FIGURE 10.4   To create a database, use the Works Tools folder of the Task Launcher and choose Database.

When creating a database, each field for the database must be defined. The items that must be specified for each field are the name of the field, the field format, appearance, and the default value for the field. These items are specified using the **Create Database window** shown in Figure 10.5.

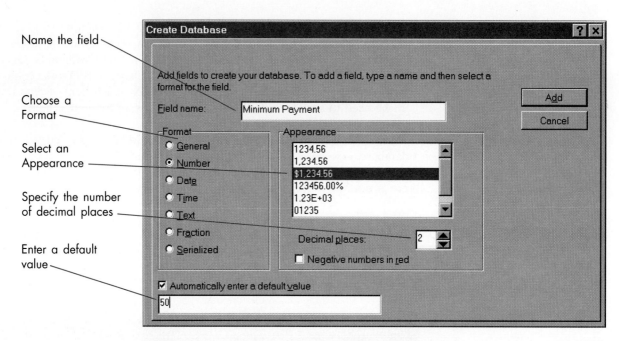

Name the field

Choose a
Format

Select an
Appearance

Specify the number
of decimal places

Enter a default
value

FIGURE 10.5   Initial fields are defined using the Create Database window.

Name the Field

The first step is to name the field. This is done by entering the name in the **Field name** entry at the top of the Create Database window. Field names can contain letters, numbers, spaces, or some special characters. The field name cannot contain more then 15 characters.

Choose a Format

The second step to defining a database field is to select the field's format. This is done by clicking one of the options in the Format area of the Create Database window.

Select an Appearance

Most formats also allow you to select an appearance for the data. Available appearances for a format appear in the **Appearance** area after a format is selected. The appearance is different for each format.

For most number formats you can also select the number of decimals displayed to the right of the decimal point. The total number of digits is determined by the field's width. The default field width is 10 characters, but this width can be changed later.

If the **Negative numbers in red** option is checked for a number format, any number less than zero will be displayed as red text on the screen.

Enter a Default Value

If a **default value** is desired for a field, check the "Automatically enter a default value" option at the bottom of the screen and enter the default value. A default value must be consistent with the selected format. For example, if the format is a number and letters are entered as the default value, the default value will not be entered in the field.

Once a field entry has been completed, click the Add button and the window will be reset for the next field. Continue creating fields until all fields for the database have been added. Once a field has been added, the Cancel button in Figure 10.5 will change to Done. To complete the database creation stage, click the Done button.

When creation of the database is competed, the screen displays an empty database in List View as shown in Figure 10.6. The field names are displayed above each column and record numbers are displayed to the left of each row.

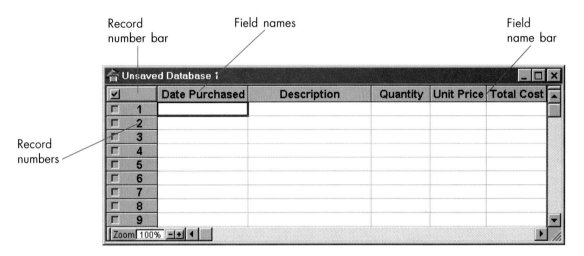

FIGURE 10.6   An empty database in List view.

CHANGING A COLUMN'S FORMAT

After the fields have been created, their **format** may need to be changed. When a format is set for any cell in a column, the format will be set for all cells in that column. This is different from the Spreadsheet module where the format can be set for individual cells within a column.

Some of the column formats can be changed using the Toolbar. The Toolbar allows you to change the font, font size, and the bold, underline, and italic attributes for the column. Other formatting must be changed using the Format menu shown in Figure 10.7.

Choose Field
or
Choose a
specific
formatting
option

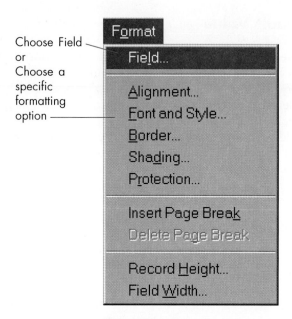

FIGURE 10.7   Use the format menu to
change column formats.

If the Field option is selected, the formatting folder tabs are displayed and
the **Field folder** is displayed on top as shown in Figure 10.8. When the Alignment,
Font and Style, Border, or Shading option is selected from the Format menu, the
formatting folders are displayed and the selected option's folder appears on top
of the other folders.

Click tabs to
change folders

Set new
formatting
options

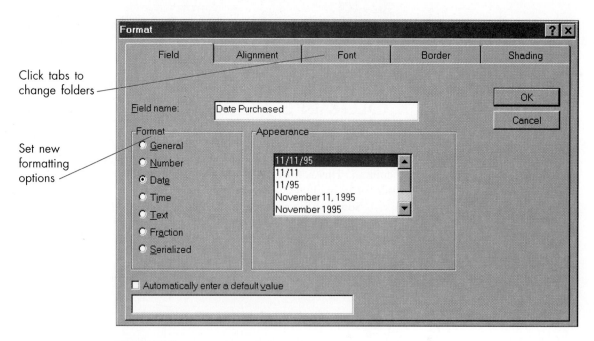

FIGURE 10.8   The Formatting folders to change a column's format.

Once the formatting folders are displayed, you can make the appropriate changes to the options. Click a different folder's tab to move to another formatting folder. All the formatting options work in a similar way as they did in the word processing and spreadsheet chapters.

Remember, a formatting option is assigned to an entire column. To change the format for a column, place the cursor in any cell of the column and use the Format menu or toolbar. To change several columns at once, select a cell in each column before changing the format.

Changing the Field Width and Record Height

The **field width** and height will be the same for all cells in the column when the database is created. These options work the same here as they do in a spreadsheet.

The Field Width option on the Format menu can be used to change a field width. The window for this option is shown in Figure 10.9. The number entered for the field width should be the number of characters in the largest cell of the field. When a field has a numeric format, editing characters such as commas, decimal point, and dollar signs must be considered when determining the field's width. The field must be wide enough to include the digits for the largest number plus these editing characters. If the **Standard button** is selected on the Field Width window, 10 characters will be used. If the **Best Fit** option is selected on the Field Width window, the field width will be set to the number of characters in the current cell or the value in a set of selected cells.

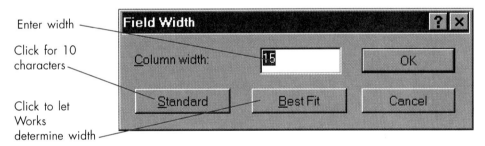

Enter width

Click for 10 characters

Click to let Works determine width

FIGURE 10.9 The Field Width window.

The mouse can also be used to change a column's width. Move the mouse pointer to the column separators on the field name bar. The pointer will change to a double arrow pointing to the left and right with the word **adjust** as shown in Figure 10.10. To make a column wider, click the column's right margin marker and drag it to the right. To make a column narrower, drag the column's right margin to the left. A dotted line will be displayed as you drag the column separator to indicate the size of the column.

Hold down the
left mouse
button and
drag the
column border

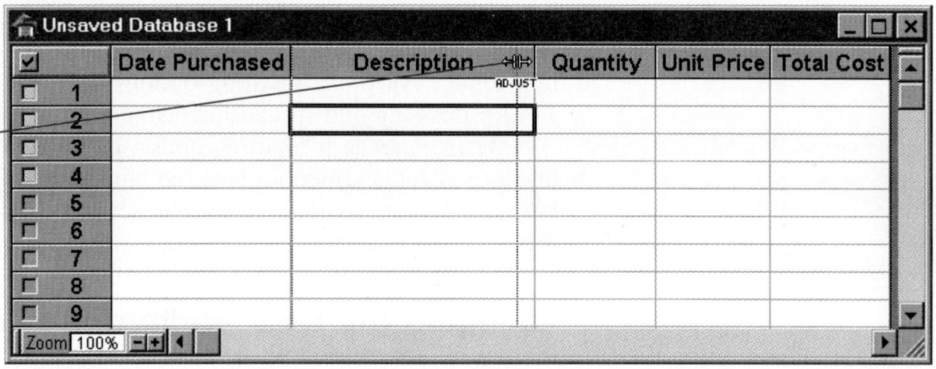

FIGURE 10.10   Column width can also be changed by dragging a column's border.

Just as you can change the width of a column, you can change the height of a row. To change a row's height use the **Record Height** option on the Format menu or use the mouse. When the Record height option is used, the number is entered in points. Remember, a point is ½nd of an inch.

To use the mouse to set a record's height, move the mouse pointer to the record separator lines on the record number bar. It will change to a double arrow similar to the one shown in Figure 10.10. To make the record's height smaller, drag the bottom line up. To make the record taller, drag the line down. To set the height for multiple records at one time, select the records to be changed and use the Record Height option from the Format menu.

ENTERING DATA INTO A DATABASE

Once the fields for a database have been defined, the data can be entered. Using the List view, the data are entered the same way as in a spreadsheet. Place the cursor in a cell and type the data. To move from field to field, use the Tab key. To move from record to record, use the arrow keys.

Default Value Fields

If the "Automatically enter a default value" option had been set on when the field was created, all new records will display the **default value**. If the "Automatically enter a default value" option is set on after records have been created, the default value will only be applied to new records. Existing records will not have the default value. The default value can be changed for any record by editing the cell that contains the default value.

Using the Fill Options

The Edit menu of the Database module has three fill options. These are the same options that are available in the Spreadsheet module. **Fill Down** is used to copy the contents of one cell into the cells below it. **Fill Right** is used to copy the contents of one cell into the cells to the right. **Fill Series** is used to fill a set of cells with a series of numbers or dates.

Copying the Previous Record's Data

In the Works database, the contents of a cell can be copied from the previous record. For example, suppose you are entering a long list of names and addresses and several consecutive records have North Carolina as their state name. You would type North Carolina in the first record's state name. To enter the state name for the next record, press **Ctrl/'**. The contents of the previous record's cell will be copied into the current cell. This would avoid having to type North Carolina in each record.

Editing a Field or Record

To edit the contents of a field within a record, first click the cell to be changed. Next, click inside the formula bar and change the cell contents. If you double click a field or press the F2 function key, the data can be edited in the cell, rather than on the formula bar. A change can be canceled with the Esc key if the Esc key is pressed before the change is completed. If the change is completed, the Undo entry option on the Edit menu can be used to undo the change.

Inserting and Deleting Fields and Records

To insert a new field, first click any cell in the column to the right or left of where the new field is to be placed. Next, click the right mouse button and click **Insert Field** from the displayed menu as shown in Figure 10.11. On the "pull-down" menu click Before to insert the new field to the left of the current field or After to insert the new field to the right of the current field. A window similar to the Create Database window is displayed. Enter the field name and formatting options for the new fields, and click the Add button. You can continue adding new fields until the Done button is clicked. The Record menu on the top line menu can also be used to insert fields the same way.

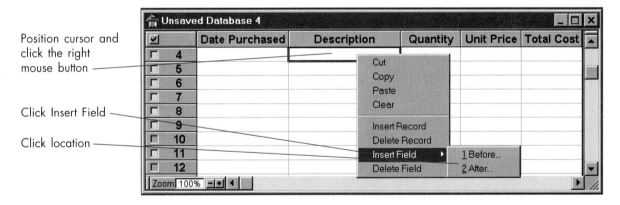

FIGURE 10.11   Use the right mouse button to insert new fields.

To insert a new record, position the cursor in any cell of the record immediately below where the new record is to be inserted and click the **Insert Record tool** on the Toolbar. The new row will be inserted immediately above the cursor. To insert multiple records, select the number of records to be inserted before clicking the Insert Record tool. For example, to insert three records, select a block of cells in three records, then click the Insert Record tool. The Record menu on the top line menu can also be used to insert records the same way.

To delete a field, position the cursor in the field to be deleted and click the right mouse button. Choose the **Delete Field** option from the menu. A message will appear that asks you to confirm the deletion. Choose OK and the field will be deleted. If more than one field is selected, all selected fields will be deleted. Records can be deleted using the same technique, except that you choose the **Delete Record** option from the right mouse button's menu.

Moving and Copying Fields and Records

Fields can be moved by using a cut and paste operation. First, click the field name of the field to be moved. This will select the entire column. Next, use the Cut option from the Edit menu or the Cut tool on the Toolbar. Then, click the field name of the field to the left of where you want the field placed and use the Paste option from the Edit menu or the Paste tool on the Toolbar.

A field can also be moved using the drag and drop method. First, click on the field name to be moved. This will select the entire column. Move the cursor over the selected field name. When the mouse pointer changes to the arrow with the word drag, drag the field to its new location.

Entire records can also be moved. To move an entire record, first click the record's number in the left margin of the database. This will select the record. Next, use the Cut option from the Edit menu or the Toolbar. Now, click the number of the record directly below where you want the record moved and choose the Paste option from the Edit menu or the Toolbar. This is the same process used in the Spreadsheet module to move a column or row.

Records can also be moved using the drag and drop method. First, select the records to be moved. Move the cursor over the selected record's number. When the mouse pointer changes to the arrow with the word drag, drag the record to its new location.

To copy records and fields, first use the Copy option from the Edit menu or the Copy tool on the Toolbar. Next, paste the record or field the way you would to move a record or field.

When a record or field has been placed on the clipboard with the Cut option, the Paste option will insert a new record or field. If the record or field has been placed on the clipboard with the Copy option, the Paste option will replace the existing data in the record or field with the copied data.

USING DATABASE FORMULAS

Database **formulas** are entered similarly to the way spreadsheet formulas are entered. Click the cell that is to contain the formula, press the equals sign (=), and enter the formula.

The database uses formulas in a different way than the spreadsheet uses them. In a spreadsheet, a formula is assigned to a specific cell. It is considered local to that cell and would need to be copied to other cells that need to use the formula. In a database, a formula is assigned to every blank cell in a field for all the records in the database and is used to compute the value of every empty cell in that field. The formula is considered global to all blank cells in the field.

A formula can be replaced with a value for a specific cell in a field. Any new formula will not affect the contents of the cell that has a value entered. The formula is assigned only to blank cells in the field. To get a formula back in the cell of a field that has been changed, select the cell and use the **Clear** option from the Edit menu.

If a formula is in any cell of a record, this creates a formula for that field in all records in the database. In general, a formula is applied to all records. A value is applied to only one record.

Database formulas use field names rather than cell coordinates like spreadsheets. For example, to compute a Total Cost field by multiplying a field named Quantity by a field named Unit Cost, enter =Quantity*Unit Cost in Total Cost field. This is shown in Figure 10.12.

Formula for Total Cost

Total Cost

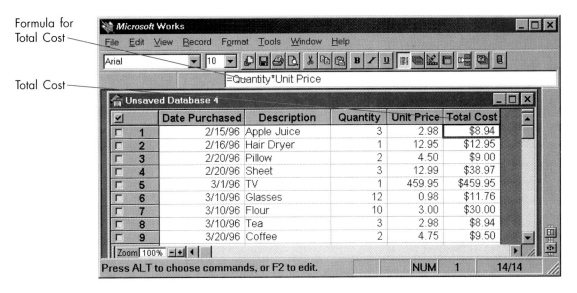

FIGURE 10.12 Formulas use field names and apply to all empty cells in a column.

To remove a formula from a field, select the entire field by clicking the field's name. Next, choose the **Clear Formula** option from the Edit menu.

Using Pointing to Create Formulas

Formulas can also be created using cell pointing. This approach is similar to the way pointing is used in a spreadsheet. To use this technique, click any cell in the column where the formula is to be used and press the Equals (=) key. Now, click any other cell in the record and that cell's name will become part of the formula. Type any arithmetic symbol needed for the formula and click the next field in the formula. When the formula is complete, press the Enter key.

Creating Running Totals

A **running total** is a **total** that accumulates values from one record to the next throughout the database. To create a running total, use the name of the field that contains the formula in the formula itself. When a field's name is used in its own formula, Microsoft Works will use the value from the previous record for that field's value.

For example, to create a running total of all total costs, enter the formula =Running Total + Total Cost in the field called Running Total. Works would add the value of the Total Cost field of the current record to the value of the field called Running Total from the previous record to compute the value of the Running Total field in the current record. Running totals are illustrated in Figure 10.13.

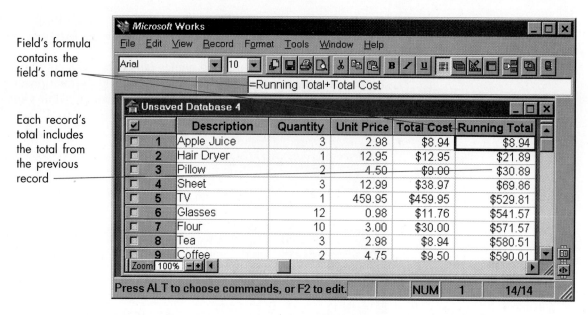

Field's formula contains the field's name —

Each record's total includes the total from the previous record —

FIGURE 10.13   A running total is created by using a field's name as part of the formula for the field.

PROTECTING DATABASE FIELDS

Certain fields in a database may need to be protected from being changed. For example, if the contents of a field is defined with a formula, you would not want people to enter data into this field accidentally. If they did, the new data would destroy the formula. To prevent this from happening, the field can be protected by using the **Protection** option on the Format menu. When database protection is turned on for a cell, the data in the cell, and many of the field options such as the cell format, cannot be changed. The Format Protection window is shown in Figure 10.14.

Click Protect field to prevent field editing —

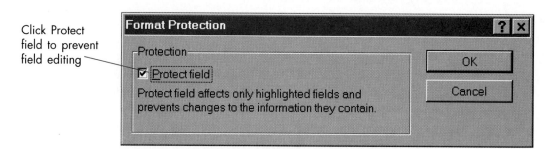

FIGURE 10.14   Protection window.

When **field protection** is set on and the Tab key or Shift/Tab key to tab backward is used, the protected cells are skipped and the cursor moves to the first unprotected cell. If a protected cell is clicked with the mouse, new data can be typed, but an error message is displayed. Remember, entire fields are protected. If protection is set on for any cell in a field, all cells in that field are protected.

Records in a database can be **sort**ed in ascending or descending sequence based on some key field. A **key field** is a field or combination of fields in the database. When records are sorted in an ascending sequence, they are ordered from low to high, based on the contents of their key field cells. When records are ordered in descending sequence, they are ordered from high to low.

Records in a database can be sorted using up to three different key fields. When more than one sort key field is used, records are ordered based on primary, intermediate, and minor key fields. The primary field is the most inclusive sort field. The intermediate field is the next most inclusive, and the minor field is the least inclusive. As an example, assume you wanted to sort records by a person's last name (see Figure 10.15). If this is your only requirement, then the Last Name field would be the primary or first sort field. Suppose you wanted all people with the same last name sorted by first name. In this case, the First Name field would be the intermediate or second sort field. Now, suppose you wanted all people with the same first and last name to be sorted by their middle initial. This would make the Initial field the minor or third sort field. This sort is shown in Figure 10.15.

Records sorted by Last Name —
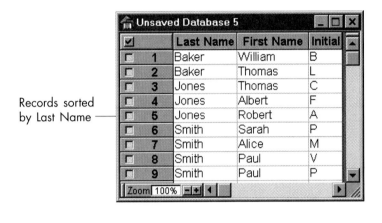

Records sorted by Last Name, First Name, and Initial —
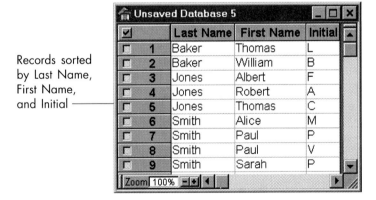

FIGURE 10.15   Records can be sorted on multiple fields.

To sort records in the database, use the **Sort Records** option on the Tools menu. The window for this option is shown in Figure 10.16 The primary sort field is the first sort field, the intermediate sort field is the second sort field, and the minor sort field is the third sort field.

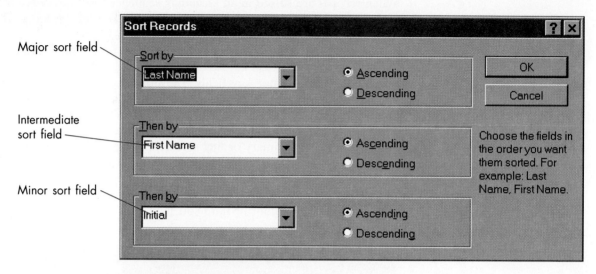

Major sort field

Intermediate sort field

Minor sort field

FIGURE 10.16   Sort Records window.

PRINTING A DATABASE

Printing a database is similar to printing any other document in Microsoft Works. Use the Print option of the File menu, the Printer tool on the Toolbar, or Print from Print Preview. The only additional options are on the Other Options folder of the Page Setup window accessed from the File menu. This folder is shown in Figure 10.17. Choose the Print **gridlines** option to print the lines between records and fields. Choose the **Print record and field labels** option to print the field names over the columns and the record numbers on the left side of each record. Both of these options work the same way here as they work in the Spreadsheet module.

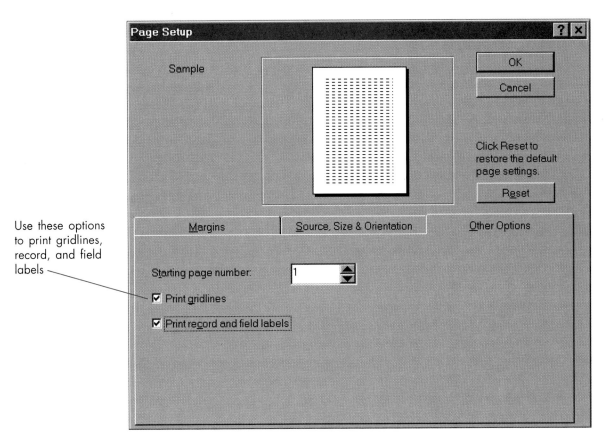

Use these options to print gridlines, record, and field labels

FIGURE 10.17   The Other Options folder of the Page Setup option.

For wide databases, those with many columns or very wide columns, the database prints like a spreadsheet. The leftmost columns print first with as many cells as will fit on a page. Then the columns to the right of those already printed will print. There are several approaches to making a database fit on a single page. They include changing the left, right, top, and bottom page margins, changing the font and font size so columns can be narrower, and printing in Landscape mode.

CHAPTER 10 SELF-TEST

1. Define the terms record, field, and cell as they apply to a Microsoft Works database.
2. Which database view displays records as a series of rows? Which view displays one record at a time?
3. What is the difference between a source field and a calculated field?
4. List five things you should consider when designing a database.
5. Explain what a default value is. When is the default value specified?
6. How do you tell Works to copy the contents of a field from the previous record?
7. How do you insert a new field into a database?
8. Write the formula to compute a Commission field in a database. Assume the commission is calculated by adding the fields named Services and Contracts, then subtracting the field named Cancels, and multiplying this answer by 10%.
9. How do you use Cursor Pointing to create a database formula?
10. Explain what a running total is. How do you create a running total?
11. What happens when you set "Protection on" for a database field?
12. Assume that you wanted to sort database records so that ZIP codes were sorted in ascending order by city, cities were sorted in ascending order by state, and states were sorted in ascending order. What would be the major, intermediate, and minor sort fields?
13. What do the Print record and field labels option on the Page Setup folder do?

TUTORIAL

In this tutorial, you will create a database to keep track of contributions for the American Cancer Society.

START THE TUTORIAL

1. Start Microsoft Works.
2. Click Works Tools tab on the Task Launcher.
3. Click the Database button.

CREATE THE DATABASE

The **Create Database window** shown in Figure 10.18 should now be displayed. The first three fields require no special options, so we will create these fields quickly.

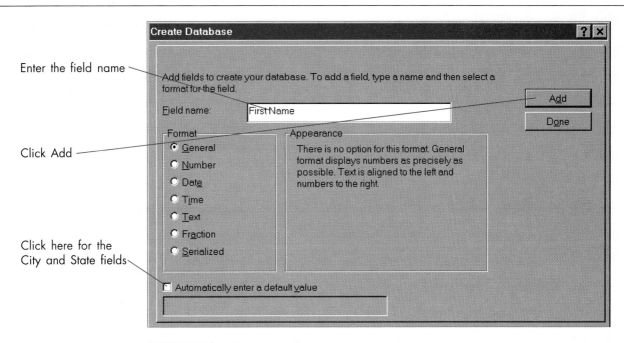

Enter the field name

Click Add

Click here for the City and State fields

FIGURE 10.18   The Create Database window.

1. Enter First Name for the Field name of the first field.
2. Click the Add button.
3. Enter Last Name for the Field name of the second field.
4. Click the Add button.
5. Enter Street for the Field name of the third field.
6. Click the Add button.

The next two fields will be the city and state fields. Since we are creating this database for the city of Bakersfield, CA, we will use **default values** for these two fields.

7. Enter City for the field name.
8. Click the "Automatically enter a default value" option at the bottom of the window.
9. Enter Bakersfield in the default value text area.
10. Click the Add button.
11. Enter State for the field name.
12. Click the "Automatically enter a default value" option at the bottom of the window.
13. Enter CA in the default value text area.
14. Click the Add button.

The next field will be the ZIP code field. Since ZIP codes are normally written as five digits, including leading zeros, we will select an Appearance for this field and assign a default value. See Figure 10.19.

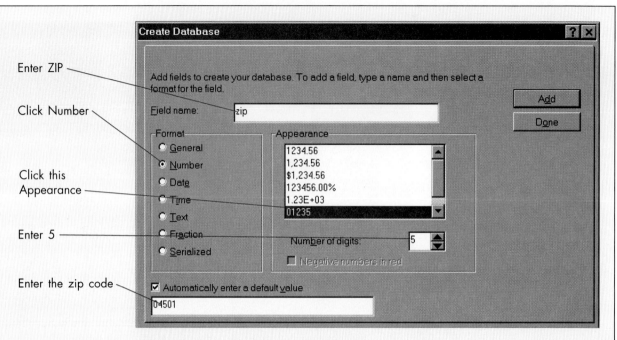

Enter ZIP

Click Number

Click this
Appearance

Enter 5

Enter the zip code

FIGURE 10.19   Completed window for the Zip field.

15. Enter ZIP for the field name.
16. Click the Number format option.
17. Click the 01235 Appearance option.
18. Enter 5 in the Number of digits area.
19. Click the "Automatically enter a default value" option at the bottom of the window.
20. Enter 04501 in the default value text area.
21. Click the Add button.

The final field to create is the Contribution field. We want a comma format with two decimals for this field.

22. Enter Contribution in the Field name area.
23. Click the Number format option.
24. Click the second Appearance option (1,234.56)
25. Click the Add button.
26. Click the Done button.

This should complete the creation of the database. You should now be in List view with an empty database like the one shown in Figure 10.20.

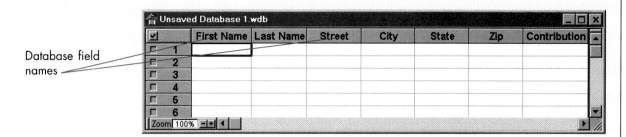

Database field names

FIGURE 10.20   The empty database after creating fields.

Enter the Database Data

The next step is to begin entering data into the database. We will enter the first record, then adjust any field formatting required.

1. Enter Nancy in the First name field of record 1 and press the Tab key.
2. Enter Samuelson in the Last Name and press the Tab key.
3. Enter 202 S. Hillcrest Dr. in the Street field and press the Tab key.

Notice that the next three fields have already been entered. Works used the default values we defined when the fields were created as the values for these fields.

4. Press the Tab key three times to move to the contribution field.
5. Enter 1000 in the Contribution field and press the tab key.

This should complete the first record. If you made a mistake in any cell, click the cell and reenter the data. Your screen should now look like the one shown in Figure 10.21.

Field widths too small

Data for first record

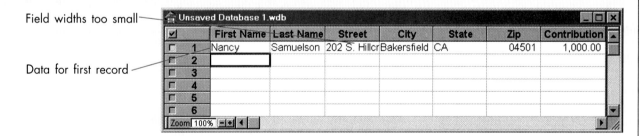

FIGURE 10.21   The database after entering the first record.

Widen the Street and City columns

Notice that the street field does not display all of the data entered. This is because the field width is too small. The next step is to widen the Street field and the City field.

1. Place the cursor in any cell in the Street column.
2. Click Field Width on the Format menu.
3. Enter 20 and press the Enter key.
4. Place the cursor in any cell in the City column.
5. Click Field Width on the Format menu.
6. Enter 15 and press the Enter key.

This should correct these two fields to hold our data. Now move to the first cell of the second record and enter the next two records.

7. Enter the following data in records 2 and 3. Tab from field to field. Tab over the City, State, and ZIP fields since the default data are correct.
   Tammy   Jones   214 Willshire Blvd. Bakersfield CA 04501 250
   Allison Micheals   311 Thomas La.   Bakersfield CA 04501 350.5

Copy Values from Previous Records

Now we want to add two more records, but this time the addresses are not in Bakersfield. We will need to enter new values in the default fields for the first record, but we can copy the values from the fourth record to the fifth record.

1. Enter the following record. This time, enter new data in the City, State, and ZIP fields.
   Brenda   Jones   314 Walnut St.   Carsonville NM 89101 500

The next record will be for the same city and state (Carsonville, NM) so use the **Ctrl/'** keys to copy these fields from record four. Remember, Ctrl/' means hold down the Ctrl key and press the single quote key.

2. Enter the following record.
   Frank   Michaels   472 Lucy Long Dr.   Ctrl/'   Ctrl/'   Ctrl/'   1200

Your database should now look like the one in Figure 10.22. All the fields may not be displayed due to font sizes. Use the horizontal scroll bar to see fields on the right.

FIGURE 10.22 Database after entering the first five records.

ADD TWO NEW FIELDS

Now add two **calculated fields** to the end of your record. The first field will compute a monthly payment if the contributor wants to pay his or her contribution in 12 equal payments. The second field will keep a running total of contributions.

1. Place the cursor in any cell of the Contribution column.
2. Click the right mouse button.
3. Click Insert Field and click the After option.
4. Enter Monthly as the field name on the insert field screen.
5. Click the Number format and the comma Appearance.
6. Click the Add button.
7. Enter Totals for the field name of the next field.
8. Click the Number format option and the Appearance that has the dollar sign.
9. Click the Add button.
10. Click the Done button.

Create a Formula for Monthly Contribution

Now, enter a **formula** that will compute a monthly amount for the contribution.

1. Tab to any cell in the Monthly column.
2. Enter =Contribution/12.
3. Press Enter to complete the formula.

The Monthly contribution should now be displayed in all five records.

Create a Running Total

Now, create a running total for all contributions.

1. Tab to the Totals field.
2. Enter =Contribution + Totals as the field's formula.

The last two fields should now look like the ones shown in Figure 10.23.

Calculated field ⎯

Running total ⎯

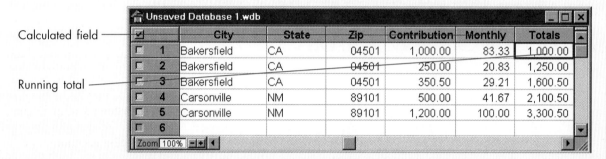

		City	State	Zip	Contribution	Monthly	Totals
☐	1	Bakersfield	CA	04501	1,000.00	83.33	1,000.00
☐	2	Bakersfield	CA	04501	250.00	20.83	1,250.00
☐	3	Bakersfield	CA	04501	350.50	29.21	1,600.50
☐	4	Carsonville	NM	89101	500.00	41.67	2,100.50
☐	5	Carsonville	NM	89101	1,200.00	100.00	3,300.50
☐	6						

FIGURE 10.23   Database after entering formulas for the Monthly and Totals field.

ENTER RECORDS USING FORM VIEW

As mentioned earlier, when a database is first created, a default form is also created. You will enter three more records using the default form for your database. To change to **Form View**, click the Form View tool. Before changing to this view, move the cursor to the first field of the first record.

1. Press Ctrl/Home to move to the first cell.
2. Click the Form View tool on the Toolbar or choose Form from the View menu.

The screen should now contain a form like the one shown in Figure 10.24. The default form assigns a field width of 20 characters to each field. This may not be the same width as you assigned the fields in the List view, but it will be fine for now. For this reason, the form does not look as neat as it should. You will work with form design in Chapter 11. Use this form to edit, view, or add records.

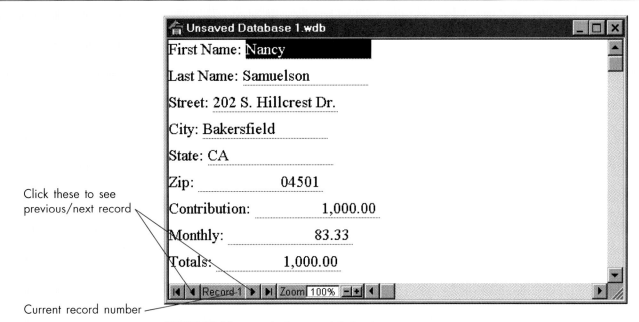

Click these to see
previous/next record

Current record number

FIGURE 10.24 First database record displayed in Form view.

Notice the record number displayed at the bottom left of the Form View window. This indicates which record is being displayed. In Figure 10.24 it is the first record in the database. Now notice the small arrows to the left and right of the record number. These arrows can be used to move from one record to the next in Form View. The left two arrows move to the first record and previous record respectively. The right two arrows move to the next and last record respectively. Use the arrows to review the database records.

3. Click the arrows at the bottom left of the form window to review the records.

To add records to the database, make sure you are on the first blank record. This will be record 6. Watch the lower-right corner of the window to make sure you are on this record.

Enter the following records. Remember to use the Tab key to move to the next field. Use the Ctrl/' key if the previous record contains the same data for a field. Tab past the Monthly and Total fields since these fields contain formulas.

4. Move to the first blank record, record 6. Make sure the cursor is in the first cell of the form.

5. Enter the following records:

Record 6	Record 7	Record 8
Mary	Bill	Charles
Jones	Michaels	Jones
210 N. Maple	111 North Ave.	33 W. Palmbeach Ave.
Bakersfield	Millsburg	Millsburg
CA	NM	NM
04501	89022	89022
75.00	444.50	100

This should complete the data for the database. To complete the last few steps, change back to List view.

1. Click the List View tool on the Toolbar.

PROTECT THE FIELDS

Some fields need to be protected, especially those with formulas. When a field is protected, the contents of the field cannot be changed. Having the fields with formulas protected will guarantee that the formulas are not accidentally destroyed.

1. Move the cursor to the Monthly column in any row.
2. Hold down the shift key and press the right arrow key to select this cell and a cell in the next column.
3. Choose the **Protection** option from the Format menu.
4. Click the Protect Field option. (See Figure 10.25.)
5. Click OK.

Check Protect field

Click OK

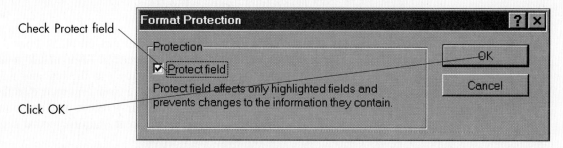

FIGURE 10.25   Protection window.

Protection should now be turned on for the last two fields. To see if the protection works, press the Tab key to move through the database. The cursor should skip the protected fields.

6. Press the Up Arrow key and press the Tab key to move through the fields. Notice the protected fields are skipped.

Now, use the mouse or arrow keys to move to different cells that are locked, and try to enter data into these fields. A message like the one in Figure 10.26 should be displayed.

7. Click a protected cell.
8. Enter a value in the cell.
9. Click OK when you get the error message.

FIGURE 10.26   This error message box appears when you try to change a protected cell.

SORT THE DATABASE

Assume you want the records sorted first by city. Then for each city, you want the records sorted by last name. For people with the same last name, you want the records sorted by first name. This would make City the primary sort field, Last Name the intermediate sort field, and First Name the minor sort field.

Sort the database. Refer to the **Sort Records** window in Figure 10.27.

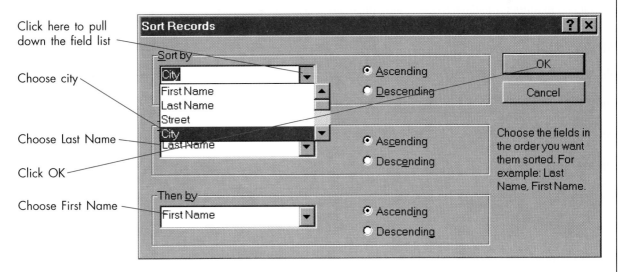

FIGURE 10.27   Sort Records window to sort the tutorial records.

1. Choose Sort Records from the Record menu.
2. Click the arrow on the right of the "Sort by" text area.
3. Select City as the sort field.
4. Click the arrow on the right of the first "Then by" text area.
5. Select Last Name as the sort field.
6. Click the arrow on the right of the second "Then by" text area.
7. Select First name as the sort field.
8. Click OK.

Check your screen to make sure the records are sorted correctly. Your screen should look like the one shown in Figure 10.28.

☑		First Name	Last Name	Street	City	State	Zip	Contribution	Monthly
☐	1	Mary	Jones	210 N. Maple	Bakersfield	CA	04501	75.00	6.25
☐	2	Tammy	Jones	214 Wilshire Rd.	Bakersfield	CA	04501	250.00	20.83
☐	3	Allison	Michaels	311 Thomas La.	Bakersfield	CA	04501	350.50	29.21
☐	4	Nancy	Samuelson	202 S. Hillcrest Dr.	Bakersfield	CA	04501	1,000.00	83.33
☐	5	Brenda	Jones	314 Walnut St.	Carsonville	NM	89101	500.00	41.67
☐	6	Frank	Micheals	472 Lucy Long Dr.	Carsonville	NM	89101	1,200.00	100.00
☐	7	Charles	Jones	33 W. Palmbeach Ave.	Millsburg	NM	89022	100.00	8.33
☐	8	Bill	Michaels	111 North Ave.	Millsburg	NM	89022	444.50	37.04
☐	9								

Zoom 75%

FIGURE 10.28   Your database after sorting the records.

PRINT THE DATABASE

Change the Page Orientation

The records in the database are too long to print on a single line in portrait orientation. Change the orientation to landscape before printing.

1. Choose the Page Setup option on the File menu.
2. Click the Source, Size & Orientation folder's tab.
3. Click the Landscape orientation option.

Set the Other Options

To print the record gridlines and the field and record labels, these options must be set on in the **Other Options folder** of the Page Setup folder.

1. Click the Other Options tab.
2. Click the Print gridlines option.
3. Click the **Print record and field labels** option.
4. Click the OK button.
   You are now ready to print the database. Preview and print the database.
5. Click the Print Preview Tool.
6. Click the Print button on the Print Preview screen.

SAVE THE DATABASE

When the database completes printing, save the database with the name Chapter 10 Tutorial.WDB. Since you have just created the database, use the Save As option from the File menu.

1. Select the Save As option on the File menu and save your database with the name Chapter 10 Tutorial.WDB.
2. Exit Works.

Exercise 10-1

Select a class of items, such as cassette tapes, CDs, books, sports teams, or classes you have completed. Create a database you can use to keep track of the items. Use several fields, such as title, author or artist, publisher, edition, purchase price or purchase date, subject, instructor, and grade.

Enter at least ten records in the database. Print two copies of the database, sorted in two different orders.

Exercise 10-2A

Create a database for the data shown at the end of this exercise. This database keeps track of business expenses. Use the following requirements.

1. Name and format the fields appropriately; you may want to use different field names.
2. Use a default value of Transportation for the Expense.
3. The Allowance field is the amount allowed for the expense. The Actual field is the amount actually spent for the expense.
4. The Total Actual field is the sum of all money actually spent. This field is calculated as the running total of the Actual field. Create these data using a formula. Do not type the data shown. This is shown only so you can check your formula.
5. The Budget is the current status of the expense budget. It is the running total of the Allowance field minus the Actual field. Create these data using a formula. Do not type the data shown. This is shown only so you can check your formula.
6. Protect the Total Actual and Budget fields.
7. Print the database after entering the data in the order shown.

Date	Expense	Company	Allowance	Actual	Total Actual	Budget
7/10/96	Meals	Fuddruckers	20.00	12.90	12.90	$7.10
7/11/96	Transportation	USAir	135.00	200.00	212.90	($57.90)
7/11/96	Lodging	Marriott	110.00	135.50	348.40	($83.40)
6/12/96	Transportation	Yellow Cab	20.00	12.00	360.40	($75.40)
6/9/96	Entertainment	Belle Theater	90.00	55.95	416.35	($41.35)
10/15/96	Meals	Thomas Rest.	35.00	16.95	433.30	($23.30)
9/21/96	Transportation	USAir	350.00	290.00	723.30	$36.70
7/11/96	Meals	Days Inn	20.00	14.95	738.25	$41.75
10/15/96	Transportation	Delta Airlines	240.00	325.00	1,063.25	($43.25)
7/15/96	Meals	Pancake House	12.00	14.36	1,077.61	($45.61)

Exercise 10-2B

1. Change the data for record 2 so that the value of the Actual field is 125.00.
2. Delete Record 7.
3. Sort the database by Expense. Print the database.
4. Sort the database by Expense within Date (sort by date, and for each different date, have the records sorted by expense). Use a Descending sequence for the Date field and an Ascending sequence for the Expense field. Print the database with gridlines and field and record labels.

Exercise 10-3

Create a database for the data below. Use the following requirements.

1. Name and format the fields appropriately.
2. Use formulas for the following fields.
   a. BO: This is the back-ordered field. It is the Ordered field minus the Received field. Create these data using a formula. Do not type the data shown. This is shown only so you can check your formula.
   b. Total: This is the total cost of the order and is computed as the Ordered field multiplied by the Unit Price field. Create these data using a formula. Do not type the data shown. This is shown only so you can check your formula.
   c. Net: This is the actual amount owed. It is the Received field multiplied by the Unit Price field. Create these data using a formula. Do not type the data shown. This is shown only so you can check your formula.
3. Protect all fields that contain formulas.
4. Print the database with gridlines and field and record labels.
5. Sort the database by Date. Print the database with gridlines and field and record labels.
6. Sort the database by Class within Date (order by date and within each date, have the items ordered by Class). Print the database with gridlines and field and record labels.
7. Sort the database by descending Item number within Class within Date (order by date and within each date, have the items ordered by Class and within each Class, have the items ordered by descending Item number). Print the database with gridlines and field and record labels.

tem	Date	Class	Description	Ordered	Received	BO	Unit Price	Total	Net
0130	8/14/96	Toy	Spiderman	100	90	10	2.75	275.00	$247.50
1678	8/17/96	Apparel	Shirts	48	36	12	19.25	924.00	$693.00
1340	8/14/96	Kitchen	Glasses	144	96	48	1.98	285.12	$190.08
0457	8/14/96	Toy	Lego Table	26	24	2	29.50	767.00	$708.00
2390	9/1/96	Apparel	Baseball Hat	144	144	0	2.00	288.00	$288.00
4175	9/17/96	Apparel	Socks	250	250	0	3.00	750.00	$750.00
0130	8/22/96	Toy	Spiderman	100	90	10	2.75	275.00	$247.50
2391	9/1/96	Apparel	Team Hat	200	150	50	2.50	500.00	$375.00
3299	8/14/96	Kitchen	Can Opener	60	30	30	29.00	1,740.00	$870.00
0013	9/1/96	Toy	Video Game	24	24	0	45.00	1,080.00	$1,080.00
0178	8/22/96	Kitchen	Steak Knives	24	12	12	14.00	336.00	$168.00
4175	8/22/96	Toy	Rocking Horse	12	12	0	59.00	708.00	$708.00

FORM DESIGN AND DATABASE FILTERS

When you've completed this chapter, you will be able to:

- Modify a default database form.
- Use color, rectangles, and clipart on a form.
- Print database data on a form.
- Create Easy filters.
- Create filters using OR and AND conjunctions.
- Create filters using ranges.
- Create filters using formulas.
- Name, rename, and save filters.
- Mark records.
- Print the results of a filter.

In the previous database chapter, a database for the American Cancer Society was created. Works automatically created a **default database form** that was used to enter and view records. Although the form is sufficient for most needs, it may need to be changed to make it easier to use or to make it look different. It may also be necessary to print records to look like a specific form. Works will allow a form to be modified in many different ways to create a custom form. Figure 11.1 shows a default form and a customized form for a used car dealer.

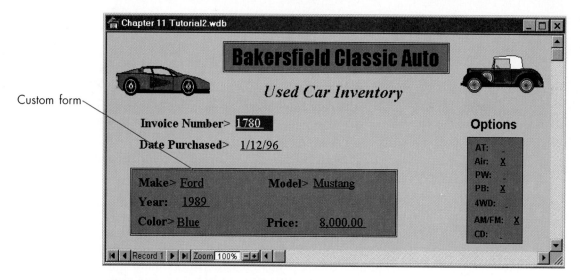

Default form

Custom form

FIGURE 11.1 Default and custom database forms.

The easiest way to create a **custom form** is to modify the default form. This is the approach we will use in this chapter. Before discussing how a form is changed, we need to explain two general concepts.

When Microsoft Works creates the default form, two items are created for each field (column) in the database. The first item is the **field name**. The field name is placed to the left of the field area and ends with a colon. This field name can be hidden and other text that better explains the data in the field can be displayed. In fact, you can enter text anywhere on the form.

The second item is the actual database field area. The value for the database field is entered and displayed in this area. Works assigns a default width of 20 characters to all field areas in Form view. This default width can be changed with the Format menu or the mouse.

When the form is created, all items on the form are treated as objects. Each field and field name is treated as an object and can be moved, shaded, colored, or otherwise formatted independently. Other types of objects can also be added to the form.

ALTERING A DEFAULT DATABASE FORM

To alter a form, use the **Form Design** option on the View menu or click the **Form Design tool** near the right side of the Toolbar. Once you are in the Form Design view, you can use the mouse to drag items on the form to different locations. To move a field, click the field. The field will be highlighted to indicate it is selected. Once the field is selected, use the mouse to drag the field to a new location. When the field is moved, both the field name and the entry area move.

To move a field using the arrow keys, click the field to be moved and choose the **Position Selection** option from the Edit menu. Use the Left, Right, Up, and Down arrows to position the field on the form. Sometimes it is easier and more accurate to use the arrow keys when moving a field.

As a field is moved, **X and Y coordinates** in the upper-left corner of the window will indicate the position of the field on the form. These coordinates are measured in inches. Use the coordinates to position a field or text in an exact location on the form. Figure 11.2 shows these coordinates.

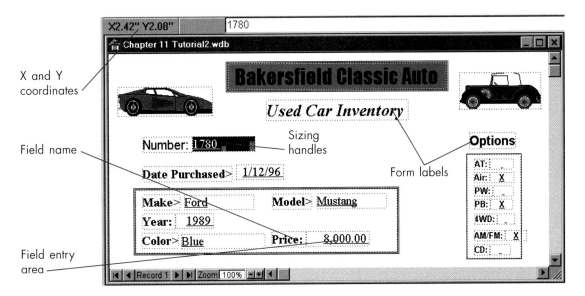

FIGURE 11.2   X and Y coordinates of a selected field are displayed at the top of the database window.

When a field is selected, handles will appear on the field much like the handles on a picture described in Chapter 5. These handles can be used to change the field's width and height.

Each field has the field name displayed to the left of the data entry area. To change the text that indicates a field, this field name must be hidden and a new **label** entered. To hide the field name, select the field and set the **Show Field Name** option off from the Format menu. When this option is set off, the field name will not be displayed. New labels to indicate the field can then be entered anywhere on the screen. Once the new label is entered, it can be moved so that it is near the field entry to identify the field.

Decorating A Form

Titles and other labels can be added to the form. To create a title, click anywhere on the form and enter the title. This creates a text block that can be selected and dragged anywhere on the form. The font, size, color, and format of the text block can be changed by using different options on the Format menu or by using the Toolbar. A text block can also be assigned border and shading options using the right mouse button menu options.

There are several other options that can be used to dress up a form. One possibility is to place a picture on the form. To insert a picture, choose the **Clip-Art** option from the Insert menu. This will start the **ClipArt Gallery** program. Select a picture from the ClipArt Gallery and the picture will be inserted. The handles on the picture or the Picture option on the Format menu can be used to change its size. The picture can be moved to different locations using the drag and drop technique. Refer to Chapter 5, Advanced Word Processing Features, for more information on working with pictures and clipart.

Another possibility is to use the **Border** option on the Format menu. You can apply an outline border to a field that has been selected. You can also shade a field entry by using the **Patterns** option on the Format menu. The font, font size, and style such as bold, italic, and underline can be changed on any field or text label on the form.

The entire form background can be shaded and colored by placing the cursor on the form, but not in a text block, and selecting the **Shading** option from the Format menu. If a text block or field is selected when the Shading option is chosen, the shading will only apply to the selected object.

A rectangle can be placed on the form by choosing the **Rectangle** option from the Insert menu. The rectangle will have handles that can be used to change its size. When a rectangle is placed on the form, it is placed in front (on top) of the fields within the rectangle. In order to access the fields that are within the rectangle's area, choose the **Send to back** option from the Format menu. Fields and other items on the form can be dragged into the rectangle to partition or separate different areas of the form.

It is also possible to place spreadsheet data and charts on the form. When the database is opened, any changes that have been made to the original spreadsheet or chart can also be applied to the spreadsheet or chart on the form.

By moving fields and changing the text used to identify the field, a form can be created that is customized to your individual needs.

Ordering Fields for Data Entry

When using the form to enter or edit data, the Tab key is used to move from one field to the next. The **tabbing order** for the fields is defined by the order in which the field was added to the database. If the Tab key does not move to the fields in the desired order, use the **Tab Order** option on the Format menu to change the order. Figure 11.3 shows the Format Tab Order window.

Click to move a field up or down in the tabbing order

Cancel any changes made in the tabbing order

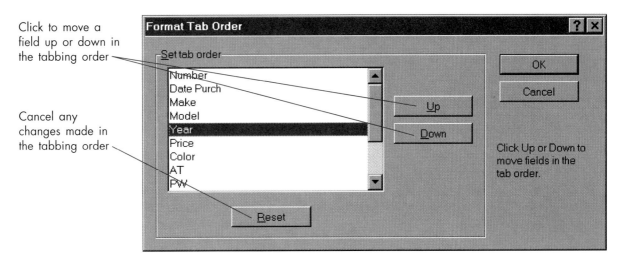

FIGURE 11.3   Use the Format Tab Order window to change the order in which fields are accessed when using the tab key.

To change the tabbing order, select the field name to be changed, then click the Up or Down button to move the selected field before or after its current position. Click the Reset button to cancel any changes made to the tabbing order.

A Note on Printing Color

Color can be used extensively in Works. It is especially useful to dress up a form and make certain areas stand out from other areas. Although color has its advantages, several problems may occur when printing.

First, printing may be much slower. If the background on a form is white, no actual printing of the background occurs. This allows the printer to only print the text. If the background has a color, the entire background will need to be printed; this will take much longer.

The second problem occurs with black and white printers. Since the printer cannot print colors like red, yellow, or blue, most printers will try to print them in some shade of gray or not print them at all. Suppose you had yellow text on a blue background. The black and white printer might print both colors as black. This would place black text on a black background, thereby making the text impossible to see. Or maybe you have red text on a white background. If the red text prints as white, it would appear as if the text is not printed at all.

In the tutorial you will use some color to dress up a form. Be aware that you may need to change the colors if you want to print the form.

DATABASE FILTERS

The function of a database is to store information about objects. These objects are things that you need to know about at some later time. The database will usually contain information concerning more objects than you need to know about at any one point in time. One of the advantages of storing information in a database is that the database will allow you to ask questions about the data within it. The question is formed by telling Works what you are looking for. Works then filters the data so that only those records you want to see are displayed. For example, assume you were a used-automobile dealer and had a customer who wanted to purchase a 1992 Ford Escort. A filter could search through the database and find only those automobiles that met that condition.

Filters can be as simple and straightforward as the one just described, or they can be complex. For example, you could ask for all automobiles that were made after 1985, cost between $5,000 and $6,500, and were not blue. In either case, Microsoft Works would search through the database and display only those records that meet the conditions specified.

Remember that there are two ways to view the database, the **List view** and the **Form view**. A filter can be created from either view. Exactly how the filter displays the selected records depends on which view is being used at the time the filter is started. If the database is in Form view, records will be displayed one at a time using the database form. If the database is in List view, all matching records are displayed as a listing. Once the filter has been completed and the records have been selected, the database can be switched between views.

Microsoft Works uses two types of filters: **Easy Filters** and **Filters using formulas**. To create a filter, choose Filter from the Tools menu or click the Filters tool on the Toolbar. This will display the Filter window. From the Filter window you specify which type of filter you will be creating.

USING EASY FILTERS

To create a filter, open the database and click the **Filters tool** on the Toolbar, or choose Filters from the Tools menu. If this is the first filter created for the database, you will be asked to name the filter. Once the filter is named, a Filter window like the one shown in Figure 11.4 is displayed.

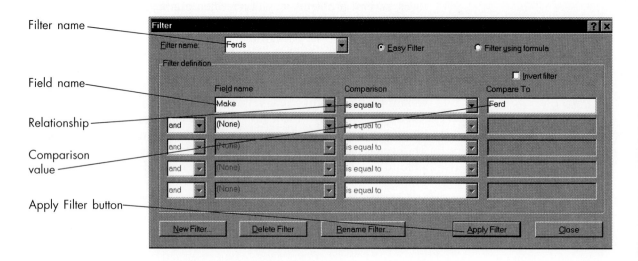

FIGURE 11.4 An Easy Filter window.

An **Easy Filter** window will allow up to five conditions for the filter. Each condition has three parts:

1. The first part of a condition is the name of a field on the database. This is the field being compared. For example, if you are looking for autos that are Fords, Ford is contained in the Make field, so Make would be the field name.
2. The second part of a filter is the relationship or type of comparison. This part of the filter determines how the value of the filtered field is being compared. For example, a condition might test the field to see if it is equal to a value or if it is less than some value.
3. The third part of the filter is the value or field to which the first field is being compared. In the example above, Ford would be the value for this area.

The example in Figure 11.4 is comparing the field named Make to the value Ford and testing for an equal condition. Thus, the filter is saying, find all autos where the make is a Ford.

Testing Multiple Conditions

Sometimes more than one condition must be evaluated. For example, suppose you wanted to see all Fords that cost less than $10,000. This would require a condition to test for the Ford and a condition to test for the $10,000.

To test multiple conditions, the criteria must be connected by an **AND** or an **OR** conjunction. If the AND connector is used, both criteria must be true for a record to pass the test. If the OR condition is used, a record will pass the test if either condition is true.

If, for example, you need to see all Fords made before 1990, an AND connector would be required. In English, the filter would be: Find all automobiles where the Make is equal to Ford and the Year is less than 1990. Figure 11.5 shows the Easy Filter for these conditions.

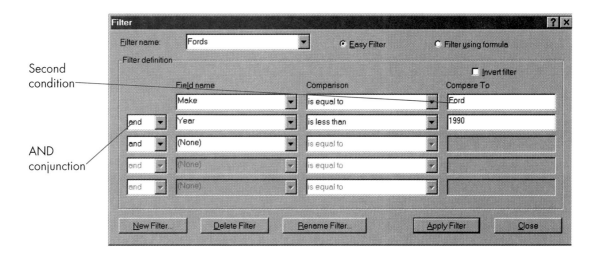

FIGURE 11.5   The Easy Filter to find Fords made before 1990.

If you wanted to find any Ford or any automobile made before 1990, the criterion would be the same, except that the two conditions would be connected by an OR conjunction rather than an AND conjunction.

Using Relational Operators

Figure 11.6 shows the options available for relationships between the field being compared and the value the field is being compared to. The first six options are fairly straightforward. For example, the **is equal to** option compares the field in the Field name entry to see if it is equal to the value in the Compare To entry. The **is less than** option tests the field to see if it is less than the value in the Compare To entry.

Click here to pull down the list

Relational operators

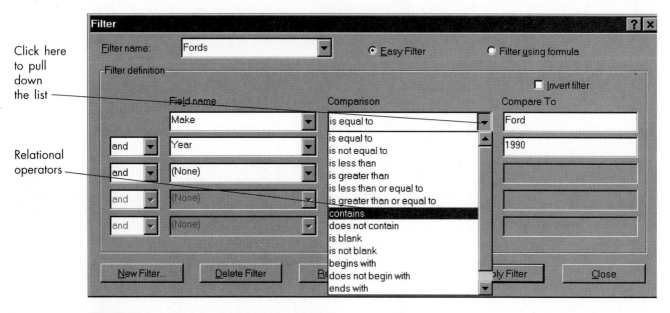

FIGURE 11.6   Relationship operators for the filter window.

A few options need explaining. The **contains** relational operator will search the field to see if the value in the Compare To entry appears anywhere in the field. For example, if the word red were entered in the Compare To entry, records would be found if the field being compared contained red, redhead, referred, spared, or any other value that contained the word red.

If the **does not contain** relational operator were used, none of the values above would be found. Suppose there were several X type autos (EXP, 240-ZX, etc.) and you did not want to see these autos. The filter to use would be: Model does not contain X.

The **is blank** and **is not blank** operators look for a field that is empty (is blank) or a field that contains anything (is not blank). Assume the options on an auto were marked with an E, P, and I for Excellent, Poor, or Inoperable. If the auto did not have the option, the field would be left blank. To find autos that have power windows in any condition, use: Power Windows is not blank. To find autos that did not have power windows, use: Power Windows is blank. These two conditions do not have a Compare To value.

The last three relational operators look for characters at the beginning or the end of a field value. The **begins with** and **does not begin with** look for characters on the left of the value. The **ends with** and **does not end with** (not shown in Figure 11.6 because it is below the scroll bar) look at the right side of a field value. For example, suppose a database contained item codes. The first character in the item code indicated the type of item (M for meat, C for canned, V for vegetable, etc.). The remainder of the code is used to indicate the particular item. Now assume these two codes exist; V173A and M135V. To find all vegetable items, you would use Code begins with V. You could not use the contains comparison because the second code contains a V, but it is not at the beginning of the code.

Using the Filter Window

Notice the arrows in the first Field Name area of the Filter window. If the arrow is clicked, a list of all fields in the current database will be displayed. To choose a field for the filter criteria, simply click the field's name.

An arrow is also beside the Comparison entry. If this arrow is clicked, a list of possible relationship options is provided. To choose a relationship, simply click the one desired. This list was shown in Figure 11.6.

The Compare To area is used to enter the value to compare to. The entries in this box must be typed. When comparing a field to characters, the case of the characters is ignored by Works. This means that if the word Blue is entered in this area, Blue, BLUE, blue, and BlUe would all be considered equal.

To see the results of the filter, click the **Apply Filter** button at the bottom of the filter window.

FILTERS USING FORMULAS

There are times when a filter needs to be developed that cannot be completed using an Easy Filter. An Easy Filter only allows five comparisons. For most filters this would be enough, but there may be times when more are needed. If more than five comparisons are needed, the filter must be written using a formula.

Even some fairly simple filters must be written using a formula. For example, suppose you wanted to buy a Ford. You have $2,000 for a down payment and you do not want to finance more than $10,000. In English, the question would be: Which Fords will cost less than $10,000 after subtracting a $2,000 down payment? The first comparison would be Make is equal to Ford. The second comparison cannot be written as an Easy Filter because the Field name entry would need to be Price-2000. The Field name entry only allows a field name. The full formula for the second comparison would be Price-2,000 < 10,000.

To enter a filter as a formula, click the **Filter using formula** option at the top of the Easy Filter window. A filter window similar to the one shown in Figure 11.7 will be displayed. The entire formula to be used by the filter must be entered in the formula area.

Choose this option to enter a formula

Enter the filter formula

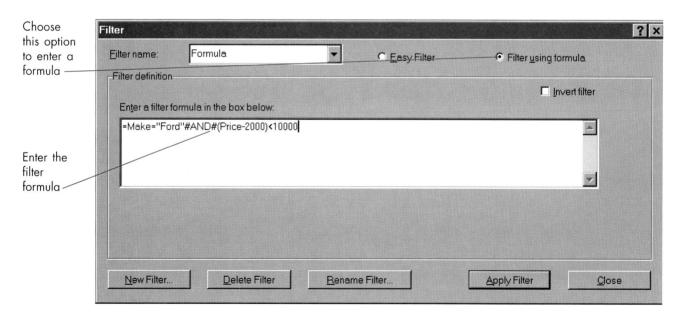

FIGURE 11.7   When filters are complex, a filter must be written using the **Filter using formula** window.

Formulas can be complex and must be written using a precise syntax. **Syntax** refers to sentence structure, and means that the formula must be written in a form that can be interpreted by Microsoft Works. Because Works converts all Easy Filters to formulas, the best way to develop a formula is to enter as much of the formula as possible as an Easy Filter, then click the **Filter using formula** option. The conditions in the Easy Filter are converted to a formula. The formula can then be changed to add the necessary requirements. Figure 11.8a shows an Easy Filter. Figure 11.8b shows the resulting formula for the filter. The formula shown in Figure 11.8b was created by Microsoft Works from the Easy Filter in Figure 11.8a, and shows some of the syntax required for certain conditions.

Easy Filter conditions

Filter			? X
Filter name:	Formula ▼	● Easy Filter	○ Filter using formula

Filter definition

☐ Invert filter

	Field name	Comparison	Compare To
	Make ▼	is equal to ▼	Ford
and ▼	Model ▼	is equal to ▼	Escort
and ▼	Year ▼	is greater than ▼	1990
and ▼	Price ▼	is less than ▼	12,000
and ▼	Color ▼	contains ▼	Blue

New Filter... | Delete Filter | Rename Filter... | Apply Filter | Close

FIGURE 11.8A

Resulting formula for Figure 11.8

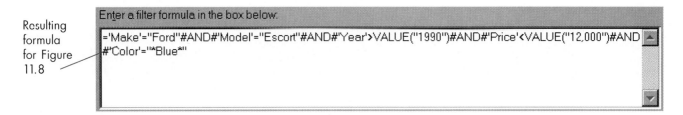

Enter a filter formula in the box below:

='Make'="Ford"#AND#'Model'="Escort"#AND#'Year'>VALUE("1990")#AND#'Price'<VALUE("12,000")#AND#'Color'="*Blue*"

FIGURE 11.8B   Use the Easy Filter window to create complex filter formulas.

Filter Formula Requirements

Remember that a formula must use a specific syntax when it is written. The syntax rules for writing formulas are as follows:

1. The formula must begin with an equals sign (=).
2. Field names must be entered as they are defined in the database. The case of the field name is not important, but spaces and special characters must appear exactly as they appear in the database field names.
3. Relational operators are entered using symbols rather than words. Figure 11.9 shows the Comparison entry using the Easy Filter form and the corresponding approach using a formula.
4. When comparing to a text field, the value being compared to must be enclosed in double quote marks. When comparing to numbers or dates, the values do not need to be enclosed in quotes.
5. When performing arithmetic in the formula, enclose the arithmetic operations in parentheses to indicate the order of operations.
6. The conjunctions AND and OR must be enclosed in pound symbols (#AND#, #OR#).

EASY FILTER	FILTER USING FORMULA
is equal to	=
is not equal to	<>
is less than	<
is greater than	>
is less than or equal to	<=
is greater than or equal to	>=
contains	="*characters*" (use wild card)
does not contain	<> "*characters*" (use wild card)
is blank	=""
is not blank	<> ""
begins with	="*characters" (use wild card)
does not begin with	<> "*characters" (use wild card)
ends with	="characters*" (use wild card)
does not end with	<> "characters*" (use wild card)

FIGURE 11.9   Symbols used as relational operators in formulas.

When a filter is written as a formula, Microsoft Works may make some changes to the filter. For example, if you enter a field name, Works will place single quotes around the field name. If you enter a number, Works will change the number to a VALUE function.

In some cases, a filter may be written and a message will appear when you try to apply the filter. The message will indicate that Works is correcting the filter to conform to an understandable syntax. In most cases, the filter will be changed correctly. In some cases, the change may be incorrect and the filter will need to be changed by you to make it correct.

Using Wild Cards in Filter Criteria

Wild cards must be used in a filter formula in place of using a *contains, does not contain, begins with, does not begin with, ends with, or does not end with* comparison. The **asterisk** (*) is the wild card used in place of any number of characters. For example, to find any model of car that begins with the letter C, use the criterion C*. To find all automobiles that are blue, such as dark blue, misty blue, royal blue, or blue/green, use the criterion *blue*. Figure 11.10 shows examples of formulas using different wild cards.

FORMULA	MEANING
'Model' = "*100"	Find any auto where the model ends in the number 100.
'Model' = "*100*"	Find any auto where the number 100 appears anywhere in the model (contains).
'Model' = "100*"	Find any auto where the model starts with 100.

FIGURE 11.10   Filter formulas and wild cards.

UNDERSTANDING AND and OR

The **AND** and **OR** conjunctions are used to allow multiple conditions in a filter. The AND conjunction requires that both conditions be met and the OR conjunction requires that either condition be met. When the AND and OR conjunctions are used together in a single filter, the filter can be quite confusing. For example, assume the following filter conditions:

	Make	is equal to	Ford
or	Make	is equal to	Pontiac
and	Price	is greater than	10,000

Does the filter above ask for any Ford or Pontiac that costs more than $10,000 or does it ask for any Ford and only Pontiacs that cost more than $10,000?

In the example above, the filter asks for any Ford or Pontiac that costs more than $10,000. This is because the OR condition is written before the AND condition. The point being made here is the order in which the conditions are specified is important. If you wanted any Ford and only Pontiacs that cost more than $10,000 conditions would need to be specified as:

	Make	is equal to	Pontiac
and	Price	is greater than	10,000
or	Make	is equal to	Ford

You may need to try a filter several different ways before you get the query to perform exactly the way you want it to.

DEFINING A RANGE OF VALUES

A filter can also be used to select a **range** of values. A range specifies a lower and an upper limit for the values for which you are searching. A range can be defined using either an Easy Filter or a formula.

Suppose you are willing to pay between $8,000 and $10,000 for an automobile. The range would be between eight and ten thousand dollars. This would require two conditions on the same field as illustrated in Figure 11.11. The first condition specifies the lower limit of the range. The second specifies the upper limit of the range.

Lower
range
limit

Upper
range
limit

AND
conjunction

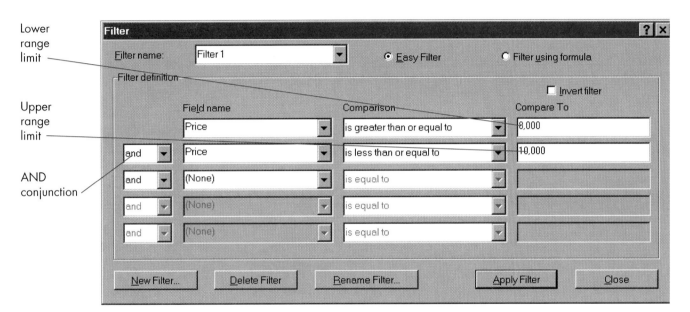

FIGURE 11.11 To check a range of values, connect a condition for the lower limit to a condition for the upper limit with an AND conjunction.

Notice that the two conditions are connected by an AND conjunction.

CALCULATING DATA IN FORMULAS

Works will also allow calculated data as the search criterion. Assume that you have $8,000 to buy an automobile. Next, assume that all autos are on sale and the prices are reduced by 15%. To find the autos you could afford, you would need to find all autos where the price minus 15% is less than or equal to $8,000. This filter could not be written using an Easy Filter. Examine the filter formula in Figure 11-12.

Formula to
compute
sale price

Amount
you have

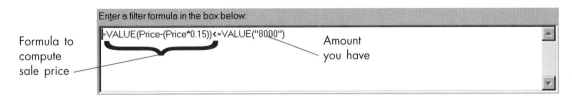

FIGURE 11.12 The **Filter using formula** window must be used whenever computations are made as part of the filter.

The first entry uses the **VALUE function** to compute a value of Price - (Price*.15). This would be the sale price of the auto, the original price minus the 15% sale amount. The **less than or equal to** symbol is used to compare with the value of 8000, the amount you are willing to pay.

The rule here is: If the first value is not a field name, it must be specified as a value using the VALUE function or some other function that generates a value, for example SUM or MIN. The second part of the filter is also specified using the VALUE function. This is not absolutely necessary, but Works will change any number to a VALUE function if it is not specified this way.

Filtering Date Fields

Dates can also be used in filters. When a **date field** is compared to a value for a date, the value must use a valid date format. For example, the condition **less than 5/15/96** would look for any date before May 15, 1996. The condition **less than 5/96** would look for any date before May 1, 1996.

Date functions and formulas can also be used as filter conditions. For example, to find any due date that is more than 60 days past due, compare the due date to see if it is greater than NOW()-60. **NOW()** is the function to obtain the current date. The allowed functions are the same as those explained in Chapter 7.

INVERTING A FILTER

When a filter is inverted, all records that pass the filter conditions are hidden and all records that fail the filter conditions are displayed. Sometimes it is easier to use an inverted filter than it is to create a filter directly. For example, suppose you want to find all autos that are not red Fords. You could look for all red Fords, then invert the filter.

To invert a filter, simply click the **Invert filter** option on the Filter window.

NAMING, DELETING, AND SAVING FILTERS

When the first filter is created for a database, Works will ask you to name the filter and make it the default filter. Any time you click the Filter tool on the Toolbar, the default filter is displayed. When changes to the filter are made, the changes are applied to the current default filter.

To create a new filter, click the **New Filter button** at the bottom of the filter window. You will be asked to name the new filter. A blank filter window will then be displayed. This filter will become the current default filter.

You may want to change the name of a filter. To change a filter name, choose the **Rename Filter button** on the Filter window and enter a new name.

Works will save only eight filters for a single database. If you try to create more than eight filters, an error message will be displayed. For this reason, you may want to delete some filters after they have been used. To delete a filter, choose the **Delete Filter** button on the filter window.

When the database is saved, the filters are also saved. They will be available the next time the database is used but remember, only eight filters can be saved.

REVISING FILTERS

Since only eight filters can be saved for a database, you may find it necessary to revise an existing filter. To revise a filter, click the filter tool on the Toolbar. The current filter will be displayed. To change the filter, click the arrow on the right of the filter name area and select the filter to revise. Make any changes to the conditions. The revised conditions will replace the original conditions in the filter.

APPLYING FILTERS

Once the filters have been created and named, they can be applied to the database at any time. To apply a filter, use the Record menu and choose the **Apply Filter** option. A list of available filters will be displayed as shown in Figure 11.13. Click the appropriate filter name and it will be applied to the database.

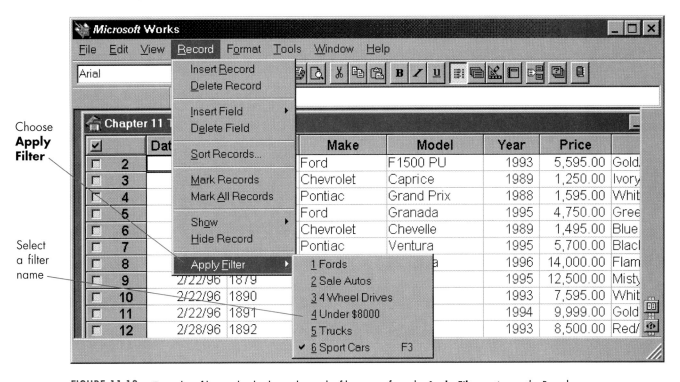

FIGURE 11.13   To apply a filter to the database, choose the filter name from the **Apply Filter** option on the Record menu.

MARKING RECORDS

One other technique that can be used to restrict the records viewed is to **mark records**. When records are marked, they can be hidden or displayed using the Record menu. There are several techniques used to mark records. The first technique is to click the check box to the left of the record number as shown in Figure 11.14. The second technique is to select the record to be marked and choose the **Mark records** option from the Record menu. To mark a record in Form view, you must move to the record to be marked and use the Mark record from the Record menu. To **unmark records**, use the same techniques. Both the check box and the Mark Records option work as toggles.

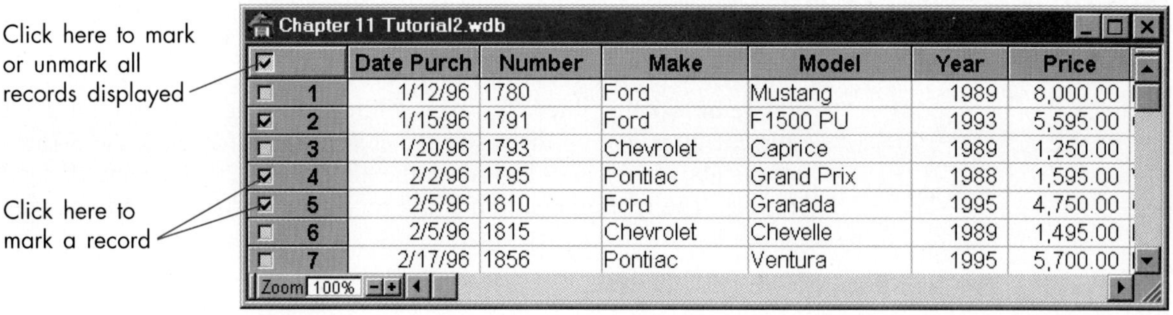

Click here to mark or unmark all records displayed

Click here to mark a record

FIGURE 11.14   Use the check boxes on the left of a record number to manually mark a record.

There are several reasons to mark records. First, assume you only wanted to print three specific records. To write a filter to display only those three records might be too difficult. The easiest way would be to simply mark the records, then show only marked records.

Next, assume you want to print records that satisfy one of two different filter conditions, but you do not want a record to be printed twice. Apply the first filter, then mark all records found by the filter. Now apply the second filter and mark the records found by that filter. Now display all marked records.

Showing Marked and Hidden Records

Once records are marked, the **Show** options on the Record menu can be used to change the records shown. The first option on the Show menu is the **All records** option. Use this option if some records have been hidden by a filter, but you now want to see all records.

The second option is the **Marked Records** option. This choice will show all records that are marked and hide all unmarked records. The next option, **Unmarked Records**, is the opposite of the Marked Records choice. It displays all records that are not marked.

The final choice is **Hidden Records**. This displays all records that have been hidden by a filter and hides all records that are found by the filter. This is the same as Inverting the filter.

When a database is printed, only those records that are not hidden by a filter or other technique are printed.

PRINTING RECORDS

When the database is printed, only those records that are displayed are printed. To print selected records from the database, first define a filter so that only the records you want are displayed, or mark the records and display only marked records. Next, print the database. Only those records displayed will print.

To print records as forms, use a filter or mark records and display only marked records. Next, change to Form view and print the records. One database record will be printed on each page along with any formatting on the form.

CHAPTER 11 SELF-TEST

1. A database default form has two items for each field in the database. What are these two items?
2. What do the X and Y coordinates indicate on a database form?
3. How do you change the tabbing order for a form?
4. Explain what a **filter** does.
5. Each condition in an Easy Filter has three parts. Explain what each part is.
6. Explain the difference between an OR conjunction and an AND conjunction in a database filter.
7. Explain what the **Contains** relationship operator looks for when it is used in a database filter.
8. Write a filter to list all books costing more that $20, but less than $30.
9. Write a filter to list a book that was the first edition (1Ed) or the third edition (3Ed) of a book.
10. Write a filter that will list all accounts where the balance is less than one half the purchase price.
11. Why would you want to mark records?
12. How does Works determine which records to print when a database is printed?

CHAPTER 11 TUTORIAL

In this tutorial, you will be using the Chapter 11 Tutorial file stored on the tutorials diskette. You will modify the database form, create several filters for the database, and print the results of filters.

STARTING THE TUTORIAL

Start the tutorial by starting Microsoft Works and opening the database Chapter 11 Tutorial.

1. Start Microsoft Works and open the database named Chapter 11 Tutorial on your Tutorial disk.

The screen should have a list of automobiles and prices. This is the database used in the tutorial.

MODIFYING THE FORM

Change to the **Form Design view** of the database.

1. Click the **Form Design tool** on the Toolbar or choose Form Design from the View menu.

A form similar to the one shown in Figure 11.15 should now be displayed. Note that much of the form has been customized. To keep this tutorial simple, only a few changes will be made to the form.

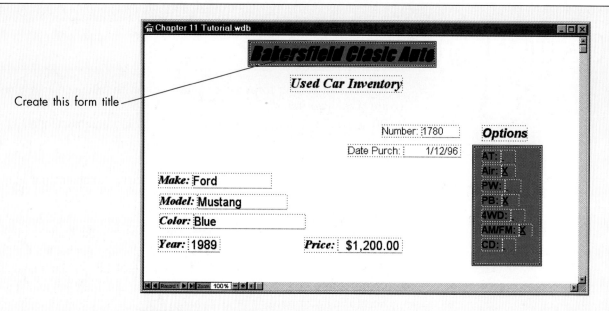

Create this form title

FIGURE 11.15 Tutorial database in Form view.

Add a Form Title

The first step will be to add the form title **Bakersfield Classic Auto** to the form as shown in Figure 11.15.

1. Click in an empty area near the top of the form.
2. Choose the **Label** option on the Insert menu.
3. Enter **Bakersfield Classic Auto** in the text box.
4. Click the Insert button.

Notice that a dotted box appears around the title. This is the text box for the title object. If you need to correct the spelling in the text box, click on the text box and make the changes in the edit area at the top of the screen.

Now change the font and size of the title label.

5. Make sure the label you just entered is selected.
6. Click the right mouse button and choose the Font and Style option.
7. Select the Impact font from the Font list.
8. Select 18 points from the size list.
9. Mark the Bold and Italic styles.

Now shade and border the text box. Refer to Figure 11.16.

10. Click the Shading tab.
11. Choose the Solid shading pattern.
12. Select the Dark Cyan color for the foreground.
13. Click the Border tab.
14. Click the double line Line Style.
15. Click OK.

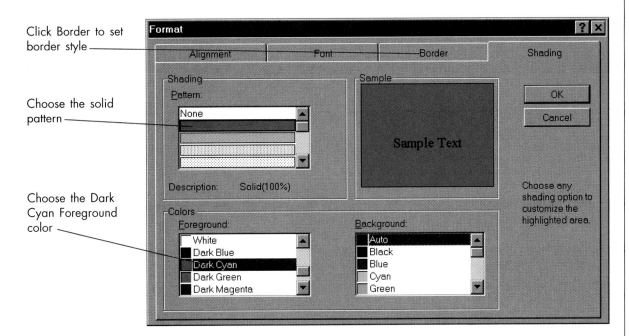

Click Border to set border style

Choose the solid pattern

Choose the Dark Cyan Foreground color

FIGURE 11.16 The Shading folder for the form title.

Now, position the label 2.7 inches from the left margin and 1.07 inches from the top margin.

16. Click the title label text box.
17. Use the mouse to drag the label to approximate coordinates X2.53 and Y1.07. Watch the upper-left corner of the screen for the correct position.

Change the Number and Date Purch Fields

The next step is to change the label and location for the Number and Date Purchased fields. Refer to Figure 11.17 for the final appearance of these fields.

Change the label and
location of these two
fields

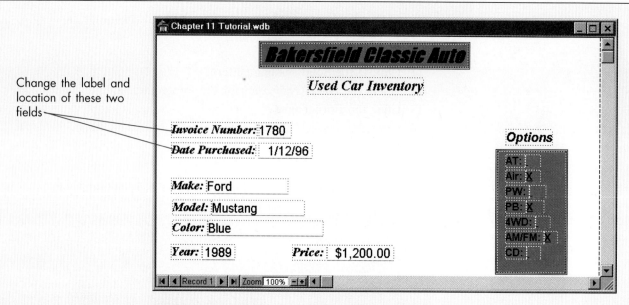

FIGURE 11.17   Tutorial form after changing the Number and Purch Date fields.

1. Click on a clear area of the screen.
2. Choose Label from the Insert menu, enter **Invoice Number:** in the text box, and click the Insert button.
3. Click the right mouse button and choose the Font and Style option.
4. Set the font to Times New Roman, size 12, Bold and Italic, and click the OK button.
5. Use the mouse to drag the label to approximate location X1.2 and Y2.13.

This creates the label for the Number field. Now set the field name for the Number field off and move the Number field beside the new label.

6. Click on the Number field to select it.
7. Choose the Show Field Name option on the Format menu to turn this option off. The field name should no longer appear.
8. Use the mouse to drag the value for the field to the right of the Invoice Number caption as shown in Figure 11.17.

Now change the width of the Number field. The easiest way to change the width is to use the **Field Size** option on the Format menu, but remember, the size can also be changed with the mouse.

9. Make sure the Number field is still selected and choose Field Size from the Format menu.
10. Enter 6 for the Width and click OK.

The label should match Figure 11.17. To see how well you have understood what you have done, we will leave the next changes for you to complete.

11. Create the label **Date Purchased**.
12. Change the Font to Times New Roman, size 12, Bold Italic, and position the label as shown in Figure 11.17.
13. Turn off the field label for the Date Purchased field and drag the field value to the right of the new label.

Dress Up the Form

We will perform a few more steps to dress up the form before finishing. First add some **clipart** to the form.

1. Click the ClipArt option on the Insert menu.
2. Click the Transportation category, click the antique car image (see Figure 11.18) and click the Insert button.
3. Use the picture handles to reduce the size of the picture, then drag the picture to the upper right side of the form. (See Figure 11.18.)
4. Use the ClipArt Gallery to insert the red sports car on the left side of the form. Size and move the sports car to fit the form as shown in Figure 11.18.

Now place a rectangle around the four lines that describe the automobile. Refer to Figure 11.18.

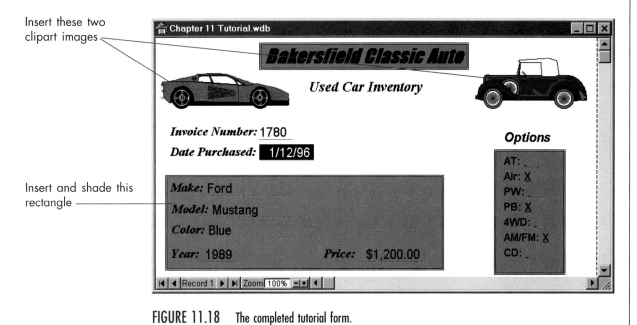

Insert these two clipart images

Insert and shade this rectangle

FIGURE 11.18   The completed tutorial form.

5. Choose Rectangle from the Insert menu.
6. Use the handles to move and size the rectangle until it surrounds the four lines that describe the automobile (see Figure 11.18).
7. Make sure the rectangle is selected (the handles are visible), and click the right mouse button. Choose Shading from the menu.
8. Click the solid Pattern and the Dark Cyan foreground color.
9. Click the Border folder tab.
10. Select the double line border and click OK.

The rectangle should now cover the lines that describe the automobile. This is because the rectangle is now on the top layer of items on the form. To correct this you must move the rectangle to the back layer.

11. Click on the rectangle to select it.
12. Choose the **Send to Back** option from the Format menu.

The description of the auto should now be on the top layer and the text should be visible.
We will show one more technique for shading the entire form.

13. Click any blank area of the form.
14. Choose Shading from the Format menu.
15. Click the solid Format and the Cyan foreground.
16. Click OK.

The entire form should now be shaded blue. This approach can be used to make a form look better, but remember, if you print the form, the printer must try to print the blue shade on the entire page. Since this would take too long, undo the shading.

17. Choose Undo Format Field from the Edit menu or choose Shading from the Format menu, click the None option for the Pattern, and click OK.

Print a Record using the Form

The last step is to print a record using the form.

1. Choose Form from the View menu.
2. Choose Print from the File menu.
3. Click the **Current Record Only** option in the What to Print area at the bottom left of the Print dialog box.
4. Click the OK button.

Save the Changes

You should now save the database so the changes made to the form will be saved.

1. Save the database.

MAKE A SIMPLE FILTER

Before you begin to make filters, move back to the List view.

1. Click the List View tool.

   To create a filter for the database, click the **Filter tool** on the

   .

2. Click the Filter tool.

   The Filter window is displayed with a Filter name window on top. Enter a name for the filter.

3. Enter **Old Fords** for the filter name and press the Enter key.

The first filter will be simple, but we will create it in two steps. The first step will be to find all Fords. The completed Filter window is shown in Figure 11.19.

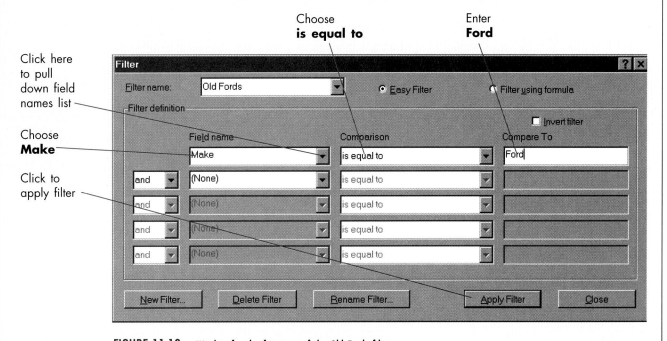

FIGURE 11.19   Window for the first step of the Old Fords filter.

1. Click the arrow to the right of the first text box. This will pull down the field name list.
2. Click the "Make field" name.
3. Click the "is equal to" option in the Comparison area.
4. Enter Ford in the "Compare To" area.
5. Click the Apply Filter button.

The database should now display only cars whose make is Ford. Examine the Make column and make sure only Fords are listed.

On your screen, notice the status line at the bottom of the screen. In the right corner of the status line, the record number the cursor is on is displayed. This should be the first record in the list, 1. The status line also shows that you have 15 of 49 records displayed (15/49).

Notice the record numbers on the left side of the screen. These indicate the actual record numbers for the records displayed (1, 2, 5, 8, 18, 25, 26, 27, 31, 34, 35, 39, 42, 47, and 49).

The entire query should list Fords made before 1993. To do this you need to add the condition that the year is less than 1993. Since you want both conditions met, the **and** conjunction is used to connect the conditions. See Figure 11.20.

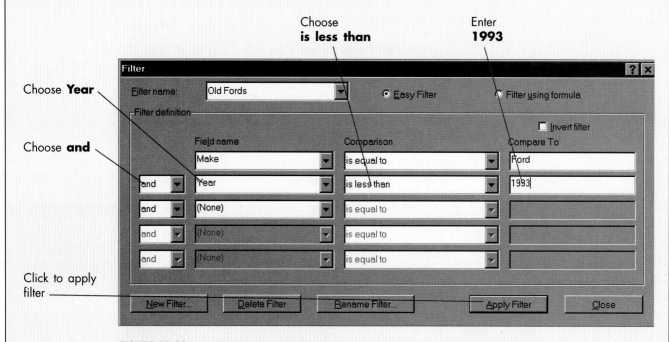

FIGURE 11.20   Filter for Fords made before 1993.

1. Click the Filter tool.
2. Choose the AND conjunction on the left of the second condition line.
3. Pull down the Field name list and choose "Year".
4. Pull down the Comparison list and choose "is less than".
5. Enter 1993 in the "Compare To" area.
6. Click the Apply Filter button.

Seven records should now be displayed. There should be three 1989 Fords and four 1992 Fords. The record numbers should be 1, 18, 26, 27, 35, 47, and 49.

USE AN OR CONJUNCTION

Or conjunctions work differently than **and** conjunctions. An **and** conjunction requires that both conditions be met. An **or** conjunction requires that only one of the conditions be met. Suppose that you would accept either a Jeep Cherokee or a Jeep CJ 10. In English you would say, show me all Cherokees and CJ 10s, realizing that an automobile cannot be both a Cherokee and a CJ 10. You are really asking for Cherokees or CJ 10s. Try this filter. Refer to Figure 11.21.

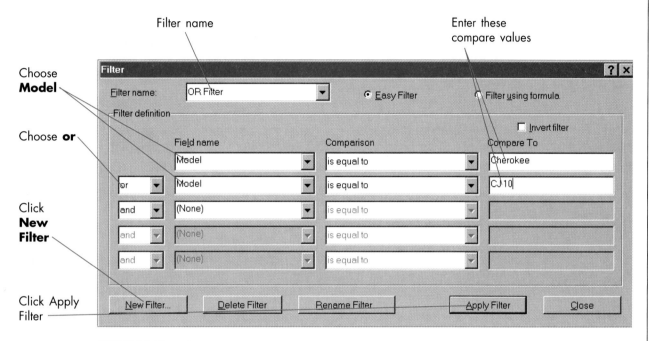

FIGURE 11.21   Filter to find Jeep Cherokees or CJ 10s.

1. Click the Filter tool.
2. Click the New Filter button.
3. Name this filter OR Filter.
4. Pull down the Field name list and choose "Model".
5. Choose the "is equal to" option in the Comparison area.
6. Enter Cherokee in the first "Compare To" entry.
7. Choose the "or" conjunction to connect the two comparisons.
8. Pull down the Field name list and choose "Model".
9. Choose the "is equal to" option in the Comparison area.
10. Enter CJ 10 in the "Compare To" entry.
11. Click the Apply Filter button.

The screen should display five records. There should be three Cherokees and two CJ 10s. The records displayed are 15, 16, 21, 37, and 44.

FINDING A RANGE

A **range** is a set of values that has an upper limit and a lower limit. For example, suppose you were willing to pay between $7,000 and $8,500 for an automobile; this would be the range of prices you are willing to pay. Ranges specify the low and high limits and are connected by an **and**. Try the filter in Figure 11.22 to find these autos.

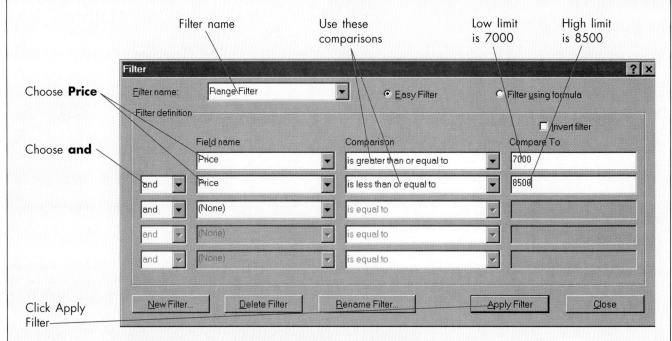

FIGURE 11.22   Filter to find autos that sell between $7,000 and $8,500.

1. Click the Filter tool.
2. Click the New Filter button.
3. Name this filter Range Filter.
4. Pull down the Field name list and choose "Price".
5. Pull down the Comparison name list and choose "is greater than or equal to".
6. Enter 7000 in the "Compare To" entry.
7. Choose the "and" conjunction to connect the two comparisons.
8. Pull down the Field name list and choose "Price".
9. Pull down the Comparison name list and choose "is less than or equal to".
10. Enter 8500 in the "Compare To" entry.
11. Click the Apply Filter button.

There should be eight records displayed. All prices should be between $7,000 and $8,500 The records displayed are records 8, 10, 12, 14, 22, 28, 37, and 47.

DEFINE A COMBINATION
AND/OR FILTER

Suppose you are willing to accept any Ford or Chevrolet that cost between $7,000 and $8,500. There are two sets of comparisons in this filter. First, the Ford **and** Chevrolet comparisons would need to be connected by an **or**. The second comparison is a range, so the $7,000 and $8,500 would need to be connected by an and. The two comparisons would then need to be connected by an and. This filter is shown in Figure 11.23.

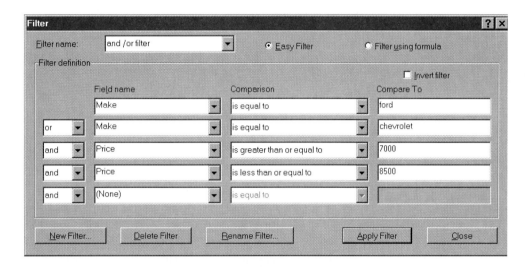

FIGURE 11.23   Filter to find all Fords or Chevrolets that cost between $7,000 and $8,500.

1. Click the Filter tool.
2. Click the New Filter button.
3. Name this filter **And/Or Filter**.
4. Pull down the Field name list and choose "Make".
5. Choose the "is equal to" option in the Comparison area.
6. Enter Ford in the "Compare To" area.
7. Choose the "or" conjunction to connect the next comparison.
8. Pull down the Field name list and choose "Make".
9. Choose the "is equal to" option in the Comparison area.
10. Enter Chevrolet in the "Compare To" area.
11. Choose the "and" conjunction to connect the next filter.
12. Pull down the Field name list and choose "Price".
13. Pull down the Comparison name list and choose "is greater than or equal to".
14. Enter 7000 in the "Compare To" entry.
15. Choose the "and" conjunction to connect the two comparisons.
16. Pull down the Field name list and choose "Price".
17. Pull down the Comparison name list and choose "is less than or equal to".
18. Enter 8500 in the "Compare To" entry.
19. Click the Apply Filter button.

This filter should find three autos. They are 8, 28, and 47.

USE CONTAINS AND IS BLANK

Suppose you want a blue auto, but don't care what color blue it is. If the color field is compared to only blue automobiles, you would not get royal blue, navy blue, blue/green, or the other blues. Since the word blue may be anywhere in the color, you would want to use the **contains** comparison. Also assume you do not want an automatic transmission. If the transmission type is automatic, the AT option field has been marked with a character. To find these autos, use the filter shown in Figure 11.24.

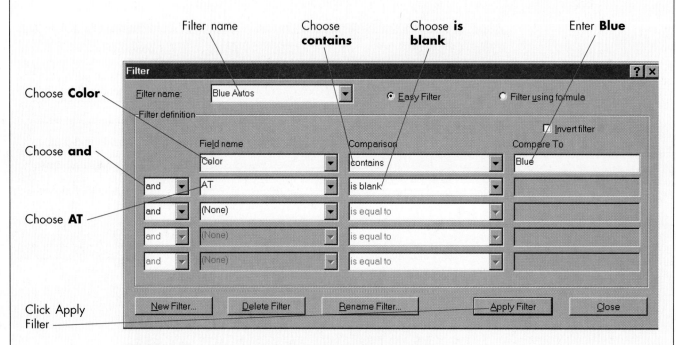

FIGURE 11.24   Filter to find Blue autos without automatic transmissions

1. Click the Filter tool.
2. Click the New Filter button.
3 Name this filter **Blue Autos**.
4. Pull down the Field name list and choose "Color".
5. Pull down the Comparison name list and choose "contains".
6. Enter Blue in the "Compare To" entry.
7. Choose the "and" conjunction to connect the two comparisons.
8. Pull down the Field name list and choose "AT".
9. Pull down the Comparison name list and choose "is blank".
10. Click the Apply button.

Examine your screen. There should be four records displayed. These are records 1, 6, 20, and 25. Check the records to make sure the color of the cars is blue and that the AT field is blank.

USE A FORMULA IN A FILTER

Assume you have a trade-in that is worth $2,500 and you are willing to pay up to $5,000 in cash for another car. This would mean you want to see any automobile where the price minus your trade-in ($2,500) is less than or equal to $5,000. Also assume that you want to buy a Ford. This filter cannot be made using an Easy Filter because the filter contains a formula.

To examine how the formula is developed by Microsoft Works, we will start with an Easy Filter, then modify the filter to add the formula. Use the Easy Filter in Figure 11.25 to start the filter.

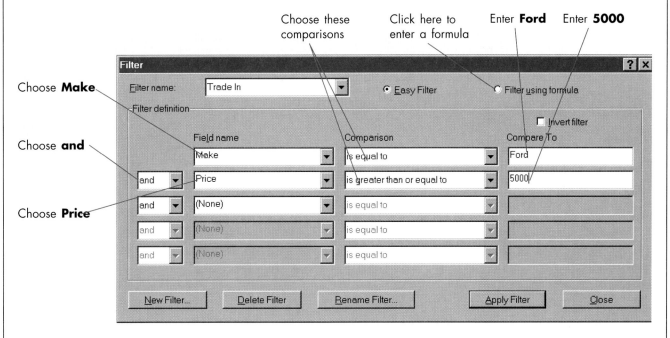

FIGURE 11.25 Easy filter to start looking for Fords that cost less than $5,000 after a $2,500 trade-in.

1. Click the Filter tool.
2. Click the New Filter button.
3. Name this filter **Trade In**.
4. Pull down the Field name list and choose "Make".
5. Pull down the Comparison name list and choose "is equal to".
6. Enter Ford in the "Compare To" area.
7. Choose the "and" conjunction to connect the comparisons.
8. Pull down the Field name list and choose "Price".
9. Pull down the Comparison name list and choose "is greater than or equal to".
10. Enter 5000 in the "Compare To" area.

Note that this would only provide Fords that cost less than $5,000. To complete the formula, click the **Filter using formula** option at the top of the Filter window.

11. Click "Filter using formula".

Note that the formula starts with the equals sign, the Make field name is in single quotes, and the value **Ford** is in double quotes. Also note that the **AND** connector begins and ends with the # symbol. Finally, note that the second comparison uses the VALUE function to convert the 5000 to a numeric value. This is because the Price field is defined with a number format.

The second part of the filter cannot be written as it currently exists. What we want is a formula where $5,000 is greater than or equal to Price minus $2,500. To complete the formula, edit this formula as shown in Figure 11.26.

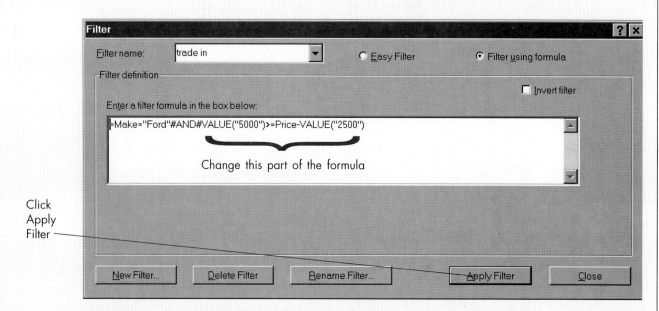

Click
Apply
Filter

FIGURE 11.26   Completed filter formula for figure 11.25.

1. Press the End key to move to the end of the filter formula.
2. Use the backspace key to delete everything up to the # at the end of the word #AND#.
3. Enter: VALUE("5000")>='Price'-VALUE("2500").
4. Click the Apply Filter button.

Thirteen records should be displayed. They are records 1, 2, 5, 18, 25, 26, 27, 34, 35, 39, 42, 47, and 49. Examine your screen and make sure you have the correct records.

USE THE HIDDEN RECORDS OPTION

When Works applies a filter to a database, all records that do not meet the filter requirements are hidden. The hidden and displayed records can be switched to form a type of **NOT condition**. For example, is you wanted to see all autos that you did not want, choose the **Hidden records** option from the Record menu's Show option as shown in Figure 11.27.

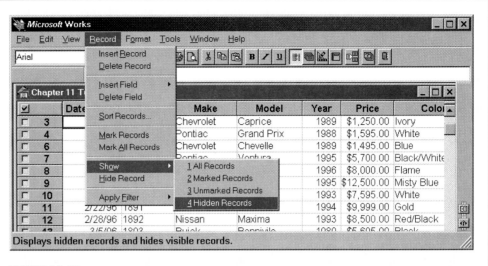

FIGURE 11.27   Use the Hidden records option from the Records menu to get results that do not meet filter requirements.

1. Click the Record menu.
2. Click the Show option.
3. Click the Hidden Records option.

You should now have all the automobiles that did not meet the original filter. This would be the other 36 automobiles out of the 49 that are available in the database.

PRINT FILTER RESULTS

When you print a database, only those records that are displayed are printed. Therefore, if a filter is applied to the database, only those records that satisfy the filter criteria are printed. When you are in **List view** the records will print in a column format.

Change the Page Setup

Before printing the results of the filters, change the page setup.

1. Choose Page Setup from the Print menu.
2. Change the left and right margins to 1 inch.
3. Change the Orientation to Landscape.
4. Use the Other Options folder to set the Print gridlines and Print record and field labels options on.

Apply a filter

Apply the first filter you created and print the results of the filter.

1. Click the Filter tool.
2. Click on the Filter name and choose the Old Fords filter.
3. Click the Apply Filter button.
4. Click the printer tool on the Toolbar.

    Now print the results of each of your other filters.

5. Apply each of the other five filters and print their results.

SAVE THE DATABASE

When the database is saved, all filters and form changes are also saved.

1. Save your database.

    This completes the tutorial. You can now exit Microsoft Works.

HANDS-ON PRACTICE

Exercise 11-1A

For this exercise, use the file Exercise 11-1.WDB on your tutorial disk. The file contains records about employees for a company.

1. Modify the default form so that it looks like the one shown in Figure 11.28. Use your name for the name of the company.
2. Mark record number 1 and choose Marked records from the Show option of the Records menu.
3. Print the form with the data for the marked record.

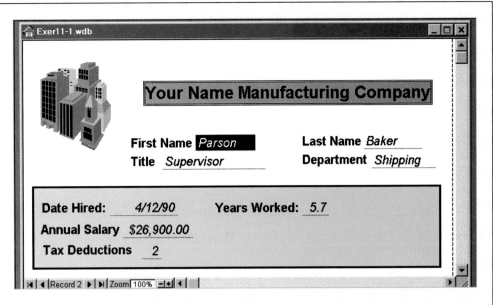

FIGURE 11.28   Custom form for Exercise 11.1.

Exercise 11-1B

Create the following filters. Name each filter. Print the results of each filter in List View with gridlines and record and field labels.

1. Find employees with a Title of Packer.
2. Find employees with a Title of Operator and a Salary greater than $25,000.
3. Find all employees that were hired between January 1, 1990 and December 31, 1993.
4. Find employees with a Title of Operator who have worked more than five years.
5. Find employees that have a salary more than $1500 per month. Note the salary is an annual salary. You will need to use a formula to divide the salary by 12 to get a monthly salary.
6. Find employees who have the letters *son* at the end of their Last Name.
7. Assume a $700 tax deduction is allowed for each dependent. Find all employees where the total deductions are more than 10% of their salary.

Exercise 11-2A

For this exercise, use the file Exercise 11-2.WDB on your tutorial disk. The file contains records about books ordered for a bookstore.

1. Modify the default form so that it looks like the one shown in Figure 11.29. Use your name for the bookstore name.
2. Mark record number 1 and choose Marked records from the Show option of the Records menu.
3. Print the form with the data for the marked record.

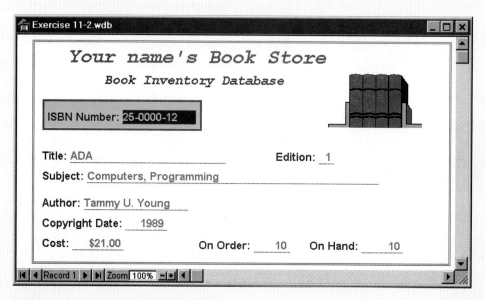

FIGURE 11.29 Custom form for Exercise 11.2.

Exercise 11-2B

Create the following filters. Name each filter. Print the results of each filter in List View with gridlines and record and field labels.

1. Write the filter to find all books where the author is Karen King.
2. Write the filter to find all books that have a copyright between and including 1990 and 1993.
3. Write the filter to find all books that have a copyright date before 1990 and are in Edition 1.
4. Write the filter to find all books where the Number On Order is greater than the Number On Hand.
5. Write the filter to find all books that have a subject that contains the word **computers**.
6. Write the filter to find all books that have a subject that contains the words **tax** or **income**.
7. Write the filter to find all books where the Number On Hand and the Number On Order are zero.
8. Write the filter to find all books where the Number On Order is more than twice the Number On Hand.

Exercise 11-3A

For this exercise, use the file Exercise 11-3.WDB on your tutorial disk. The file contains checks written against a checking account.

1. Modify the default form so that it looks like the one shown in Figure 11.30. Use your name and address on the check in the upper left corner.
2. Mark record number 1 and choose Marked records from the Show option of the Records menu.
3. Print the form with the data for the marked record.

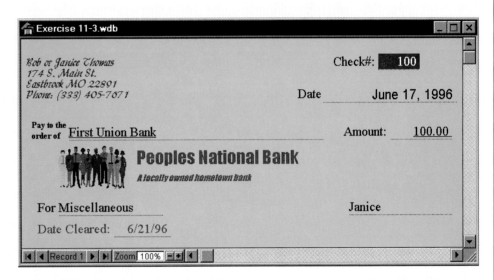

FIGURE 11.30   Custom form for Exercise 11.3.

Exercise 11-3B

Create the following filters. Name each filter. Print the results of each filter in List View with gridlines and record and field labels.

1. Find all checks written to First Union Bank.
2. Find all checks written by Janice for Food.
3. Find all checks that have not cleared the bank.
4. Find all checks written for Gas or in July. (Hint: Look for dates after 6/30/96 and before 8/1/96.)
5. Find all checks written by Bob that are between $25 and $50.
6. Find all checks written for any type of utilities.
7. Find all checks that have taken more than ten days to clear the bank.
8. Find any check that was written by Janice for Food or Gas.

12

CREATING DATABASE REPORTS

LEARNING OBJECTIVES

When you've completed this chapter, you will be able to:

- Create a simple Works report with titles and column headings.
- Create a Works report with totals and other statistics.
- Customize a standard Works report.
- Sort database data for reports.
- Name, delete, duplicate, and save Works report definitions.

This chapter will introduce the report routines of the Database module of Microsoft Works. These routines will allow you to create **reports** that contain all the records and fields in the database or only certain fields and records. The reports can contain new fields that do not exist in the database as long as the new data can be derived from existing data. The report records can be sorted and report statistics can be printed. Statistics can be created for all records in the report or they can be created for a selected set of the records. The report can also be previewed before being printed and the report definition can be saved with the database.

As we discuss how to generate reports in the following sections, we will use the American Cancer Society database. This database will contain eight fields: Contributor ID, First Name, Initial, Last Name, City, State, Contribution Last Year, and Contribution This Year.

REPORT CONCEPTS

Reports are more explicit than filters. Normally, filters are used to examine a database. Reports are used when a formatted copy of the database data that lists specific fields, reorders the fields, or indicates totals or other statistical information is needed. Reports can be used by managers to analyze data or distribute to members of a team. Since reports can contain information that is calculated from other data in the database, a report may need to be created to generate this new information.

In Microsoft Works, a report is not actually created. A **report definition** is created. When a report is printed, the data currently in the database are used by the report definition to create the report. This technique of creating a report definition rather than a report, allows the data in the database to change and each time the report is printed, allows the report definition to use the changed data.

Up to eight report definitions can be created for each database. All report definitions are saved with the database when the database is saved. This makes the report definition available for future use.

CREATING A REPORT DEFINITION

Creating a simple report definition consists of five basic steps.

Step 1: Name the report.
Step 2: Enter a report title, select a font and font size to be used, and select the print orientation — Portrait or Landscape.
Step 3: Select the fields to be printed on the report.
Step 4: Select the sort order for the records in the report.
Step 5: Select any report totals or statistics desired.

Steps three and four above are not required, but are so common that we include them here. These steps will create the report definition. The only thing left is to print the report.

Step1: Name the Report

To create a report definition, open the database and choose the **ReportCreator** option from the Tools menu. If no report definitions have been defined for the database, you can click the **Report View** tool on the toolbar to create a new report. The Report View tool and the ReportCreator option on the Tools menu are shown in Figure 12.1.

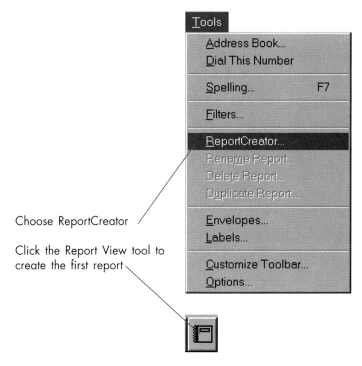

Choose ReportCreator

Click the Report View tool to create the first report

FIGURE 12.1   Tools menu and the Report View tool.

When a report is created, a **Report name** window is displayed. Enter a name for the report and the ReportCreator window is displayed.

Step 2: Complete the Report Title options

The first folder presented is the **Title folder** shown in Figure 12.2. This folder allows you to enter a report title, select the default font and font size for the report, and set the printing orientation for the report. The default report title will be the database file name followed by the report name. To change this default title, delete the title in the Report title entry and enter a new title. The title will only be printed at the top of the first page of the report, even if the report is longer than one page.

Next, select the printing orientation for the report. Click either the **Portrait** option or the **Landscape** option.

Finally, select the report's font and font size. The selected font will be used for all lines in the report unless they are changed using techniques discussed later in this chapter.

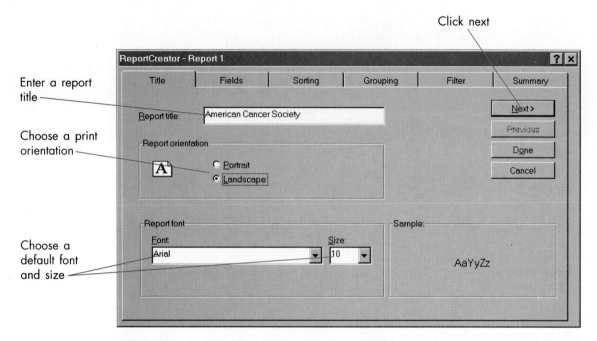

FIGURE 12.2   The Title folder of the ReportCreator.

Step 3: Select the Fields for the Report

When the Title options have been completed, click the Next button and the **Fields folder** will be presented. This folder is shown in Figure 12.3.

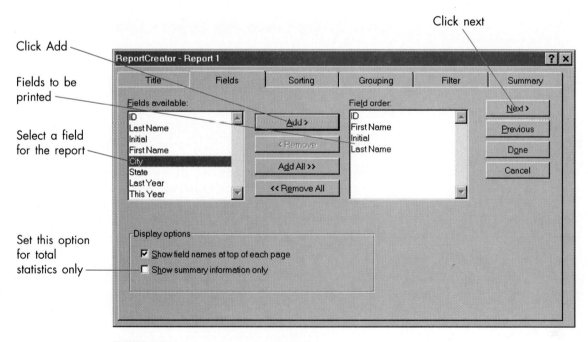

FIGURE 12.3   The ReportCreator Fields folder.

To identify the fields for the report, select each field name from the Fields available list and click the Add button. As the fields are added, they will be listed in the Field order list. Select and add the fields in the order that you want them to appear on the report, moving from left to right. For example, if you want the fields to appear as First Name, Initial, Last name, select the fields in this order. Continue selecting and adding fields until all the required fields are listed in the Fields order list.

If the report is to contain all fields in the database, you can use the **Add All** button. If a mistake is made and a field is added that is not wanted on the report, select the field name in the Fields order list and click the **Remove** button.

The first option at the bottom is used to provide column headings for the report. If the **Show field names at top of each page** option is selected, a heading is provided for each column. The headings will be printed at the top of each page.

The **Show summary information only** will print totals and statistics only. The individual records in the database will not be printed.

When all the options for this folder have been completed, click the Next button.

Step 4: Select the Sorting Order

The next step is to specify the sort order for the records on the report. This is done by using the **Sorting folder** shown in Figure 12.4. Use the arrow beside the Sort by list to pull down the field names and select a field name to use for the sort. Up to three fields can be used for **sorting**.

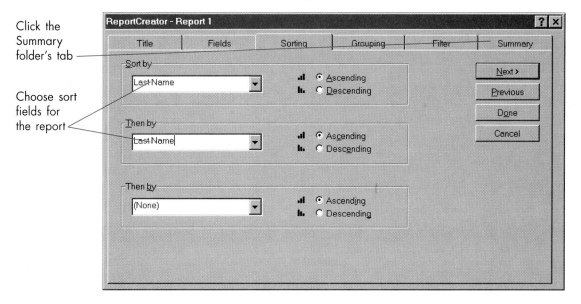

Click the Summary folder's tab

Choose sort fields for the report

FIGURE 12.4   The ReportCreator's Sorting folder.

The next two folders allow you to specify Grouping and Filter options. These options will not be covered in this text. When the Sorting folder is complete, click the Summary folder's tab.

Step 5: Select Report Summaries

The final folder on the ReportCreator is the **Summary folder** shown in Figure 12.5. This folder is used to select **summary statistics** for each field printed on the report. These summary **statistics** are printed once at the end of the report. There are seven different summary statistics:

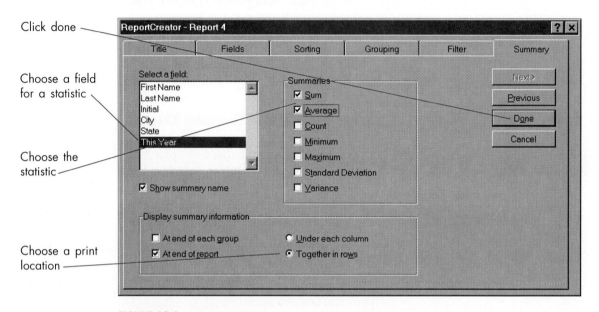

FIGURE 12.5   The Summary folder.

Sum: Print the total of all entries in the column. The column must contain numeric data.

Average: Print the average of the entries in the column. The column must contain numeric data.

Count: Print the number of entries in the column. Records that do not contain an entry in the column are not counted. This is the only summary that does not require numeric data.

Minimum: Print the smallest entry in the column. The column must contain numeric data.

Maximum: Print the largest entry in the column. The column must contain numeric data.

Standard Deviation: Print the standard deviation of entries in the column. The standard deviation is a measure of the variability of the numbers in the column. The column must contain numeric data.

Variance: Print the variance of the numbers in the column. The variance is the square of the standard deviation. The column must contain numeric data.

Each summary statistic must be associated with some field on the report. To specify the summary statistic and the field it is associated with, first select the field, then select that statistic. More than one summary statistic can be associated with a field.

The location of the summary statistics printed in the report is specified in the Display summary information area of the **Summary folder**. If the **Under each column** option is selected, the statistics will be printed beneath the appropriate column. If the **Together in rows** option is selected, each statistic will be printed on a different line. The results of both options are shown in Figure 12.6. After setting the required summary statistics, click the Done button. An information window indicating the report definition has been created appears. Click Preview to see the report or click Modify to make changes to the report definition.

American Cancer Society

First Name	Last Name	City	State	This Year
Donald	Applebaum	Pittsburgh	PA	$50.00
Carol	Jones	Silver Springs	MD	$25.00
Phillip	Jones	Silver Springs	MD	$410.00
Lawrence	Martin	Richmond	VA	$750.00
Jason	Miller	Philadelphia	PA	$10.00
Larry	Miller	Philadelphia	PA	$30.00

COUNT OF First Name: 6
TOTAL This Year: $1,275.00
AVERAGE This Year: $212.50

American Cancer Society

First Name	Last Name	City	State	This Year
Donald	Applebaum	Pittsburgh	PA	$50.00
Carol	Jones	Silver Springs	MD	$25.00
Phillip	Jones	Silver Springs	MD	$410.00
Lawrence	Martin	Richmond	VA	$750.00
Jason	Miller	Philadelphia	PA	$10.00
Larry	Miller	Philadelphia	PA	$30.00

COUNT: **SUM:**
6          $1,275.00
         AVG:
         $212.50

FIGURE 12.6   Summary statistics printed as rows and as columns.

After a report definition has been created, it can be displayed and modified. The report definition identifies the different types of rows that will be printed on the report. A sample Works report definition is shown in Figure 12.7.

Title Rows

The first type of row is the **Title row**. Title rows print once on the first page of the report. In Figure 12.7 there are two Title rows. The first row displays the Title entered in the Title folder of the ReportCreator. The second Title row is blank. This row is used to provide a blank line between the report title and the report column headings.

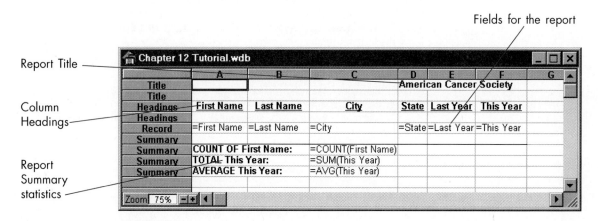

FIGURE 12.7   A sample report definition showing row types.

Headings Rows

The second type of row is the **Headings row**. Headings rows will print at the top of each page. Notice that the report definition has two headings rows. The first one contains the field names. Works uses this Headings row for column headings. Headings for any column can be changed by clicking the cell and typing a new heading. The second Headings row is blank. Works uses this row to provide a blank line between the column headings and the record lines.

Record Rows

The third type of row is the **Record row**. This row contains formulas to print the field contents. When Works prints a report, all Record rows are printed for each record displayed in the database. The standard report uses only one record row. More Record rows can be inserted to get different types of reports. For example, to double space a report, a blank Record row could be inserted. To print records on more than one line, create multiple record rows with different fields on each row.

Notice in Figure 12.7 that the field names in the Record row are preceded by the equals sign (=) which indicates they are formulas. The equals sign is used to indicate that the contents of a field are to be placed in the record cell. These formulas are normally used on the Record and Summary rows. If cell contents are not preceded with the equals sign, the data in the cell are treated as a heading or label, as in the Title and Headings rows.

Summary Rows

The final type of row is the **Summary row**. This type of row prints once at the end of the report. Summary rows are normally used to print report statistics. In Figure 12.7 there is one summary row for each summary statistic.

Figure 12.8 shows the relationship between the different types of rows and a sample report.

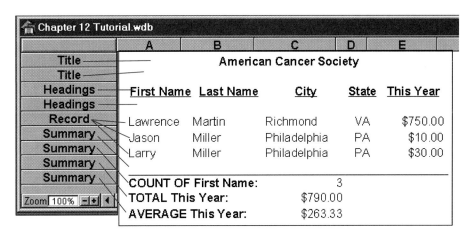

FIGURE 12.8   Each type of row produces one or more lines on a report.

CUSTOMIZING A REPORT

Once a report definition has been created, it can be customized. New rows can be added, existing rows can be changed, some rows can be moved, and rows can be deleted. Row formats can also be changed, such as changing their height, and columns formats can be changed as well.

Changing Entries in Rows

To change an entry, click the cell that contains the entry to be changed. Then use the **F2 function key** or type new text in the edit bar. This process is similar to the way you edit data in a database or spreadsheet cell.

Formatting Cells

You can change formatting of individual cells with the Toolbar or the Format menu options. To change the format for a cell, select the cell or a series of cells, then set the format. You can assign cells the bold, italic, and underline attributes using the Toolbar. You can change the font and font size using the Toolbar. Use the **Number** option on the Format menu to change the format used to display numbers in a cell.

To specify the alignment of cell contents, use the **Alignment** option on the Format menu. These alignments work the same way they work in the Spreadsheet module of Works. If you are not familiar with the alignment options, refer to Chapter 6, An Introduction to Computer Spreadsheets.

The **Borders** option and the **Shading** option on the Format menu can be used to apply borders to the report or shade specific cells.

Remember, the **Record row** is used to print all records in the database. If you change a cell format in the Record row, each record that prints will use the cell format. For example, if the Last Name cell in the Record row is formatted as bold, all last names will print as bold.

The formatting options for cells are also available using the right mouse button. Click the right mouse button and choose the Format option. All the formatting folders will be available.

Changing Column Width and Row Height

A **column's width** and **row's height** are changed in the report definition the same way they are changed in the **List view** of the database. If the Format menu options are used, the width is entered as the number of characters and the height is set as the number of points. If the mouse is used, drag the separator lines to change a column's width or row's height.

Inserting and Deleting Rows and Columns

To insert new rows and columns in a report definition, click the right mouse button and select the Insert Row or Insert Column option on the menu. To insert a column, click a cell immediately to the right of where the column is to be inserted and choose the **Insert Column** option. The column will be inserted to the left of the current cell.

To insert a row, select the **Insert Row** option from right mouse button menu. A window like the one in Figure 12.9 will be displayed. Select the appropriate row type and click Insert. A row of that type will be inserted. Rows are inserted so they will occur in the correct order. Title rows always come first, then Headings rows, then Record rows, and finally Summary rows. If the active cell is in a row that is the same type as the row being inserted, the new row will be inserted above the current row.

Select the row type to be inserted

Click Insert

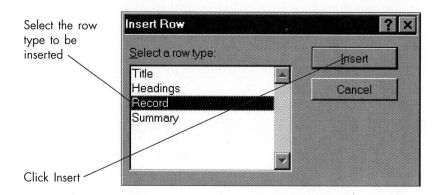

FIGURE 12.9 The Insert Row window.

To delete a row or column, place the cursor in any cell of the row or column to be deleted and click the right mouse button. Choose the **Delete Row** or **Delete Column** option and the row or column will be deleted.

Moving Rows, Columns, and Cell Entries; Clearing Entries

To move a row or column from one location to another, use the Cut and Paste operations. To move a row, click the row name to select the row. Next, use the Cut option on the Edit menu. Now, select the row you want the cut row placed above, and use the Paste option on the Edit menu to paste the row back into the report definition. If you try to paste a row at a location that would place it in the wrong order (Title, Headings, Record, Summary), Works will move the row to the nearest location that would maintain the proper order.

To move columns, use the same technique, but select the column name rather than the row name. Select the column to the right of where the cut column is to be placed before pasting the column back into the report definition.

To move a cell entry from one location to another, select the cell and cut it to the clipboard. Click the cell you want the entry moved to and paste it into the new cell. To clear an entry, click the cell and use the **Clear** option from the Edit menu.

Entering Field Contents

When new rows or columns are inserted into a report definition, entries will need to be made in the new cells (unless you are inserting the row to get a blank line).

The options on the Insert menu shown in Figure 12.10 can be used to create the cell entries. If the **Field Name** option is selected, the **Insert Field Name** window is displayed. The window lists the fields available in the database. This option will place the field name in the cell. For example, if you choose the **First Name** field from the list, the words First Name will print when the cell is printed, not the first name of a person in the database.

If **Field Entry** is selected from the Insert menu, the Insert Field Entry window is displayed. This window also lists the fields available in the database. This option will place a formula to print the contents of the field in the cell. For example, if you choose the First Name field from the list, the first name of a person in the database will be printed in the cell.

To insert a field, click the cell in which the entry is to be inserted, select the Field Name or Field Entry on the insert menu, select the field name, and click the OK button.

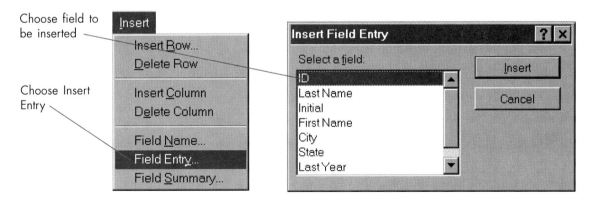

FIGURE 12.10   Use the Field Name or Field Entry on the Insert menu to place data in a cell.

Another option on the Insert menu is the **Field Summary** option. This option is used to select summary statistics for the cell. This option should be used only in Summary rows. When the Field Summary option is selected, the window shown in Figure 12.11 is displayed. Select a field name on the left side of the folder and the statistic from the right side of the folder, then click OK. The selected statistic will be applied to the field and the formula for the statistic will be inserted into the active cell.

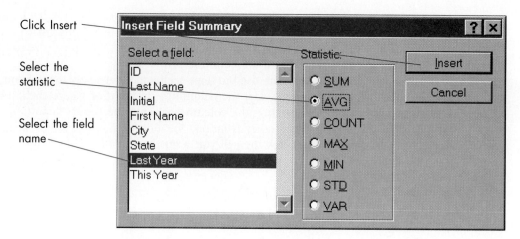

Click Insert

Select the
statistic

Select the field
name

FIGURE 12.11   Insert Field Summary window.

All three insert options discussed above are also available from the right mouse button menu.

Field names, values, and summaries can also be inserted by entering them directly into the cells rather than choosing them from the folders. To enter a field name, type the field name in the cell. To enter a field value, enter the field name preceded by an equals sign (=). To enter a field summary statistic, precede the summary statistic name by the equals sign (=) to indicate it is a formula, then enter the statistic name followed by the field name enclosed in parentheses. Each of these techniques is shown in Figure 12.12.

Field name

Precede a field
content entry with
an equals sign

Precede a statistic with an
equals sign and follow it with
a field name in parentheses

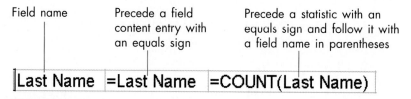

FIGURE 12.12   Formats for cell entries.

Changing the Sort Order

If the sort order for the records needs to be changed from the order specified when the report was originally created, choose **Report Settings** from the Format menu. This option will provide access to the **Sorting folder** shown in Figure 12.4. Make the correct Sort by settings and click the Done button to change the sort order.

PRINTING A REPORT

To print a report, you must be in Report View with the report definition displayed. To print the report, use the **Print Preview tool** or the **Print** option from the File menu. The Page Setup windows can be used to specify margins, page size, orientation, and other printing options.

Copying Report Output To The Clipboard

The report output can also be copied to the clipboard using the **Copy Report Output** option on the Edit menu. Once the report output is on the **clipboard**, the Paste tool can be used to place the output into a word processing document or spreadsheet. Once the report output has been pasted into another document, it can be treated as if it were originally typed into the document.

An easy way to place database data into a report in the word processor is to quickly create a report that contains the needed data, copy the report output to the clipboard, then paste the clipboard to the word processing document.

USING FILTERS FOR A REPORT

A filter can be applied to the database before the report is printed. If this is done, only the records that meet the filter requirements are printed on the report. To set a filter for the report, choose Report Settings from the Format menu and click the **Filter folder**'s tab. This will provide the folder shown in Figure 12.13.

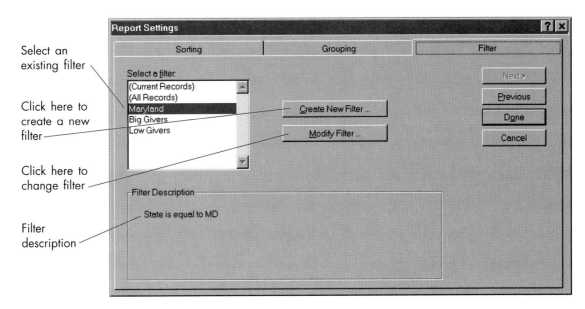

FIGURE 12.13 The Filters folder.

The filters that have been created for the database are displayed in the **Select a filter** list. To use an existing filter, select the filter and click the Done button. To modify an existing filter, select the filter and click the **Modify Filter** button. To create a new filter click the **New Filter** button.

NAMING, DELETING, AND DUPLICATING REPORTS

Reports can be renamed, deleted, and duplicated by selecting the appropriate option from the Tools menu. An easy way to create a report is to start by duplicating an existing report, then making the necessary changes to the copy of the report.

SAVING A REPORT

To save a report, save the database. All reports that are defined for the database are saved when the database is saved.

CHAPTER 12 SELF TEST

1. In Microsoft Works you do not create an actual report, you create a report definition. Explain what the report definition is.
2. How often will a report title row print?
3. How often will a report headings row print?
4. What type of report row prints the data from the database?
5. What type of report rows use report statistics?
6. How would you get a report to double space report record rows?
7. What is the difference between choosing the Field Name option and choosing the Field Entry option on the Insert menu?
8. Explain how you would insert a new summary row in a report that has already been created.
9. If you insert a new record row and your cursor is on the record row of the report definition, where will the new record row be inserted?
10. What option is used to place the report output on the clipboard?

CHAPTER 12 TUTORIAL

In this tutorial, you will be using a database that has already been created to generate a simple report.

START THE TUTORIAL

Start Microsoft Works, then open the database Chapter 12 Tutorial.WDB which is on your tutorials and exercises diskette.

1. Start Microsoft Works and open the database named Chapter 12 Tutorial.WDB.

When the file has been loaded, you should have a list of names, addresses, and contributions like those in Figure 12.14. This will be the database used in the tutorial.

✓		ID	Last Name	Initial	First Name	City	State	Last Year	This Year
□	1	12451	Thomas	C	Marylin	Baltimore	MD	$0.00	$25.00
□	2	14452	Miller	D	Jason	Philadelphia	PA	$10.00	$10.00
□	3	16781	Smith	K	Marcia	Baltimore	MD	$200.00	$225.00
□	4	17891	Smith	J	Thomas	Baltimore	MD	$150.00	$150.00
□	5	18672	Jones	M	Phillip	Silver Springs	MD	$500.00	$410.00
□	6	18910	Thomas	O	William	Baltimore	MD	$100.00	$0.00
□	7	19902	Miller	U	Samuel	Philadelphia	PA	$55.00	$50.00
□	8	21441	Jones	R	Gayle	Silver Springs	MD	$0.00	$50.00
□	9	23411	Miller	B	Anne	Philadelphia	PA	$75.00	$100.00
□	10	25671	Jacobs	C	William	Pittsburgh	PA	$150.00	$150.00

Chapter 12 Tutorial.wdb

Zoom 100%

FIGURE 12.14   Chapter 12 Tutorial database.

CREATE A SIMPLE REPORT

We will begin this tutorial by creating a simple report. To create the report, choose the **ReportCreator** option from the Tools menu.

1. Choose the ReportCreator option on the Tools menu.
2. Enter **All Records** as the report name for this report and press the Enter key.

The ReportCreator's Title folder should now be displayed.

Enter the Report Title

Enter the report title in the **Report Title** area and set the report orientation. Refer to Figure 12.15.

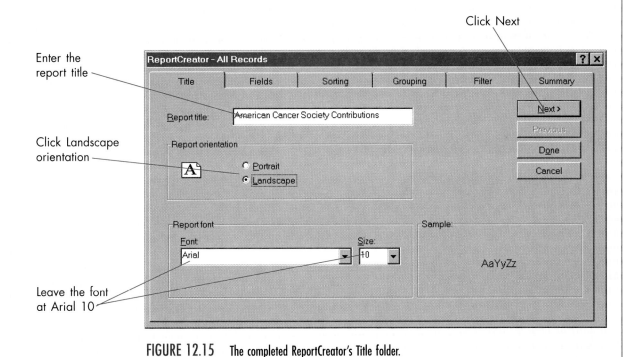

Click Next

Enter the report title

Click Landscape orientation

Leave the font at Arial 10

FIGURE 12.15   The completed ReportCreator's Title folder.

1. Enter: **American Cancer Society Contributions** in the Report Title area.
2. Click the Landscape option in the Report orientation area.
3. Click the Next button.

Add the Report Fields

The Fields folder should now be displayed. To specify the fields to be included in the report, click the field name, then click the Add button. Check the **Field order** list box to make sure the fields have been added. See Figure 12.16.

1. Click **Last Name** in the Fields available list.
2. Click the Add button to insert the field into the report definition.
3. Use the same procedure to add the First Name, City, State, Last Year, and This Year fields to the report definition.
4. Check the Show field names at top of each page option.
5. Click the Next button.

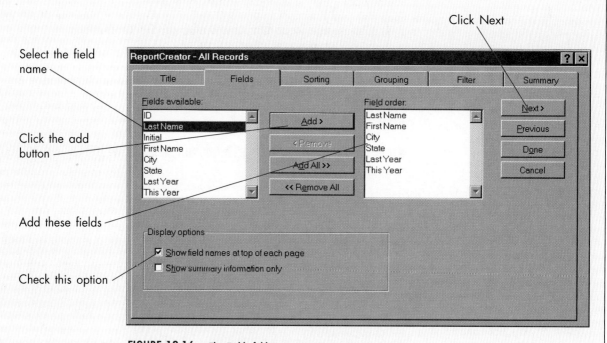

FIGURE 12.16   The Fields folder.

Check the Field order list box. If you have added an incorrect field, select the field name in the Field order list and use the Remove button to remove the field. If necessary, add any missing fields. If the fields are in the wrong order, click the Remove all button and add the fields again.

Define the Sort Order

The next step is to define the **Sorting** order for the records in the report. For this report we will sort by first name within last name. See Figure 12.17.

Click the summary tab

Choose Last Name

Choose First Name

Choose Ascending

Choose Ascending

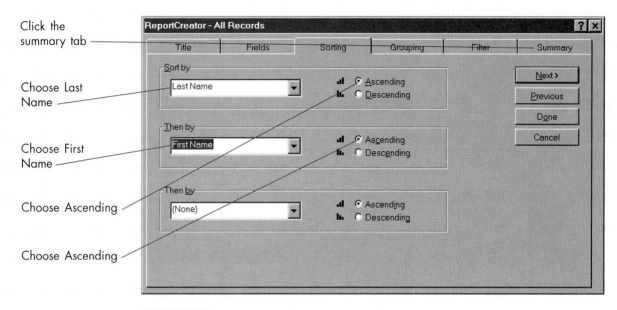

FIGURE 12.17 The Sorting folder.

1. Click the arrow on the right of the Sort by list and choose **Last Name**.
2. Click the Ascending button to the right of the Sort by list.
3. Click the arrow on the right of the first Then by list and choose **First Name**.
4. Click the Ascending button to the right of the Sort by list.

For this report we will not need to set grouping options or a filter, so click the Summary tab.

5. Click the Summary tab.

Choose the Summary Statistics

The **Summary** folder should now be displayed. This folder is shown in Figure 12.18. In this tutorial you want to count the number of contributors and print the sum and average of the contributions last year and this year.

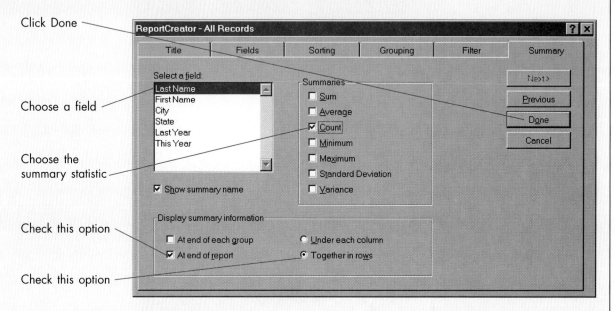

Click Done

Choose a field

Choose the summary statistic

Check this option

Check this option

FIGURE 12.18   The Summary dialog box.

1. Click the **Last Name** field name, then click the **Count** statistic.
2. Click the **Last Year** field name, then click both the **Sum** and **Average** statistics.
3. Click the **This Year** field name, then click both the **Sum** and **Average** statistics.

Since you want the summary statistics in rows at the bottom of the report, make sure the **Together in rows** option is set on in the **Display summary information** area.

4. Click the **At end of report** option in the Display summary information area.
5. Click the **Together in rows** option in the Display summary information area.
6. Click the Done button.

You should now have a question box with a Preview and Modify button.

7. Click the Preview button.

Your report preview should look like the one in Figure 12.19.

8. Click the Next button to see the report summaries.

Last Name	First Name	City	State	Last Year	This Year
			American Cancer Society Contributions		
Applebaum	Alice	Pittsburgh	PA	$210.00	$500.00
Applebaum	Donald	Pittsburgh	PA	$75.00	$50.00
Jacobs	Gary	Pittsburgh	PA	$500.00	$1,000.00
Jacobs	Jim	Pittsburgh	PA	$275.00	$175.00
Jacobs	William	Pittsburgh	PA	$150.00	$150.00
Jones	Carol	Silver Springs	MD	$25.00	$25.00
Jones	Gayle	Silver Springs	MD	$0.00	$50.00
Jones	Phillip	Silver Springs	MD	$500.00	$410.00
Kline	Everett	Silver Springs	MD	$1,000.00	$1,500.00

FIGURE 12.19   First few records of the report preview.

After examining the report, cancel the preview.

9. Click the Cancel button.

The report definition is now created. It should look like Figure 12.20.

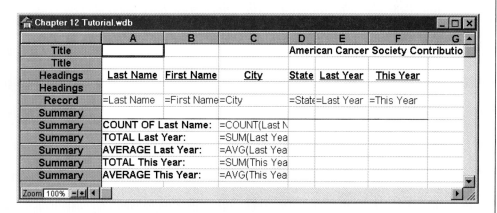

FIGURE 12.20   The tutorial's report format.

CUSTOMIZE THE REPORT DEFINITION

The next step is to make a few changes to the report definition. The changes include a different font and font size for the title, a new field for the report, and different headings.

Customize the Report Title

To change the report title, do the following.

1. Move the cursor to the cell that contains the report title. This should be column D of the first report title row.
2. Set the font to Times New Roman.
3. Set the font size to 16.
4. Use the Alignment option on the Format menu and choose **Center across** selection. Click the OK button.

Add a Net Change Field

The next step is to create a new report field. This field will calculate the difference between last year's contribution and this year's contribution.

1. Click cell G of the Record row.
2. Enter: **=This Year - Last Year**.
3. Press the Enter key.

Change the Column Headings

For this report you need two column headings. The first step is to insert a new Headings row.

1. Click anywhere in the first Headings row.
2. Click the right mouse button.
3. Choose **Insert Row** from the right button menu.
4. Choose **Headings** from the **Insert Row** window.
5. Click the Insert button.

You should now have a new empty Headings row above the original Heading row. Enter the following heading in this row. See Figure 12.21 for the report definition after the next several changes.

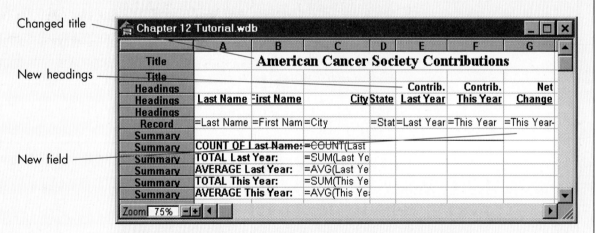

FIGURE 12.21   Report definition after adding a field and customizing the heading rows.

6. Enter **Contrib.** in cell E of the first Headings row, press Enter, and click the Bold Tool on the Toolbar.
7. Enter **Contrib.** in cell F of the first Headings row, press Enter, and click the Bold tool on the Toolbar.
8. Enter **Net** in cell G of the first Headings row, press Enter, and click the Bold tool on the Toolbar.
9. Enter **Change** in cell G of the second Headings row, press Enter, and click the Underline and Bold tools on the Toolbar.
10. Select cells E, F, and G of both Headings rows. Use the Alignment option on the Format menu to set a Right alignment for these cells.
11. Select cells A, B, and C of the second Headings rows. Use the Alignment option on the Format menu to set a left alignment for these cells.

Set the New Column's Format

1. Click cell G of the Record row.
2. Use the Number option on the Format menu to set the format to Currency with two decimal places.

Print the Report

1. Click the Preview tool on the Toolbar. Use the Zoom In button to get a clearer view of the report.

The top part of the report should look like Figure 12.22. There should be two pages of the report with the second page containing the summary statistics. Use the Next button to see the second page.

Click to see the second page —

Click to print —

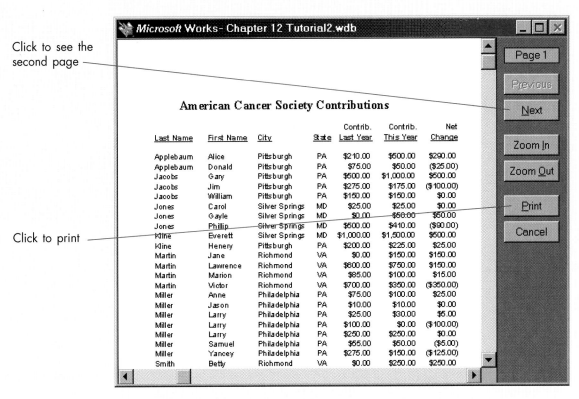

FIGURE 12.22   The changed report's preview.

2. Click the Next button.

You are now ready to print this report.

3. Click the Print button.

USE A FILTER FOR THE REPORT

Remember that filters can be used to restrict the records used for the report. There has been a filter created that lists only those contributors that have given less this year than they gave last year. This filter is named Low Givers. Print the report again using this filter.

1. Choose the **Report Filter** option from the Tools menu.

   You should have the Filters folder shown in Figure 12.23

Choose **Low Givers**

Click Done

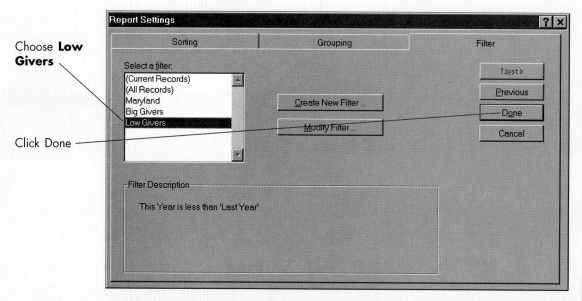

FIGURE 12.23   The report Filter folder.

2. Click **Low Givers** in the Select a filter list.
3. Click Done.

   Now preview and print this report.

4. Click the Preview tool

   This report should list 12 contributors on a single page.

5. Click the Print button.

SAVE THE REPORT

When you save the database, you also save your report definition. To save the report, use the **Save** or **Save As** option from the File menu.

1. Save the database.

> Note: When you save the database, all report options are also saved. Since the Low Givers filter was applied to the report when that database was saved, this filter will still be applied to the database the next time it is opened. To gain access to all the database records, change the filter to (All Records) or choose All Records from the Show option of the Record menu in List View.
>
> This completes the tutorial. You can now exit Microsoft Works.

HANDS-ON PRACTICE

Exercise 12-1

For this exercise, use the database named Exercise 12-1.WDB. This database is stored on your tutorials and exercises diskette.
Create the report shown in Figure 12.24.

1. Use the report title shown in Figure 12.24. Use a Landscape orientation.
2. Use only the fields shown in Figure 12.24. Make sure the fields appear in the order shown.
3. Sort the records by **Department**.
4. Create a **Sum** and an **Average summary** statistic for the **Salary** field.
5. Change the format for the **Date Hired** field to the **Month, Year** format as shown in Figure 12.24. You may need to change the field width for this column to get the entire date to print properly.
6. Use the alignments shown in Figure 12.24.
7. Print the report.

Employee Listing

Last Name	First Name	Department	Salary	Dependents	Date Hired
Alberts	John	Maintenance	$25,000.00	2	March 1985
Danson	Tammy	Maintenance	$17,600.00	1	April 1990
Miller	Sarah	Maintenance	$27,000.00	3	July 1983
Payne	Shea	Maintenance	$17,550.00	1	March 1985
Ramsey	Jessica	Maintenance	$24,355.00	1	July 1995
Shank	Micheal	Maintenance	$17,550.00	2	April 1990
Smith	Wes	Maintenance	$19,750.00	3	December 1993
Turner	Brittney	Maintenance	$16,500.00	4	November 1966
Zale	Gary	Maintenance	$21,000.00	4	March 1985
Carson	Sonia	Production	$19,790.00	2	December 1994
Hanks	Kathey	Production	$19,000.00	5	August 1955
Johnson	Whittney	Production	$25,000.00	4	December 1994
Jones	Adam	Production	$25,500.00	5	December 1969
Jones	Jacob	Production	$33,000.00	3	November 1994
Kline	Drew	Production	$16,000.00	2	July 1995
Lane	Jason	Production	$12,000.00	3	December 1991
Miller	Mary	Production	$22,000.00	6	July 1989
Pills	Joe	Production	$13,790.00	1	March 1985
Viers	Thomas	Production	$29,900.00	2	August 1988
Wilson	Becky	Production	$14,500.00	3	April 1988
Baker	Parson	Shipping	$26,900.00	2	April 1990
Benke	Robert	Shipping	$25,000.00	3	April 1984
Frankel	Quincy	Shipping	$23,500.00	3	October 1995
Parker	Bob	Shipping	$18,675.00	2	May 1983
Sonner	Logan	Shipping	$28,000.00	3	October 1985

SUM:
$538,860.00
AVG:
$21,554.40

FIGURE 12.24 Sample report for Exercise 12.1.

Exercise 12-2

For this exercise, use the database Exercise 12-2.WDB on your tutorials disk. The database consists of orders from different departments within a department store. Create the report shown in Figure 12.25.

Note: Not all records are shown in Figure 12.25.

1. Use the report title shown in Figure 12.25. Use a Portrait orientation. Use a default font of Times New Roman and a font size of 12 points.
2. Use only the fields shown in Figure 12.25. Make sure the fields appear in the order shown.
3. Sort the records by **Item #**, then by **Department**.
4. Create a **Sum** and an **Average summary** statistic for the **Total** field. These totals are not shown in Figure 12.25. Print these summary statistics together in rows.
5. Change the report title to an 18 point Arial font.
6. Use the alignments shown in Figure 12.25.
7. Print the report.
8. Apply the filter named **Sporting Goods** and print the report a second time.

Department Order Report

Dept	Item#	Description	Unit Price	Quantity	Total
Electronics	2671	Toaster, 2 Slice	22.89	12	$274.68
Electronics	2856	Toaster, 4 Slice	29.50	6	$177.00
Electronics	2864	Knife Sharpener	17.50	24	$420.00
Electronics	2891	Gas Grill	345.00	10	$3,450.00
Electronics	2894	Air Conditioner	879.50	5	$4,397.50
Electronics	2904	Can Opener	12.00	24	$288.00
Electronics	2331	Coffee Maker	45.90	12	$550.80
Electronics	2465	Toaster Oven	39.99	12	$479.88
Electronics	2774	Gas Grill	256.00	10	$2,560.00
Electronics	2009	Air Freshener	65.90	12	$790.80
Electronics	2222	Blender	39.90	12	$478.80
Electronics	2345	Mixer	39.77	6	$238.62
Electronics	2376	Gas Grill	300.00	6	$1,800.00
Electronics	2672	Sandwich Griddle	32.30	24	$775.20
Electronics	2890	Iron, Steam	19.00	12	$228.00
Electronics	2970	Humidifier	496.00	24	$11,904.00
Sporting	4222	Tent, 2 man	195.00	6	$1,170.00
Sporting	4333	Tent, 4 man	345.00	4	$1,380.00
Sporting	4690	Sleeping Bag, Small	56.90	12	$682.80

FIGURE 12.25   Sample report for Exercise 12.2.

Exercise 12-3A

For this exercise, use the database named Exercise 12-3.WDB on your tutorials disk. The database contains a set of records about invoices and items ordered on the invoice.

1. Create the report shown in Figure 12.26. Use the following requirements.
    a. Report only the fields shown. Report the fields in the order shown. Sort the report by **Date**, then by **Invoice #**, then by **Item #**.
    b. Insert a second **Title** row as shown. Format both **Titles** using a Times New Roman, bold italic, 16 point font.
    c. Change the report Heading rows so they appear as shown. Make sure you use two heading rows as shown.
    d. Align each field as shown in Figure 12.26.
    e. Add the field titled **Number Backordered** using a formula. The number backordered is the **Quantity** minus the **Number shipped**.
    f. Use a **Summary** statistic to count the number of line items. (You can use the **Count** statistic on any field to do this.) Use the **Together in rows** option for this statistic.
    g. Print the report using Landscape orientation.

Hudson Wholesalers
Invoice/Shipping Report

Date	Invoice #	Item#	Unit Price	Quantity	Number Shipped	Number Backordered	Amount Billed
3/15/96	0101	0211	19.95	24	24	0	478.80
3/15/96	0101	0314	22.00	100	100	0	2,200.00
3/15/96	0101	0410	320.00	10	10	0	3,200.00
3/15/96	0101	0412	195.00	90	70	20	13,650.00
3/15/96	0101	0577	55.95	50	50	0	2,797.50
3/15/96	0113	0211	19.95	48	36	12	718.20
3/15/96	0113	0314	22.00	90	50	40	1,100.00
3/15/96	0113	0444	69.90	60	60	0	4,194.00

FIGURE 12.26   Sample report for Exercise 12.3.

Exercise 12-3B

1. Modify the report created in Part A. Add the following requirements.

   a. Insert a column between the **Invoice #** and the **Item #**. The new column should print the field named **Salesperson**. Add an appropriate entry to the Headings rows to indicate the **Salesperson** column.

   b. Add a column to the to the right of the **Amount Billed** column. This column should show a **Commission Amount**. The commission amount is to be computed as the **Amount billed** multiplied by 10%. Use an appropriate heading for the column. Format this column using a currency format.

   c. Add a **Summary** row to the end of the report. The summary row should have three statistics. Sum the **Quantity Ordered**, sum the **Number Shipped**, and sum the **Amount Billed**. Place each summary statistic under the appropriate column.

   d. Print the report.

INTEGRATING WORKS APPLICATIONS

When you've completed this chapter, you will be able to:

- Use multiple windows.
- Copy data between Works tools.
- Copy database and spreadsheet data into a word processing document.
- Link data in one application to another application.
- Insert charts in a word processing document and change a chart's size.
- Create form letters.
- Create labels from database data.

Integration refers to the ability to use information from one Microsoft Works tool in another Works tool. Examples of integration are the ability to copy data from a spreadsheet into a database and from a database into a word processing document. Another example is copying a chart from a spreadsheet into a word processing document or linking a chart to a word processing document. To integrate applications, you place each of the documents to be integrated in a separate window.

INTEGRATION CONCEPTS

The concept of windows is the foundation for integration between Works applications. **Windows** in Microsoft Works are similar to windows in the Windows operating environment. Before learning how to perform the integration steps, you will need to know how to use windows within Works.

Using Windows

Works allows multiple windows to be open at one time. Each window is a file that has been loaded into memory. Each window can contain a different kind of application. For example, one window may contain a word processing document, another window a spreadsheet, and a third window a database. When several windows are open, one will be the active window and the others inactive windows. The active window will be the one with which you are currently working. Figure 13.1 shows several Works windows.

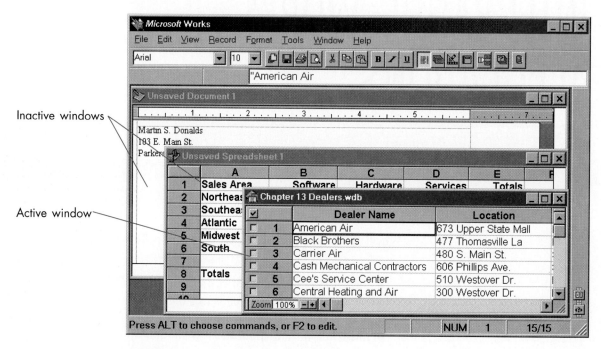

FIGURE 13.1   Multiple windows in Microsoft Works.

To work in a particular window, you must first make that window active. To make a window active, select the appropriate file name from the **Window menu** or use the **Ctrl/F6** keys to move between windows. When the window is active, it comes to the front of the desktop and the previously active window moves to the back.

Most integration of Microsoft Works applications involves copying data or linking information from one window to another. The window that contains the original data is called the **source window**. The window the data are being copied to is called the **destination window**.

COPYING TO WORD PROCESSING WINDOWS

Copying From Another Word Processing Window

To copy data from one word processing window to another, both windows must be open. The easiest way to copy data between two word processing windows is to use a copy and paste operation. To begin the copy, move to the **source window** and select the text to be copied. Next, choose the Copy option from the Edit menu or click the Copy tool on the Toolbar. This will place the text on the Windows **clipboard**.

Once the text is on the clipboard, use the Window menu or the Ctrl/F6 keys to move to the **destination window**. Move the cursor to the location where the text is to be copied and paste the contents of the clipboard into the document.

You can also use the drag and drop method to copy data between windows. To use the drag and drop method, make sure some part of the target window can be seen on the screen. If necessary, move a window or use the Window menu to **tile** the windows. When the windows are tiled, they are placed side-by-side. Start the copy process in the source document by selecting the text to copy, then move the mouse pointer over the selected text. When the pointer changes to a drag pointer, press the left mouse button. Now drag the mouse to the target window. When the drag pointer moves into the destination window, the window will move to the front and the move pointer will change to the copy pointer. Move the copy pointer to the location where the text is to be placed and release the mouse button. This approach is illustrated in Figure 13.2.

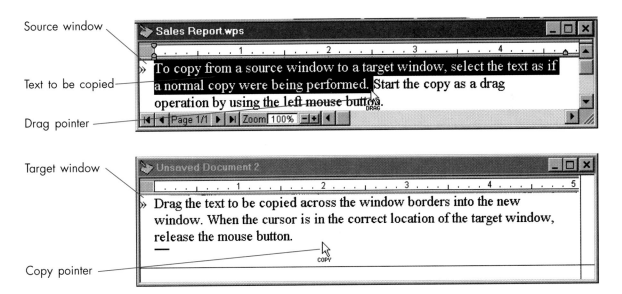

FIGURE 13.2 Using drag and drop to copy between windows.

When text is copied from one word processing document to another, the original formatting is also copied. This includes any special character fonts, paragraph formats, underlines, bold, italics, and tab markers.

Copying from a Spreadsheet

There are several ways to copy data in spreadsheet cells to a word processing document. To start any copy procedure, move to the source spreadsheet's window and select the cells to be copied. Choose the Copy option from the Edit menu or use the Copy tool to copy the cells to the clipboard.

Next, use the Window menu or the **Ctrl/F6** keys to move to the destination window and move the cursor to the location where the spreadsheet cells are to be placed. From the Edit menu, choose Paste or click the Paste tool. The selected spreadsheet will be placed in the document as a table.

When you select the table, sizing handles like those in Figure 13.3 are displayed. These handles can be used to decrease or increase the amount of the spreadsheet displayed. Drag one of the right or left **handles** to display or hide columns, or drag the top or bottom handles to display or hide rows. To edit the contents of the table, double click the table. The spreadsheet menus will appear and you will be able to use any of the spreadsheet options to change the table. To return to the word processor, click anywhere outside the table.

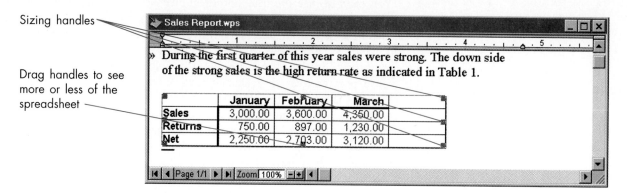

Sizing handles

Drag handles to see more or less of the spreadsheet

FIGURE 13.3   Inserted spreadsheet cells appear with handles when selected.

Any changes to the original source spreadsheet, i.e., changes to values, formatting, fonts, etc., will not be reflected in the document's copy. Likewise, changes in the copy stored in the word processing document will not be reflected in the original source spreadsheet. Use this option when a duplicate copy of the spreadsheet needs to be stored with a word processing document.

Another approach to copying spreadsheet data into a document is to use the **Paste Special** option from the Edit menu. The Paste Special window is shown in Figure 13.4. The format options available on the Paste Special window depend upon what is on the clipboard at the time the Paste Special option is chosen. The exact way the spreadsheet cells are copied depends upon the option selected in the **As** list.

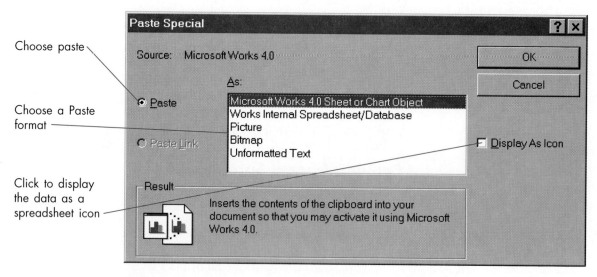

Choose paste

Choose a Paste format

Click to display the data as a spreadsheet icon

FIGURE 13.4   Paste Special window is used to specify how spreadsheet cells are copied to a document.

The first option on the Paste Special window when spreadsheet data are on the clipboard is the **Microsoft Works 4.0 Sheet or Chart Object**. Choosing this option is the same as using the Paste option on the Edit menu or using the Paste tool. If this option is selected, the **Display as Icon** option is available. If this option is checked, an icon representing the spreadsheet is displayed rather than the spreadsheet data.

The **Works Internal Spreadsheet/Database** option will insert the contents of the selected cells as text separated by tabs. Each row from the spreadsheet becomes one paragraph in the word processing document, and each column from the spreadsheet becomes one column in the word processing document. Tab markers are inserted to align and space the cell data. The results of this option are shown in Figure 13.5.

The copied data can be treated as if they were typed into the document. Fonts and font sizes can be changed; bold, italic, or underlined attributes can be changed; borders can be added; and any other formatting changes can be made. Use this approach when the data need to be copied to the document, but does not need to be used as a spreadsheet.

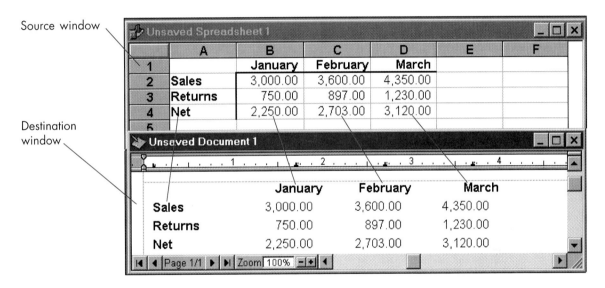

FIGURE 13.5   The Works Internal Spreadsheet/Database option copies the spreadsheet cells as a set of rows and columns.

Both the **Picture** and the **Bitmap** options insert the copied cells as a clipart image. The primary difference is the type of image inserted. The Picture option inserts an image of the cells as a draw image. The Bitmap option inserts an image of the cells as a paint image.

Both images display handles when selected. The handles can be used to enlarge or reduce the picture's image. All other options that are available to format and position pictures are available to the spreadsheet image.

Generally, if you want an image of the cells, paste the cells as a Picture. Enlarging and reducing this type of image produces a better quality image as long as the height and width of the picture remain proportional in relation to the original picture. If you want to distort the image of the spreadsheet, for example make it taller but not wider, use the Bitmap option to insert the image.

The **Unformatted Text** option pastes the contents of the cells as text. This is like the Works Internal Spreadsheet/Database option, except that the font and other formatting are not copied from the spreadsheet, and tab marks are not inserted.

Copying a Chart

To copy a spreadsheet **chart** into a document, first open a window that contains the spreadsheet and the chart (recall that the chart is stored with the spreadsheet). Then use the Chart option on the View menu to display the chart to be copied. Next, use the Copy option from the Edit menu or the Copy tool to copy the chart to the clipboard. Now, move to the word processing document and use the Paste tool or the **Paste Special** option on the Edit menu to paste the chart into the document.

When a chart is on the clipboard, three paste formats are available on the Paste Special window. The first format, **Microsoft Works 4.0 Sheet or Chart Object**, copies the chart and the spreadsheet used to create the chart into the document. The chart is displayed as an object within the document.

Since the spreadsheet is also copied, the spreadsheet or chart can be edited from within the word processing document. To edit either the spreadsheet data or the chart, double-click the chart. This will open the spreadsheet module within the word processing document. When the chart window is opened, the chart menu bar is the menu bar used by Works. Use the chart menu bar or Toolbar to make any changes required to the chart. An example of the window is shown in Figure 13.6.

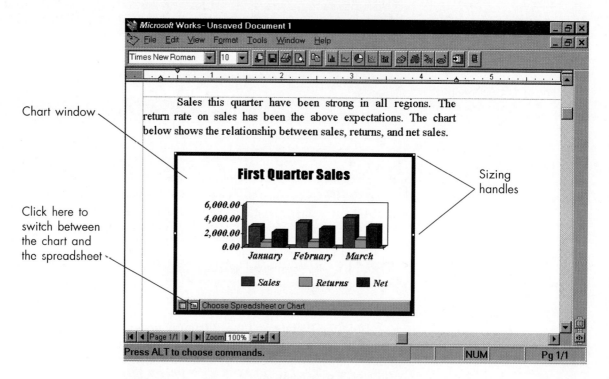

FIGURE 13.6　A Works chart copied to a word processing document.

The bottom of the chart window displays two icons. To switch to the spreadsheet and change the data, click the spreadsheet icon. To return to the chart, click the chart icon. To close the chart window and return to the word processing document, click anywhere outside the chart's frame.

The other two formats on the Paste Special window are the **Picture** and **Bitmap** formats. These formats work the same way for a chart as they do for spreadsheet cells except they only copy the chart. The chart is copied as a picture and can be sized using the picture handles. Sizing and text wrap can also be set using the **Text Wrap** and Picture options on the Format menu.

COPYING DATA FROM A DATABASE

Copying from a database to a word processing document works the same as copying from a spreadsheet. Select the cells to be copied, move to the word processing document, choose Paste Special, select a paste format, and choose the OK button. The difference is that only the Works Internal Spreadsheet/Database, Picture, Bitmap, and Unformatted Text formats are available when copying from a database window. See the **Copying from a Spreadsheet** section earlier in this chapter for details about how these formats work.

Copying a Database Report

Copying a **database report** into a word processing document is a little different than copying the database data. This is because the database report is not stored as data directly. It is created from the database report definition.

To copy a database report, start in the database **Report View** with the correct database report definition displayed. While in this view, click the **Copy Report Output** option from the Edit menu. This option will write the report to the clipboard. Once the report is on the clipboard, move to the word processing window and use the Paste Special option from the Edit menu to paste the report into the word processing document. Only two format options are available for pasting reports. The **Works Internal Spreadsheet/Database** will paste the report output with the fonts and spacing set by the report format. The **Unformatted Text** option will use the word processing document's font and spacing.

LINKING OBJECTS

The techniques discussed above copy spreadsheet data or database data into a word processing document. When changes are made to the original spreadsheet data, the changes will not be reflected in the copy of the data. Sometimes this is desirable. In other cases, you may want any changes made to the original spreadsheet data to be reflected in the data in the word processing document. If this is the desired result, the data should be **linked** to the word processing document. When data are linked, the document that contains the original data is referred to as the **server document**. The document that contains the linked data is called the **client document**. Only spreadsheet ranges and charts can be linked to a word processing document.

To link a named **spreadsheet range** to a word processing document, open the spreadsheet document. Move to the word processing document and place the cursor where the range is to be inserted. Next, choose Spreadsheet from the Insert menu. An Insert Spreadsheet window like the one in Figure 13.7 will be displayed. Click the **Use a range from an existing spreadsheet** option. Next, select the name of the spreadsheet that contains the range to be linked. When the spreadsheet name is selected, all range names in the spreadsheet will be displayed. Choose the range name to be copied and click the OK button. The range will be displayed in the word processing document and linked to the original source document.

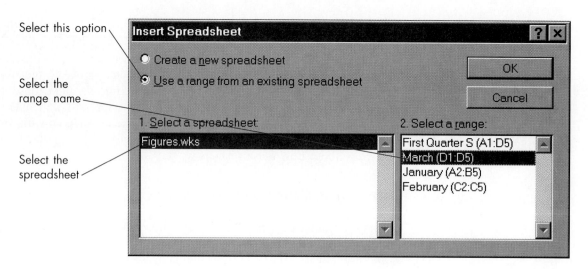

Select this option

Select the range name

Select the spreadsheet

FIGURE 13.7 Use the Spreadsheet option from the Insert menu to link a named spreadsheet range to a word processing document.

To link a range of cells that are not named, move to the server document and select the cells to be placed in the client document. Copy the selected cells to the clipboard. Next, move to the client document, then move the cursor to where the cells are to go, and choose the Paste Special option from the Edit menu. The Paste Special window was shown in Figure 13.4. Set the **Paste Link** option on. The only format available in the **As** list box when the Paste Link option is selected will be Microsoft Works 4.0 Sheet or Chart Object. Select this format from the list box and choose the OK button. The data on the clipboard will be displayed in the word processing document and will be linked to the server document.

To link a spreadsheet chart, use the Insert menu from the client document and choose the Chart option. The Insert Chart window, which is similar to Figure 13.7, will be displayed. This window will list all available spreadsheets. Select the spreadsheet and a list of all charts in the spreadsheet will be displayed. Select the chart to be linked and choose the OK button. The chart will be displayed and linked to the document.

Although linked spreadsheet ranges and charts are displayed and printed as part of the word processing document, cells and charts are not actually copied into the document. Only a reference to the spreadsheet cells are placed in the document. Any changes to the original spreadsheet or chart will be reflected in the word processing document. These changes include fonts, cell formatting, cell sizing, gridlines, and text.

Setting Link Options

Objects that have been linked to a word processing document can be updated automatically anytime a change occurs to the original object, or they can be updated manually. To specify how the object is to be updated, use the **Links** option on the Edit menu. When you choose this option, the Links window shown in Figure 13.8 appears. The Links window lists all linked objects in the document. It shows the object's location, name, and updating method.

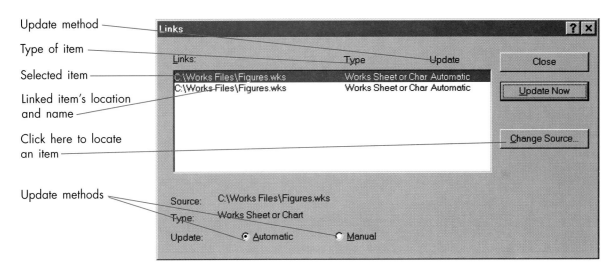

Update method

Type of item

Selected item

Linked item's location
and name

Click here to locate
an item

Update methods

FIGURE 13.8   Links window.

To change the update method, select the object in the list box and choose the **Automatic** or **Manual update** option at the bottom of the window. If the Automatic option is selected for a linked object, any change to the original object is automatically reflected in the linked object. If the Manual option is selected for a linked object, changes will not be reflected in the document until the item is selected in the Links list box and the **Update Now** button is selected.

Special Considerations for Linked Objects

There are a few special considerations for linked objects. First, since a document does not contain the object (it only contains a reference to the object), if a document that contains linked object is moved from one machine to another, the linked objects must also be moved.

Second, if a linked server document is moved or renamed, the new location and name must be reflected in the client document. To reflect the change, click the **Change Source** button on the Links window. A window similar to an Open File window will be displayed. Use this option to locate the file that contains the linked item and click the OK button. The reference to the server document will be updated to reflect the new name and location.

Opening a Document that Contains Linked Data

When a document is opened that contains linked objects, such as a spreadsheet range or a chart, a message appears that asks if you want to update the linked objects. If you choose the **Yes** button, Works will check the server document and make necessary changes to the client document. If you choose the **No** button, changes to the linked document will not be reflected in the client document. If, for any reason, the server document cannot be found, no changes will be made to the client document. A server document may not be found if it has been moved or deleted, or if its name has been changed.

Copying from a Word Processing Document

You can also copy data from a word processing window into a database window. To avoid confusion, the word processing data to be copied should be organized in a row and column format. Each column should be separated by a tab and each row should be a paragraph. Each tab mark will be used to separate the data into cells in a row, and each paragraph mark will be used to specify a new record. See Figure 13.9 for an example.

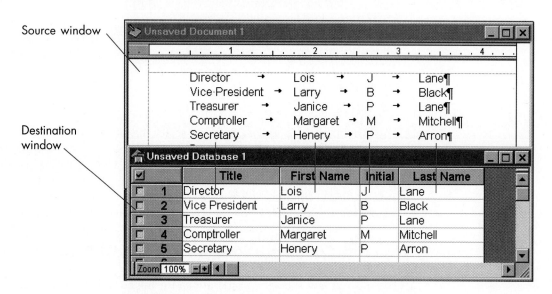

FIGURE 13.9 Results of copying word processing data to a database.

To make the copy, first select the data in the word processor that are to be copied. Next, select the Copy option from the Edit menu. Make the destination database the active window. Position the cursor in the database in the upper-left corner of the area you want the word processing data copied into, and choose the Paste option from the Edit menu.

Since the new data will replace any data in the cells in the paste area, you should insert enough empty rows into the database to hold the new data before performing the paste. Figure 13.9 shows the results of a paste operation.

Copying from Another Database

Copying from one database window to another database window is very direct. Each row in the source database is inserted as a record in the destination database. The copied data will replace any data in the destination rows, so new rows should be inserted before data is copied into an existing database. When data are copied to the destination database, only values are copied. If formulas are used in the source columns being copied, the result of the formula is copied, not the actual formula.

To copy cells from one database to another database, select the data in the source database that are to be copied. Next, select the Copy option from the Edit menu. Now make the destination database the active window. Position the cursor in the destination database in the upper-left corner of the area you want the data copied into, and select Paste from the Edit menu.

Copying from a Spreadsheet

Copying from a spreadsheet to a database works like copying from a database to a database. Rows from the spreadsheet become rows in the database. The copied data will replace any data in the destination rows and only values are copied. Results of formulas are computed, and the results, not the formulas, are copied.

COPYING TO A SPREADSHEET

Copying to a spreadsheet works exactly like copying to a database. When copying from a word processing document, format text as columns separated by tabs. Make each row a paragraph.

When copying from a database, each field in the database will be a column in the spreadsheet and each record in the database will become a row in the spreadsheet.

CREATING FORM LETTERS

One of the advantages of integrating information from different Works modules is the ability to create **form letters** and **mailing lists**. Form letters can be created by merging data from a database with a letter created in the word processing module. A customized form letter is simply a letter that contains standard text in most of the letter and tailored text for a particular person or event in specified parts of the letter. For example, you may want to mail a personalized letter to all your customers informing them of a special sale. The body of the letter, which describes the sale, is the same for every customer, but the names and addresses are different for the individuals receiving the letters. The contents of the letter are typed as a standard word processing document, and the names and addresses are inserted from a database.

The letter is created as a normal word processing document. Special **field place holders** are inserted where the individualized data are to be printed. These field place holders refer to data in a specific database.

To create a form letter, start by creating a new word processing document. Next, choose the **Form Letters** option from the Tools menu. Works will display the **Form Letters** window with the Instructions folder as show in Figure 13.10. The Form Letters steps will guide you through each step necessary to create the form letter. To perform the first step, click the Next button.

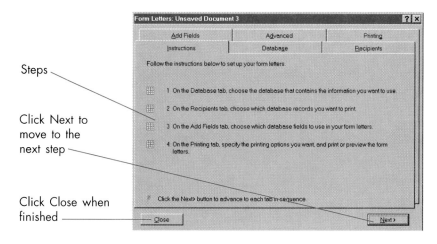

Steps

Click Next to move to the next step

Click Close when finished

FIGURE 13.10   The Instructions folder of the Form Letters window.

Select The Database

The first step in the form letter is to select the database to be used with the form letter. When the Next button is selected, a **Database folder** like the one in Figure 13.11 is displayed. Select the database name to be used with the form letter. If the database name is not in the list of databases, click the **Open a database not listed here** option. You can then search through the drives and folders to find the database. To examine the database data, click the **View Database** button. When you have the correct database selected, click the Next button.

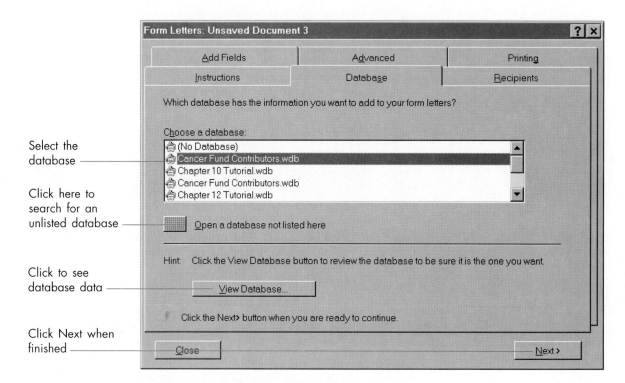

FIGURE 13.11   The Database folder of the Form Letters menu.

Select the Recipients

When you click the Next button on the Database folder, the Instructions folder is displayed again and the first step is checked. Click the Next button again and the **Recipients folder** is displayed as shown in Figure 13.12. The Recipients folder allows you to select which records in the database will be used to print the form letter. A form letter will be printed for each record displayed in the database.

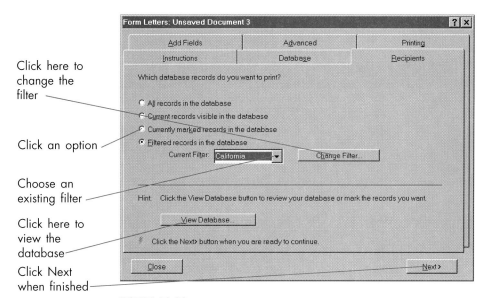

Click here to change the filter

Click an option

Choose an existing filter

Click here to view the database

Click Next when finished

FIGURE 13.12   The Recipients folder of the Form Letters window.

The first step is to select one of the options on the left of the folder. If the **Filtered records in the database** option is selected, the Current Filter list is available. You can use this list to select the appropriate filter. If a filter is selected, you can use the Change Filter button to change the criterion for the filter. If an appropriate option or filter is not available, choose the **View Database** button and create a new filter for the database. When the correct option is selected, click the Next button.

Add the Database Fields

After the Recipients folder is complete the next step is to add database fields to the form letter. The **Add Fields folder** is shown in Figure 13.13. To add a field to the database, select the field name to be added, then click the **Insert field** button.

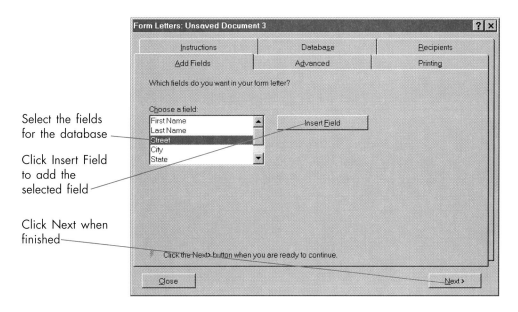

Select the fields for the database

Click Insert Field to add the selected field

Click Next when finished

FIGURE 13.13   The Add Fields folder of the Form Letters window.

At this point you may want to diverge from the set sequence of steps provided by the Next button. You could insert all the fields needed from the database now and enter the text for the form letter later. If this approach is used, you will need to use the cut and paste operations to get the field names in the correct places in the form letter.

The other approach to creating the form letter is to switch between the adding of the fields and the editing of the form letter. Using this approach, you enter the text for the form letter until a database field is needed, come back to the Add Fields folder, insert a field, then move back to enter more of the form letter. We will introduce the Advanced folder that will allow you to edit the letter before completing the form letter steps.

Edit the Letter

To enter text or otherwise edit the contents of the form letter, click the **Advanced folder** tab on the Form Letters window. The only button on this folder is the Edit button. Click this button and the form letter document is displayed. A window is placed on top of the document with a **Go Back** button as shown in Figure 13.14. Click inside the document to enter text or edit the document. Click the Go Back button to return to the Form Letter window.

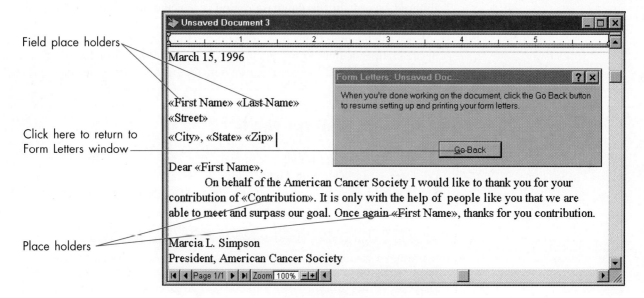

FIGURE 13.14 A form letter with field place holders inserted.

You can use the Advanced and Insert Fields folders to create the form letter. Use the Edit button on the Advanced folder to edit the document. Use the Go Back button and Insert Fields folder to add a field. When the form letter is complete, click the Next button on the Insert Fields folder. This will display the Instructions folder again. Click the Next button to print the form letters.

Print the Form Letters

The **Printing folder** of the Form Letters window is shown in Figure 13.15. Click the Preview button to preview the form letters. A small window may appear that indicates which records will be printed. Click the OK button to preview the letters.

Click here to preview

Click here to print

Enter number of copies for each record

Select grouping option

Click Close to Finish

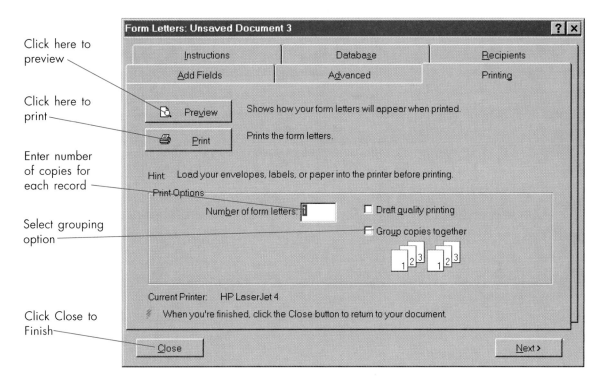

FIGURE 13.15   The Printing folder of the Form Letters window.

To print the letters, click the Print button. A message will appear that indicates the form letters are being printed. Normally, one form letter will be printed for each record available by the database filter or other database selection option set on the Database folder. If more than one letter is needed, set the number of copies using the **Number of form letters** option on the Printing folder.

To complete the form letter, click the Close button on the printing window. This will return you to the form letter document. Changes can still be made to the document. If changes need to be made to the form letter options discussed above, click the Form Letters option on the Tools menu. All the folders will be available and changes can be made.

Note the symbols **<< >>** placed around the field names in the document (see Figure 13.14). These symbols show that this is a **field place holder** for the database field; the word(s) inside the symbols is/are the name of the field in the database. The field place holder will be replaced by the data from the database when the form letter is printed. Any number of place holders can be inserted in a document, but all place holders must come from a single database. If all the data are not in a single database, copy needed fields from one database into another using the procedures discussed earlier.

The field place holders can be aligned with the Left, Right, and Center tools and can be formatted with bold, italic, and underlined attributes. You can also change the font and size and apply other formats to the place holders. When the place holder is replaced by the database data, the data will use the format and font applied to the place holder. Any spacing or punctuation must be inserted into the document as word processing text.

Once the place holders are inserted, they can be moved or copied by using the Cut, Copy, and Paste tools.

It is important to remember that the place holder consists of the two symbols plus the field name. If any part of the place holder is deleted or changed, the entire place holder should be deleted and inserted again.

CREATING LABELS

Labels can also be created from the data in a database. Labels are printed using a customized mailing labels form in the word processor, much the same way a form letter is created. The primary difference between a form letter and a label is that you can print multiple database records on a single page of labels. Form letters print one entire copy of the document for each record. Each copy of the document will be printed on different pages.

The process for creating labels is similar to the process used to create a form letter. First choose the **Labels** option from the Tools menu. The window shown in Figure 13.16 is displayed. If you want to create the labels for several records in a database, click the **Labels** button. If you want several copies of one label, for example, you want to create 50 address labels for yourself, click the **Multiple copies of one label** button.

Click here to create labels from a database

Click here to create a special label

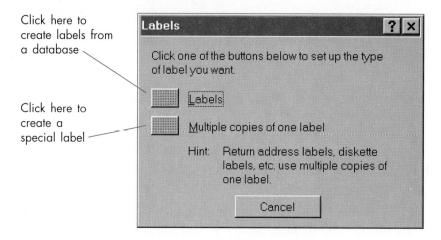

FIGURE 13.16   The Label option window.

Select the Label Size

The first folder on the Labels window is the instructions folder. Click the Next button on this folder to display the **Label Size folder** shown in Figure 13.17. Works has most of the information necessary for label sets sold by Avery Dennison. If the labels being used are produced by Avery and you know the style number, select the format from the **Choose a label size** list and click the Next button.

Choose a label size

Click here to specify your own style

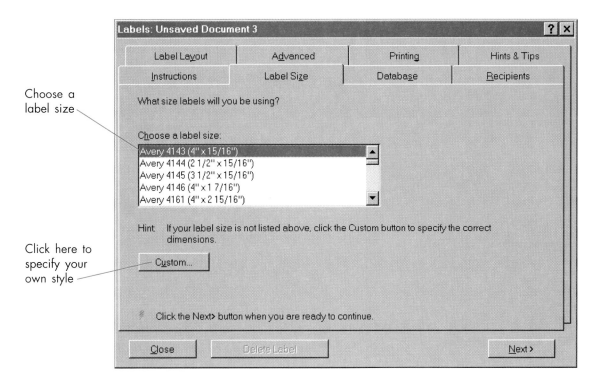

FIGURE 13.17   The Label Size folder of the Label window.

If your labels are not listed or the style is unknown, choose the **Custom** button. This button will present the Custom Labels window shown in Figure 13.18.

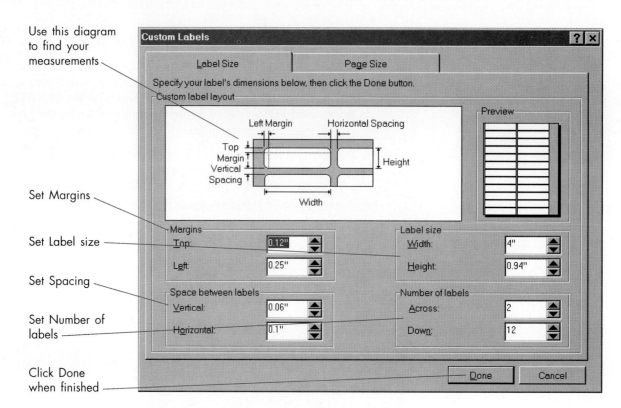

Use this diagram to find your measurements

Set Margins

Set Label size

Set Spacing

Set Number of labels

Click Done when finished

FIGURE 13.18   The custom Label Size folder.

To specify a custom label format, measure the margins and spacing according to the diagram shown in the custom Label Size folder. Enter these measurements in the **Margins and Space between labels** areas. Specify the size of the labels in the **Width** and **Height** entries of the **Label size** area. Enter the number of labels across the label page in the **Across** entry of the **Number of labels** area. Enter the number of label rows on the label page in the **Down** entry of the Number of labels area. When the entries are complete, click the Done button, then click the Next button.

Select the Database and the Recipients

The next step is to select the database. This step is the same as selecting the database for a form letter. Select the database and click the Next button. The Recipients folder will be displayed. These options are set the same way they are set for the form letters. These folders are shown in Figures 13.11 and 13.12.

If the **Multiple copies of one label** option is selected from the Labels window in Figure 13.16, these two folders will not be available.

Complete the Label Layout

The next step is to insert the fields and text for the labels using the **Label Layout folder** shown in Figure 13.19. To insert a field, select the field name and click the Add Field button. To start a new line, click the **New Line** button. If text needs to be placed on the label, type the text exactly as you want it to appear.

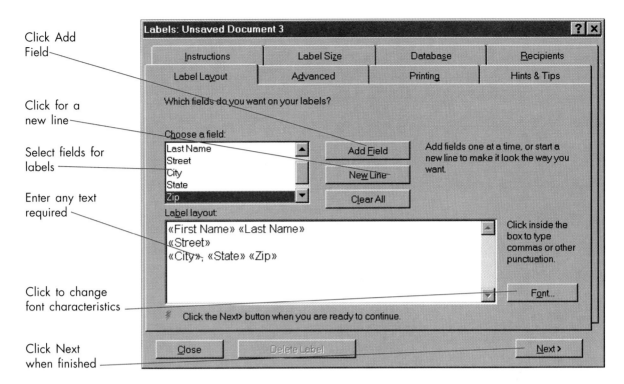

Click Add
Field

Click for a
new line

Select fields for
labels

Enter any text
required

Click to change
font characteristics

Click Next
when finished

FIGURE 13.19   The Label Layout folder of the Labels window.

If the **Multiple copies of one label** option was selected, no database fields will be displayed. Simply type the text for the label into the **Label Layout** area.

To change the font and style of the printing on the label, click the Font button. The Font and Style window will be displayed. Change any font characteristics necessary and click the OK button. When the label layout is complete, click the Next button.

Print the Labels

The final step is to print the labels. The print folder is shown in Figure 13.20. To preview the labels, click the Preview button. To **test print** the labels, click the Test button. This button will only print the first two rows of labels. Use this button to see that the labels print correctly. If they do not print correctly, you may need to change the label layout.

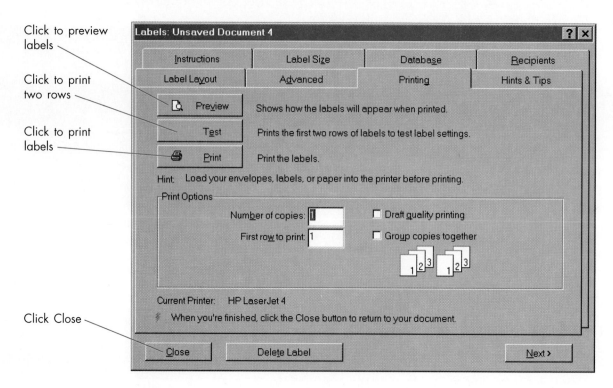

Click to preview labels

Click to print two rows

Click to print labels

Click Close

FIGURE 13.20 The Printing folder of the Labels window.

When you know the labels are correct, click the print button. When you have completed printing the labels, click the Close button.

Note: When the labels are printed, a message indicating which database records are being printed will appear. You may also get an error message indicating that the labels may not print correctly because the margins for the printer do not match the margins for the labels. If this happens, you will need to change the top, bottom, left, and right margins on the Page Setup for the printer.

Working with a Form Letter or Labels Document

When a form letter or label format is created, it is created as a word processing document. When the **Close** button is selected, you are placed in the word processing window used to print the form letter or labels. All the word processing tools are available to modify the form letter or label. For example, you could assign borders, shading, or colors to the text, insert pictures, insert a spreadsheet, charts, or database data into either the form letter or the labels.

You can also save the document to be used later.

CHAPTER 13 SELF-TEST

1. Explain the concept of a window as it applies to Microsoft Works.
2. How do you switch between windows in Microsoft Works?
3. List the steps required to copy a block of text from one word processing window to another word processing window.
4. Explain the difference between how cells appear in a document when it is pasted using the **Microsoft Works 4.0 Sheet or Object** format and the **Works Internal Spreadsheet/Database** format.
5. How do you copy a chart into a word processing document?
6. What is the difference between pasting a chart with the **Microsoft Works 4.0 Chart Object** format and the **Picture** format?
7. What is the difference between copying and linking data?
8. What is the difference between a client document and a server document?
9. What happens when a server document that is linked to a client document is moved or renamed?
10. Explain how Microsoft Works determines what data are placed in which cells of a spreadsheet when the data are copied from a word processing document into a spreadsheet.
11. When a spreadsheet is copied into a database, what happens to the spreadsheet formulas?
12. What is a field place holder?
13. How do you test print labels? How many labels are printed when you test print?
14. How do you restrict the records that will be used when printing a form letter?

TUTORIAL

In this tutorial you will create a form letter and print a copy of it for a selected set of sales managers. The form letter will contain data from a spreadsheet, a chart from the same spreadsheet, and data from a database. You will also print mailing labels for each sales manager in the database.

START THE TUTORIAL

1. Start Microsoft Works.
2. Click the Word Processor button on the Works Tools folder of the Task Launcher.

START THE FORM LETTER

You should now have an empty document. This empty document will be used to create the form letter. Rather than going directly to the form letter, we will enter some of the text for the document now.

Enter the Letterhead

Begin the form letter by entering the following letterhead. Put the **letterhead** in the **Header** area to conserve space on the letter. Refer to Figure 13.21.

1. Click inside the Header area of the document
2. Click the Center Alignment tool on the toolbar.
3. Enter: **Bakersfield Appliance Center** and press the Enter key.
4. Enter: **390 W. Oak Street** and press Enter.
5. Enter: **Bakersfield, WA 45771.**

A professional letterhead would have the company name highlighted to make it stand out.

6. Select the company name (the first line you entered).
7. Assign the Impact font, 16 points.
8. Make the name bold and italic using the toolbar.

Insert the **current date** in the body area of the document.

9. Click in the document work area.
10. Select Date and Time from the Insert menu.
11. Select month name, day, and year date format from the Date and Time window and click the OK button.
12. Press the Enter key four times.

Your document should now look like the one in Figure 13.21.

FIGURE 13.21 Tutorial Document after creating the letterhead and date.

Start the Form Letter

When you develop a form letter, the mailing address of each letter needs to be individualized for the person receiving the letter. The names and addresses for these letters are stored in a database named **Chapter 13 Customers** on your tutorial disk. We can use the **Form Letters** option on the Tools menu to create the form letter. Choose this option now.

1. Click **Form Letters** on the Tools menu.

The **Form letter instructions** should now be displayed. The first step is to choose the database that contains the information we want to use.

2. Click the Next button.

Choose the Database

The **Database folder** like the one in Figure 13.22 should now be displayed. Look in the **Choose a database** list and select the database named Chapter 13 Customers if it is shown. If it is not shown, locate the database on your tutorials diskette using the Open a database not listed here button.

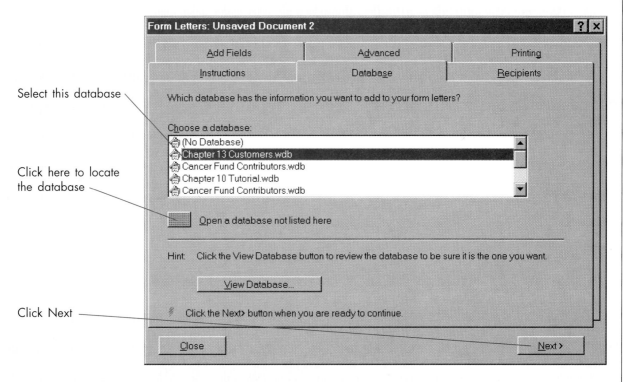

Select this database

Click here to locate the database

Click Next

FIGURE 13.22   The Database folder.

1. Select the database named **Chapter 13 Customers**. If this database is not shown, perform the next five steps.
2. Click the **Open a database not listed here** button.
3. Click the **Look in** area of the **Use Another File** window.
4. Click the drive letter that contains your data diskette. The database should now be shown.
5. Click the **Chapter 13 Customers** database name.
6. Click the Open button.

The database should now be in the Choose a database list.

7. Click the Next button.

Set the Recipients Option

The Form Letter Instructions folder should now be displayed. The next step is to set the options on the **Recipients folder**.

1. Click the Next button.

The **Recipients folder** should now be displayed. A **filter** has been placed in the database for each city in which there are customers. To avoid printing a lot of pages, use the Franklin filter that has been created for the database. This will only provide two records. Refer to Figure 13.23.

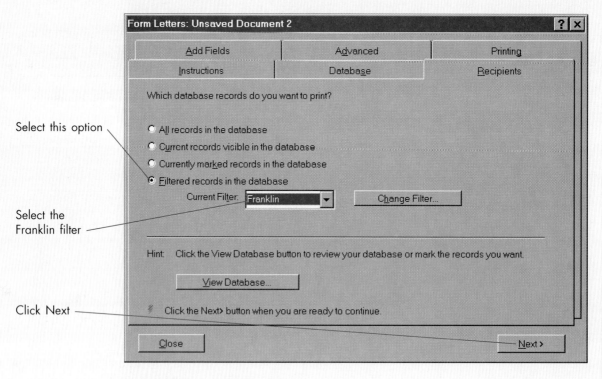

FIGURE 13.23   The Recipients folder.

2. Click the **Filtered records** in the database option.
3. Select the **Franklin** filter.
4. Click the Next button.

Add the Database Fields

The next step is to add the database fields.

1. Click the Next button on the Instructions folder.
2. For each field in the **Choose a field** list, click the field name, then the Insert button. There should be a total of eight fields inserted.
3. When you have inserted each field, click the Close button.

Modify the Mailing Address

The form letter should now be displayed in the word processing window. Because of the way we inserted the database field names, all field names are on one line. The fields should be on separate lines for a mailing address as shown in Figure 13.24. A period also needs to be placed after the **Initial** field and a comma should be placed after the **City** field.

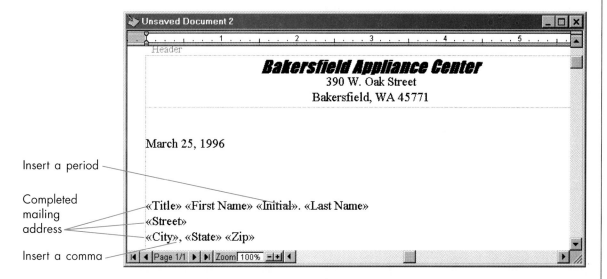

FIGURE 13.24   Completed mailing address for the tutorial form letter.

1. Place the cursor immediately after the **Initial** field marker and type a period.
2. Place the cursor immediately to the left of the **Street** field marker and press the Enter key.
3. Place the cursor immediately to the left of the **City** field and press the Enter key.
4. Place the cursor immediately to the right of the **City** field and type a **comma**.
5. Place the cursor immediately to the right of the **ZIP** field marker and press the Enter key twice.

Enter a Salutation

You want a salutation line in the letter that uses the recipient's title and last name. To insert the field place holders, we will use the Database Field option from the Insert menu.

1. Enter **Dear**.
2. Choose the **Database Field** option from the Insert menu.
3. Click the **Title** field name and click the Insert button.
4. Click the **Last Name** field name and click the Insert button.
5. Click the Close button.
6. Enter a **comma** and press the Enter key.

CREATE THE BODY OF THE LETTER

The database field entries are complete. Now enter a few introductory sentences for the body of the letter.

1. Press the Enter key to insert a blank line.
2. Press the Tab key and enter the following sentences:

   Last fall you purchased a Thompson Air Conditioner from our store. A recent survey indicates that you purchased one of the best air conditioners on the market. The survey results are shown below.

3. Press the Enter key.

Insert the Spreadsheet Data

You are now ready to insert data from the Chapter 13 Spreadsheet file into the document. Before inserting the **spreadsheet** data, the document needs to be open.

1. Make sure the cursor is at the bottom of the document.
2. Select Open from the File menu.
3. Open the **Chapter 13 Spreadsheet** from your data disk.

   The spreadsheet is now displayed on the screen and can be copied to the word processing document.

4. Select cells A1 through F5 as a block.
5. Click the Copy tool.
6. Enter Ctrl/F6 to move back to the word processing document.
7. Select **Paste Special** from the Edit menu.
8. Click the Paste option.
9. Select the **Microsoft Works 4.0 Sheet or Chart Object** format.
10. Click the OK button.

   The spreadsheet data should now be displayed in the word processing document. To make the document look better, center the spreadsheet.

11. Click on the spreadsheet object.
12. Click the Center tool on the toolbar.

Your document should look like Figure 13.25.

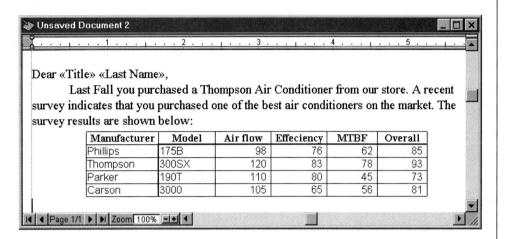

FIGURE 13.25   The tutorial with the spreadsheet inserted.

Insert the Chart

The next step is to enter an introductory paragraph for the chart.

1. Place the cursor to the right of the spreadsheet and press the Enter key twice.
2. Click the Left Align tool on the Toolbar.
3. Press the Tab key and enter the following sentences:

   The results of this survey are charted below. As you can see, the Thompson Air Conditioner has the highest rating in all four categories.

4. Press the Enter key twice.

Now paste a **chart** into the document. The chart has already been created and is stored with the Chapter 13 Spreadsheet.

5. Use the Ctrl/F6 keys to move back to the Chapter 13 Spreadsheet.
6. Choose **Chart** from the View menu.
7. Choose the **Manufacturers** chart and click the OK button.
8. Click the Copy tool to copy the chart to the clipboard.

Move back to the form letter document and paste the chart in as a picture. See Figure 13.26.

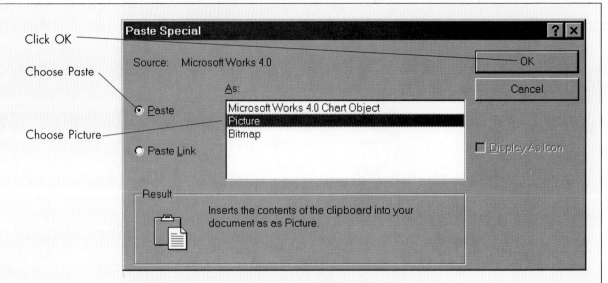

Click OK

Choose Paste

Choose Picture

FIGURE 13.26   The Paste Special window with a chart on the clipboard.

9. Use the Crtl/F6 keys to move back to the word processing document.
10. Choose Paste Special from the Edit menu.
11. Click the Paste option.
12. Click the Picture format.
13. Click the OK button.

The chart should be displayed in the document. Use the chart handles to reduce its size, then center it.

14. Click anywhere on the chart. This will select the chart picture and display its handles.
15. Drag one of the corner handles to reduce the chart to 75%. Watch the lower left side of the screen to see the chart size.
16. With the chart still selected, click the Center Align tool on the toolbar.

Your screen should look like Figure 13.27.

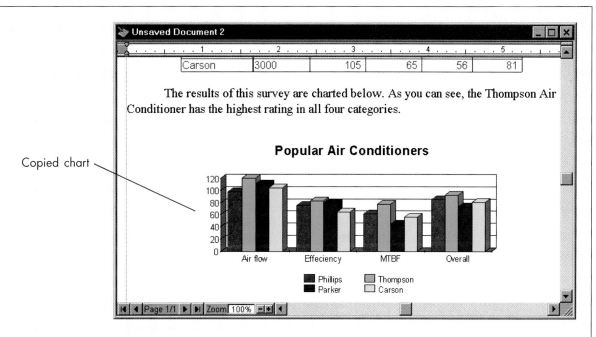

| Carson | 3000 | 105 | 65 | 56 | 81 |

The results of this survey are charted below. As you can see, the Thompson Air Conditioner has the highest rating in all four categories.

Copied chart

Popular Air Conditioners

FIGURE 13.27   The tutorial document with the chart inserted.

Copy the Database Data

Insert a blank line and enter the next paragraph.

1. Place the cursor to the right of the chart and press the Enter key twice.
2. Click the Left Align tool.
3. Press the Tab key and enter: **Since scheduled maintenance will ensure the maximum efficiency and life for your product, we have compiled a list of dealers in your area that service the Thompson Air Conditioners.**
4. Press the Enter key.

The next step is to insert the dealer names and addresses from the **Chapter 13 Dealers** database.

5. Choose Open from the File menu.
6. Open the file **Chapter 13 Dealers** from the tutorials disk.

You only want the records for those dealers that are in the city of Franklin. A filter has been designed to display these dealers. First apply the filter then copy the selected records into the report.

7. Select **Filters** from the Tools menu.
8. Click the **Filter name** list on the filter window and choose the **Franklin** filter.
9. Click the **Apply Filter** button.
10. Select all three fields of the five records displayed.
11. Click the Copy tool.

Now move back to the word processing document and paste the records into the document.

12. Use the Ctrl/F6 keys to move back to the word processing document.
13. Click the Paste Tool.

The dealer names and addresses should now be in the document as shown in Figure 13.28.

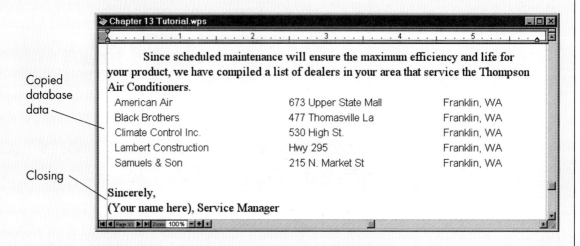

Copied
database
data

Closing

FIGURE 13.28   The tutorial after copying dealers from the database.

Complete the Letter

Now complete the document by entering the closing.

1. Press Ctrl/End and press the Enter key.
2. Enter the following closing lines:
3. Enter: **Sincerely**, and press Enter.
4. Enter: **(your full name), Service Manager**.

PREVIEW AND PRINT THE LETTER

We can now return to the **Form Letters** window to preview and print the form letters.

1. Select Form Letters from the Tools menu.
2. Click the Printing tab to move to the Printing folder.
3. Click the Preview button.
4. Click the OK button on the box that says Preview all records.

Use the next and previous buttons to see the documents to be printed. Each document should be printed on a single page. Use the next section to make any corrections necessary.

Make any Necessary Changes

Check each page of the form letters and make sure the recipient is from the city of Franklin. If they are not:

1. Press Esc to cancel the preview.
2. Click the **Recipients** tab.
3. Select the **Franklin** Filter.
4. Click the Printing tab and the Preview button.

   If each document does not fit on one page:

1. Press Esc to cancel the preview.
2. Click the Close button.
3. Choose Page Setup from the File menu.
4. Change the left, right, and bottom margins to provide less space.
5. Use the Form Letters option to preview the document again.
6. If necessary, change the margins again until each document fits on a single page.

Print the Documents

Once you have three documents of one page each, print the documents.

1. Click the Print button.

Save the Form Letter

1. Click the close button.
2. Use the **Save As** option on the File menu to save the document.

CREATE THE MAILING LABELS

Now assume that you will need mailing labels for the envelopes. The technique we will use creates a mailing label format that is embedded as part of the form letter. This technique will keep the labels format and the form letters together in the same file.

To create a mailing label format, use the **Labels** option on the Tools menu.

1. Make sure the word processing window is the active window.
2. Choose Labels from the Tools menu.
3. Click the Labels button on the small Labels window that appears.

Choose the Label Size

The first step in the instructions is to choose the **label size**. We will use the Avery 5160 label form. This format has labels of 1″ x 2 5/8″ with three labels in each row and ten rows on a page.

1. Click the Next button on the Instructions folder.
2. Select the **Avery 5160** label style (see Figure 13.29).
3. Click the Next button.

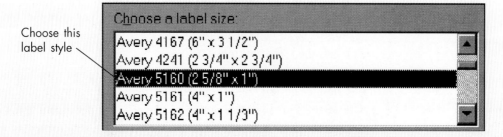

Choose this label style

Choose a label size:

Avery 4167 (6" x 3 1/2")
Avery 4241 (2 3/4" x 2 3/4")
Avery 5160 (2 5/8" x 1")
Avery 5161 (4" x 1")
Avery 5162 (4" x 1 1/3")

FIGURE 13.29   The Choose a Label Size list area of the Label Size folder.

Choose the Recipients

Notice on the Instructions folder that the directions to choose the database is already checked. This is because the labels are being created for the form letter and the form letter is using the Chapter 13 Customers database. If we wanted to change the database, we would use the Database tab to select a different database.

The next step for us is to select the recipients. We want a mailing label for all customers in the database.

1. Click the Next button.
2. Click the **All records in the database** option.
3. Click the Next button.

Define the Label Layout

The next step is to define which fields will be used on the labels and where on the label they will print. This is the **Label Layout**. Refer to Figure 13.30 when completing these steps.

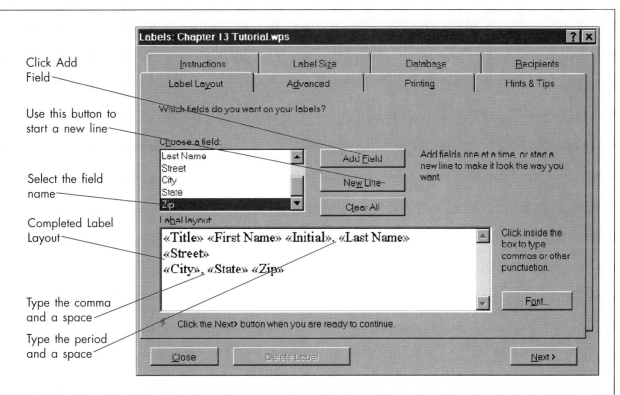

Click Add
Field

Use this button to
start a new line

Select the field
name

Completed Label
Layout

Type the comma
and a space

Type the period
and a space

FIGURE 13.30   The completed Label Layout folder.

1. Click the Next button.
2. Click **Title** and click the **Add Field** button.
3. Click **First Name** and click the **Add Field** button.
4. Click **Initial** and click the **Add Field** button.
5. Type a period and a space.
6. Click **Last Name** and click the **Add Field** button.
7. Click the **New Line** button.
8. Click **Street** and click the **Add Field** button.
9. Click the **New Line** button.
10. Click **City** and click the **Add Field** button.
11. Type a comma and a space.
12. Click **State** and click the **Add Field** button.
13. Click **ZIP** and click the **Add Field** button.

Review your label layout and compare it to Figure 13.30. If you have errors, edit the **Label layout** area or click the **Clear All** button and start over.

14. Click the Next button.

Preview and Print the Mailing Labels

The labels should now be ready to print.

1. Click the Next button on the Instructions folder.
2. Click the Preview button.

The preview should show one page of labels with three labels across the page. There should be eight rows of labels with only two labels on the last row.

3. Click the Print button.
4. Click the Close button.

Notice the Label format displayed on the screen. This label format is now part of the form letter. You can change the font, size, apply borders, insert clipart, or otherwise format the label in any way you want.

Use the page down or arrow keys to move to the document.

SAVE THE FORM LETTER AND LABELS

Since you have created a label format since the last save, you will need to save the document again.

1. Save the form letter to your disk.
2. Close all files and exit Microsoft Works.

HANDS-ON PRACTICE

Exercise 13-1A

For this assignment, you will be using the files Exercise 13-1A, Exercise 13-1B, and Exercise 13-1C. You will also be creating a new word processing document.

Create the form letter shown in Figure 13.31. To create this document, use the following requirements:

1. Use the Insert menu to insert the date printed.
2. Use the fields from the database in Exercise 13.1A on your tutorials disk.
3. Copy this paragraph from the file named Exercise 13-1B on your tutorials disk.
4. Copy cells A1 through E7 from the spreadsheet Exercise 13-1C on your tutorials disk. Center the spreadsheet cells on the page.
5. Type the next paragraph shown in Figure 13.31. Then insert the chart named **Average** from the spreadsheet named Exercise 13-1C on your tutorials disk.
6. Type the paragraph shown in Figure 13.31. Insert the chart named **Increase** from the spreadsheet named Exercise 13-1C on your tutorials disk.
7. Type the next paragraph shown in Figure 13.31.
8. Open the Exercise 13-1D database. Apply the filter named **Bakersfield**. Copy the records displayed by the filter to the word processing document where shown in Figure 13.31. Create the following headings so they appear over each column:
   Street   Style   Rooms   Baths   Price
9. Insert the remainder of the document as shown in Figure 13.31. Insert your full name as the company president.
10. Print one copy of the letter for each person displayed by the **Bakersfield** filter in the Exercise 13-1A database. This filter should display three records.

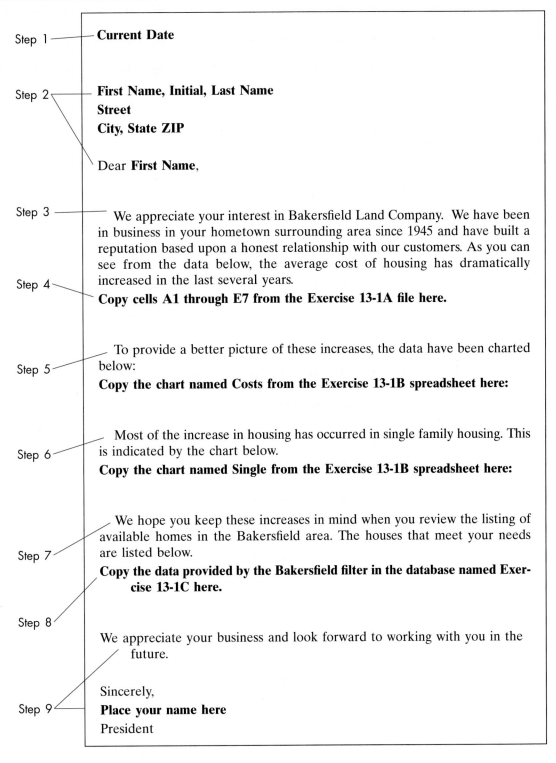

Step 1 — **Current Date**

Step 2 — **First Name, Initial, Last Name**
Street
City, State ZIP

Dear **First Name**,

Step 3 — We appreciate your interest in Bakersfield Land Company. We have been in business in your hometown surrounding area since 1945 and have built a reputation based upon a honest relationship with our customers. As you can see from the data below, the average cost of housing has dramatically increased in the last several years.

Step 4 — **Copy cells A1 through E7 from the Exercise 13-1A file here.**

Step 5 — To provide a better picture of these increases, the data have been charted below:
Copy the chart named Costs from the Exercise 13-1B spreadsheet here:

Step 6 — Most of the increase in housing has occurred in single family housing. This is indicated by the chart below.
Copy the chart named Single from the Exercise 13-1B spreadsheet here:

Step 7 — We hope you keep these increases in mind when you review the listing of available homes in the Bakersfield area. The houses that meet your needs are listed below.
Copy the data provided by the Bakersfield filter in the database named Exercise 13-1C here.

Step 8 — We appreciate your business and look forward to working with you in the future.

Sincerely,

Step 9 — **Place your name here**
President

FIGURE 13.31   Sample Document for Exercise 13-1.

Create a set of mailing labels similar for all records in the Exercise 13-1A database. Place the **First Name**, **Initial**, **Last Name**, **Street**, **City**, **State**, and **ZIP** on the label. Use the Avery 5161 label style. Sort the database by **Last name** within **ZIP Code** before printing the labels.

Exercise 13-2

1. Create the memorandum form letter shown in Figure 13.32. Pay particular attention to the text shown in italics and parentheses. When you see italic text, insert a database field place holder. The database you will be using is named Exercise 13-2 and is stored on your tutorials disk.

2. Apply the filter named **Freshman** to the Exercise 13.2 database and print one copy of the form letter for each student displayed by this filter.

3. Create a set of mailing labels for all students in the database. Have the mailing labels print the **Student ID** centered on the first line of the label. Print the student's full name, street, city, state, and ZIP code on the next three lines. Use a 10 point Arial font and the Avery 4144 label style.

Memorandum

To: *(insert First name, Initial, and Last name place holders from the database)*

From: *(insert your name here)*, Chair
(insert Department database field place holder)

Subject: New Students

Date: *(insert current date)*

Welcome to the Department of *(insert Department place holder here)*, *(insert First Name place holder here)*. We are glad you have decided to major in *(insert Major place holder here)*. We have many majors from *(insert City and State place holders here)*; some may be your neighbors.

You will enjoy living in the *(insert Dorm place holder here)* dorm. This is one of the newest and most active dorms on campus.

Your academic advisor will be *(insert Advisor place holder here)*. You should make an appointment to see your advisor during the first week of classes. Since schedules are completed early, you will need to determine your classes for next semester.

If I can be of any help during the semester, don't hesitate to stop by the *(insert Department place holder here)* department's office. Again, welcome to the department, *(insert First name place holder here)* and good luck with your first year.

FIGURE 13.32   Sample Document for Exercise 13-2.

For this assignment, you will be using the files Exercise 13-3A, Exercise 13-3B, and Exercise 13-3C. You will also be creating a new form letter.

Create the document shown in Figure 13.33. To create this document, use the following requirements:

1. Insert the ClipArt image shown at the top of the document.
2. Enter the **Thank You** line. For the name, insert place holders from the Exercise 13-3B database. Use the **First Name** and **Last Name** fields. Change the font for the entire line to Arial 16.
3. Copy the first paragraph from the Exercise 13-3A file.
4. Delete the comments, that are in parentheses from the paragraph you just copied. In place of the comments, insert field place holders from the Exercise 13-3B database.
5. Type this line. Use a 12 point bold Arial font.
6. Insert the chart named **MIXED** from the Exercise 13-3C spreadsheet.
7. Copy the last paragraph in the Exercise 13-3A document here.
8. Apply the filter named **Increase** from the Exercise 13-3B. Copy the **Last Name**, **Initial**, and **First Name** of those people found by the **Increase** filter.
9. Enter this line and your name on the final line.
10. Apply the filter named **Print Me** to the Exercise 13-2B. This filter should provide only three records.
11. Use the print preview to review the form letter. Make any changes to the print margins that may be necessary to get the document to print on a single page.
12. Print one copy of the letter for each person displayed by the **Print Me** filter from step 10 above.

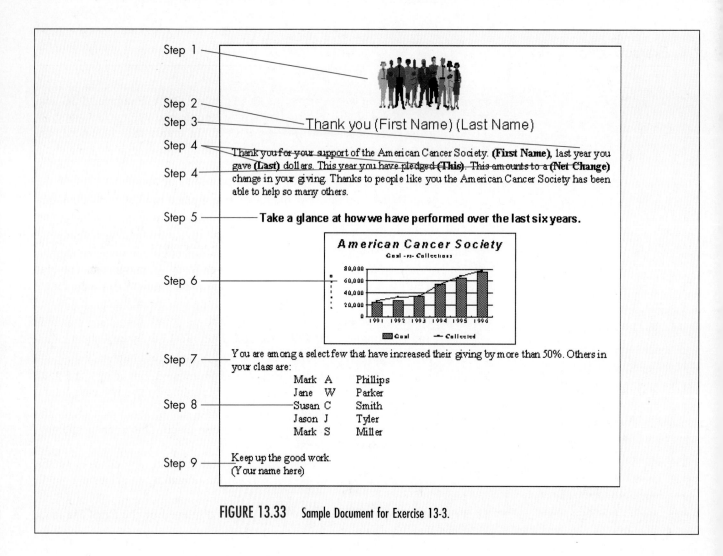

Step 1

Step 2

Step 3 — Thank you (First Name) (Last Name)

Step 4 — Thank you for your support of the American Cancer Society. **(First Name)**, last year you
gave **(Last)** dollars. This year you have pledged **(This)**. This amounts to a **(Net Change)**

Step 4 — change in your giving. Thanks to people like you the American Cancer Society has been
able to help so many others.

Step 5 — **Take a glance at how we have performed over the last six years.**

Step 6

Step 7 — You are among a select few that have increased their giving by more than 50%. Others in
your class are:

Mark	A	Phillips
Jane	W	Parker
Step 8 —	Susan	C	Smith
Jason	J	Tyler
Mark	S	Miller

Step 9 — Keep up the good work.
(*Your name here*)

FIGURE 13.33   Sample Document for Exercise 13-3.

APPENDIX A: TELECOMMUNICATIONS

One of the most exciting uses of personal computers is the ability to communicate with other computers and information services. This process is called telecommunications, since telephone lines are usually used to connect the computers together. When you are connected to other systems, you can communicate with many people on a wide variety of topics. You can even access new and exciting programs for use on your own computer.

USING THE COMPUTER AS A TERMINAL TO A HOST COMPUTER

One of the most common ways to use Microsoft Works to communicate is as a terminal, or remote computer. When using your personal computer as a terminal, it is acting as an input and output device to another computer system. Normally, the other computer, which is often called the host computer, will be a large, sophisticated, mainframe computer. When connected to a host computer, you will be able to run programs stored on the host and transfer information from the host to your computer. You can also transfer information from your computer to the host. This ability is handy, since mainframes can store vast amounts of information that you can access when needed.

Communicating with Another Personal Computer

Another way to use Microsoft Works to communicate between computers is to connect to another personal computer. You can then transfer data from one machine to another. You can use this peer-to-peer communications setup when you want to transfer data from one PC to another, but cannot readily exchange disks between the systems because of distance or incompatible disk types. This use of telecommunications allows you to exchange information between different kinds of computers, such as an IBM personal computer and the Apple Macintosh computer.

405

TELECOMMUNICATIONS HARDWARE REQUIREMENTS

Typically, computers are connected to one another via telephone lines and require special equipment to operate correctly. Figure A.1 provides an overview of most of the components required for computer telecommunications.

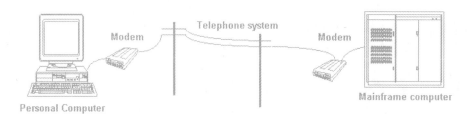

FIGURE A.1 Typical telecommunications components.

Modem

The computer stores data as a series of digital bits, which are either on or off. These digital bits are usually represented by a **1** when they are on and a **0** when they are off. By storing a group of bits (usually eight) together, it is possible to store a character, or byte, of information.

Telephone lines typically do not recognize digital signals. The phone system was designed to transmit voice frequencies, which are analog in nature. You can see in Figure A.2 that analog signals are transmitted in a continuous wave that varics with the frequency of the data. This is the same concept we use when we talk and use high and low frequencies in our speech.

10100101

Digital data   Analog data

FIGURE A.2 Digital signals must be converted to analog signals before transmitting.

Figure A.2 shows that the digital **1**'s and **0**'s sent by the computer are not compatible with the analog signal needed by the phone, so some conversion must be made between the two modes. This conversion is accomplished by the modem. A modem is a hardware device used to translate the data signals from digital to analog or vice versa. When the modem translates from digital to analog, it is referred to as modulation. When it translates from analog to digital, it is referred to as demodulation. These terms provide the modem with its name, which is an acronym of *MOD*ulation *DEM*odulation.

You can purchase either external or internal modems. An external modem is housed in a small box that is usually connected to the computer via a plug called the serial port. An internal modem is installed inside the main unit of the computer.

Since a computer can only use digital data, you must have a modem on both sides of the communications link: one at the transmitting remote computer and one at the host computer.

Serial Port

A computer port is a special socket or plug that allows devices such as a modem or printer to be connected to the computer. The serial port transmits and receives data one bit at a time. When data are sent in this serial fashion, one bit of information is sent after another in a horizontal line. The serial port is referred to as an RS-232 serial port, or just a serial port, and normally has either a 25-pin connector or a 9-pin connector located on the back of the computer. These ports are shown in Figure A.3.

9-pin connector   25-pin connector

FIGURE A.3   Serial ports are used to connect the computer to an external modem.

The parallel port is another type of port used on personal computer systems. The parallel port gets its name from the bits of information that travel in a parallel fashion through the port. This port is used primarily for connecting the printer to the computer. The difference between serial and parallel data is illustrated in Figure A.4.

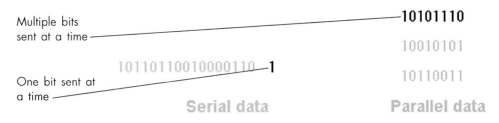

Multiple bits sent at a time

10101110
10010101
10110011

One bit sent at a time

10110110010000110 1

Serial data   Parallel data

FIGURE A.4   Parallel versus serial communication.

TELECOMMUNICATIONS SOFTWARE REQUIREMENTS

In addition to the hardware components required for communications, you will also need communications software. This software controls the data transmission from one computer to another and provides the means to transfer data between computers. The communications component of Microsoft Works does a good job in this area and can handle most requirements for computer communications.

Function of Communications Software

To understand the functions performed by communications software, consider the problems that can arise in our normal voice communications. When you talk to a friend over the phone, you are communicating in a manner similar to computer communications, except that you are the host computer and your friend is the remote computer. You communicate by speaking words (in a language your friend understands), which consist of a series of syllables followed by a very short pause. These words are usually parts of sentences, which are separated by a longer pause. If you do not include these pauses or if you talk too fast or too slow, your friend on the other end of the telephone line will have a difficult time understanding what you are saying. If for any reason your friend cannot understand your statements, he or she will ask you to repeat what you have said. These factors of transmission speed, message length, and error control are all present in computer communications and are handled by the communications software.

Baud Rate (Transmission Speed)

One of the most critical components of any communication is the speed at which a message is transmitted and received. This idea can be illustrated when you play a record too fast or too slowly; the message is garbled and you probably will not understand all of what is said. The same thing happens with computers, which use baud rate to specify the speed at which data are to be sent and received.

To avoid errors, both machines must send and receive data at the same speed. Whereas each computer has a maximum speed at which it can operate, the modem is usually the constraining factor because it operates at a lower speed than the computer. The modem speed, or baud rate, is used to define the number of bits transferred per second (bits per second, or BPS). Some common rates include 300, 1200, 2400, 4800, 9600, 14,400 and 28,800 BPS. Usually, if your modem supports a higher BPS rate, it will also support the lower rates.

Setting Communications Parameters in Microsoft Works

Before you connect to another computer, you will need to set a few parameters on your computer. The most common settings you will need to make are found under the Settings menu as well as on the communications Toolbar illustrated in Figure A.5.

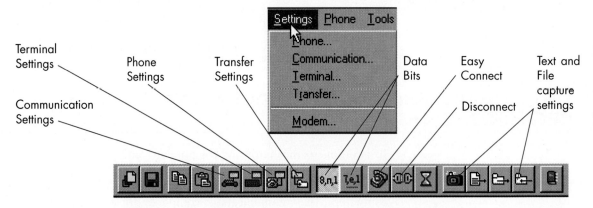

FIGURE A.5   Enter communications parameters with the Settings menu or Toolbar.

Specifying the Serial (COM) Port

The port specification is needed to identify which RS-232 serial communications port on the computer you will be using. Ports are named COM1, COM2, COM3, and COM4 depending on the number of ports the machine has. Most computers have at least two COM ports.

To determine if your computer is equipped with a modem, click the Communication option on the Settings menu. This will display the Settings window seen in Figure A.6. The Communications settings will be displayed and let you know which devices are available. Highlight the entry for Standard modem, then click the Properties button to display the settings for your modem, as shown in Figure A.7. The modem Properties window shows which COM port is used by the modem and the maximum speed supported by the port. Please note that this speed is not the same as the modem speed, rather it is the maximum speed supported by the communications connection in the computer. Your modem will likely be quite a bit slower than this, and the COM port will automatically adjust to your modem's slower speed.

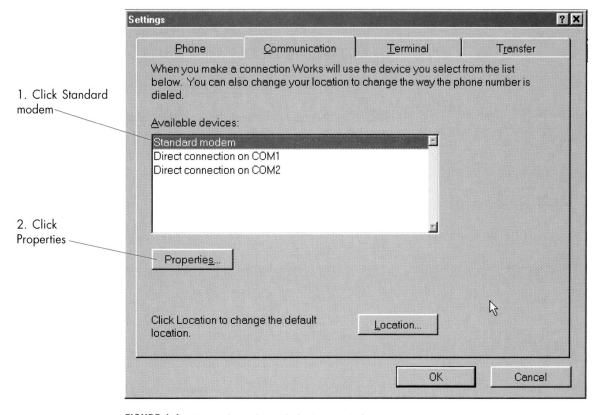

FIGURE A.6   Locate the modem with the Settings window.

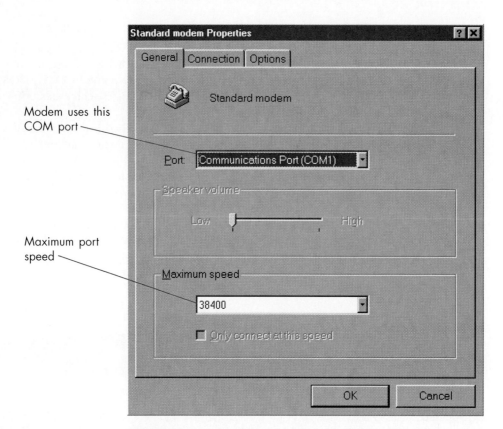

Modem uses this COM port

Maximum port speed

FIGURE A.7   The properties window displays the COM port and port speed available to the modem.

Connection Preferences

The Connection folder of the modem Properties window that you used to determine the modem COM port also allows you to specify the number of digital bits that the host computer uses to denote a character. Typically, this value is either 7 or 8 bits and can be selected by clicking the desired value in the Data bits box as shown in Figure A.8. It is important that both the transmitting computer and the receiving computer use the same number of bits, so you need to find out how many bits the computer that you are calling uses. Should you not have this information, try to communicate using the 8-bit option, which is most commonly used. If you see unreadable characters, try the 7-bit option. You can also select 7 or 8 data bits by clicking the Toolbar buttons as shown in Figure A.5.

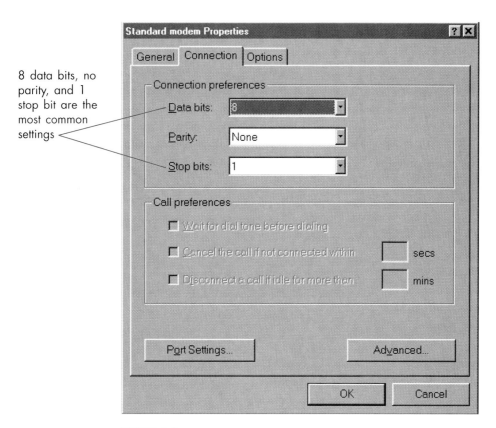

8 data bits, no parity, and 1 stop bit are the most common settings

FIGURE A.8 Click the Connection folder in the Standard modem Properties window to change connection preferences.

Establishing Parity

When we communicate verbally with another person, we can easily ask for the message to be repeated if we do not understand something, or if an error has been made. This ability to check for errors is also required for computer communications. The parity system is an available error-checking method.

Errors can occur when you send data across a telephone line because of noise or static on the line. This static may be interpreted as real data by the receiving computer, which would then result in the receipt of incorrect data. The parity system adds a given number of bits to each character sent; when the character is received, the receiving computer checks it for the correct pattern. If the pattern is not correct, the receiving computer asks the sending computer to resend the message until the message is received correctly.

Although the parity method offers some protection against errors, many computers are now using more sophisticated methods that are automatic. For this reason, unless you know the parity setting for the computer with which you are communicating, first try to communicate with parity set as **None**. This setting is displayed in the modem Properties Connection window seen in Figure A.8.

Stop Bits

The next option displayed in the modem Properties Connection window specifies the number of Stop bits. A stop bit acts like a pause in verbal communications. It tells the receiving computer system that you have completed sending a specific character. Again, this parameter must be the same on both communicating computers. If you are uncertain as to the correct value, start with the Stop bits set to 1.

Terminal Emulation

The Microsoft Works communications software allows you to specify certain characteristics of your computer to imitate a specific computer terminal. This process is known as terminal emulation and is useful when you want to connect to a large computer that uses standard terminals of a specific type.

The emulation process specifies such terminal characteristics as the clearing of the screen, positioning the cursor, and drawing lines. Since various terminal types operate differently, you will need to specify the kind of terminal you want Works to mimic. The choices are found in the Terminal option of the Settings menu and are illustrated in Figure A.9. Ideally, you should find out from the computer center of the host computer what kind of terminal is used; in the absence of this information, you might try the ANSI specification first, as it is a commonly-used standard.

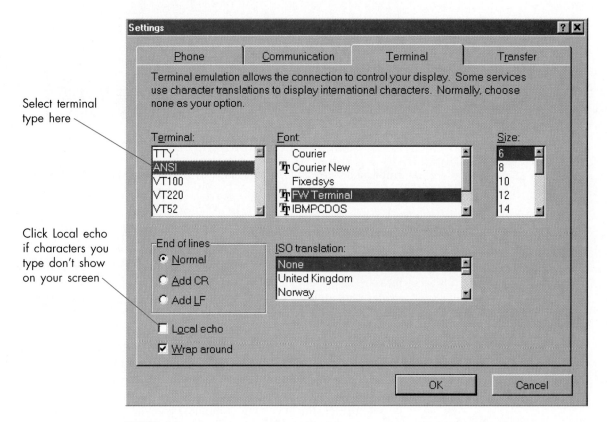

Select terminal type here

Click Local echo if characters you type don't show on your screen

FIGURE A.9   Choose the Terminal option from the Settings menu to change Terminal emulation.

The other options in the Terminal window are normally set correctly; however, here is a suggestion if you have problems:

Problem: You connect to the host computer normally, but when you type, nothing shows on your screen.

Answer: The host computer needs the Local echo option activated on your computer. Activate it in the Settings Terminal window.

DISABLING CALL WAITING AND DIALING TYPE

Before you can communicate over a telephone line, you must call and connect to the other computer system. The modem Dialing Properties window displayed in Figure A.10 will allow you to specify the important setup commands for your modem. You will only need to do this once, and it will allow your modem to dial the other computer for you automatically.

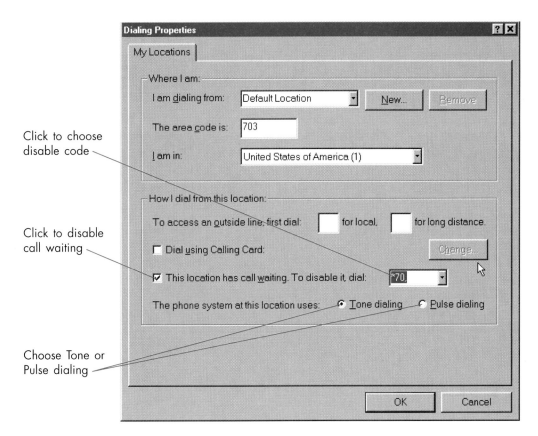

Click to choose disable code

Click to disable call waiting

Choose Tone or Pulse dialing

FIGURE A.10   The modem Dialing Properties window.

The first section of the Properties window allows you to create several locations from which you place your computer call. Most users will leave these entries as is. The second set of entries allows you to select special dialing features.

A common phone option is Call Waiting, which beeps to let you know another call is on your line. This beep will cause errors when using the modem, so call waiting should be disabled when using the computer to make a call. By clicking the **disable** box shown in Figure A.10, you can have Works automatically disable call waiting as the modem dials. To use this feature, click on the down arrow and select the disable code for your area. Try *70 if you are unsure, or call the phone company and ask for the correct code. Call waiting will be disabled only for the call made by the computer and will automatically be reactivated when you complete the computer call.

The dialing type section specifies the kind of telephone line you are using. The Tone option is used with the Touch Tone system; the Pulse option refers to the older, rotary dial phones.

USING EASY CONNECT TO PLACE A CALL

Once the initial parameters are set, you can use the Works Easy Connect feature to place the call to the remote computer. To use Easy Connect, select it from the Phone menu or click the Phone button on the Toolbar. The Easy Connect window seen in Figure A.11 will be displayed. Enter the phone number and a short description of the computer you wish to call. These entries will be saved automatically when you click OK, so if you want to call the same location in the future, all you will have to do is click the name of the service displayed in the lower window of the Easy Connect screen. Click OK to complete the call and click on the Dial button in the confirmation box that appears. You will now hear the modem dial the phone and begin the connections to the remote computer. If the remote system responds with a busy signal, use the Dial Again option under the Phone menu to redial.

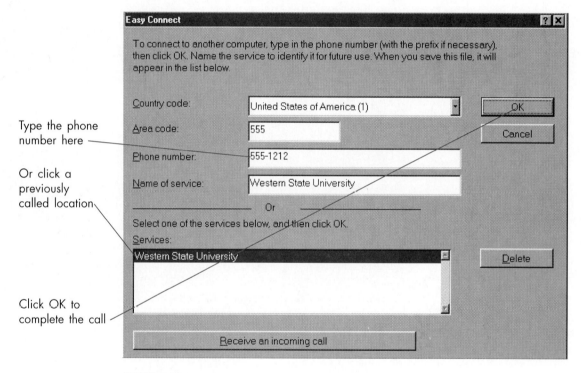

Type the phone number here

Or click a previously called location

Click OK to complete the call

Easy Connect

To connect to another computer, type in the phone number (with the prefix if necessary), then click OK. Name the service to identify it for future use. When you save this file, it will appear in the list below.

Country code: United States of America (1)

Area code: 555

Phone number: 555-1212

Name of service: Western State University

_____ Or _____

Select one of the services below, and then click OK.

Services:
Western State University

OK
Cancel
Delete

Receive an incoming call

FIGURE A.11   Use Easy Connect to place the computer call.

SAVING THE COMMUNICATIONS PARAMETERS

Once you have established all the parameters using the Settings menu, you will want to save them as a file so you do not have to enter them each time you decide to communicate. You can save different files, each containing a different selection of options for different computers with which you usually communicate. For example, you might have one file that you use to connect to the university system and another that you use to connect to a friend's computer.

To save the communications parameters you just entered, select the Save option under the File menu as you would to save a word processing file or spreadsheet. Works will then prompt you to enter a name for the file.

TRANSFERRING FILES BETWEEN COMPUTERS

One of the most useful benefits of communications is the ability to transfer files of information from one computer to another and thus easily share information between two computer users. This type of communications also uses the terms host and remote computers to identify each system.

When you transfer data between computers, you will upload or download data, depending on the direction of the transfer. When you upload data, you send data from the remote computer to the host. When you download data you transfer data from the host to the remote computer. You may find that you want to download information when you want access to data or programs stored on a large mainframe or information service. There may also be times when you will need to use the power of the large mainframe to process data stored on your machine. In this case, you would need to upload the data.

The upload ability can be especially useful when developing a new program or taking programming courses that use the mainframe computer for processing. In this situation, you could create the program using Microsoft's word processor, then upload the file to the mainframe for testing. This would allow you to use all of the powerful word processing features for data entry and editing, but still use the mainframe for actual program execution.

Preparing for File Transfer Using ASCII or TEXT Formats

When you begin to transfer files from one computer to another, you will probably see the term ASCII files used. ASCII is an abbreviation for American Standard Code of Information Interchange and specifies a standard kind of file that can be used by many computer systems. The ASCII format removes special codes or control characters used by word processors and other software programs to align tabs, underline, change fonts, and so forth. If these codes were left in the file to be transferred, they could be interpreted differently by the other computer system's software, and unpredictable results could occur.

You can have Microsoft Works save files in the ASCII format by choosing the Save As option on the File menu and selecting the Text (or Text and Commas in the Spreadsheet module) option in the **Save as** type list. Save the files in the Works module in which the document was created; for example, word processing documents should be saved in the text format in the Word Processing module and spreadsheets should be saved in the Text and Commas format in the Spreadsheet module.

Downloading Files Using an Error Checking Protocol

To download or receive files from the host computer, you should already be connected to the host and be somewhat familiar with the host operation. Most host computers that offer files for downloading will have a help function that will describe the method the host computer uses to download information. Usually, this procedure will have you first specify the name or identification number of the file you want to download. The host will then ask you to choose the download method or protocol you would like to use. These protocols provide error-checking to be sure the file is transferred correctly. You will need to be sure to choose one supported by Works. The two most commonly used protocols are XMODEM and KERMIT.

The use of these two protocols is similar. We will look at transferring a file using the XMODEM protocol; should you need to use a different one, the steps will be virtually the same.

First, pull down the Settings menu and select the Transfer option. Select the XMODEM/CRC option as shown in Figure A.12. This sets up your computer to accept the XMODEM protocol.

Select transfer protocol here

The received file will go in this folder

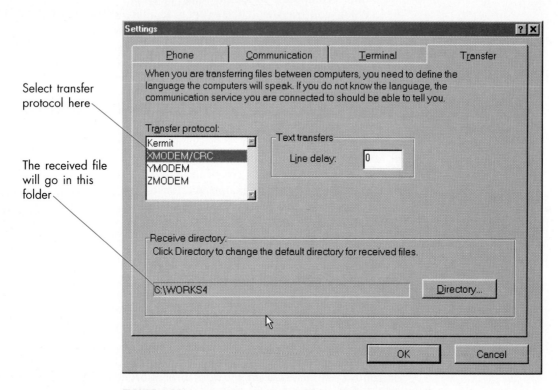

FIGURE A.12   The Settings Transfer window controls file transfers.

Next, making sure you are connected to the host computer, begin the XMODEM download process on the host computer. If you are not sure how to do this, check with the host computer help facility. Once you have specified to the host that you would like to transfer the file using a specific protocol such as XMODEM, the host will wait for you to prepare the Works software on your computer to receive the file.

To instruct Works to receive a file using the XMODEM protocol, click the Receive Binary File button on the Toolbar or select Receive File from the Tools menu as seen in Figure A.13. You will be prompted to enter a name for the file to be stored as on your disk. You then see the Receive File window shown in Figure A.14. The file transfer will now proceed automatically with Works updating you of the progress.

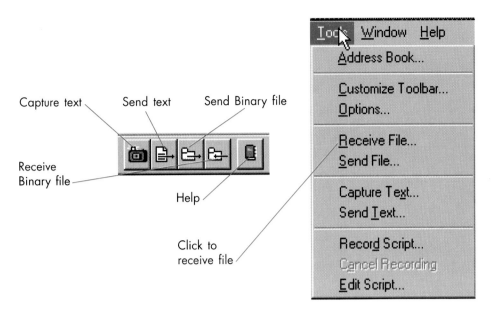

Capture text   Send text   Send Binary file

Receive
Binary file

Help

Click to
receive file

Tools Window Help

Address Book...

Customize Toolbar...
Options...

Receive File...
Send File...

Capture Text...
Send Text...

Record Script...
Cancel Recording
Edit Script...

FIGURE A.13   Select the Transfer option from the Tools menu, or use the Toolbar
buttons to send and receive files.

Enter the name
you want to call
the file when
prompted

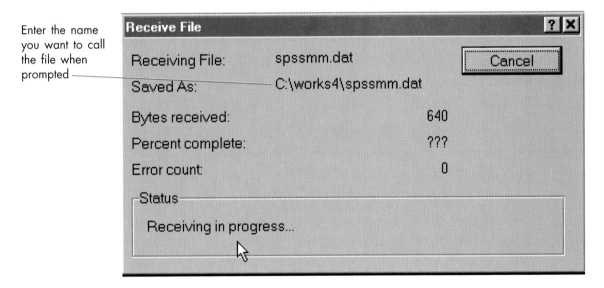

Receive File   ? X

Receiving File: spssmm.dat   Cancel

Saved As: C:\works4\spssmm.dat

Bytes received: 640

Percent complete: ???

Error count: 0

Status

    Receiving in progress...

FIGURE A.14   The Receive File status box informs you of the file reception progress.

Works will notify you in the Receive File status box when the file transfer is
complete; just press Enter to proceed. The file is transferred to your computer and
stored under the name you specified.

Uploading Files to the Host Computer Using XMODEM

Uploading files to the host system works much the same as downloading, except that you will send files to the host rather than receive them. Again, you will first need to determine how the host system handles file uploads. Before continuing, you might want to check the help screens, on the host system. Once you have informed the host that you want to upload, you will need to tell it the file name and the protocol you will use, which will again be XMODEM. Next, select the Send File option from the Tools menu. Works will now provide a list of all the files that are available. You can select the file you want to transfer by tabbing to the file box and using the arrow keys to select the file to upload. When you press Enter, the transfer will begin, and the transfer Status box will appear on your screen as shown in Figure A.14. In this case, **Send** will replace **Receive**. When the transfer is complete, press the Enter key to finish the procedure.

TELECOMMUNICATIONS SELF-TEST

1. To what do the terms host and remote computer systems refer?
2. When should you use the Local Echo function on your computer?
3. What is the function of a modem in telecommunications?
4. What is the difference between digital and analog data?
5. Explain what each of the following refers to:
   a. Baud rate
   b. Data bits
   c. Stop bits
   d. Parity
   e. Port
6. List the steps required to transfer a file from your computer to a host mainframe computer.
7. What is meant by downloading or uploading a file?
8. What are file transfer protocols used for?

APPENDIX B:
USING ADD-INS

Microsoft Works, as well as other Windows programs, include add-in accessories that use an approach known as **Object linking and embedding** (OLE). **OLE** applications create objects that are stored in Windows application documents. The program that creates the object is referred to as the **server application**. The document that stores the object is called the **client document**. When an OLE object is stored in a client document, all information about the server application that created the object is stored with the object. This information is used to find the server application when the object needs to be edited or changed.

To see which installed applications on your system support OLE, choose the **Object option** on the Insert menu of the Microsoft Works word processing module. The **Object Type** list box will list all available OLE applications.

Some OLE applications that come with Microsoft Works are shown at the bottom of the Insert menu in the word processing module and the database Form Design view. We will discuss only those applications that are supplied with Microsoft Works and listed on these Insert menus.

USING WORDART

WordArt is an OLE accessory that allows you to add special effects to text characters. These special effects can be used to create headlines, titles, and logos. This tutorial will walk through the creation of a simple WordArt object. Although you will be using an empty word processing document, remember that WordArt objects can be created and inserted into any word processing document.

1. Start Microsoft Works.
2. Open a new word processing document.
3. Choose WordArt from the Insert menu.

The WordArt accessory program is started and a WordArt text box is displayed on the screen. Figure B.1 shows the WordArt screen.

Enter WordArt Text

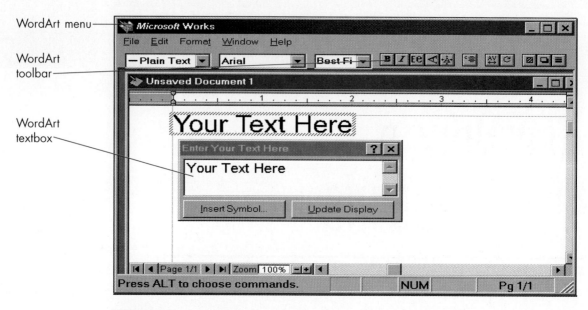

WordArt menu

WordArt toolbar

WordArt textbox

FIGURE B.1   WordArt text box, menu, and Toolbar.

The text for the WordArt is entered in the text box. Create a text entry for the WordArt.

1. Type: **Jill's Express** and press Enter.
2. Type: **Service**.

Throughout this tutorial we will use the toolbar to create the WordArt object. A table describing **WordArt tools** and their functions is shown in Figure B.2.

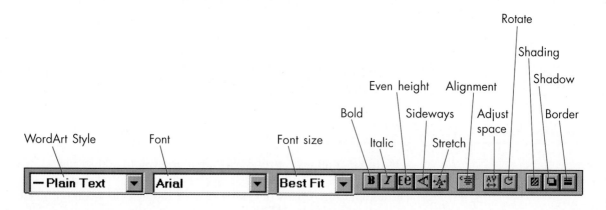

FIGURE B.2   The WordArt Toolbar.

TOOL	DESCRIPTION
Style tool	Select a WordArt style.
Font tool	Select a WordArt font.
Font size tool	Change the size of the select font.
Bold tool	Apply the bold format.
Italic tool	Apply the italic format.
Even height tool	Make all letters in the text an even height.
Sideways tool	Turn characters so the text reads sideways.
Stretch tool	Stretch the text to fill the WordArt frame.
Alignment tool	Select an alignment for the text.
Character spacing tool	Adjust the space between characters.
Rotate tool	Rotate or incline the text.
Pattern tool	Choose a shading pattern and color.
Shadow tool	Add one of several shadow effects.
Border tool	Change the thickness of the character's border.

Change the Font and Size

To see the WordArt better, increase the size of the font. If you get a Size Change box that asks if you want to resize the text box, click the Yes button.

1. Choose the Impact font from the WordArt fonts list.
2. Click the down arrow next to **Best Fit** on the Toolbar.
3. Change the font size to 30 points.
4. Click the **Yes** button on the **Size Change** box.

Select a WordArt Style

The **WordArt styles** are on the left side of the Toolbar. The current style is Plain Text. Click the arrow beside this entry to see the available WordArt styles.

1. Click **Plain Text** on the left side of the Toolbar.

The styles shown in Figure B.3 are displayed. These style shapes indicate the way the WordArt text will be displayed. To select a style, click the desired shape.

Choose this style

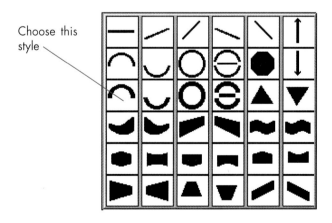

FIGURE B.3   Choose a style from the WordArt style options.

2. Click different styles to see how they look. If you get a Change Size window, click the Yes button to allow Works to change the size of the display.
3. Choose the **Arch Up** style as shown in Figure B.3.

Set the Character Spacing

The character spacing can be set from close together (Very Tight) to far apart (Very Loose). To change the spacing, use the **Adjust Space** tool on the Toolbar. This is the fifth tool from the right side of the Toolbar. When you click the Adjust Space tool, the **Spacing Between Characters** window appears. See Figure B.4.

Set the spacing to Loose

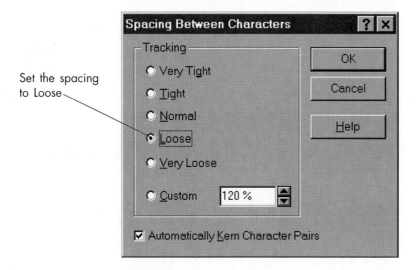

FIGURE B.4   Choose a spacing for characters in the WordArt.

1. Click the **Adjust Space** tool. The **Spacing Between Characters** window appears.
2. Try several settings to see how the spacing changes.
3. Set the spacing to **Loose** and click the OK button.

Change the Character Shading

Shading patterns define how the text appears on the screen. The shading patterns consist of a **Foreground** that is the front or major color of the text, and a **Background** that is the minor or back color of the text. The text also has a pattern. The pattern defines how the foreground and background colors are combined to fill the text characters. Change your text to a Red foreground with a Navy background. See Figure B.5.

1. Click the Shading tool. The **Shading** window appears as shown in Figure B.5.
2. Click the **Foreground** entry and change the color to Red.
3. Click the **Background** entry and change the color to Blue.
4. Experiment with different patterns to see their effect.
5. Click the stripe pattern indicated in Figure B.5 and click the OK button.

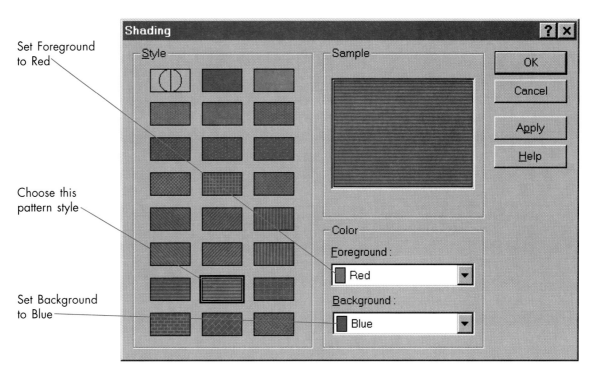

Set Foreground to Red

Choose this pattern style

Set Background to Blue

FIGURE B.5   Shading defines the colors and pattern of the character.

Set a Character Border

The **border** is the character's outline. Change the text border to a medium black line. See Figure B.6.

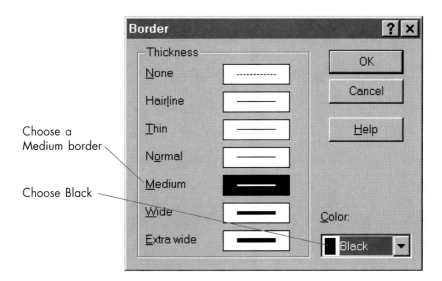

Choose a Medium border

Choose Black

FIGURE B.6   Use the Border tool to outline the characters.

1. Click the **Border** tool. The Border window shown in Figure B.6 appears.
2. Choose the **Medium** line thickness.
3. Set the border color to **Black**.
4. Click OK.

Apply a Shadow

To apply a shadow to the WordArt, use the **Shadow** tool on the Toolbar. This is the second tool from the right.

1. Click the **Shadow** tool. The **Shadow options** window appears as shown in Figure B.7.
2. Try several different shadow options to see their effect.
3. Choose the third shadow style from the right .
4. Select a Navy Shadow Color and click the OK button.

Choose this
shadow

Choose Navy

FIGURE B.7   Use the Shadow tool to add shadow effects.

Set the Stretch to Frame Option

To change the size of the WordArt object from within the Works document, the **Stretch to Frame** option must be set on. This is the seventh button from the right. See Figure B.2.

1. Click the **Stretch to Frame** tool.

Exit the WordArt Accessory

To exit the WordArt accessory, click anywhere outside the **Enter Your Text Here** box. The WordArt is then inserted into the document as an object. Your WordArt object should look like Figure B.8.

FIGURE B.8   Completed WordArt object.

1. Click anywhere outside the **Enter Your Text Here** box.

Size the WordArt

To change the size of the WordArt, click the object to expose the handles. Drag the handles to change the size.

1. Click the object to expose the handles.
2. Drag the handles to see their effect on changing the size of the WordArt.

To make changes to the WordArt, double click the WordArt object. The WordArt accessory will be started and you can use the menu bar or the Toolbar to make changes. Click outside the text box to return to the document. When the document is saved, the WordArt is saved with the document as an embedded object.

Remember, WordArt can be placed in any document that will accept a picture. When the WordArt is placed in the document it is treated as a picture image. Use the **Text Wrap** and **Picture** options on the Format menu to change the way the text and the WordArt appear.

USING MICROSOFT DRAW

Microsoft Draw is another OLE accessory that comes with the Microsoft Works package. This draw program can be used to create pictures or drawings that can be embedded in a Works document.

Open a Document

1. Choose **New** from the File menu.
2. Click the Word Processor button.

Insert a Draw Object

1. Choose **Drawing** from the Insert menu.

A draw window like the one in Figure B.9 is displayed. The left side of the window contains a set of drawing tools. Each tool is used to draw a different geometric shape. Figure B.10 shows each tool.

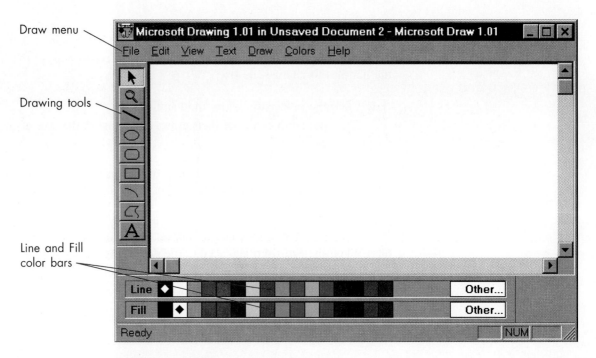

Draw menu

Drawing tools

Line and Fill
color bars

FIGURE B.9   The Microsoft Draw window.

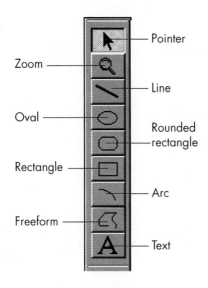

Zoom

Oval

Rectangle

Freeform

Pointer

Line

Rounded
rectangle

Arc

Text

FIGURE B.10   The Microsoft Draw drawing tools.

TOOL   DESCRIPTION

Tool	Description
Pointer tool	Used to select one or more objects and to move and size objects.
Zoom tool	Magnifies the screen to show greater detail.
Line tool	Draws straight lines.
Oval tool	Drag this tool to draw an ellipse. Drag the tool while pressing the Shift key to draw a circle.
Rounded rectangle tool	Drag this tool to draw a rectangle with rounded corners. Drag the tool while pressing the Shift key to draw a square.
Rectangle tool	Drag this tool to draw a rectangle with square corners. Drag the tool while pressing the Shift key to draw a square.
Arc tool	Drag to draw an arch. Turn on the fill command and drag to draw a pie wedge.
Freeform tool	Freehand drawing pencil.
Text tool	Click to type a line of text.

Draw an Oval

To use a drawing tool, click the tool and move the mouse pointer into the draw window's work area. The mouse pointer will change to a cross hair. Move the cross hair where the object is to be placed, and drag the mouse while holding down the left mouse button. Release the button when the object is complete.

1. Click the Oval drawing tool.
2. Move the mouse pointer into the work area. It changes to a cross hair. Move the cross hair near the location where the oval is to be placed.
3. Hold down the mouse's left button and drag the mouse. Release the button when you have drawn the oval.

Moving and Sizing an Object

Notice the handles around the object you just drew. (Figure B.11). When the handles are displayed, the object is selected. To change the size of an object, drag one of the handles.

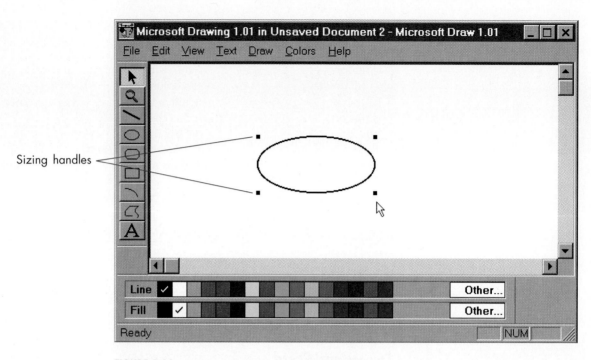

Sizing handles

FIGURE B.11 Drag an object's handles to change its size.

1. Click the Pointer tool.
2. Click inside the oval to select it.
3. Click one of the handles and drag the mouse while holding down the mouse button. Change the oval's size and release the button.

   To move an object, select the object and drag it with the mouse.

4. Click anywhere inside the oval. Drag the mouse while holding down the mouse button to move the object. Release the mouse button.

Change the Fill and Line Colors

The two rows of colors at the bottom of the window are used to set an object's colors. Change the inside of the oval to turquoise and the border to red.

1. Click the object to select it.
2. Click the Red color in the Line row.
3. Click the Turquoise color in the Fill row.

Change the Line and Fill Pattern

The **Line Style** and **Pattern** options on the Draw menu are used to change the line style and the fill pattern. Change the line to 2 points and the fill pattern to a hatch pattern. Figure B.12 shows the object after the changes.

1. Click the object to select it.
2. Choose Line Style from the Draw menu.
3. Click the 2 point option.
4. Choose Pattern from the Draw menu.
5. Click the hatched (bottom left) pattern.

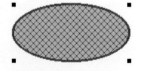

FIGURE B.12 The draw object with line and pattern changes.

Draw a Paned Window

A paned window is actually a square divided into four parts, or panes. The frame is created with a square and the panes are created with a vertical and a horizontal line. See Figure B.13.

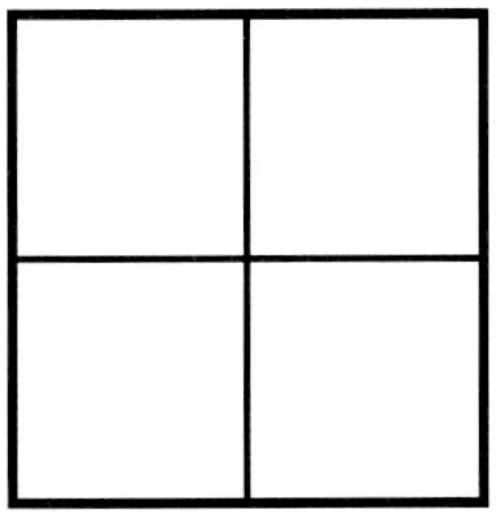

FIGURE B.13   Completed paned window.

1. Click the Oval you just drew and drag it to the upper left corner of the window.
2. Click the Square corner drawing tool. Move the pointer into the draw window.
3. Drag the cross hair while holding down the Shift key to draw a square. Release the mouse button.
4. Use the Line Style option on the Draw menu to set the line width to 2 points.
5. Use the Pattern option on the Draw menu to set a plain fill (top left) pattern.
6. Use the Line and Fill color bars to set the line color to Black and the fill color to White.
7. Click the Line tool.
8. Use the Line Style option on the Draw menu to set the line width to 1 point.
9. Draw a line down the center of the square.
10. Draw a line across the center of the square.

Grouping Objects

Each of the three objects used to draw the window, the square, and two lines, are currently independent. Each object can be moved, colored, patterned, or otherwise changed independently. To treat the window as a single object, the parts must be grouped. To group items, select each item to be grouped and choose the **Group** option from the Draw menu.

1. Click the Selection Arrow tool.
2. Move the mouse pointer into the **Draw** window. Press the mouse button and drag the arrow. As you drag the arrow, a dashed selection box appears. Drag the selection arrow so the box encloses all three parts of the window you just drew. This will select all the objects used to make up the window.
3. Choose the Group option from the Draw menu.

The entire window pane can now be treated as a single object. Try moving and coloring the window.

4. Click the window to select it.
5. Drag the window to a new location.
6. Click the Dark Blue line color.

To work with the individual parts of the group, select the grouped item and choose the **Ungroup** option from the Draw menu. Make sure the window parts are grouped before continuing.

Turn Snap To Grid Off

Notice when an object is drawn or moved, it appears to jump. This is because of the **Snap To Grid** option. Microsoft Draw uses invisible grid lines to align objects. There are twelve grids per inch. The **Snap To Grid** option can be used to help align objects. To get greater control of the drawing, turn the **Snap To Grid** option off.

1. Choose the **Snap To Grid** option from the Draw menu to turn the option off.
2. Move the paned window. Notice that it now moves more smoothly and can be moved shorter distances.

Rotate the Oval

Objects can be rotated left or right and flipped horizontally or vertically. Rotate the oval to the left.

1. Select the oval drawing. Drag the oval back toward the center of the Microsoft Draw window.
2. Choose **Rotate/Flip** from the Draw menu.
3. Choose **Rotate Left** from the **Rotate** submenu. If you get an error message indicating the object cannot be rotated, drag the oval to the center of the screen and try again.

Layering Objects

Objects in a drawing are in layers. Each layer is in front of or behind another layer. To see the layering, move the filled oval on top of the paned window. See Figure B.14.

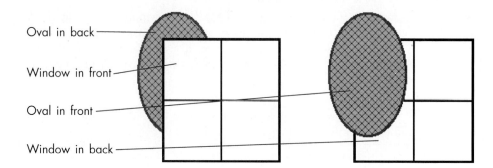

Oval in back
Window in front
Oval in front
Window in back

FIGURE B.14   Layered draw objects.

1. Drag the patterned oval on top of the paned window. The window should now cover part of the oval because the window is the top layer.
2. With the oval selected, choose **Bring to Front** from the Edit menu. The patterned oval should now cover part of the window because the oval is the top layer.

Layering is the way most pictures are created. Individual geometric shapes are created and layered over each other.

Use the Framed and Filled Options

The **Framed** option on the Draw menu displays an object's borders. If this option is turned off, the border will not show. The **Fill** option on the Draw menu displays an object's fill pattern.

To see how the framed option works, do the following:

1. Click the **Selection Arrow** tool.
2. Click the paned window.
3. Hold down the Shift key and click the oval. This will select both objects.
4. Choose the Framed option on the Draw menu to turn the option off. Notice that the frame disappears.
5. Choose the Framed option again to turn the option on.
6. With both options still selected, choose the Fill option from the Draw menu to turn the Fill option off. Notice that the frame from the object behind shows through the object in front.
7. Choose the Fill option again to turn the option back on.

Create an Arched Window

The two objects you have created can be combined to create the arched window shown in Figure B.15.

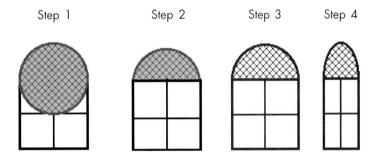

Step 1   Step 2   Step 3   Step 4

FIGURE B.15   Steps to create an arched window.

1. Select the oval. Use the handles to change the oval to a circle. Size and move the circle so its edges are aligned with the edges of the window. See Step 1 in Figure B.15.
2. Use the Edit menu to send the circle to the back so it looks like Step 2 in Figure B.15.
3. Select both objects, the windows and the filled circle. Use the Group option on the Draw menu to group the two objects.
4. Use the Line color bar to change the line color to Dark Blue.
5. Use the Fill color bar to change the fill color to White. See Step 3 in Figure B.15.
6. Use the sizing handles to make the window taller and narrower. See Step 4 in Figure B.15.

Duplicating Objects

Now use the Copy and Paste options to create four windows. See Figure B.16.

1. Select the new arched window.
2. Choose Copy from the Edit window.
3. Choose Paste from the Edit Window three times.
4. Drag the windows until they are aligned horizontally as shown in Figure B.16.

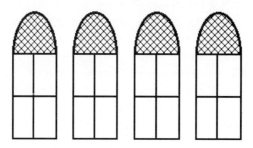

FIGURE B.16   Copied windows aligned.

Exit Draw

To exit the Microsoft Draw program and return to the Works document, choose Exit and Return from the File menu.

1. Choose Exit and Return from the Edit menu.
2. Click the Yes button in the Update window.

The drawing is now embedded in the document. To make changes to the drawing, double-click the drawing's image. The Microsoft Draw program will be started and the image will be copied to the drawing work area. Make the changes and exit to the document to save the changes.

The drawing can be sized and moved within the document using the drawing handles.

Microsoft Draw can be used to create drawings that help illustrate ideas or concepts in a document. Many of the illustrations in this text have been created with Microsoft Draw. If you would like to practice using the draw program, use the arched windows as a beginning point to create the picture in Figure B.17.

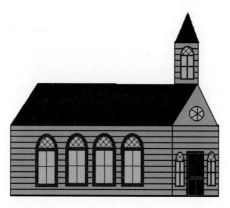

FIGURE B.17   Practice drawing by creating this picture.

Note-It is an OLE application used to add pop-up notes to a document. Note-It messages are an ideal way to include reminders, annotate a document, or provide instructions on how to use a document. Note-It messages can be added to word processing documents or database forms.

Insert a Note-It Pop-Up Message

1. Open any existing document or choose the New option from the File menu and click the Word Processing button.
2. Choose Note-It from the Insert menu.

The Note-It window shown in Figure B.18 is displayed. Three steps are used to insert a note: select a note symbol, type a caption for the note, and enter the note message.

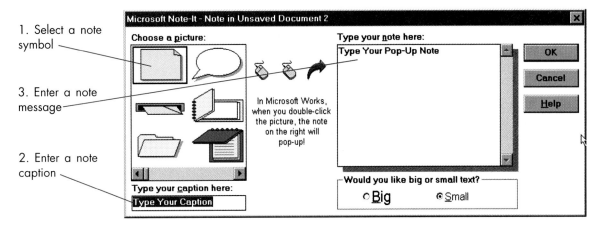

FIGURE B.18 Note-it window.

Select a Note Symbol

To select a note symbol, click any symbol on the left side of the dialog box.

1. Select the symbol in the lower-righthand corner.

Enter a Caption

The caption appears in the document with the note symbol. The caption should indicate the contents of the note.

1. Click the caption text box below the label **Type your caption here:**.
2. Replace any text in the text box with the following: **Note Instructions**.

Enter a Message

The note's message is entered in the **Type your note here:** text area.

1. Click the note message text area.
2. Replace the existing text with this note: **To read the note, double-click the note's symbol. To edit the note, select the note's symbol. Then choose Microsoft Note-it Object from the Edit menu and choose Edit from the submenu.**
3. Click the OK button.

The word processing document should now be displayed with the Note-It symbol.

Read the Note

To read the note, double-click the note symbol.

1. Double-click the note symbol.

   Figure B.19 shows a document with the note displayed.

   To edit a note, select the note symbol and choose Microsoft Note-It Object from the Edit menu. Choose Edit from the submenu. The Note-It program will start with the selected note in the note text box. Make the necessary changes and click the OK button.

Note displayed —

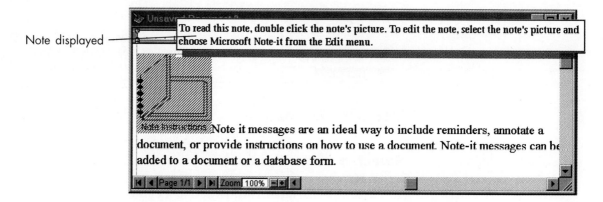

FIGURE B.19   The note message shows up when the note symbol is double-clicked.

To delete a note, select the note symbol and press the Delete key. To move a note, use the drag and drop technique. To size a note symbol use the symbol's handles. When a document is printed, only the note's symbol and the caption are printed.

USING TASK WIZARDS

Task Wizards are automated routines that perform common tasks within Works. The Wizard procedure uses cue cards to step through the creation of a document, database, or spreadsheet. We will guide you through the Wizard used to create a letterhead. You should try some other Wizards on your own.

Start the Letterhead Wizard

1. Choose New from the File menu.
2. Click the Task Wizards tab on the Task Launcher window.
3. Click Common Tasks.

The list of Wizards shown in Figure B.20 is displayed. Choose the **Letterhead Wizard.**

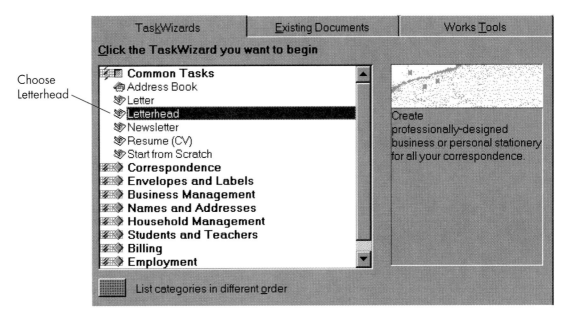

Choose Letterhead

FIGURE B.20   Choose Letterhead from the list of Task Wizards.

4. Double-click **Letterhead** in the **Task Wizard** list.

The first screen allows you to select the letter style. You can click the three different style buttons to see how they look.

5. Click each of the three style buttons on the left side of the screen.
6. Click the **Simple** style button.
7. Click the Next button at the bottom right of the screen.

Create the Letterhead

You should now have the screen shown in Figure B.21. Each of these options allows you to set different characteristics of the letter. We will only concern ourselves with the Letterhead portion.

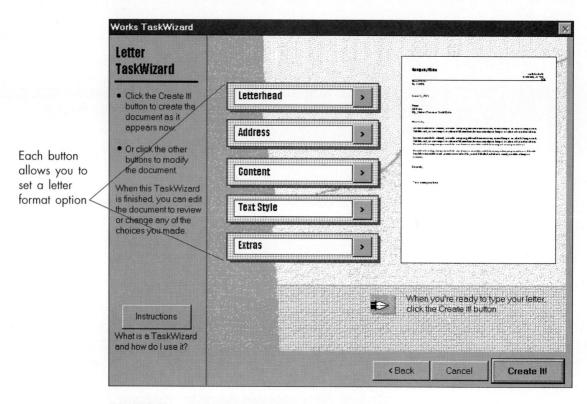

Each button
allows you to
set a letter
format option

FIGURE B.21   Click the Letterhead option to set up the letterhead.

1. Click the **Letterhead** entry on the **Letter Task Wizard** window.
2. Click the **I want to design my own** option.
3. Click the Next button.

The window shown in Figure B.22 should now be displayed. Click the different
styles to see the style.

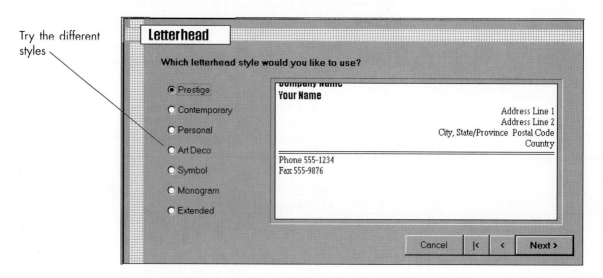

Try the different
styles

FIGURE B.22   You can choose from seven different predefined letterhead styles.

4. Click each of the style options to see the style.
5. Click the **Prestige** style.
6. Click the Next button.

The letterhead window should now display two options—**Company name** and **Personal name**. Since you do not want the company name, turn this option off. Enter your name as the **Personal name**.

7. Click the **Company name** option to turn it off and click the **Personal name** option to turn it on.
8. Enter your full name in the **Personal name** area.
9. Click the next button.

Enter your address in the next four lines. If a line does not apply, leave it blank.

10. Enter your address in the next series of lines.
11. Click the Next button.

Now turn off all numbers except your home phone number.

12. Click an option to turn it on or off. Turn off all phone numbers except the **Home phone number**.
13. Enter your home phone number.
14. Click the Next button.

The letterhead is now complete. If it is not correct, use the buttons at the bottom of the window to move back to previous windows where you can make corrections. When everything is displayed correctly, click the Next button.

15. Make any corrections necessary.
16. Click the OK button.
17. Click the **Create it** button on the Letterhead window.
18. Click the **Create Document** button.

You should now see a window that says **Works is creating the document**. Wait a few seconds and the document will be created.

You should now be in the word processor with an unsaved document. The letterhead is displayed at the top of the screen. The letterhead is simply text, so you can edit any part of it.

Save the Letterhead

To use the letterhead in future documents, save it as a template. To save the document as a template, use the **Save As** option and choose the **Template** button.

1. Choose **Save As** from the File menu.
2. Click the **Template** button.
3. Enter **MYLETTER** as the template name.

The letterhead is now saved as a template. The next time you need to write a letter, choose **Use A Template** from the Startup menu and select the **MYLETTER** template from the **User Defined Templates** at the bottom of the Task Wizards list.

4. Close the letterhead file.
5. Click the **No** button when asked if you want to save the document.

USING TEMPLATES

A **template** is a ready-made document, database, or spreadsheet that has the basic layout, formats, and formulas for a particular task. Works comes with several templates to help you with basic personal and business needs.

1. Choose New from the File menu.
2. Click the Task Wizards tab on the Task Launcher window.

Select a Template

Open the **MYLETTER** letterhead template created under the section **Using Task Wizards**.

1. Click the **User Defined Templates** group.
2. Click the **MYLETTER** template.
3. Click the OK button.

The letterhead or other document should now be opened and ready to use. If you opened the letterhead, you could create a letter now. When templates are used, the document that uses the template is treated as a new document. When the document is saved, you will be asked to name the document. This will create a new word processing document without changing the template.

Templates provide a fast and easy way to start a common word processing document, spreadsheet application, or database. Look at the different Wizards in Works. Each wizard will help you create a template that can be used to save a tremendous amount of time and effort.

GLOSSARY

Absolute cell address   Retains the current cell address or contents when the cell is copied or filled to a new location.

Active cell   The highlighted cell shows which is currently in use.

Active column   The column that houses the active cell. The intersection of the active column with the active row forms the active cell.

Active row   The row that houses the active cell. The intersection of the active column with the active row forms the active cell.

Alignment   Alignment indicates how a line of text is positioned on a line or in a cell. Examples of alignment are left, right, centered, and justified.

All Character option   This option displays special characters, such as tab keys, spaces, and paragraph markers on the screen.

AND   AND is a conjunction used to relate two conditions in a spreadsheet IF statement or a database filter criteria. If the AND conjunction is used, the conditions on both sides of the AND must be true for the IF test or filter condition to be true.

Banner   A banner is normally a set of lines that appears at the top of a printed page. An example of a banner is the image that appears across the top of the first page of most newspapers.

Bitmap   A bitmap is a technique used to storage graphic images. Each dot used to create the graphic image is stored as one bit in the computer's memory. These on and off bits are used to represent the image.

Block of cells   A block is a group of cells that have been selected with the mouse or the F8 Extend key. Once selected, you can work with all the cells in the block at the same time.

Bookmark   A Bookmark is a marked location in a document. To create a Bookmark use the Bookmark option on the Edit menu. To move to a defined bookmark use the GO TO option on the Edit menu.

Border   Borders are lines that can be printed on the left, right, top, or bottom of a paragraph or cell. Borders are used to outline text or data.

Bullet   A bullet is a character that is placed on the first line of a paragraph. Normally, the remainder of the text in the paragraph is indented to the right of the bullet. Bullets are often used to indicate a list of items.

Caps Lock   When the Caps Lock key is up, normal typing is in lower case letters. Use the shift key to upper case letters. When the Caps Lock key is down, normal typing is in upper case letters. Use the shift key to get lower case letters.

Cascading menu A sub-menu displayed when a menu option is selected. Menu options that have cascading menus will have a small arrowhead on the right of the menu option.

Cell The intersection of a row and a column forms a cell.

Cell borders A box or border that can be drawn around a group or block of cells.

Cell coordinate Cells are identified by combining both the letter of its column and the number of its intersecting row. This forms the cell coordinate.

Client document The client document is the document that displays linked information. The actual information is stored in the server document.

Clipart Clipart is pictures. Clipart pictures can be placed in a document using the Microsoft Clipart Gallery. Clipart that has been placed on the Windows clipboard can also be pasted into a document using the Paste tool.

Clipboard The clipboard is used to store data temporarily. To place data on the clipboard, select the data then use the Copy or Cut tools. To place the data on the clipboard into a document, use the Paste tool.

Column labels Letters positioned at the top of the spreadsheet used to identify the columns.

Column Width Determines how wide the spreadsheet column is and is changed from the Format menu.

Columns Columns run vertically down the screen.

Copy tool In Microsoft Works, the Copy tool appears as two documents on the toolbar. This tool places the selected text on the clipboard.

Cursor In Microsoft Works, the cursor is a blinking vertical bar that indicates where typed text will be placed.

Custom form A custom form is a database form designed by the user.

Cut tool In Microsoft Works, the Cut tool is a pair of scissors on the toolbar. This tool deletes the selected item from a document and places it on the clipboard.

Database A database is a collection of rows or records and columns or fields that contain data about common objects, such as people, places, things, events, etc.

Default value A default is a value used for an option if no value has been defined by the user.

Destination window When copying from one Works application to another the destination window is application the information is to be copied into.

Document Ruler The ruler is displayed across the top of a word processing document. It is used to measure the documents page width, mark the left and right margins, and hold the tab markers. The Ruler option on the View menu is used to turn the ruler display on and off.

Document Title This is the name of the file that contains the document. It is displayed at the top left of the document's window.

Drag and Drop A technique used to move or copy data. To use the drag and drop to move data, select the data to be moved, place the cursor over the selected block and hold down the left mouse button. When the mouse pointer changes to drag, drag the mouse until the cursor is at the location where the text is to be moved and release the mouse button. To copy data using drag and drop, follow the steps above and hold down the Ctrl key while dragging the mouse.

Easy Format An Easy Format is a predefined format for text. A format can be created using a combination of different formatting options and stored as an

Easy Format. The next time the format needs to be used, the Easy format can be applied rather than assigning each formatting option individually. In many word processors, these are referred to as Styles.

Easy Text Easy Text is used to quickly enter text that is commonly used in a document, such as a company title. To use Easy Text, enter the Easy Text's name and press the F3 function key. Associated text will replace the Easy Text name.

Editing cells To edit the contents of a cell, position the cursor on the cell and press the F2 Edit key. The content of the cell, such as a formula or a label, is displayed on the formula bar.

Field In a database, a field is column that contains the same type of data for each record in the database. For example, the First Name field would contain first names of all the people in the database.

Field labels Field labels are field names that are displayed and printed above each column in a database.

Field marker Field markers indicate where special data, such as current date, time, page number, or database data will be placed when a document is printed. If special data, such as date or time, is replaced by the field marker, the marker will be bracketed by asterisks on each side such as *date*. If it is a database field, the field name will be bracketed by << and >>, such as <<First Name>>.

Filter A filter is a set or criterion used to describe which records in a database are to be displayed when the filter is applied. For example, to display one record where the last name is Smith, the filter would use the criterion Last name is equal to Smith.

Font A font defines the shape of characters and numbers in a document.

Footers Footers are lines that are printed at the bottom of each page of a document. Footers can contain text, clipart, and special characters.

Footnote A footnote is a cited reference to a work used to indicate the true source of the work. In Microsoft Works, a footnote consists of a number or symbol in the text of the document and a citation at the bottom of the page or the end of the document.

Form letter A form letter is a letter that contains the same basic information for each recipient of the letter. Certain information, such as the name and address, is changed for each recipient.

Form View In a database, this view displays one database record at a time.

Formatting Formatting changes the way text and numbers are displayed. Examples of formatting are bold, italic, and underlined text. There are many more types of formatting.

Formatting cells Cells can be formatted to take on special appearance. They can assume different decimal positions, date formats, currency formats and many more.

Formula (database) In a database a formula is used to create fields from existing data. The formula is normally expressed using field names and arithmetic operators. For example Unit Cost * Quantity ordered.

Formula (Spreadsheet) Formulas are numeric operations performed on values. Formulas can contain cell coordinates, numbers, or a combination of both. For example A1*C4/2.

Gridlines Gridlines are lines used to outline cells when they are displayed or printed. They help the user when viewing a database or spreadsheet.

Handle A handle is a small square that appears around a picture or other object when the picture or object is selected. The handles can be dragged to reduce or enlarge the image.

Hanging indent A hanging indent moves the first line of a paragraph to the left of the left Margin. The paragraph appears as though all lines except the first line of a paragraph are indented.

Header Headers are lines that are printed at the top of each page of a document. Headers can contain text, clipart, and special characters.

Headings row Headings row are used in report definitions. The contents of the readings rows print at the top of each page of the report and normally indicate what data is printed in each column of the report.

Horizontal scroll bar This bar is displayed at the bottom of the screen and shows the relative position of the cursor on a line.

IF statement Allows conditional logic to be used in a spreadsheet by determining IF this action occurs, then this result is displayed.

Insert typing mode Insert typing mode insert new characters in a document or cell and pushes existing characters to the right. To shift between overstrike and insert typing mode, press the Insert key.

Inserting rows and columns Allows additional rows and columns to be added between occupied cells in an existing spreadsheet.

Key field In a database, a key field is a field that is used for sorting database records. A database can be sorted on up to three different key fields at one time.

Labels A label can be made up of alphabetic, numeric, or alphanumeric (a combination of both alphabetic and numeric characters) data. Labels, by their nature, cannot be used in any kind of arithmetic function or formula.

Landscape orientation Landscape orientation prints a document sideways, the right side of the page is used as the top and the bottom of the page is used as the right.

List View In a database, this view displays all records in the database in the form of rows and columns.

Magnifying glass Tool on the toolbar used to execute the Print Preview option. In print preview the magnifying glass is used to zoom the preview screen.

Margins The margins define the white space at the left, right, top, and bottom of a printed page. The margins are set using the Margins folder of the Page Setup option on the File menu.

Menu bar The top bar of a Microsoft Works tool. The menu bar is used to pull down the tool's menus.

Microsoft Draw Microsoft Draw is a drawing program that is provided with most Microsoft application programs. This program allows you to create drawings, consisting of geometric shapes and text, and embed these drawings in other documents.

Note-it Note-it is a Microsoft application that allows you to insert notes or comments into a document. The notes or comments can be viewed on the screen but they do not print when the document is printed.

Num Lock When the Num Lock key is on the numeric keypad on the keyboard types numbers. When the Num Lock key is off the numeric keypad is used to move the cursor.

OLE Object Linking and Embedding is a technique used by Windows 95 to connect an object to the application program that created the object. When an object that is linked or embedded in a document is double clicked, the application that created the object is started and the linked or embedded object is loaded into the application for editing.

OR OR is a conjunction used to relate two conditions in a spreadsheet IF statement or a database filter criteria. If the OR conjunction is used, either condition on each side of the OR can be true for the IF test or filter condition to be true.

Overstrike typing mode Overstrike typing mode replaces existing characters as they are typed. To shift between overstrike and insert typing mode, press the Insert key.

Paragraph In the word processor a paragraph is the amount of text that appears between two paragraph marks. Paragraph marks are inserted each time the Enter key is pressed.

Paste tool In Microsoft Works, the Paste tool appears as a clipboard on the toolbar. This tool inserts the contents of the clipboard into a document.

Point A point is 1/72 of an inch and is used to define the height of a character.

Portrait orientation Portrait orientation prints a page the way the page is normally defined. The top of the page is printed at the top. Compare this to Landscape orientation.

Protection In both spreadsheets and databases, cell and field protection prevents a user from changing the contents of the protected cells. Protection is normally used to prevent accidental destruction of data and formulas.

Pull Down menu A pull down menu lists a set of options that perform certain tasks. To pull down the menu, place the mouse pointer over the menu name and click the left mouse button. You can also pull down a menu by pressing the ALT key followed by the underlined letter on the menu name.

Range In a database filter, a range is a set of inclusive values. The range specifies the lowest and highest value. All values between the upper and lower values are included in the range.

Recalculation modes Automatic calculation (the default) re-computes spreadsheet formulas each time an entry is changed while manual re-computes only when instructed by the user.

Record In a database, a record contains all the information about a single item in the database. Each record is composed of several columns or fields.

Record labels Record labels are numbers that are displayed and printed to the left of each record in a database.

Record rows Record rows are used in report definitions and normally print the data from the records in the database. Each record row in a report definition will print one time for each record available in the database.

Relational operator Relational operators are used in IF statements of Database filters to specify how values are to be compared. For example the = relational operator tests two values to see if they are equal.

Relative Cell Address Allows the automatic update of cell contents when copied or filled to a new location.

Report definition A report definition is used to describe how a report will look when it is printed. It consists of Title rows, Headings rows, Record rows and Summary rows. Each row contains data that will be printed when the report is printed.

Report view In a database, this view displays a report definition. The report definition describes the data to be printed on the report.

Right mouse button This mouse button is used to display a context sensitive menu. Works displays a different menu depending upon the type of data selected.

Row Height Determines how tall the spreadsheet row is and is changed from the Format menu.

Row labels Numbers positioned along the left side of the spreadsheet used to identify the rows.

Rows Rows run horizontally across the screen.

Running Total A running total is a total that accumulates from one database record to the next. For example if three consecutive records had totals of 10, 15, and 20, the first record's running total would be 10, the second record's running total would be 25, and the third record's running total would be 45.

Server application The server application is the application used to create an object that is linked or embedded in another document.

Server document The server document is the document that contains the information when data is linked to another document. The document that displays the linked information is referred to as the client document.

Sort Rows Allows rows to be sorted based on the contents in one or more cells.

Source window When copying from one Works application to another the source window contains the information to be copied.

Splitting the spreadsheet screen Permits the spreadsheet screen to be divided into sections enabling you to view different parts at the same time.

Spreadsheet A popular application for personal computers which allow you to calculate and compare all sorts of data, in a manner similar to a manual accounting ledger sheet. A spreadsheet is composed of rows and columns that intersect to form cells.

Spreadsheet navigation You can move around in the spreadsheet through the use of the arrow keys, the mouse, scroll bars or with a combination of these methods.

Subscript A subscript is text that is printed lower that the normal characters on a line. The subscript is also normally printed smaller than the normal text.

Summary Row Summary rows are used in report definitions and print one time at the end of the report. Summary rows normally contain statistics for the report.

Superscript A superscript is text that is printed higher that the normal characters on a line. The superscript is also normally printed smaller than the normal text.

Syntax Syntax is the sentence structure required to form a condition in a database filter.

Tab Leader A tab leader is a set of characters that are printed to the left of a tab stop. They are used to guide a reader's eye across a page to the tabbed text.

Tab stop A tab stop is a marker on the document ruler that indicates where the cursor should stop when the tab key is pressed. Text can be aligned to the left, right, or center of the tab stop. A decimal alignment aligns the text on a decimal point.

Tabbing order The tabbing order is used on a database form to indicate the next field on the form when the tab key is pressed. To change the tabbing order use the Tab order option on the Format menu of Forms Design view.

Table A table is composed of a set number of rows and columns and is normally used to display related and comparative data.

Table Lookup functions Instructs the spreadsheet to search a table of values and find a value to automatically enter into a cell.

Task Launcher The task launcher is used to select a task wizard, open an existing document, or select a Works tool to create a new document.

Task Wizard A Task Wizard is a predefined routine used by Microsoft Works to help you create certain types of documents, spreadsheets, or databses. The Task Wizard leads you though several steps, then, through an automated routine, creates the document.

Template A template is a document, spreadsheet, or databse that provides a starting point for a specific type of task. The document, spreadsheet, or database will normally contain the formatting and formulas required. The remainder of the document is then entered or modified by the user.

Thesaurus The thesaurus provides a list of substitute words or synonyms for commonly used words. To use the thesaurus in Microsoft Works, place the cursor on a word and choose the Thesaurus option on the Tools menu.

Thumbnail A thumbnail is a small reduced view of a clipart image.

Tile A technique used to arrange windows. When windows are tiled, each window is reduced in size and the windows are displayed side by side.

Title row The Title row of a report definition prints one time on the first page of a report. The title row normally contains values to print the report name or company name.

Toggle A toggle is turned on if it is off and off if it is on. Many Works options work as toggles. For example, if the bold format is on and bold is selected, the bold format is turned off. If the bold format is off and it is selected, the bold format is turned on.

Toolbar The Toolbar is located below the menu bar and displays several icons that can be used to execute Microsoft Works options. To use a tool on the toolbar, click the tool's icon.

Undo Undo is an option on the Edit menu. When this option is used, the last operation performed is reversed, returning the document to the condition it was before the operation was performed. The Ctrl+Z key will also execute the Undo option.

Values Values consist of numbers and special numeric characters such as dollar signs, commas, and decimal points. Since values are numbers, they can be used in any type of arithmetic function and in formulas.

Vertical scroll bar This bar is displayed at the right of the window. It can be used to move quickly through a document.

Wild Card A wild card is a symbol, either * or ?, used to substitute for any character when searching text. The * wild card will substitute any number of characters while the ? will only substitute one character.

WordArt WordArt is art work that consists primarily of words or text characters. The WordArt application program is used to create a wordart object.

Word-wrap Word-wrap will push a word to the next line when new text is inserted in a paragraph.

X coordinate On a database form the X coordinate defines the distance from the top of the form.

Y coordinate On a database form the Y coordinate defines the distance from the left margin of the form.

Zoom Zoom is used to magnify or reduce the display of the document. Use the plus button (+) or minus button (-) at the right of the Zoom display at the bottom of the screen to magnify or reduce the display.

INDEX

DOS, 6
Dot matrix printer, 5
Download, 415
Drag and drop, 43, 61, 188

Easy Calc, 221
Easy Connect, 414
Easy Filter, 310–311
Easy Format, 77, 89, 96, 113,–114, 131
Easy Text, 112, 137
Editing cells, 156
Ellipsis, 36
Ends with, 312
Enter, 4
ERR, 190
Esc, 4
Existing Documents, 63
Exit Works, 63
Explorer, 24
Exponential format, 159
EXT, 39
Extend indicator, 35
Extension, 9

F2 Edit key, 156
F2 function key, 349
F3 function key, 112
F5 key,154
F6 (Next Window) key, 225
F6 function key, 84
F7 function key, 110
F8 Extend key, 156
F8 function key, 39
Field Entry, 351
Field folder, 282
Field Marker, 81
Field Name, 280, 306, 351
Field place holder, 378, 381
Field protection, 287
Field size, 324
Field Summary, 351
Field width, 283
Fields, 276
Fields folder, 344
Fields order, 356
File name, 9
File, 9
Fill, 431
Fill Down, 174, 189, 284
Fill Right, 189, 284
Fill Series, 284
Filter folder, 353
Filter tool, 310, 327
Filter using formula, 313–314, 333
Filter, 278, 310, 390
Filtered records in the database, 379
Filters using formulas, 310
Find, 110
Find Next, 110, 112
Find option, 128
Find whole words only, 110
Fixed format, 159
Floppy disk drives, 3
Floppy disks, 3
Folders, 9, 18
Font and Style, 116
Font, 75, 87
Footer area, 34
Footer, 69, 82, 99,120, 138
Footnotes, 83, 98
Foreground, 422
Form Design tool, 307, 321, 278

Form Design view, 321
Form Design, 307
Form letter instructions, 389
Form letter, 377–378, 389
Form view, 277, 298, 310
Format, 157, 281
Formatting, 8, 37
Formula, 150, 155, 286, 297
Formula bar, 153
Fraction format, 159
Framed, 431
Freeze Titles, 223
Function keys, 4
Functions, 193

General, 160
General format, 159
Go back, 380
Go To key, 154
Go To, 117
Go, 380
Gridlines, 229, 259, 290

Handles, 125, 369
Hanging Indent, 72, 78
Hard disk drive, 3
Hard disks, 3
Header area, 34
Header, 69, 82, 99, 120, 138, 388
Headings row, 348
Help, 15
Help buttons, 35
Help facility, 47
Help index, 48
Hidden Records, 320, 334
HLookup, 220
Horizontal (X) Axis, 259
Horizontal lookup, 220
Horizontal scroll bar, 34
Host computer, 405
Hot zone, 121
Hyphenate CAPS, 120
Hyphenate, 142
Hyphenating words, 120
Hyphenation, 120, 142

Icons, 13
In-line, 125
Indents and Alignment, 80, 90
Insert Column, 187, 350
Insert Field Entry window, 351
Insert Field Name window, 351
Insert Field, 285
Insert mode, 37
Insert Record tool, 278, 285
Insert Row, 186, 350, 360
Inserting Text, 37
Integrated programs, 6
Invert filter, 318
Is blank, 312
"Is blank", 332
Is equal to, 312
Is less than, 312
Is not blank, 312
Italics, 39

Justified alignment, 41, 55

Keep paragraph with next option, 116

Keep paragraph with next, 130
KERMIT, 415
Key field, 289
Keyboard, 4

Label Layout folder, 384
Label Layout, 385, 398
Label Size folder, 383
Label size, 398
Labels, 150, 155, 308, 322, 382, 397
Landscape orientation, 69, 121, 140
Landscape, 262, 343
Laser printer, 5
Leading zeros, 159
Left, 160
Left alignment, 41
Left margin, 68
Legend, 247
Letterhead Wizard, 435
Letterhead, 388
Li, 116
Line Between, 120
Line Chart, 249
Line Spacing, 56, 116
Line Style, 428
Linked, 373
Links, 374
List View, 277, 310, 335
Lookup Value, 218

Magnifying glass, 44, 62
Mailing lists, 377
Manual calculation, 226
Manual update, 375
Margin markers, 71
Mark records, 319
Marked Records, 320
Mark records option, 319
Match case, 110
Maximum, 346
Megahertz, 2
Menu bar, 34, 153
Menu button, 50
Microsoft ClipArt Gallery, 123
Microsoft Draw, 425
Microsoft Works 4.0 Sheet or Chart Object,
    371–372, 392
Minimum, 346
Modem, 406
Modify Filter, 353
Modulation, 406
More Info, 50
Mouse pointer, 15
Mouse, 5, 14
Move text, 43
MS-DOS, 11
Multiple copies of one label, 382, 384
Multiple-column document, 119

Negative numbers in red, 280
Nesting IF statements, 195
New Chart, 253
New Easy Text, 112
New Filter button, 318
New Filter, 353
No footer on first page, 82
No header on first page, 82
Nonbreaking hyphen, 81
Nonbreaking space, 81
Normal view, 52
NOT condition, 334